The Lithium Economy

The Lithium Economy

A CRITICAL ANALYSIS OF THE GLOBAL LITHIUM VALUE CHAIN

Eric Lyon

Contents

Introduction

I first became interested in conserving and preserving our environment as a young man participating in the Boy Scouts of America. While I would later spend my adult career in the U.S. Army, those youthful ideals stuck with me. On occasion, they would resurface. For instance, as a Major attending a mid-career professional development program, I wrote my mandatory paper about the Earth Liberation Front and their use of clandestine methodology. This is where my interest in our environment and my previous tour as a Guerrilla Warfare instructor came together. I'm not sure what the school staff thought of this as everyone was expected to re-fight WWII or some other great campaign where we inevitably emerged victorious.

At the end of my career, I had the opportunity to attend the Harvard National Security Fellowship. Again, it was expected that we would write our thesis on some suitably strategic topic that the Army War College found acceptable. "Great Power Competition" seemed to be a popular topic. At the age of 50, I was still not that far removed from my younger Eagle Scout self, so I wrote about catastrophic climate change as a national security threat and the need to transition to a global green economy.

Having spent 35 years in the military, I naively thought only federal agencies had the power to make changes in our society. I mistakenly confused my narrow life experience with how the rest of the world worked. As I studied the topic, I realized that it wasn't just governments that could spur change, but also companies, private organizations, and individuals. Consequently, I took an interest in how private companies were deeply involved in low-carbon solutions. I found the topic fascinating and I still do.

I also found it important to put my money where my mouth was. I didn't want to be the guy talking about climate change at the local coffee shop but then drove a gas guzzling Hummer around town. I didn't want to talk the talk, I wanted to walk the walk. Like many of my peers in my former industry, I served six tours in Iraq and

Afghanistan – many did far more than I did. Since I astutely suspected a life in special operations probably wouldn't amount to much for me in the private sector, I put everything I made from each warzone deployment in the bank which collectively became our life savings.

After discussing it with my wife, I made the decision to invest in low-carbon businesses. Seeing as how I had researched green energy companies during my studies, I thought I might know which ones could be successful and which ones would not. Consequently, I invested our life savings, every nickel of it, in a variety of public companies focusing on renewable energy. This, of course, was a calculated risk, but so is life. I believe one can reduce (not eliminate) risk through preparation, hard work, and research. After having made my initial investments, I stuck with the discipline and continued to study the industry. This book is my attempt to share with the reader what I have learned in my pursuit of knowledge. As such, I consider my efforts a continuation of public service.

Since the larger green industry is dynamic, the material in this book is merely a snapshot in time. While some historical information may be enduring, other data will be irrelevant next week. Take it for whatever it's worth to you. While I sought to find the most accurate and representative information for any given topic, invariably I would find other data from one or even a dozen other sources that contradicted it. Data depends on sourcing, the methodology leading to the assessment, and the inherent biases of the authors. Accordingly, be skeptical of my stats and numbers. In fact, I ask that you question everything in this book and draw your own conclusions.

Not only is this industry dynamic, but it is also expansive. Every chapter of this project covers a topic so vast that it could be its own 300-page book. However, no one is going to read or buy a 6,000-page work. Please approach each chapter as an overview that provides trends and general concepts, a basic starting point that might spark your own quest for more detailed knowledge on the subject.

I have pursued a critical analytical approach to this topic so it is filled with my own opinions that the reader may or may not agree with. I have intentionally focused on strategy, leadership, and decision making at many levels. If I believe an institution, company or person has made a bad decision relating to their industry, I let the reader know this quite clearly. Although I label myself a critical thinker, others have used less complimentary adjectives to describe me.

While I have no formal education or extensive experience on the matter, I have a keen interest in supply chains and making them more intelligent, efficient, and less costly. I also believe they should be aligned with stated strategy and meet desired end goals. However, business processes can evolve over time for reasons that have nothing to do with efficiency. So, it's not surprising to find many of the supply chains relating to the critical mineral and battery metals space perplexing. The reader will find this a common thread I address throughout the book.

I wrote this book on my own, so every mistake, mischaracterization or incomprehensible math solution is my own. I wouldn't have it any other way. I've also introduced my own brand of humor into the book on occasion, which can be a dangerous thing, but I kept it to a minimum. I've purposely kept the book informal to make it easier to read as digesting hundreds of pages about battery chemistries and global shipping rates may not fulfill everyone like it does me.

Easily my proudest achievement while writing this book was being thrown out of the Reno-Tahoe Industrial Park by Tesla security guards. As I drove up to the Giga Nevada entrance, I took a picture of the Tesla symbol displayed on the side of the road. I asked the security guard if I could speak to someone at the front office to schedule a tour of the facility. He advised that this could only be done online. I thanked him, made a U-turn, and drove back down Electric Avenue and parked in front of a nearby office building to figure out where I was going to have lunch in Reno.

A few minutes later, two Tesla security guards arrived in white pick-up trucks (no, they were not BEVs). Instantly, my SERE training kicked in. I got out of my car to speak with them. They stated that the other security guard had seen me take a picture while driving up and they asked me to delete the photo as it was of "private property". I advised them that I was a Tesla shareholder, was writing a book on the lithium industry, and wanted a tour of the plant. They seemed unimpressed and said to request a tour online. I told them I was going to Thacker Pass the next day as part of my research. Judging from the looks on their faces, they had no idea what I was talking about.

I then asked if I could take a selfie with them as this dramatic incident would be great PR for my book. They declined. Then, they advised me that I needed to leave the industrial park too since it was private property. I said goodbye and drove off (observing the speed limit) with tears streaming from my eyes. Only then did I realize that Elon and I were not as tight as I thought we were. More importantly, it occurred to me that maybe the guards thought I was working for Lucid??? I'm still waiting for them to schedule my tour.

On a separate note, this book is not investing advice and should not be misconstrued as such. Investing is a personal activity and the reader should do their own homework on every investing decision they make. Superior investing outcomes are the result of superior research. As I mentioned, I do invest in the green energy space. Of the publicly traded companies I mention in this work, I am long on TSLA, BYDDY, NIO, LLKKF, VUL and FREYR. If I exhibit bias (like "endowment bias") in my writing, then that speaks poorly to my qualities as a critical thinker. Use my failings as an example to improve your own decision making.

Finally, I humbly present this work to you, the reader. I sincerely hope it was worth both your time and money. It has been my absolute pleasure. Eric.

Author and family at their home in Tucson, AZ in November 2022. Their dog, Clover, is a Black Labrador.

CHAPTER 1

A Global Lithium Overview

In 1817, a young Swedish chemist, Johan August Arfvedson, discovered a previously unknown mineral at an iron mine outside of Stockholm. He named the specimen after the Greek word for "stone" which was "lithos". The lithium he discovered was in petalite, which itself is a mineral of pegmatite. At the time, the modern world had no use for the newly discovered mineral. However, 200 years later, it would be the key ingredient that revolutionized the global auto industry.[1]

Lithium is the New Oil

Many a financial analyst or clean energy expert has described Lithium as the "new oil". This provocative comparison is based on their very real observation of the hurried expansion of the lithium mining industry as it toils to keep up with the thirst for lithium-ion batteries (LIBs) required by the global electric vehicle (EV) industry. Just as the venerable Internal Combustion Engine (ICE) uses refined oil to propel it forward, then the refined lithium required for EV batteries must be its direct replacement. Right? Well, yes and no.

Lithium may be the new oil in that LIB powered EVs are on pace to replace almost all ICE vehicles presently used for ground transportation. However, present day LIB chemistry and technology is not advanced enough to replace ICE powered transportation like airplanes and ships. Someday, a more advanced solid-state LIB

---

[1] https://www.chemistryviews.org/details/ezine/10225971/225th_Birthday_Johan_August_Arfwedson/

with much improved energy density may push out these stubborn ICE modes of transportation as well, but it won't happen at scale until the year 2030 at the earliest (my best estimate).

An important distinguishing feature of the two commodities is that oil itself creates chemical energy when exploded inside ICE devices. LIBs do not in themselves propel EV's forward, they must first be charged by an external energy source. Ideally, our LIBs batteries are charged by renewable energy sources like wind, solar, geothermal and hydropower. Ironically, depending on the grid and the utility's operating model, these batteries are most commonly charged from polluting fossil fuels (i.e. coal, natural gas) that contribute directly to our manmade global warming.

For lithium chemistry batteries to be anointed the new oil, they must become cheaper, lighter and more energy dense. While LIBs continue to improve every year and large amounts of capital are rapidly being injected into battery research, we aren't there yet. For the time being, at least, oil is oil, lithium is lithium and they will have different roles to play in society's energy consumption. But let's be clear, the expansion of LIBs to power vehicles and the grid will result in the accelerating demand destruction of oil products. Almost half of all global oil consumption is used to power vehicle ground transportation. When the world achieves 100% adoption of battery powered vehicles, one half of oil demand will be destroyed. Oil companies know this. They are now in the position of making the strategic decision to transition to a low carbon economy or continue to watch their antiquated business model increasingly erode by clinging to antiquated thinking.

As lithium gains greater importance in our world as a crucial commodity needed in our daily lives, it is of course open to international manipulation, national control and use as a *casus belli* just like oil. As we know all too well, the Middle East and OPEC (Organization of the Petroleum Exporting Countries) are a focal point for international relations and security dilemmas because of their oil producing capacity. Moving forward, we will see South America's Lithium Triangle – a brine rich area encompassing parts of Chile, Argentina, and Bolivia – gaining more political significance.

Is this idea far-fetched? In March 2023, Bolivia's President Luis Arce called for the creation of a lithium cartel that included Bolivia, Chile, Argentina, and Peru. Arce stated, "The objective is clear: to position our countries, Bolivia, Chile, Argentina and Peru, as potential promoters of our forms of energy storage that allow us to overcome the use of fossil fuels; minerals like lithium are one way to do it."[2] Perhaps we will see the eventual creation of OLEC – Organization of the Lithium Exporting Countries in our future. As an aside, while Peru is conducting initial lithium exploration, they do not have any active operations.

While there isn't an OLEC yet, there is the International Lithium Association (ILiA) which stood up in 2021 and describes itself as "…the global trade association for the lithium industry and represents the entire lithium value chain." The ILiA is an international not-for-profit industry association run by and for its members. The organization seeks to be the recognized voice of the international lithium industry while promoting ESG (Environmental, Social, Governance) and sustainability principles and cementing itself as a trusted source of knowledge reference all aspects of the industry.[3]

The three countries with the largest estimated lithium reserves in the world are Bolivia, Argentina and Chile – in that order.[4] If these countries can effectively harness their lithium resources and bring this commodity to market at scale, we can expect a corresponding global shift in economic and political influence to the Lithium Triangle. And if we can develop an economic way to extract lithium from the oceans which has 5,000 times more of the soft white metal than exists on land, any country with a coast has the potential to be a contributor to the ongoing lithium expansion.[5]

When these new lithium sources and extraction methods are discovered, the limiting factors become access to the requisite technology, the capital needed to set up large scale operations and the political will and strategy to pursue this course of action. The countries that cannot execute such a plan will find themselves at the mercy of those who can, much like the present-day oil industry. However, the opportunity for the global dispersion and relative democratization of lithium driven energy systems is very real.

2   Flores, Yuri. "Bolivia proposes regional policy on lithium and an organization of producing countries". La Razon, March 23, 2023.

3   https://lithium.org/about/

4   https://pubs.usgs.gov/periodicals/mcs2022/mcs2022-lithium.pdf

5   Lewis, Michelle. "Scientists have cost-effectively harvested lithium from seawater." https://electrek.co, June 4, 2021.

What is Driving the Lithium Explosion

The global automobile industry is transitioning from internal combustion engine (ICE) models to battery electric vehicles (BEV) at an accelerating rate. There are many reasons for this transition but the primary one is the need to decarbonize the transportation sector which contributes immensely to manmade global warming and its resulting catastrophic climate change. In 2020, the U.S. alone emitted some 6 billion metric tons of carbon dioxide (CO2) into our atmosphere. Of this, the transportation sector accounted for 27% of these emissions or 1.62 billion metric tons of CO2.[6]

The chief culprit of these transportation sector CO2 emissions are light vehicles, of which 81 million were sold around the globe in 2022. China led world sales with close to 27 million vehicles, followed by the United States with 13.7 million and then all of Europe with about 14.6 million vehicles.[7] An estimated 7.8 million BEVs were sold worldwide in 2022, which was quadruple 2019 sales and triple 2020 sales.[8] This means there are another 73 million light vehicles a year that will transition to BEVs in the future – that's going to require a lot of batteries.

Let's pause here briefly and discuss the ongoing demand destruction of the existing OEM (original equipment manufacturer) ICE industry. Established OEMs like Toyota, VW, Ford, GM and Stellantis are confronted with the reality that new BEV companies like Tesla and BYD are destroying their dated business models based on antiquated technology. The OEMs are under financial stress as they divest of their old ICE production lines (representing billions of dollars in stranded assets) while developing entirely new BEV processes. Successful BEV companies like Tesla and BYD have nothing but growth ahead of them, while the OEMs are only replacing their old ICE units with newer BEVs.

There is also a phenomenon in industry when transitioning to new products called the Osborne Effect. When a company or industry announces that it has a newer, better product becoming available soon, customers will stop buying the old product and wait to get the new one. When an OEM like GM starts making a new electric pickup truck, people will stop buying the gas ones while they wait for the new BEV model. This also works across brands as purchasers will stop from buying a new Ford ICE truck

---

[6] https://www.epa.gov/ghgemissions/sources-greenhouse-gas-emissions

[7] "Global car sales projected to rebound in 2023." https://evertiq.com, Feb 09, 2023.

[8] Irle, Roland. "Global EV Sales for 2022." https://www.ev-volumes.com

while they wait for Tesla's Cybertruck or Rivian's new models to become available. This effect contributes to the demand destruction of the existing ICE business model.

Additionally, there is the Ratner Effect where a company's self-admission that their products are not competitive in the market encourages customers to leave the brand and go elsewhere. For example, GM recalled every Chevy Bolt BEV ever made in 2022 due to potential fire hazards from its batteries (made by LG Chem). While recalls are common in the car industry, many people chose to look elsewhere for a BEV with a better battery safety record. In another example, Ford CEO Jim Farley recently discussed Ford losing $2 billion USD in potential profits in 2022 due to its own mismanagement. As an investor, do you want to put your money into a company that grossly mismanages its own business or one that gets it right through competent management?

With these ideas in mind, let's transition our discussion back to BEVs and what kind of batteries these tens of millions of vehicles are going to use. For now, and as far out as 2030, these BEVs will use some form of LIB. This LIB dominance is for several reasons including lithium being a very light-weight metal, it has a high energy density, is relatively inexpensive and abundant. LIBs also have the advantage of being firmly established as the global leader in propelling BEVs with an accompanying worldwide value chain that is growing every day (or one could argue just as well it is growing supply chain dependencies).

To be sure, LIBs use other metals as well, depending on a whole host of factors, to include: nickel, cobalt, manganese, iron, aluminum, cadmium and graphite (not a metal!). While many of these other materials can be substituted for whatever reason the manufacturer has (cost, supply chains, human rights concerns) lithium is the one component that cannot be replaced – it's the most valuable component of the battery. Battery manufacturers understand this.

As a result of the global BEV industry expansion, the LIB manufacturing industry has exploded as well. According to SNE Research, 518 GWh of battery capacity for was delivered worldwide in 2022.[9] The battery industry is dominated by Asian companies with China, South Korea and Japan (in that order) leading the way. China absolutely dominates the global battery market and no one else is even a close second. Europe

---

[9]   "2022 EV Battery Report." SNE Research, Feb 08, 2023.

and North America have largely ignored the battery revolution until just recently and are far behind in every aspect.

Globally, the Chinese BEV market drives Chinese lithium-ion battery manufacturing which in turn drives lithium refinement. It is important to note that EV batteries use either battery grade lithium hydroxide or lithium carbonate in their chemistry. Hence, mining lithium is just the first stage since a company must then refine it into useable form. However, if a country dominates the midstream processing of lithium like China does, they have a strangle hold on the entire value chain.

This raises the question of how we identify the lithium value chain and how we capture it (or don't). To start, the lithium value chain includes hard rock mining and the resulting lithium concentrate. If a company mines brine, they produce lithium carbonate equivalent (LCE). Hard rock and lithium brine are further refined into battery grade material which is sold by the ton. LIB manufacturing is a critical piece of the value chain as are BEVs and BESS (Battery Energy Storage Systems) that use them. Many people are unaware that an increasingly critical piece of the overall value chain is battery recycling which we discuss in depth in Chapter 17.

While this is the tangible value chain driven by lithium, the extended chain goes further. Let us consider: electric charging solutions & infrastructure, EV fleet operations, autonomous driving, supply chain efficiencies & disruption, robotaxis, BESS, virtual power plants (VPPs) and utility-scale disruption of the larger energy generation industry. It's simpler just to conceptually envision the electrification of everything. The companies, region, country, or societies that can capture the majority of this value chain have the most to gain.

Now let us bring the value chain back full circle because it all starts with lithium mining. Presently, Australia, Chile and China dominate global lithium mining, accounting for some 91% of all lithium mined in 2022. In 2010, the world only produced about 160,000 tons of LCE (Lithium Carbonate Equivalent) and growing moderately to just 195,000 tons of LCE in 2015. In 2022, global lithium production had accelerated greatly to 690,000 metric tons of LCE as mining companies tried to keep up with EV and associated battery demand.[10]

---

[10]   U.S. Geological Survey, Mineral Commodity Summaries (Lithium), January 2011, 2016, 2023

Australian Lithium Industry

Australia leads the world in lithium extraction, producing 323,000 tons of LCE in 2022. Why does Australia dominant global lithium mining? There are several reasons. First, Australia has a historic, established mining sector that accounted for 10% of its national GDP (Gross Domestic Product) in 2020.[11] There are at least 483 mining companies operating in the country working 350 active mining operations.[12] In contrast, U.S. mining accounted for less than 1% of its GDP in 2020.

Because mining contributes so much income to Australia's national revenue, the industry has political pull at both the national and state level. Naturally, Australia mining companies must navigate national and state permitting regulations like every other country, but they are able to get mining projects approved reasonably fast, with 3.5 years being the norm. However, even this was not deemed fast enough and new regulation was put forward in 2021 that would reduce waiting time to under two years.[13] Compare this to the U.S. mining industry where permitting approvals take up to ten years.[14] (We'll discuss the U.S. permitting process in-depth in Chapter 6.)

Over the past decade, the Australia mining industry has had easy access to large amounts of capital to pursue its mining projects, receiving some $246 billion in investments from 2012–2022.[15] Investors see Australian mining as a good place to park their money as the industry exported $303 billion USD worth of minerals in 2022 which included $21.8 billion USD of battery metals including lithium, nickel and copper (wiring harnesses). With a combination of extensive industry expertise, a permissive environment with short permitting times and ready access to large amounts of investment capital, Australia has taken advantage of the lithium boom. However, with lithium exports accounting for an estimated $10.5 billion USD in 2022, lithium remains a small player in their overall mining industry.[16]

---

[11] https://www.trade.gov/country-commercial-guides/australia-mining

[12] "Australia – Mining by the numbers". S&P Global. Feb 8, 2022.

[13] https://www.mining.com/australia-approves-one-touch-approvals-for-projects/

[14] Discussion with a senior U.S. lithium mining executive confirmed that permitting times in the U.S. are much longer than other countries and are considered excessive and counterproductive to the industry as a whole.

[15] https://www.minerals.org.au/trade-and-investment

[16] "Resources and Energy Major Projects." Australian Government. Dec 2022.

From a strategic value perspective, Australia has missed out on most of the lithium value chain. While Australia produced most of the world's lithium in 2022 (and 6% of world nickel supplies) the profits end as soon as the container of pulverized lithium, measured in tons, gets shipped off to the Asia market. Why is this? Presently, all operating lithium mines in Australia are open pit, hard rock operations located in the state of Western Australia – they have no lithium brine resources at scale.[17] There are five major operational lithium mines in Australia with Greenbushes Mine being by far the most important since it is the highest producing hard rock lithium mining operation in the world.

Greenbushes is owned by Talison Lithium, an Australian company, which operates the mine, running its day-to-day operations. However, when you dig deeper, we find that Talison Lithium is a Joint Venture (JV) owned 51% by Tianqi Lithium (a Chinese company) and 49% by Albemarle (an American company). The resulting spodumene offtake is sold directly to these two stakeholders. So, in essence, Tianqi and Albemarle are selling their own lithium, which they mined, to themselves.[18]

Until very recently (2022), Australia missed out altogether on the lithium refinement phase where lithium hard rock is processed into useable battery grade material like lithium hydroxide monohydrate. It is this midstream processing phase that brings in the highest prices per ton of product. Australia simply didn't have the industrial history, expertise or desire to process its mined lithium into a battery grade form. Instead, they shipped it out to the battery producing countries of Asia: China, South Korea and Japan.

But this is understandable because Australia has no automotive industry to speak of with not a single active automobile manufacturing plant on the continent. Consequently, Australia has no BEV manufacturing capacity either, importing all purchased BEVs from abroad. With no domestic BEV industry, they have no related battery industry either. Now we see that with no BEV industry to drive a battery industry

---

[17] https://www.ga.gov.au/scientific-topics/minerals/mineral-resources-and-advice/australian-resource-reviews/lithium

[18] https://www.igo.com.au/site/operations/lithium-holdco-joint-venture. Of note, Tianqi operates in Australia as part of a Joint Venture (JV) formed in 2021 with Australian mining company IGO. In this JV, Tianqi is the majority owner at 51% while IGO is the minority owner at 49%.

to in turn drive a battery grade lithium refinement industry, Australia sold its hard rock lithium concentrate abroad where others benefited from the downstream lithium value chain.

The Lithium Triangle

No, the Lithium Triangle is not some mysterious place where airplane navigation systems stop working and people disappear and are never heard from again as they are absorbed into a dark pool of lithium brine. It is the converging area between Bolivia, Argentina and Chile, where the largest known lithium brine deposits in the world reside. Importantly, the lithium in this area exists in the form of brine salars (Spanish for "salt lakes"). Most of the Earth's lithium resources, around 60%, are in the Triangle.

These salars are located at high elevation in the driest parts of the Earth and are remote. These underground lakes are filled with a variety of minerals to include lithium. The common method of extracting this lithium is by pumping the brine to the surface and filling a series of evaporation ponds. As the brine evaporates, various minerals remain that are filtered out until just lithium remains which in turn is refined into battery grade material (lithium carbonate, lithium hydroxide). This process is slow and deliberate, taking up to two years to produce the needed lithium.[19]

Importantly, lithium brine margins (profits) are significantly higher than lithium hard rock margins, meaning, a brine extraction operation is more profitable and captures more of the value chain as opposed to hard rock operations. Therefore, by luck of geography and geology, the countries of the Lithium Triangle have a strategic opportunity to realize far more of the value chain than their hard rock competitors. For example, spot lithium spodumene (hard rock) prices in China for November 2022 averaged $5,800.00 USD per ton while spot lithium carbonate prices averaged $67,000.00 USD per ton.[20]

Bolivia's Lithium Coup?

Let's take a look at what Bolivia has done with its estimated 21 million tons of identified lithium resources centered around its Salar de Uyuni, believed to be the

---

[19] https://piedmontlithium.com/why-lithium/lithium-101/where-lithium-comes-from-does-make-a-difference-brine-vs-hard-rock/

[20] U.S. Geological Survey, Mineral Commodity Summaries (Lithium), January 2023.

single largest brine deposit in the world. Despite this massive lithium wealth, they extract very little lithium. From 2018-2021, Bolivia produced an estimated 1,800 tpa of LCE from their small evaporative pond operations in the Salar de Uyuni.[21] Bolivia, as a nation, has completely missed the ongoing lithium revolution. Like Australia, Bolivia has no auto industry and is not in the BEV manufacturing game so they are missing that obvious piece that could drive lithium extraction. But there is more to it.[22]

Bolivia's lithium salar has several quality issues compared to neighboring Chile and Argentina in that their salar is at a lower elevation, meaning evaporation is slower which raises traditional extraction costs. Also, lithium concentrations are relatively smaller, meaning that you extract less lithium for the same effort of neighboring countries, again, raising costs. And high levels of magnesium present in the brine add to production costs due to more intensive filtering measures.

On the political front, President Evo Morales' term from 2006-2019 fostered an environment that created obstacles to outside lithium mining investment. For example, Morales essentially nationalized the natural gas industry, making gas companies pay 82% of their annual profits to the State. Importantly, this decision reflected a long-time mistrust by Bolivians for transnational companies who had previously stripped them of their national resources. Most importantly, at different times during his presidency, Morales expressed his intent to nationalize the mining industry.

In 2012, the Bolivian government seized the assets of Canadian mining company South American Silver Corporation (SASC) after continued protests and escalating violence from local indigenous communities. In a move to quell the violence (several mining employees were taken hostage) and show his support for the indigenous communities who helped elect him, Morales announced, "the mine will be nationalized via a Supreme Decree."[23]

Before the government takeover, SASC traded as high as $3.35 a share. Immediately

---

[21] Morse, Ian. "Bolivia looks to opaque methods, firms to build lithium powerhouse". Mongabay, Dec 12, 2022.

[22] https://restofworld.org/2022/quantum-motors-bolivia-electric-cars/ (Bolivia does have a small EV company, Quantum Motors, that can hand make 60, one-person, micro-EVs a month.)

[23] https://climateandcapitalism.com/2012/09/06/behind-bolivias-nationalization-of-canadian-mine/

after news of the decision, stocks plunged to a mere $0.32 a share.[24] In 2014, SASC changed its name to TriMetals Mining Incorporated. Six years after the nationalization of SASC, in 2018, an arbitration tribunal awarded the company a $28 million settlement, much less than the $307 million they were seeking.[25] In 2019, TriMetals changed its name to Gold Springs Resource Corporation. In 2022, Gold Springs traded on the Toronto Stock Exchange (TSX:GRC) at $00.17 a share with a $42 million market cap. With this kind of experience on the public record, it's not surprising that foreign mining companies would be less than enthusiastic investing in the country.

To make the Bolivia/lithium drama even more intriguing, there were persistent conspiracy rumors that Evo Morales was forced out of office in late 2019 in a coup by either the British or U.S. government to, ultimately, gain control of their national lithium deposits. I've researched both theories and couldn't find any credible evidence to support them, especially taken in context of Great Britain's and America's general apathy regarding the lithium industry in 2019. However, these unfounded rumors do illuminate the attitudes of a large section of Bolivian society and their mistrust of foreign mining companies.[26]

To muddy the lithium brine even more, Evo Morales' successor, President Arce, later accused Tesla and Elon Musk of financing the coup against Morales. Elon Musk allegedly supported the ouster of Morales and was encouraged to set up business in Bolivia by National Unity Front leader Samuel Doria Medina. Medina tweeted on February 22, 2020, "@jairbolsonaro will discuss Tesla plant in Brazil with @elonmusk I suggest we should add to this initiative: build a Gigafactory in the Salar de Uyuni for their lithium batteries."[27]

That sounds less like planning a Tesla generated lithium coup and more like an offer to do business. Right? However, (and I cannot make this stuff up) Elon Musk tweeted the below masterpiece of international relations on Twitter on July 25, 2020, between himself and a person named 'Armani'. Musk later deleted the tweet.[28]

24 https://www.mining.com/bolivia-seizes-vancouver-based-south-american-silver-corp-assets/
25 https://www.bnamericas.com/en/news/south-american-silver-wins-arbitration-case-vs-bolivia
26 https://foreignpolicy.com/2019/11/13/coup-morales-bolivia-lithium-isnt-new-oil/
27 https://twitter.com/sdoriamedina/status/1231308142153273346?lang=en
28 https://www.carscoops.com/2021/03/bolivian-president-accuses-elon-musk-and-tesla-of-being-involved-in-countrys-2019-coup/

Elon Musk: Another government stimulus package is not in the best interest of the people imo

Armani: You know what wasn't in the best interest of people? The U.S. government organizing a coup against Evo Morales in Bolivia so you could obtain lithium there.

Elon Musk: We will coup whoever we want! Deal with it.

No, I don't think Elon Musk and Tesla's team of secret lithium hitmen orchestrated a coup in Bolivia, but we can understand why outside lithium mining companies have yet to get any traction in the country. It is obvious that most companies made the strategic decision to pursue extraction operations elsewhere. Presently, Bolivia's state lithium mining company YLB extracts small amounts of lithium from the Uyuni Salar. In November 2021, Bolivia's new government-initiated discussions with eight different foreign mining companies to pursue Direct Lithium Extraction (DLE) operations.[29]

In January 2023, Bolivia signed a $1 billion USD deal with the Chinese consortium CBC consisting of CATL (largest battery manufacturer in the world), BRUNP (CATL's battery recycling subsidiary) and CMOC (an international mining company with battery metals operations). CBC, in coordination with Bolivia's state mining company YLB, will build two lithium conversion plants capable of producing 25,000 tpa (tons per annum) each. If Bolivia sells 50,000 tpa at a price of $50k per ton, they will realize revenues of $2.5 billion USD annually. Importantly, CBC will build all necessary infrastructure required (roads, bridges) to make the lithium operations viable.[30]

It is no coincidence that Bolivia had already signed onto China's Belt and Road Initiative (BRI) where China provides access to cheap loans in order for Bolivia to develop various infrastructure projects. (We'll discuss this more in Chapter 11 about the China mining industry). China uses the BRI to gain access to countries across the globe by creating a favorable environment for Chinese companies. This lithium project illustrates exactly how it is supposed to work: Chinese companies build infrastructure for

---

[29] https://www.argusmedia.com/en/news/2283947-bolivia-takes-another-shot-at-lithium

[30] Bouchard, Joseph. "In Bolivia, China Signs Deal For World's Largest Lithium Reserves." The Diplomat, Feb 10, 2023.

Bolivia which allows China to more readily extract needed raw materials like lithium to advance the Chinese economy. This lithium deal is textbook BRI. Keep your eyes and ears open whenever you hear about a new mining deal struck by a Chinese company in a foreign country. Most likely, that country has already signed onto the BRI and, therefore, the skids have already been greased for the mining company. There was no doubt who would be getting the contract.

Argentina – Most Investment by New Companies

Argentina is the next lithium powerhouse in the Triangle with an estimated 14 million tons of LCE located in brine reserves, just slightly less than that of neighboring Bolivia. In contrast to Bolivia, Argentina has an established and growing lithium brine extraction industry – and a more stable and receptive political environment. United States Geological Survey estimates that Argentine mining operations extracted a modest 6,200 tons of lithium in 2022.

The largest lithium brine operation in Argentina today is the one run by Livent, an American company spun off from FMC Corporation in 2019. Livent's local Argentinian subsidiary, Minera del Altiplano, runs the day-to-day operations of the mine located at Salar del Hombre Muerto. The operation has been open since 1998, producing LCE and lithium chloride. They use traditional brine extraction methodology, pumping up underground brine into a series of evaporation ponds.[31] (Lithium chloride can be used to make lithium metal which was priced by Shanghai Metal Market in March 2023 at $385,000.00 USD per ton.)

Australian mining company Allkem (formerly Orocobre, which merged with Galaxy in 2021) runs the only other active lithium carbonate brine evaporation operation at the Salar de Olaroz. The plant has been productive since 2015, producing 13,000 tons of LCE in 2022 although they have plans to ramp production to 42,500 tpa. Daily operations are run by an Argentinian company, Sales de Jujuy S.A. (SDJ). SDJ is a joint venture with Japanese company Toyota Tsusho Corporation (TTC) and JEMSE (an Argentine mining investment company).[32]

Here we see TTC, which is the trading arm of Toyota Group, securing its lithium

---

[31] https://www.nsenergybusiness.com/projects/fenix-lithium-mine-salar-del-hombre-muerto/

[32] https://www.allkem.co/projects/olaroz

supply via the Triangle. Of note, TTC is the executive sales agent for the lithium produced. In 2021, 86% of the lithium sold went to the EV battery supply chain. Some $192 million USD in debt financing was provided to the original Orocobre operation in 2014 by the Mizuho Financial Group, a Japanese firm.[33] While Japan and their car industry are LIB and BEV laggards, this is one of several modest projects that they are pursuing in the lithium space.

In 2021, TTC signed a Memorandum of Understanding (MOU) with BHP (an established Australian mining and oil company) and Prime Planet Energy & Solutions (PPES) for the creation of a Green Electric Vehicle (EV) Ecosystem. PPES is a joint venture (JV) between Toyota Motor Corporation and Panasonic, both Japanese companies, focused on the production of LIBs for EVs. One could probably guess that the majority of the lithium offtake from the Salar de Olaroz project is being directed by TTC to PPES.[34] Overall, from the debt financing to local JVs and subsequent offtake sales, this is largely a Japanese operation.

Argentina's brine salars are where we see the increasing global competition for lithium production and offtake sales. For example, Rio Tinto, an Australian-Anglo mining giant, has its hands into a lot of metals like iron ore, copper, and gold. With a $111 billion USD market cap as of 2023, they are a Big Dawg for sure. However, despite their depth and breadth as a business, they have never been into lithium mining.

This changed in early 2022 when Rio Tinto finalized a deal to acquire a lithium mining project in Argentina from Rincon Mining for $825 million USD. Rincon Mining itself was a JV between Australian company Argosy Minerals and Argentine company Puna Mining. As a side note, Argosy Minerals continues ownership of its other Tonopah, Nevada lithium brine project. This project is located just down the road from Albemarle's existing Silver Peak lithium brine operation which we will discuss more in Chapter 7.

The Rio Tinto acquisition illustrates the trend of big, traditional mining companies getting into the lithium game. They may lack historic lithium expertise, but they know the mining industry and can hire lithium-smart people to expand their enterprise. Also, a large company like Rio Tinto has the financial muscle to buy their way

---

[33] https://www.proactiveinvestors.com/companies/news/155798/orocobre-closes-us192-million-debt-financing-with-mizuho-for-lithium-project-37040.html

[34] https://www.toyota-tsusho.com/english/press/detail/211004_004898.html

into the lithium game with the application of brute force capital. In an example of a growing trend in the lithium brine space, Rio Tinto alluded to its use of direct lithium extraction (DLE) technology for its Argentine operation. We will discuss the topic of DLE in more detail in Chapter 12.

Chile – Largest Producer in the Lithium Triangle

Chile rounds out the Lithium Triangle's ABC (Argentina, Bolivia, Chile) cartel of lithium giants. Chile has reserves of 49 million tons LCE and currently produces and sells more lithium products than any other country in the world other than Australia. In 2022, USGS estimates that Chile produced 206,000 tons of LCE. Most of Chile's lithium comes from its famous brine salar and associated evaporation ponds in the Atacama Desert.

The largest producer of lithium in Chile is SQM (Sociedad Quimica y Minera), an established mining company which is also the single biggest producer of lithium in the world as a corporate entity. SQM's primary methodology of lithium brine extraction is through a series of sequenced evaporation ponds, which is currently the dominant technique for brine extraction worldwide. SQM has a steady flow of lithium carbonate and lithium hydroxide offtake agreements with major players in the lithium-ion battery industry, cementing SQM's position as a major lithium player.

Albemarle, a U.S. company, is the only other lithium player in Chile. Albemarle has been established in Chile for decades, refining lithium carbonate and lithium chloride at their onsite facilities. With their HQs in Santiago, they have extensive experience operating in-country. Albemarle has continued to upgrade and expand its lithium refinement operations in Chile as global market demand soars.

Chile has a back-and-forth history with nationalizing critical state resources, much as Bolivia has. Politically, Chile is conscious of lithium as a national resource and its growing potential as a money maker for the State. There has been continuing pressure to nationalize lithium and the legislation to do so was proposed for Chile's constitutional re-write in 2022. Ultimately, this proposal was rejected, but it is very much in their national conscious.

With this political uncertainty in the background, very few lithium mining permits have been given to outside companies. As we see, Albemarle is the only foreign entity operating in-country and they have been there since the 1980's. Chile as a nation is still working on creating clear lithium mining policy to provide a defined level of operational certainty and de-risking. Until then, additional mining projects will be limited. Increased national production will depend on how fast Albemarle and SQM can expand their present operations which they both are.

China – Largest Importer of Lithium

While China is the largest importer and midstream converter of lithium in the world, their domestic lithium operations are modest. In 2022, China produced 100,000 tons of LCE from their various brine and hard rock operations which is half of what SQM made that same year. China is aware of its limited lithium reserves located in the confines of its own soil, although it is twice what the U.S. is believed to have. Accordingly, China has implemented and executed a global lithium acquisition strategy to make up for its own domestic limitations. We'll go into detail on this topic in Chapter 11.

There is no doubt that China has developed and capitalized on the global lithium value chain more so than any other country in the world. Chinese corporate tentacles are everywhere in the lithium mining world in the form of joint ventures, debt financing, buy-outs and shareholdings. In researching this book, I quickly learned to dig deeper on any and every company to see where the hand of China might be. I usually found it. As we read previously in this chapter, China landed the lithium contract with the Bolivian government. The Chinese are also next door in Chile with Tianqi Lithium owning one quarter of SQM. To put that in perspective, Argentina signed an (MOU) Memorandum of Understanding with China as part of their BRI with Beijing promising over $23 billion USD in various investments.[35] Just like China's BRI greased the economic skids for future Chinese battery projects in Bolivia, it did the same for Tianqi Lithium.

While China will never be the world's leader in lithium mining production due to its inherent geology and geography, they are the world leader in lithium refinement of battery grade lithium products. Also, China dominates the EV battery space, where Chinese company CATL is the single largest producer of lithium-ion batteries in the world. To round out their value chain dominance, China has the largest automobile market in the world and is the largest manufacturer of BEVs. When China sneezes, the global lithium value chain catches a cold.

---

[35] Lanteigne, Marc. "Argentina Joins China's Belt and Road." The Diplomat, Feb 10, 2022.

Battery Mineral Resources

While we have discussed at length a general overview of the lithium enterprise, lithium alone doesn't make a battery. It must be used in conjunction with other battery minerals like nickel, manganese, cobalt and graphite (battery type dependent). If we estimate that lithium production will increase tenfold from where it is today to meet future battery demand, then its accompanying battery materials will also need to increase tenfold. Of course, this math will change considering that newer battery chemistries like lithium iron phosphate (LFP) eliminate the need for nickel and cobalt. But let's see what this data looks like as production of all these materials will most likely be far more than tenfold by 2050.

Let's start with lithium of which an estimated 689,000 tons of LCE were produced in 2022.[36] A tenfold increase is 6.89 million tons of LCE which is far more than current assets can produce. This means more hard rock mines and lithium brine operations need to be brought online to meet growing demand. Not every country has the geology to ramp up production, but we do know the Lithium Triangle has the reserves to meet this demand providing them outsized influence moving forward. As there is an estimated 138 million tons of LCE reserves, a tenfold ramp up will exhaust this in 20 years and a twentyfold ramp up in just ten years.

An estimated 2.7 million tons of nickel was extracted in 2021 with Indonesia being the leader by far with 1 million tons. However, only 410,000 tons of nickel was believed to be used in battery production in 2022.[37] Therefore, a tenfold ramp in production is 4.1 million tons. With an estimated total world reserve of 95 million tons, a tenfold ramp up in nickel production could last for about 24 years and a twentyfold ramp up only 12 years. If the nickel industry substituted traditional nickel uses with other metals to focus more on battery grade nickel production, they could cannibalize within the industry to make more batteries.

A whopping 20 million tons of manganese was extracted in 2022 with South Africa, Gabon, and Australia accounting for 75% of global production. The world has an estimated 1.7 billion tons of manganese with South Africa, China, Brazil and

---

[36] U.S. Geological Survey, Mineral Commodity Summaries (Lithium), January 2023.

[37] "Sumitomo Metal sees global nickel demand for battery use at 410,000 in 2022." Reuters, March 29, 2022.

Australia accounting for 85% of this.[38] However, its use in LIBs is trivial with less than 60,000 tons being deployed in batteries in 2022. The manganese industry can easily keep up with future battery deployments at either tenfold or twentyfold scale. But it should be noted that manganese cannot be substituted in the steel industry by any another metal, not that it will need to be cannibalized any time soon to support the LIB industry.

Cobalt extraction in 2022 was 190,000 metric tons with the Democratic Republic of the Congo (DRC) alone producing 68% of that. There are estimated reserves of 8.3 million metric tons of Cobalt in the world with almost half residing in the DRC and another 18% in Australia.[39] A tenfold increase in production is 1.9 million tons a year and twentyfold is 19 million. Clearly, that's a problem and not possible with present reserves. However, cobalt as a battery component can be substituted as we have seen with the increased production of LFP batteries that have no nickel or cobalt.

Graphite production in 2022 stood at 1.3 million tons with China producing 65% of this total amount. Global reserves of natural graphite are estimated at 330 million tons with two-thirds located in Turkey, Brazil, and China.[40] A tenfold increase is 13 million tpa and twentyfold is 26 million. However, natural graphite competes with synthetic graphite meaning any country with the R&D capability, capital and willingness to pursue it can produce its own graphite. Because of this, graphite is the battery material least prone to disruption and can have the shortest supply chain as one can collocate both graphite and battery manufacturing.

As we present this data on mineral reserves, we should keep in mind that these are just estimates. The majority of the world's surface has not been geologically surveyed and therefore we don't know how much total minerals sources there actually are and where they are located. Of growing importance to the battery industry, geologists believe there are considerable reserves of battery mineral nodules on our ocean floors, but extraction is costly and environmental impacts unknown.

As we can see with what a tenfold and twentyfold increase of battery minerals looks like compared to current production and estimated reserves, the numbers don't add up. As battery manufacturing accelerates across the global enterprise, low

---

[38] U.S. Geological Survey, Mineral Commodity Summaries (Manganese), January 2023.

[39] U.S. Geological Survey, Mineral Commodity Summaries (Cobalt), January 2023.

[40] U.S. Geological Survey, Mineral Commodity Summaries (Graphite), January 2023.

volume battery minerals like cobalt will need to be substituted for more plentiful ones. Another strategy to meet demand will include R&D efforts to make batteries more efficient with increased energy density that use less battery minerals. Most importantly, the comprehensive recycling of existing batteries to conserve limited resources and shorten far-flung supply chains will become a crucial industry. (We discuss this at length in Chapter 17).

Looking Ahead

1. Presently, lithium is the key ingredient for EV batteries and most likely will be for the foreseeable future. Tenfold and twentyfold increase in production means huge growth in hard rock mining, brine extraction, midstream conversion facilities and urban mining (recycling). Will we eventually find a substitute for lithium using sodium, magnesium, or zinc? If so, will lithium be phased out altogether or run in parallel to new battery chemistry? What impact would a feasible substitute have on the existing global lithium enterprise?

2. My guess is the Lithium Triangle will grow in importance as a lithium hub based on their large reserves. A tenfold increase in lithium production will require increased evaporation and DLE operations in Chile, Argentina, and Bolivia. It is likely that the Lithium Triangle countries develop a battery industry as opposed to shipping the majority of their LCE to China and losing much of the value chain. The growing North American battery industry will increasingly look to western hemisphere resources to enhance critical mineral security.

3. Will China continue its dominance of the lithium value chain? By every indication they are doubling down on their lithium acquisition, midstream conversion, and battery manufacturing. Chinese battery giant CATL alone has 12,000 people in its R&D division indicating their intent to dominate the future LIB innovation space. China recognizes growing LIB regionalization in North America and Europe and have consequently shifted to pursuing substitutes at scale like LFP batteries, expanding into Africa for battery minerals, increasing domestic extraction operations and investing heavily in battery recycling.

4. As we mentioned, most of our planet has not been geologically surveyed. Will exploration teams discover new lithium and other battery mineral deposits in previously unknown locations creating a new LIB powerhouse? Will a country discover vast amounts of battery mineral nodules off their coast and develop an environmentally sound and economic way to extract them? Will someone develop the technology to economically extract lithium from seawater, rendering the Lithium Triangle and much of the current global lithium processing architecture irrelevant?

CHAPTER 2

U.S. Lithium Policy

"...the United States does not have a coherent national materials and minerals policy."
- National Materials and Minerals Policy, Research and Development Act of 1980

Maximizing the American Lithium Value Chain

Until 2018, the U.S. had no strategic vision or policy at the national level effectively encouraging the capture of its domestic lithium value chain. In this respect, the U.S. is like other countries, such as Bolivia, who grapple with the economic significance of the lithium industry but have never been able to maximize it. To date, U.S. policy has been incomplete, reactionary and bureaucratically complex. There are many reasons for this but let's start with the lithium value chain.

First, even though the U.S. has the world's second largest automobile market, its BEV segment is relatively small compared to other countries. In a reoccurring theme, China realizes much higher BEV penetration rates and will continue to do so for many years to come. This is ironic considering that Tesla, a U.S. company, has largely driven the global auto industry's transformation from an ICE business model to a lithium-ion BEV one.

While the U.S. domestic BEV effort is quite modest compared to its competitors, its domestic LIB industry is non-existent. Except, of course, for Tesla's internal effort to grow the battery industry for its own vehicle force. And even this is done in close partnership with Panasonic who has the intellectual capital and technological skill to make the actual battery cells. Since the growth of the lithium-ion battery industry in the 1990's, the U.S. has been an uninterested bystander as Japan and South Korea initially captured most of the industry before ceding the rest of it to China. As we'll see in Chapter 16, current battery industry growth in the U.S. is led almost exclusively by foreign companies.

The U.S. has very little domestic lithium refining capacity which is dominated by just two players. Although the U.S. has modest lithium reserves estimated at 775,000 tons, its lithium resources (i.e. potential but not proven) are estimated at more than nine million tons.[41] One could reason, with a focused national effort, real incentives and a disciplined approach, the U.S. could realize massive economic rewards from its domestic lithium value chain. This would include increasing extraction operations, expanding midstream conversion capacity and investing heavily in battery manufacturing.

However, any lithium mining company looking to do business in the U.S. has to navigate a labyrinth of laws accumulated over the last 150 years. As the average mining permitting time in the U.S. is ten years, many companies make the decision to do business elsewhere in the world with a better mining environment. Thus, a key strategy for a company doing business in the U.S. is having (or hiring) a competent legal team who understands U.S. specific mining laws at the federal, state, local and tribal levels. No permit, no mine.

Most of the U.S. laws on the books address hard rock mining as that is the dominate form of mineral extraction in the U.S. (non-hydrocarbon). The U.S. did not have any specific federal law pertaining to brine mining until 1970 and that amendment is rather broad and does not recognize lithium. Currently, there is no legal momentum to modernize and improve existing federal mining laws that specifically regulate lithium hard rock and brine extraction. To do so would recognize lithium as a critical mineral that is exceptionally important to American economic prosperity and security.

General Mining Act of 1872

The basis for modern U.S. mining regulation goes back to *An Act to Promote the Development of the Mining Resources of The United States* signed into law by Ulysses S. Grant. This legislation is more commonly known as the General Mining Act of 1872. Significantly, this act only governs mining activity on U.S. federal land. The Act is a

---

[41] U.S. Geological Survey, Mineral Commodity Summaries, January 2022 (Lithium). Report prepared by Brian Jaskula.

broad document, only six pages long, written at a time when most mining efforts were concerned with gold, silver, copper, tin and lead.[42]

The Act allowed private mining concerns to conduct operations on federal land if they obeyed all existing "State, territorial and local regulation". But if the mining was on federal land, then the mining company most likely did not have any other laws to navigate. Quite simply, a mining company would file an affidavit with the office of the U.S. Surveyor-General (a position that no longer exists but was later absorbed by the eventual Bureau of Land Management- BLM). After 60 days of filing, with no legitimate counterclaim filed in protest, the miner was given a patent and awarded rights to the mine.

This extremely broad document enabled private mining companies to pursue mining rights on federal land, exploit the resources, pay no royalties and then up and leave when they were done. According to the U.S. General Accounting Office (GAO), in the last 150 years since the Act was signed into law, an estimated 140,000 hard rock mines have operated on federal land.[43] In 2018, there were 872 registered mines on federal land managed by the Bureau of Land Management (BLM) and the Forest Service. Most of these mines paid no royalties to the U.S. government – as dictated by the Act of 1872.[44] GAO data revealed only three lithium mines approved for federal lands in 2018 – two in Arizona and one in Nevada.

The U.S. federal government received $550 million in royalties from mining companies in 2018. Since 83% of known mining operations were on areas managed by BLM, they paid no royalties. However, the other 17% were located on Forest Service land. On Forest Service land, the federal government provides the mining companies a lease; the company doesn't own the claim and thus pay royalties.[45]

---

[42] *An Act to promote the Development of the mining Resources of The United States.* This is the base document that all subsequent amendments speak to. The Act itself was a reaction to an avalanche of unregulated mining in the West which often resulted in conflicting mining interests (i.e. shootouts).

[43] https://www.gao.gov/hardrock-mining-federal-lands

[44] https://www.gao.gov/products/gao-20-461r

[45] https://www.gao.gov/assets/gao-20-461r.pdf

fied person : *Provided,* That all the persons availing themselves of the provisions of this section shall be required to pay, and there shall be collected from them, at the time of making payment for their land, interest on the total amounts paid by them, respectively, at the rate of five per centum per annum, from the date at which they would have been required to make payment under the act of July fifteenth, eighteen hundred and seventy, until the date of actual payment : *Provided further,* That the twelfth section of said act of July sixteenth, eighteen hundred and seventy, is hereby so amended that the aggregate amount of the proceeds of sale received prior to the first day of March of each year shall be the amount upon which the payment of interest shall be based. Five per cent interest to be paid on what sum and for what time.

SEC. 3. That the sale or transfer of his or her claim upon any portion of these lands by any settler prior to the issue of the commissioner's instructions of April twenty-sixth, eighteen hundred and seventy-one, shall not operate to preclude the right of entry, under the provisions of this act, upon another tract settled upon subsequent to such sale or transfer : *Provided,* That satisfactory proof of good faith be furnished upon such subsequent settlement : *Provided further,* That the restrictions of the pre-emption laws relating to previous enjoyment of the pre-emption right, to removal from one's own land in the same State, or the ownership of over three hundred and twenty acres, shall not apply to any settler actually residing on his or her claim at the date of the passage of this act. Settler, transferring claims prior to, &c., not precluded from entering upon another tract, if, &c.
Certain restrictions of the pre-emption laws not to apply.

APPROVED, May 9, 1872.

CHAP. CLII. — *An Act to promote the Development of the mining Resources of the United States.* May 10, 1872.
See 1873, ch. 159. *Post,* p. 465.

Be it enacted by the Senate and House of Representatives of the United States of America in Congress assembled, That all valuable mineral deposits in lands belonging to the United States, both surveyed and unsurveyed, are hereby declared to be free and open to exploration and purchase, and the lands in which they are found to occupation and purchase, by citizens of the United States and those who have declared their intention to become such, under regulations prescribed by law, and according to the local customs or rules of miners, in the several mining-districts, so far as the same are applicable and not inconsistent with the laws of the United States. Valuable mineral deposits in public lands and the lands to be open to citizens, &c.

SEC. 2. That mining-claims upon veins or lodes of quartz or other rock in place bearing gold, silver, cinnabar, lead, tin, copper, or other valuable deposits heretofore located, shall be governed as to length along the vein or lode by the customs, regulations, and laws in force at the date of their location. A mining-claim located after the passage of this act, whether located by one or more persons, may equal, but shall not exceed, one thousand five hundred feet in length along the vein or lode ; but no location of a mining-claim shall be made until the discovery of the vein or lode within the limits of the claim located. No claim shall extend more than three hundred feet on each side of the middle of the vein at the surface, nor shall any claim be limited by any mining regulation to less than twenty-five feet on each side of the middle of the vein at the surface, except where adverse rights existing at the passage of this act shall render such limitation necessary. The end-lines of each claim shall be parallel to each other. Length of mining-claims upon veins or lodes;
width;
end-lines.

SEC. 3. That the locators of all mining locations heretofore made, or which shall hereafter be made, on any mineral vein, lode, or ledge, situated on the public domain, their heirs and assigns, where no adverse claim exists at the passage of this act, so long as they comply with the laws of the United States, and with State, territorial, and local regulations not in conflict with said laws of the United States governing their possessory title, shall have the exclusive right of possession and enjoyment of all the surface included within the lines of their locations, and of all veins, lodes, and ledges throughout their entire depth, the top or apex of which Locators of mining locations where there is no adverse claim, &c., to have what exclusive rights of possession and enjoyment.

Above, the first page of the The General Mining Act of 1872. This six-page overly broad law continues to govern mining operations located on federal lands to this day.

Mineral Leasing Act of 1920

Because the Mining Act of 1872 was so broad and encouraged anyone and everyone to stake a claim and pay no taxes, the U.S. government ran into problems reference oil and coal. So many people were staking claims, it became evident that they were claiming land that had significant energy reserves, which could undercut national energy and military security. Accordingly, *The Mineral Leasing Act of 1920* was signed into law by President Woodrow Wilson on February 25, 1920.[46]

The intent of this 17-page document was to "promote the mining of coal, phosphate, oil, oil shale, gas and sodium on the public domain". Inherent in this statement was recognizing these minerals as critical to U.S. economic and national security. In this Act, the Secretary of the Interior was given responsibility to oversee the process of providing leases to mining companies.

Therefore, companies mining these minerals on federal land did not own the claim, they merely leased it from the U.S. government (USG). Lease lengths were finite, would be re-assessed by the Department of the Interior (DOI) and quarterly royalty payments would be made to the USG. Compared to the overly broad Mining Act of 1872, this act had very specific language to prevent issues in the oil and coal industry that were present in the hard rock mining industry. From 1926 to 1990, a further 47 amendments were made to the 1920 Mineral Leasing Act.

Reference Lithium, we are interested in the subsequent amendment entitled the *Geothermal Steam Act of 1970*. This is relevant to us today, because it addresses brine and the byproducts of geothermal steam mining which could include lithium. At the time of the amendment, the U.S. had no collective understanding of the future importance of lithium. Hence, we find modern day lithium brine extraction operations regulated by a 50-year law with no idea what it would one day be regulating.

The Geothermal Act regulates geothermal steam and its byproducts much like other minerals that were commonly mined at the time of the original Act of 1920. It provides guidance on leasing timelines, royalty payments and administrative procedures for securing a permit. However, Section 24 gives the Secretary of the Interior broad powers to "protect the public interest" and provide for "the protection of water

---

[46] *Mineral Leasing Act of 1920 as Amended*. Bureau of Land Management. This 152-page PDF includes the original 1920 Act and then the subsequent 47 amendments added to it over the next 70 years.

quality and other environmental qualities".[47] The Act would obviously have to be amended to encourage the extraction of lithium through geothermal activity.

The *Federal Land and Policy Management Act of 1976*, signed by President Ford, was a document created specifically for BLM. The law updated and codified how the BLM would manage public, federal lands. The Act gave more authority to BLM within the Department of the Interior, especially when enforcing environmental concerns, which are broadly defined.

As the General Mining Act of 1872 was considered by critics as overly vague with not enough regulation, BLM, who was responsible for enforcing the Act, was seen as favoring mining companies. Critics observed that mining companies often abused the 1872 Act by harming the environment, recklessly abandoning their operations and using ostensible mining claims to conduct other business – all while paying no taxes at all to the public.

In response to these complaints, in 1994, Congress passed a moratorium on funding the provisions of patents by BLM. Meaning, BLM would receive no funds to process new claims after 1994. This meant mining companies could not actually own the mines they worked on as they had since 1872. Now, the government would retain ownership of the land and mining companies would in essence temporarily lease the land. As of the writing of this book, the moratorium on patents is still in effect.[48]

National Materials and Minerals Policy, Research and Development Act of 1980

This Act correctly determined that the U.S. did not have a coherent mineral policy. The Act also recognized that critical minerals were crucial to U.S. economic and national security. The Act directs the office of the President to coordinate with the relevant

---

[47] *Mineral Leasing Act of 1920 as Amended.* Bureau of Land Management. The geothermal amendment is critical to understanding the legal foundation for present day lithium brine mining in the U.S.

[48] https://www.blm.gov/programs/energy-and-minerals/mining-and-minerals/locatable-minerals/patents. BLM has posted on their website a laconic notice confirming the moratorium on mining patents – some 29 years after it first came into effect.

agencies to forecast critical mineral demands, secure critical mineral supply chains and to coordinate applicable research efforts.

With much irony, this Act references the *National Mining and Minerals Act of 1970* which was enacted by Congress to better regulate and coordinate mining operations nationally. Another theme we see in the 1970 Act is an effort to better protect the environment from exploitative mining practices that had no regard for the land.

It is interesting to note, that some 40 years later, the problems identified by the 1980 Act had not been fixed. The U.S. did not forecast critical mineral demands as seen by our present lithium dilemma, associated supply chains were not secured and the necessary emphasis on coordinating associated research and development efforts was never applied. We will see subsequent laws essentially repeat what was already enacted, but never followed.

Energy Policy Act of 2005

Another document we are interested in is the *Energy Policy Act of 2005*, which is long and detailed, weighing in at an impressive 551 pages. This Act updated many previous regulations and laws pertaining specifically to the realm of energy and energy conservation. Interestingly, it recognizes many modern energy technologies like hybrid vehicles. However, the Act did not exhibit any government consciousness of pure electric vehicles or lithium-ion batteries. Notably, from a lithium brine perspective, the Act updated and built on the *Geothermal Steam Act of 1970.*

From a bureaucracy perspective, it's interesting to note that the Act recognized the long delays in geothermal permitting and had a section devoted to reducing the backlog of permit requestors. In fact, Section 225 gives specific guidance to reduce permitting backlogs. From reading the backlog discussion, one can see that there are permits submitted as far back as five years prior that are still in administrative limbo.[49] The bureaucracy is so complex and under-resourced that permit approval takes more than half of a decade.

---

[49] *Energy Policy Act 2005*. Section 225. The language says that geothermal permitting backlogs must be reduced by 90% in the next five years. This means, presumably, some 10% of permit requests will still not be processed after five years.

Energy Independence and Security Act of 2007 (EISA)

The *Energy Independence and Security Act of 2007* was signed into law on December 19, 2007, by President Bush. The purpose of this 310-page document was to "move the United States toward greater energy independence and security, to increase the production of clean renewable fuels, to protect consumers, to increase the efficiency of products, buildings, and vehicles, to promote research on and deploy greenhouse gas capture and storage options, and to improve the energy performance of the Federal Government, and for other purposes."[50] Let's review some of its relevant sections.

Improved Vehicle Technology; SEC. 131. TRANSPORTATION ELECTRIFICATION. This section reveals an understanding of relevant electric vehicle technology and the different types (battery, fuel cell, hybrids, etc..). The Act approves $450 million for local administrations to promote the use of EVs. The money will be spent in the form of grants from 2008-2012, in consultation with the Secretary of Transportation. Separate electric transportation programs are further funded at $475 million from 2008-2012.

SEC. 136. ADVANCED TECHNOLOGY VEHICLES MANUFACTURING INCENTIVE PROGRAM. This program provided $25 billion in low-interest loans for new and established companies to develop low-emission vehicles. Section 136 would prove to be the single most significant piece of U.S. legislation that transformed the global lithium value chain. This is because a young entrepreneur by the name of Elon Musk took a $465 million loan from this program in 2008 and developed the commercially successful Tesla Model S.[51]

Subtitle B—Geothermal Energy. SEC. 611. SHORT TITLE.
This subtitle may be cited as the "Advanced Geothermal Energy
Research and Development Act of 2007".

SEC. 621. REPORTS. (a) REPORTS ON ADVANCED USES OF GEOTHERMAL ENERGY. This section addresses the need to research mineral recovery from geofluids.

---

[50] Energy Independence and Security Act of 2007.

[51] https://www.energy.gov/lpo/tesla; I find it interesting that the DOE still has a funded ATVM program with $16 billion available today. Nissan and Ford both used this program to fund EV programs that never met with mainstream success like Tesla. Only one other EV start-up, Fisker (which subsequently went bankrupt), met the ATVM loan requirements. U.S. battery manufacturers can also use this program like Syrah Resources, an Australian company specializing in graphite production.

A total of $450 million is provided to pursue a variety of geothermal research and technology programs to be spent over five years from 2008-2012. There is no mention of lithium brine extraction.

Energy Act of 2020

This Act became law in November 2020 as part of a larger 5,000- page omnibus bill. From a brine extraction perspective, there wasn't much. Section 614 mentions authorizing a grant to research more cost-efficient methods of removing minerals from brine during the coproduction process.

Section 7001 directs the Secretary of the Interior (SOI) to maintain a list of critical elements considered vital to U.S. economic or national security as well as surveys to determine where these minerals may be found in the geographic U.S.

Section 7002. MINERAL SECURITY. This section amends the National

Materials and Minerals Policy, Research and Development Act of 1980. Specifically, "(3) establish an analytical and forecasting capability for identifying critical mineral demand, supply, and other factors to allow informed actions to be taken to avoid supply shortages, mitigate price volatility, and prepare for demand growth and other market shifts."[52]

SOI is directed to provide estimates of quantities and locations of critical minerals on U.S. territory. SOI will conduct surveys and geological mapping to accomplish this. SOI will then collect this data and make it available for the public.

The Secretary of Energy is directed to establish a Critical Material Consortium. The existing Energy Innovation Hub that would most likely manage this is Ames National Laboratory. This effort is provided $600 million in funding from 2021-2025.

Also, the Secretary of Energy was given $75 million to establish a 'Critical Materials Supply Chain Research Facility'. The facility will advance the development and commercialization of the critical material supply chain. As lithium is listed as a critical mineral, its associated supply chain would be a topic for development.[53]

---

[52] This is an interesting directive as this very topic is what the USG failed to do reference the lithium value chain until publication of this Act although the President was directed to do so by the reference 1980 Act.

[53] As of this writing, I don't think this facility has been created. There is an existing Critical Materials Institute located at the Ames National Laboratory associated with the University of Iowa.

Section 7003 directs the Director of National Intelligence (DNI) to provide a report to congress on the critical mineral strategy of the People's Republic of China (PRC), with emphasis on their Belt and Road Initiative. The DNI will provide future reports detailing the PRC's mining activity and processing capabilities. The DNI will also address the PRC's overall control of a critical mineral, domestic and international mineral pricing and associated price volatility.[54]

What we have just reviewed in this chapter are some of the prominent historic laws that regulate the mining industry and critical minerals. However, President Trump and Biden have both given guidance in the form of Presidential Executive Orders (EO's) as well. We will start by examining several relevant Executive Orders issued by both Presidents. EO's carry the force of law unless limited by congressional action or court rulings. EO's are also used to enforce existing laws. An Executive Order is a public document and part of the government's official record that an Agency can reference. As such, it can be essential for communicating policy and coordinating interagency activity. Importantly, EO's don't provide funding.

Executive Order 13806 (EO13806) 2017

President Trump issued EO13806 (Assessing and Strengthening the Manufacturing and Defense Industrial Base and Supply Chain Resiliency of the United States) on July 21, 2017. Section 1 (Policy) provides an overview of the need to provide a secure environment for the U.S. manufacturing and industrial base along with associated supply chains. The EO recognizes that the U.S. has lost 5 million manufacturing related jobs since the year 2000.[55]

Section 2 (Assessment of the Manufacturing Capacity, Defense Industrial Base, and Supply Chain Resiliency of the United States) directs the Secretary of Defense to coordinate and consult with a dozen other agencies and provide a report on

---

[54] It is interesting to see the DNI directed to execute intelligence activity against the PRC's global lithium-ion battery supply chain. Individual investors conduct this very type of intelligence collection for their portfolio, while some do it at an organizational level like Benchmark Mineral Intelligence.

[55] Executive Order 13806 (Assessing and Strengthening the Manufacturing and Defense Industrial Base and Supply Chain Resiliency of the United States) signed July 21, 2017.

associated strategic vulnerabilities. Paragraph (a) requires identification of raw materials crucial for national security. Paragraph (b) requires identifying manufacturing capabilities necessary for identified raw materials. Paragraph (c) requests identification of economic and geopolitical conditions that could disrupt U.S. domestic production. Paragraph (d) focuses on identifying the specifics of how domestic manufacturing and their supply chains are vulnerable to single point of failure conditions.

Overall, this EO is very broad but seeks to identify specific manufacturing, industrial and supply chain vulnerabilities as reported by the relevant U.S. agencies. There is no recognition of raw materials like battery metals as being critical. The EO gives the Secretary of Defense 270 days to come back with a coordinated assessment. Five months later, President Trump issued a subsequent EO focusing on critical minerals, much different from EO13806, which was broad and vague in mentioning "raw materials".

Executive Order 13817 (EO13817) 2017

In December 2017, President Trump published EO 13817 (A Federal Strategy to Ensure Secure and Reliable Supplies of Critical Minerals). Section one correctly identified the U.S. was overly reliant on imported critical minerals vital to both national security and economic prosperity, creating strategic vulnerabilities. It also identified that the U.S. had deposits of some of these critical minerals within American borders. However, "our miners and producers are currently limited by a lack of comprehensive, machine-readable data concerning topographical, geological, and geophysical surveys; permitting delays; and the potential for protracted litigation regarding permits that are issued."[56]

Section One (Findings) further identified the need for increased domestic mining exploration, increased actual production of these minerals as well as the need to recycle and reuse critical minerals. EO 13817 also directs the U.S. to find alternatives to these minerals whenever possible. Further, the U.S. needs to reduce the amount of minerals it imports and improve its own domestic production and related manufacturing.

Section Two (Definition) leaves the definition of a critical mineral to the Secretary

---

[56] Executive Order 13817 (A Federal Strategy To Ensure Secure and Reliable Supplies of Critical Minerals) signed December 20, 2017.

of the Interior with the guidance that: 1) it is a non-fuel mineral (i.e. it's not coal or a hydrocarbon) essential to economic or national security; 2) its supply chain is vulnerable to disruption; and 3) it serves an essential function in the manufacturing of a product related to our national economy and security. Additionally, the Secretary of the Interior will coordinate with the Secretary of Defense and other relevant executive agencies to identify what is a critical mineral.

Section Three (Policy) puts forth overarching policy guidance in that the U.S. Federal Government will reduce America's vulnerability to critical mineral supply chain disruption. It will do this by identifying new sources of critical minerals to construct redundant supply chains. Second, it will intensify all aspects of the process to include exploration, mining, concentration, separation, alloying, recycling, and reprocessing critical minerals. Third, it will ensure U.S. miners have access to the most advanced topographic, geologic, and geophysical data within U.S. borders. Lastly, it will streamline leasing and permitting processes relating to the mining of critical minerals.

Section Four (Implementation) directs the Secretary of Commerce to coordinate with the Secretaries of Defense, the Interior, Agriculture Energy and the U.S. Trade Representative and provide a report on how they will collectively execute the policy described in Section Three. While this section is largely redundant to the previous EO, we should notice the specific guidance to develop "options for accessing and developing critical minerals through investment and trade with our allies and partners". I take this, from a lithium perspective, the need to develop a strategy based on the U.S., North America, Western Hemisphere then our allies located abroad.

In February 2018, as directed, U.S. Geological Survey (USGS is part of the Department of the Interior) published a draft list of 35 critical minerals. After a period of several months where USGS invited public comments on the topic, they published a finalized list in May 2018. Lithium made the list as did companion battery metals cobalt and manganese. The brief description listed next to lithium was "used primarily for batteries."[57] Now that the Department of the Interior and USGS had done its job and published the critical minerals list, Secretary of Commerce published their fifty-page strategy to execute the policy guidance in EO13817.

---

[57] https://www.usgs.gov/news/national-news-release/interior-releases-2018s-final-list-35-minerals-deemed-critical-us

A Federal Strategy to Ensure Secure and Reliable Supplies of Critical Minerals had six Calls to Action: 1) Advance Transformational Research, Development, and Deployment Across Critical Mineral Supply Chains; 2) Strengthen America's Critical Mineral Supply Chains and Defense Industrial Base; 3) Enhance International Trade and Cooperation Related to Critical Minerals; 4) Improve Understanding of Domestic Critical Mineral Resources; 5) Improve Access to Domestic Critical Mineral Resources on Federal Lands and Reduce Federal Permitting Timeframes; and 6) Grow the American Critical Minerals Workforce.[58]

After reading this strategy, a few points stand out.

- The authors recognize the critical mineral supply chain is interconnected and all aspects of it must be addressed.
- On the list of critical minerals, more than 50% of lithium consumption is imported with 25% coming from Chile, 24% from Argentina and 1% from China.
- The need to research lithium extraction from seawater.
- The need to recycle lithium-ion batteries, referencing the Department of Energy and their Vehicles Technology Office.
- The authors recognize the catastrophic supply chain shocks the U.S. could suffer if China shut down critical mineral exports.
- The importance of geographically close trading partners like Canada and Mexico.
- The need to trade with U.S. allies like Japan and South Korea.
- There is a complex labyrinth of mining approvals at every level.

After reading the strategy, I agree with every word of it. The strategy accurately recognizes in detail every challenge and problem relating to critical mineral strategy, mining, lithium and the domestic U.S. battery industry. In total, the authors identify 6 Calls to Action, 24 goals, and 61 recommendations that describe specific steps that the Federal Government must take to achieve the objectives outlined in the strategy. To do so, the U.S. government must coordinate across 30 different federal agencies

[58] https://www.commerce.gov/sites/default/files/2020-01/Critical_Minerals_Strategy_Final.pdf

and hundreds of state, local, tribal and international partners. (And that's why it is dead in the water and will never work.)

Executive Order 13953 (EO13953) 2020

Let's fast forward to Fall of 2020, September 30th, when President Trump issued EO13953 (Addressing the Threat to the Domestic Supply Chain from Reliance on Critical Minerals From Foreign Adversaries and Supporting the Domestic Mining and Processing Industries). This EO references EO13817 and provides an overview of the findings in the previously discussed federal strategy. The introduction recognizes China's dominance in rare earth elements as well as the U.S.' complete reliance on graphite, importing 100% of American consumption needs.

Section 1 begins by declaring a national emergency, referring to America's undue reliance on foreign entities for critical minerals. The Secretary of the Interior (SOI) is directed to coordinate with other relevant agencies and investigate U.S. dependence on foreign supplied critical minerals. Furthermore, the SOI is directed to "recommend executive action, which may include the imposition of tariffs or quotas, other import restrictions against China and other non-market foreign adversaries whose economic practices threaten to undermine the health, growth, and resiliency of the United States...".[59]

Section 2 directs relevant agencies to expend resources towards protecting the U.S. domestic critical supply chain. These agencies will focus on establishing critical mineral supply chains free from foreign sources and expand U.S. domestic mining and processing capabilities. Various agencies are also directed to report back on their plans to enact the guidance in the EO.

Section 3 offers new guidance for the SOI and the Secretary of Defense to consider using the authority delegated in section 306 of Executive Order 13603 of March 16, 2012 (National Defense Resources Preparedness). This EO can be used to provide grants and procure equipment for the production and processing of critical minerals in the United States.

Section 4 directs the Secretary of Energy to investigate loan guarantees pursuant to Title XVII of the Energy Policy Act of 2005 to support domestic critical mineral

---

[59] Executive order 13953 ((Addressing the Threat to the Domestic Supply Chain from Reliance on Critical Minerals From Foreign Adversaries and Supporting the Domestic Mining and Processing Industries) signed September 30, 2020.

supply chain programs. The Secretary is also directed to look at the definitions and constraints of various standing U.S. Codes to see if they can be interpreted in a manner to support the domestic critical mineral supply chain.

Section 5 asks relevant agencies to support a streamlined permitting process for projects under their authorities that supports the domestic critical mineral supply chain.

Section 6 asks several agencies to relook historic mining sites for their utility in providing critical minerals needed today.

EO13953 is a more aggressive document than EO1387, which was a request for research and solutions. EO13953 shows a willingness to take adverse economic action against a foreign competitor, specifically, China. For sure, this EO is more forceful in directing the various agencies to facilitate domestic critical mineral supply chain resilience whenever and wherever they can. Overall, EO13953 is an attempt to cut through the massive federal bureaucracy as one can assume not much had actually happened from the issuance of the previous EO almost three years earlier.

Executive Order 14017 (EO14017) 2021

Five months later, in February 2021, President Biden issued Executive Order 14017 (America's Supply Chains) which identified ongoing insecurities in U.S. strategic supply chains. Section 1 (Policy) of this far-reaching order identified a U.S. need for, "... resilient, diverse, and secure supply chains to ensure our economic prosperity and national security." EO14017 also recognizes that global economic competition can undermine critical U.S. manufacturing capacity. Also identified is the need to work with allies and partners.[60]

Section 2 (Coordination) gives guidance for The Assistant to the President for National Security Affairs (APNSA) and the Assistant to the President for Economic Policy (APEP) to coordinate all necessary actions of the Executive Branch relating to this EO. This is a tall order as agency heads are encouraged to consult with relevant stakeholders. This means labor unions, industry, academia, state, local and tribal governments. (Moving forward, as we observe actions relating to this EO, this is most likely where things grind to a halt. Stakeholder differences equal gridlock.)

---

[60] Executive Order 14017 (America's Supply Chains) signed February 24, 2021.

Section 3 (100-Day Supply Chain Review) requests a comprehensive supply chain risk analysis by relevant agencies. Of note, the Secretary of Energy is directed to address EV battery supply chains. The Department of Defense was directed to address risks with critical minerals, including rare earth elements.

In many ways this EO is redundant regarding previous published EO's as it requests updates to various supply chain vulnerabilities that were requested by the outgoing Trump administration. Significantly, there is language throughout this EO recognizing the impacts of climate change. Of interest to us and the U.S. lithium value chain, this is the first time we see language about batteries for the EV industry as a topic of strategic significance. More importantly, his EO also shows the incoming Biden Administration continuing the critical mineral strategy and momentum of the outgoing Trump Administration.

In June 2021, *Building Resilient Supply Chains, Revitalizing American Manufacturing, and Fostering Broad-Based Growth* requested by EO14017 was published by the White House. This was a 250-page document. For our purposes we are concerned with pages 85 – 148 addressing the U.S. battery value chain. The battery section recognizes the reality of the U.S. situation, "China and the European Union (EU) – in contrast to the U.S. approach – have developed and deployed ambitious government-led industrial policies that are supporting their success across the battery supply chain."[61]

The report goes on to describe how the U.S. is deficient in all five steps of the battery value chain: raw material production, refinement, battery production (two stages) and recycling. The authors recognize the importance of nickel, lithium and cobalt for lithium-ion battery production. From a mining perspective, of the 55+ recommendations to better capture the domestic battery value chain, the authors also recommend comprehensive reform of the General Mining act of 1872. Again, I agree with every conclusion in this report as the U.S. and remains far behind when compared to its chief competitor, China.

---

[61] *Building Resilient Supply Chains, Revitalizing American Manufacturing, and Fostering Broad-Based Growth.* White House Report. June 2021. This is a very detailed report, clearly written by industry experts, who understand all aspects of the game and recognize how inadequate U.S. policy has been and continues to be in relation to the lithium-ion battery valuation chain.

Infrastructure Investment and Jobs Act (IIJA) 2021

The Infrastructure Investment and Jobs Act (IIJA) was signed into law on November 15, 2021, by President Biden. Weighing in at a mere 1,039 pages, I think it is safe to describe it as 'comprehensive'. It would take a team of experienced industry experts a week to comb through this legislative encyclopedia, while taking books of notes, just to get a general understanding of its contents. And just think how 150 years ago the General Mining Act of 1872 was a mere six pages.

To begin, the word 'lithium' was used just four times and it was in reference to battery recycling assistance programs. Mining is addressed in general and mostly on the issue of mining reclamation efforts that have been previously funded for more than $11 billion USD in total. For our purposes of this chapter, we will look at the portion of the report TITLE II—SUPPLY CHAINS FOR CLEAN ENERGY TECHNOLOGIES. This part has eleven sub-sections spanning 36 pages. Let's review them and see what we find.

SECTION 40201. EARTH MAPPING RESOURCES INITIATIVE. Recognizes that USGS needs additional resources to conduct continued mapping of the U.S. territory in search of critical minerals. The Secretary of the Interior is authorized $320 million in appropriations to execute this initiative from 2022-2026.[62]

Section 40204. USGS ENERGY AND MINERALS RESEARCH FACILITY. USGS is provided $167 million to create a facility – in cooperation with an academic partner – to study energy and critical minerals.

Section 40206. CRITICAL MINERALS SUPPLY CHAINS AND RELIABILITY. This entire section gives guidance to improve the permitting process and how Congress will hold the Secretary of the Interior, BLM and Forest Service accountable for expediting the mining approval process.

Section 40207. BATTERY PROCESSING AND MANUFACTURING. Gives responsibility for advancing this to the Secretary of Energy (SOE). This section focuses on securing and improving the domestic battery supply chain and associated battery

---

[62] https://www.reuters.com/article/us-critical-minerals-ahome/column-united-states-aims-to-reshape-the-critical-minerals-world-idUKKCN1TK27L; Less than 18% of the U.S. is geologically mapped, thus USGS does not even know the real potential for critical mineral discovery for much of the U.S. Also, the data they do have is dated and not readily accessible to private mining companies because they don't have modern data sharing software.

grade minerals. SOE is given $3 billion in grants from 2022-2026 to promote battery manufacturing. SOE is provided additional funds of $60 million, $50 million and $10 million to advance the battery technology chain.

Section 40208. ELECTRIC DRIVE VEHICLE BATTERY RECYCLING AND SECOND-LIFE APPLICATIONS PROGRAM. The secretary of Energy is provided $200 million in funds to issue grants to qualified private industry partners to move this program forward from 2022-2026.

Section 40210. CRITICAL MINERALS MINING AND RECYCLING RESEARCH. To pursue this, the SOE is provided $100 million in grants, which can be awarded to eligible entities up to $10 million per project.

We see with the IIJA 2021 an evolution of U.S. government thought towards the entire battery value chain, viewing it as a strategic economic and national security concern. We also see very detailed guidance showing an in-depth and modern understanding of a host of topics. Experts with very specific knowledge created detailed plans for electric vehicles, charging infrastructure, geological mapping, recycling, associated education and research.

Combined with the June 2021 *Building Resilient Supply Chains, Revitalizing American Manufacturing, and Fostering Broad-Based Growth*, the USG as a whole displayed a comprehensive understanding of the critical mineral and associated supply chain problem. Importantly, it is in the IIJA where we see U.S. law go beyond recommendations, strategy papers and general directives. In the IIJA, we see money actually being appropriated for necessary programs and the institution of accountability measures (i.e. deadlines, reporting formats) for the agencies responsible for disbursing these monies.

The technical understanding of the overall problem is evident. However, the real questions remains – is this enough investment to move the massive ship of the USG in the right direction to develop an effective national critical mineral strategy? Another question – is there enough direction and accountability to get the massive, overlapping, U.S. bureaucracy and its competing internal stakeholders to get off the stick and execute the law as written? A final question – if this is enough investment (and let us assume there are subsequent investments), and the bureaucracy does execute this plan (even through subsequent administrations), how many years will it take to develop a resilient, domestically grounded, critical mineral value chain? Five years? Ten years? Longer?

Defense Production Act of 1950 (DPA) — Invocation

On March 31, 2022, President Biden invoked the Defense Protection Act of 1950 through Presidential Determination (PD) Number 2022-11. The *2022 Invocation of the Defense Production Act for Large-Capacity Batteries* was published in response to the U.S.' continuing critical mineral supply chain vulnerability. The invocation recognized the fundamental and ongoing U.S. deficiency in battery metals like lithium, nickel, cobalt, graphite and manganese.[63]

Specifically, this PD invoked Section 303 of the DPA which states: "To create, maintain, protect, expand, or restore domestic industrial base capabilities essential for the national defense, the President may make provision — for the encouragement of exploration, development, and mining of critical and strategic materials, and other materials..." Of note, these actions are directed through the Secretary of Defense who in turn consults with other relevant agencies like the Department of Energy.[64]

This Presidential Determination provides more strategic direction reference the battery supply chain. As such, it is another venue for government action to pursue increased security for battery metals. However, this PD provides no funding for requested actions as only Congress appropriates money. Also, the Department of Defense has little ability to increase battery metal production as they have no mining authorities, do not control any mineral deposits, and cannot influence the permitting process. However, I do see this action by President Biden as a way to continue conditioning all aspects of the expansive U.S. government to recognize the necessity of an effective national critical mineral enterprise.

Inflation Reduction Act 2022

This bill was signed into law on August 16, 2022, by President Biden. While the *Inflation Reduction Act (IRA)* didn't really have anything to do with reducing inflation, that was just a marketing ploy, it was the most sweeping climate change mitigation legislation ever signed into law. This 725-page piece of political craftsmanship covered a lot of ground including deficit reduction measures, beefing up the IRS, prescription drug pricing reform, energy security, agriculture,

---

[63] 2022 Invocation of the Defense Production Act for Large-Capacity Batteries: In Brief. Congressional Research Service. May 27, 2022.

[64] Defense Production Act of 1950, As Amended. August 2018.

conservation, forestry, electrification, climate science and greenhouse gas reduction. We are interested in Part 4, Clean Vehicles, Section 13401, page 366. To get a $3,750.00 per EV tax credit, the critical minerals in the battery must be domestically sourced or from an ally in which the U.S. has an existing Free Trade Agreement or were recycled in North America. Starting in 2024, 40% of the critical minerals in the battery must meet this requirement, 50% in 2025, 60% in 2026, 70% in 2027 and 80% in 2028.

To earn another $3750.00 tax credit, the battery components must be manufactured or assembled in North America. Starting in 2024, 50% of the battery components must meet these sourcing requirements, 60% in 2025, 70% in 2026, 80% in 2027 and 90% in 2028, and 100% in 2029 moving forward. The EV itself must be manufactured or assembled in North America. There were further requirements based on household income, vehicle class and overall price. Used EV's were eligible for a $4,000.0 tax credit if the car cost $25,000.00 or less.

Part 5, Investment in Clean Energy Manufacturing and Energy Security, section 13501, page 406. Provides $10 billion to the DOE to provide financial assistance to manufactures of clean energy storage systems (i.e. battery manufacturing or critical mineral processing).

Section 45x, Advanced Manufacturing Production Credit, page 411, states, in reference to battery manufacturing:

"(J) in the case of electrode active materials, an amount equal to 10 percent of the costs incurred by the taxpayer with respect to production of such materials,

"(K) in the case of a battery cell, an amount equal to the product of—

(i) $35, multiplied by

"(ii) subject to paragraph (4), the capacity of such battery cell (expressed on a kilowatt-hour basis),

"(L) in the case of a battery module, an amount equal to the product of—

"(i) $10 (or, in the case of a battery module which does not use battery cells, $45), multiplied by

"(ii) subject to paragraph (4), the capacity of such battery module (expressed on a kilowatt-hour basis), and

"(M) in the case of any applicable critical mineral, an amount equal to 10 percent of the costs incurred by the taxpayer with respect to production of such mineral.

Subtitle C—Environmental Reviews, SEC. 50301. DEPARTMENT OF ENERGY, page 648. DOE is provided $125 million to improve environmental reviews and authorizations.

Section 50303. DEPARTMENT OF THE INTERIOR, page 649. DOI gets $150 million to improve the environmental review and permitting process.

The Clean Air Act was amended reference Section 132. CLEAN HEAVY-DUTY VEHICLES. Page 650. $1 billion is allotted to replace Class 6 vehicle (medium-duty commercial trucks, two axles) or Class 7 vehicle (heavy-duty commercial trucks, usually three axles, like a garbage truck) with zero-emission vehicles in communities and to assist states, municipalities and tribes. Additionally, this funding can be used to develop necessary charging networks for BEVs.

Section 60115. ENVIRONMENTAL PROTECTION AGENCY EFFICIENT, ACCURATE, AND TIMELY REVIEWS. Page 691. $40 million was provided to the EPA to improve the permitting process. Specifically, the EPA will use the funds "to provide for the development of efficient, accurate, and timely reviews for permitting and approval processes through the hiring and training of personnel, the development of programmatic documents, the procurement of technical or scientific services for reviews, the development of environmental data or information systems, stakeholder and community engagement, the purchase of new equipment for environmental analysis, and the development of geographic information systems and other analysis tools, techniques, and guidance to improve agency transparency, accountability, and public engagement."

Section 70002. UNITED STATES POSTAL SERVICE CLEAN FLEETS. Page 717. The USPS received $3 billion to replace its antiquated ICE vehicle fleet with new postal EVs and charging infrastructure. The USPS fleet is easily electrified as they drive relatively short, pre-determined routes and can charge at night at their home Post Office. LFP battery chemistry would be ideal for this type of vehicle and delivery mission.

Without question, the IRA is the most important law ever passed by the U.S. to move the American battery and BEV industries forward. The incentives for EV and batteries made with a North American supply chain were enough to induce large scale investment of these industries into the country. The law immediately rendered any business not meeting the published sourcing requirements non-competitive. Also, if a BEV was close in price to a competing ICE model, the tax incentives made the BEV the better choice especially considering that the total cost of ownership of a BEV is much lower than that of an ICE model to begin with. This contributed to the ongoing demand destruction of the ICE business model.

In case you missed it in the sea of battery bureaucracy-speak *Section 45x Advanced Manufacturing Production Credit* is a gamechanger for the battery industry in the U.S. To start, a company producing electrodes (cathodes and anodes) has its material costs subsidized 10%. Battery cells are subsidized to the tune of $35.00 per kWh which is $35 million per gWh which is enough batteries to make 10,000 BEVs. The battery packs, which the battery cells are placed in, are subsidized to the tune of $10.00 per kWh per battery pack – this is in addition to the battery cells. And any mining company extracting battery minerals to include lithium, nickel, cobalt, manganese and graphite has their production costs subsidized 10% by the U.S. government.

To sum up the impact of these government incentives, a battery company would be a fool not to set up shop in the U.S. Apparently, quite a few companies in Europe thought it would be foolish not to take advantage of U.S. incentives that subsidized the entire up-stream and downstream lithium value chain as well. According to a March 2023 report by Transport & Environment, 68% of 50 planned battery gigafactories in Europe are at risk of cancelling, delaying or scaling back their plans to take advantage of the incentives offered by the IRA.[65] Some of the battery factories being planned in the U.S. include:

- Tesla Giga Nevada announced it is expanding current battery capacity
- American Battery Factory announced it will build a factory in Arizona
- Panasonic announced it is building a new battery factory in Kansas
- Northvolt announced it is prioritizing battery production in the U.S. over Germany due to the IRA incentives
- Freyr will build a battery plant in Georgia
- LG Chem will build a battery factory in Tennessee
- CATL announced plans for a battery factory in Michigan

With this shift, we see global competition in the lithium space taking place by region. China and Asia first dominated this space and have a clear and present lead. In turn, the U.S. has decided to compete and the IRA is the tool to bring battery capacity to

---

[65] https://www.transportenvironment.org/discover/how-not-to-lose-it-all/

North America. If the U.S. succeeds in attracting and building a robust LIB industry, Europe will have to institute similar or even better incentives to attract the limited intellectual and technological capacity required to build out a regional lithium value chain.

As we close out this chapter, I do have a few questions regarding the IRA's mandate for 80% sourcing of battery minerals from North America or U.S. allies by the year 2028 to qualify for incentives. I don't see the U.S. and its neighbors producing the quantities needed in that amount of time, although the incentives and pressure are there to get it moving in the right direction. I believe the U.S. will continue to rely heavily on expanded South Korean and Japanese battery production and their disruption prone supply chains to meet these requirements. Another possibility is U.S. battery production shift towards regionally sourced minerals that are inherently more secure. This might mean substituting hard-to-onshore minerals at scale like nickel and cobalt. Importantly, this will require recycling at scale of every single LIB in the country.

Looking Ahead

1. What will the long-term effects of the IRA be? Will they be as intended, shifting much need intellectual capital and talent to an American-centric battery industry? Will annual BEV sales accelerate with the given incentives? Will the mining industry be incentivized to increase production of critical and battery minerals to feed this industry? But let's expand out thinking to the larger North American battery supply chain as well. We need to ask how the IRA will affect the Canadian lithium value chain and the Mexican lithium value chain. The U.S. cannot achieve the critical minerals security it needs without working in concert with both its northern and southern neighbors.

2. We have seen numerous repeat attempts through legislation, Executive Orders and throwing money at the problem to improve the mining permitting process. Just recently, the EPA was provided $40 million in the IRA to do just this. When will we see result from this investment? 2025? Does throwing money at the problem solve it? If the money does not hire more people to manage the permitting process and if this same process is not streamlined, then the bureaucracy remains in place. Now consider if the permitting process is improved like all mining companies wish it was, but the legal process

that runs in parallel to it remains the same. Much of the extended mining approval timelines are due to drawn out legal maneuvering.

3. Will the U.S. ever get its act together and overhaul the *Mining Act of 1872*? If so, what will the new version look like? Will it tie into and support a national critical mineral strategy? Will it specifically address battery minerals as a national economic interest? To date, there is not enough inertia in the U.S. political system to move beyond the existing status quo. But maybe we are asking the wrong questions, does the *Mining Law of 1872* even really mater today? The NEPA nullified many of the most egregious parts of the Act, Congress has refused to fund other parts of the act, and states are free to charge their own royalties on mining companies as they see fit.

4. Will the U.S. continue to recognize a critical mineral supply chain as a strategic national interest? Will it continue to update, amend, and pass necessary critical mineral legislation? More importantly, what are the mechanisms in place to inform lawmakers of the national importance of critical minerals in our economy? What is being done to educate the general public on the topic who appears to be consistently ignorant and apathetic to the subject? Will the political space continue to be dominated by interested industries and their lobbyists as they work to shape the narrative?

5. Will the U.S. be able to onshore most of its battery mineral needs by 2028 as the IRA is designed to accomplish? Does allowing batteries and components from South Korea and Japan to qualify for the IRA make sense from a critical mineral strategy perspective? Where do their battery minerals originate from? In a similar vein, does allowing batteries and components from Europe to qualify for the IRA incentives make sense either? Where is the consideration for a resilient critical mineral supply chain not reliant on shipping material tens of thousands of miles before it can be used? Did we learn anything from the pandemic of 2020-2022?

A worker uses a forklift to move a 1,000-pound bag of LCE at an SQM warehouse in Chile. The lithium is stored in sealed, stackable bags in climate-controlled warehouses. *(by Science Photo Library)*

A striking view of the expansive Salar de Uyuni in Bolivia where an estimated 21 million tons of lithium resides in its underground brine deposits. Although Bolivia has the largest lithium resources in the world, they only extract 1,800 tons of LCE annually. *(by Getty Images)*

An aerial view of lithium brine evaporation ponds in the Atacama Desert in Chile, part of the Lithium Triangle. The top two clusters are SQM operations. The bottom cluster is Albemarle's operation. This is where the majority of the world's lithium brine extraction occurs. The satellite view was taken in 2018. *(by NASA)*.

CHAPTER 3

Managing the Lithium Bureaucracy

"I obey but I do not comply." – *Antonio de Mendoza, as Viceroy of New Spain when receiving official letters from the Spanish Crown who he deemed out of touch with his local reality*

Do Little and Do That Slowly

We saw in *Chapter 2: U.S. Lithium Policy* that there is a great deal going on in the mining, critical mineral, associated supply chain, and lithium space. There are many separate U.S. agencies that have different pieces of this overarching beast. And this is why it is exceedingly difficult to coordinate a whole of government approach to this or any topic – because of competing stakeholders. But if we are to fully understand the U.S. lithium value chain, then we need to know the key players.

When it comes to lithium mining, and mining in general for that matter, the U.S. has created an interlocking bureaucracy that makes unlocking the lithium value chain difficult. When it takes ten years to approve a new mining operation, that means companies will look elsewhere to do business. Over the course of a decade, people retire, companies go out of business and commodity prices change drastically. A ten-year process means that a country isn't serious about the critical minerals business. In this case, it means that the U.S. can't execute its national critical mineral strategy.

And let's be honest, it doesn't take ten years to approve a mining operation. People from the various government offices that approve the mining operation aren't working diligently five days a week, all day long to approve a permit request. The paperwork gets sent to someone and it sits on their desk or languishes in their e-mail inbox. They aren't actually working on it. We call this amazing human phenomenon "gridlock". There are many reasons for this.

A government agency may be understaffed and can be overwhelmed by the sheer volume of requests they receive. If they are understaffed, it is most likely because they are underfunded. This is because one government administration may make lithium mining a priority and then the next one doesn't. Oftentimes, what an agency can do boils down to how much funding they received for their annual budget and then what priorities they put this money against.

Also, individual federal agencies have their own cultures and fight turf wars with other agencies meaning a company's submitted paperwork becomes a casualty of bureaucratic warfare. An agency may use the approval process as a pocket veto, meaning they don't support what you are doing so they sit on it. You know you are being stonewalled when the bureaucracy tells you that your paperwork "is in staffing" or is "with legal for review" or "let me get back to you".

I worked in the U.S. federal government for 35 years and served in parts of the Department of Defense that lived for many years in a state of perpetual gridlock – literally, nothing got done. It was safer, politically, and for your own career, to do nothing. The mentality among many elements of a bureaucracy is, if I may quote our Spanish acquaintance Senor Mendoza again: Do little and do that slowly.[66]

Department of the Interior (DOI)

The Department of the Interior is run by the Secretary of the Interior (SOI), a cabinet level position within the administration. As such, the SOI is a political appointee who invariably changes with each administration. Incoming administrations select their own people for these positions who will support their views and execute their policies without unreasonable delay. In fact, this is critical for making any large bureaucracy run effectively.

DOI was officially created in 1849 and manages many functions familiar to Americans like the National Park Service, U.S. Fish and Wildlife Service and Bureau of Indian Affairs. The Department manages some 480 million acres of land[67], employs

---

[66] *Antonio de Mendoza, First Viceroy of Mexico.* Hubert J. Miller. 1973.

[67] https://www.doi.gov/ocl/s-434

70,000 people in 2,400 locations[68] and was authorized a $17.6 billion budget for Fiscal Year 2022[69]. The Department's 23-page budget overview for 2022 only briefly mentions 'critical minerals' as an area the United States Geological Survey, an office within DOI, has invested in.[70]

Office of Surface Mining, Reclamation and Enforcement (OSMRE)

OSMRE resides in the Department of the Interior, under the Assistant Secretary for Land and Minerals Management. OSMRE headquarters is in Washington, DC while three regional offices are positioned in Pittsburg, PA (covers the Appalachian Region), Alton, IL (covers the Mid-continent Region), and Lakewood, CO (covers the Western Region). OSMRE's 2022 budget request was submitted to Congress for $312 million.[71] OSMRE employs approximately 500 people.

The Office was formed in the same year and as a response to the *Surface Mining Control and Reclamation Act of 1977*. The Act was passed to regulate widespread strip mining of coal at scale. The concern was that mining was being conducted without regard to environmental considerations. In response, the Act requires mines to submit environmental and reclamation plans before receiving an approved permit. Importantly, the permitting process must occur before any actual mining happens. The mining company also must post bonds that cover forecasted reclamation costs.

Part of OSMRE's mission is enforcement of the Act's provisions through inspections, levying of fines for violations and/or shutting down violating mines. As OSMRE works in partnership with the individual States and Tribal Nations, OSMRE ensures these entities have their own internal programs that meet Act provisions. OSMRE publishes its own 147-page handbook on how to implement the *National Environmental Protection Act of 1969* into OSMRE decision making.

---

[68] https://www.doi.gov/employees/about

[69] https://www.doi.gov/sites/doi.gov/files/fy2022-bib-dh003.pdf

[70] Remember, *Executive Order 13953*, published in 2020, directs the SOI to respond to the national emergency of critical mineral vulnerabilities and even recommend executive action against China that includes tariffs.

[71] https://www.osmre.gov/sites/default/files/pdfs/FY22BudgetInvestments_0.pdf

National Mine Map Repository (NMMR)

NMMR was created in 1982 and falls under the Office of Surface Mining, Reclamation and Enforcement (OSMRE), which is under the Assistant Secretary for Land and Minerals Management, reporting to the SOI. Their office is just outside of Pittsburgh, PA. NMMR was created when the national mine map repository was transferred from the now abolished Bureau of Mines to OSMRE.

The repository has almost 250,000 images of maps that are digitally archived and accessible to the public for research. Mining companies use the repository for historical data when opening a once closed mine, learning about an area that has an extensive mining history and collecting information in preparation for the permitting process. Repository employees cannot provide assessments or analysis to its customers (they are restricted from doing so) they can only provide customers access to the data and explain the mechanics of the maps themselves.[72]

Bureau of Land Management (BLM)

The Bureau of Land Management (BLM) was created in 1946 and falls under the Assistant Secretary for Land and Minerals Management (who in turn reports to the Secretary of the Interior). BLM was created by merging the General Land Office and the Grazing Service. While DOI headquarters is in Washington DC, BLM headquarters is in Grand Junction, Colorado as most of the land it manages is in the Western states.[73]

The BLM administers 245 million acres of land, employs 10,000 people[74] with a budget of $1.6 billion in 2022.[75] BLM requested $16 million in 2022 for 'Other Mineral Resource Management' with no mention of critical mineral mining. On the topic of minerals, based on the budget overview, BLM appears to be fully focused on oil, gas and coal management. But with only one active lithium mine in the entire country producing low volume tonnage, this is understandable.[76]

---

[72] https://www.osmre.gov/programs/national-mine-map-repository

[73] The Trump administration moved the BLM HQs to Colorado under much criticism; the Biden administration intends to move it back to DC.

[74] https://www.blm.gov/careers/working-at-blm

[75] https://www.blm.gov/about/budget

[76] BLM's 13-page budget overview doesn't mention 'critical mineral strategy' although they administer most of the U.S. mining operations.

BLM has a robust mining interface on its home webpage with an overview of BLM administered mining activity and permitting process. From a permitting perspective, a mining company is going to live in the *Code of Federal Regulations, Title 43 Public Lands: Interior, Subtitle B Regulations Relating to Public Lands, Chapter II Bureau of Land Management, Department of the Interior*. BLM has 12 different geographic offices (mostly in the Western states) to interface with the public and manage mining applications among other business.[77]

United States Geological Survey (USGS)

USGS was created in 1879, is positioned organizationally under the Assistant Secretary for Water and Science who reports to the SOI. The 10,000 person USGS has their HQs in Reston, VA about 20 minutes west of Washington, DC. Their mission: "The USGS monitors, analyzes, and predicts current and evolving Earth-system interactions and delivers actionable information at scales and timeframes relevant to decision makers. The USGS provides science about natural hazards, natural resources, ecosystems and environmental health, and the effects of climate and land-use change."[78]

USGS 2022 budget was $1.6 billion with $140 million going to the Energy and Mineral Resources Mission Area. This mission area focuses in part on locating and defining mineral resources in the U.S. Specifically, the Mineral Resources program received $86 million in funding, which in part supports geologic survey and database development. This is a key aspect of overall mineral knowledge that supports critical mineral mining operations. Another $26 million was provided to fund associated supply chain research.[79]

As we saw in the Chapter 2, USGS was directed in *Executive Order 13817* (published in 2017) to provide an updated critical mineral list that included lithium, cobalt and manganese. This was the necessary foundation for moving forward with an overall national critical mineral strategy. USGS also received

---

[77] Remember, *Infrastructure Investment and Jobs Act (IIJA) 2021* instructed them to improve their mining permitting process.

[78] https://www.usgs.gov/about/about-us/who-we-are

[79] https://www.usgs.gov/news/featured-story/president-bidens-fiscal-year-2022-budget-makes-significant-investments-usgs

appropriated funds in the *Infrastructure Investment and Jobs Act (IIJA)* to conduct geologic survey of the U.S. territory, as the majority of it has never mapped and, therefore, we can't define the mineral resources of the country. All we have is an educated guess.

National Minerals Information Center (NMIC)

NMIC is an office within U.S. Geological Survey that serves as an accessible repository for mineral knowledge including worldwide supply and demand issues relating to U.S. national security. For example, their home page offers access to detailed monthly, quarterly and annual minerals commodity summaries. The annual summary is called the Minerals Yearbook Volume I. Minerals Yearbook Volume II used to provide a state-by-state summary of mineral activity. However, NMIC stopped providing these several years ago.[80]

Their 2022 Minerals Yearbook Volume I is 206 pages long and covers 84 different commodities. Major battery materials are covered like nickel, cobalt, manganese and graphite. Pages 100-101 provide their lithium overview.[81] They also publish quarterly U.S. Mineral Industry Surveys, but they don't cover battery metals in those. NMIC used to provide country and regional specific mineral industry analysis as far back as 1994, but they stopped doing this in 2018.

Bureau of Indian Affairs (BIA)

BIA was created in 1824 and is led by the Assistant Secretary of Indian Affairs who reports directly to the SOI. Their mission is to: "…enhance the quality of life, to promote economic opportunity, and to carry out the responsibility to protect and improve the trust assets of American Indians, Indian tribes and Alaska Natives." BIA headquarters is in Washington, DC with an additional 12 regional offices positioned to carry out its mission at the tribal level.[82]

BIA employs 4,100 people, had a 2022 budget of $2.7 billion and manages 56 million acres of land. The 2022 budget provided $67 million to support Mining and

---

[80] I'll guess that NMIC no longer has the staff nor funding to provide the breadth and volume of current mineral industry knowledge that it once did.

[81] I referenced their lithium data several times in Chapter 1.

[82] https://www.bia.gov/bia

Mineral activity with an estimated $27 million specifically supporting the Indian Energy Service Center (IESC). The IESC facilitates mineral development in coordination with tribal leadership, but their primary focus is oil and gas recovery. Various mining operations (non-hydrocarbon) contributed $240 million in value added for fiscal year 2019.[83]

BIA has a Division of Energy Mineral Development (DEMD) which in turn has subordinate offices of a Solid Minerals Branch and a Fluid Minerals Branch. DEMD can and does provide grants to tribes interested in pursuing mineral development on their land. In 2021, the Energy and Mineral Development Program provided $6.5 million in grants for 34 separate native projects. In 2020, some tribes received grants to pursue manganese extraction, critical metals exploration and a critical mineral survey.[84]

U.S. Forest Service (USFS)

The USFS was founded in 1905 and is an Agency within the Department of Agriculture. Its headquarters is in Washington DC and breaks down its areas of responsibilities into nine separate geographic regions. USFS manages 193 million acres of public land with a workforce of 30,000 people. The USFS budget for 2022 was $7.8 billion.[85]

USFS runs a Minerals and Geology Management (MGM) program that administers mine exploration and development occurring on National Forest Service lands. USFS coordinates this mining activity as necessary with DOI to that extent that it sends mining patent applications to BLM for review and approval. This is because USFS is responsible for surface resource management only and DOI/BLM is responsible for the actual mineral resource itself.

Mining operations on Forest Service administered land is governed by *Code of Federal Regulations (CFR) 36 – Parks, Forests and Public Property, Chapter II, Part 228. Part 228 is further divided into Subpart A Locatable Minerals; Subpart B Leasable Minerals; Subpart C Disposal of Mineral Materials; Subpart D Miscellaneous Mineral*

---

[83] Bureau of Indian Affairs. Bureau Highlights. 2022 Budget.

[84] https://www.bia.gov/news/bia-announces-over-65-million-energy-and-mineral-development-grants-awarded-34-tribes-and

[85] https://www.esa.org/esablog/science-policy/federal-budget-tracker/#usfs

Provisions; Subpart E Oil and Gas Resources. For lithium mining, a company's legal team will need to know all aspects of Subpart A.[86]

United States Environmental Protection Agency (EPA)

The *National Environmental Policy Act of 1969 (NEPA)* was signed into legislation by President Nixon. The Act was in response to widespread concerns by Americans over increasingly widespread pollution of their air, water and lands. At its heart, the Act was passed to "…encourage productive and enjoyable harmony between man and his environment…" At only six pages long, the Act was a broad, sweeping document open to interpretation just like the Mining Law of 1872.[87]

The Act stood up the Council on Environmental Quality, who advises the president on environmental affairs and provides him an annual report. The Council was also directed to consult with the Citizens' Advisory Committee on Environmental Quality (which no longer exists). One of the Council's early suggestions was for President Nixon to create a new agency that would enforce the provisions of NEPA.

Soon after, the Environmental Protection Agency was established by Presidential Order in 1970. The EPA headquarters is located in Washington, DC with an additional ten regional officers to advance the agency mission. In 2022, the EPA 927-page budget request sought $11.2 billion in funding to accomplish its mission and to pay its 15,324 full time employees.[88]

The EPA has an outsized impact on the mining approval process due to their mandate of protecting the environment. While the EPA is not an expert on the mining industry, they are expert on how the mining industry impacts the environment. They are also expert on the EPA approval process any mining company must follow to get permitted for their operations. Thus, the EPA forms a critical part of the bureaucracy mining companies must navigate.

---

[86] Code of Federal Regulations. Title 36. National Archives. https://www.ecfr.gov/current/title-36/chapter-II/part-228/subpart-A

[87] The National Environmental Policy Act of 1969, as amended.

[88] *U.S. EPA, FY 2022, Justification of Appropriation Estimates for the Committee on Appropriations.* May 2021. Of note, this massive budget request does not include the words "lithium", "critical mineral strategy" nor "mining" other than in relation to coal.

Department of Energy (DOE)

As we saw in Chapter 2 with the brief overview of relevant laws, DOE is a player in U.S. critical mineral strategy research, planning and execution. In 2022, DOE requested a budget of $46.2 billion. In this budget request, DOE speaks to the lithium battery ecosystem as well lithium processing capability and recycling. DOE also requested $45 million for Mineral Sustainability to build a resilient domestic critical mineral supply chain.[89]

DOE published its critical minerals and materials strategy for 2021-2031 that goes into detail of how they will contribute to this effort. DOE's three pillars are diversifying critical mineral supply chains, finding substitutes and reusing/recycling. A powerful tool DOE can and has employed is guaranteeing high-risk loans for qualified companies that advance low-carbon transportation technology. To date, this program has been underutilized but there have been some successes.

Here are a few examples. As I mentioned before, the biggest win to date was the $465 million loan DOE gave Tesla in 2010, which Elon Musk turned into the single largest driver of the global lithium value chain to date. In July 2022, DOE provided a $102 million loan to Syrah Technologies LLC to expand its graphite active anode material (AAM) processing facility in Vidalia, Louisiana.[90] In the same month, DOE offered Ultium Cells LLC a conditional commitment to loan them $2.5 billion to build three separate lithium-ion battery factories in Ohio, Tennessee and Michigan.[91]

Critical Materials Institute (CMI) – Ames National Laboratory

CMI is a recognized DOE Energy Innovation Hub that advances a resilient critical materials supply chain. CMI is led by Ames National Laboratory (associated with Iowa State University) and focuses part of its research efforts on battery metals to include lithium, cobalt, manganese and graphite (not a metal). CMI works in partnership with

---

[89] Department of Energy, FY 2022 Congressional Budget Request, Budget in Brief. June 2021.

[90] https://www.energy.gov/articles/doe-announces-first-advanced-technology-vehicles-manufacturing-loan-more-decade; Of note, Syrah is an Australian company and they ship in their graphite from Africa.

[91] https://www.energy.gov/lpo/articles/lpo-offers-conditional-commitment-loan-build-new-ev-battery-cell-manufacturing

other federal R&D facilities to include Oak Ridge National Laboratory, Idaho National Laboratory, and Lawrence Livermore National Laboratory.[92]

CMI studies a variety of related topics. For example, in 2019 CMI received a patent for methodology separating lithium chloride from geothermal brine solutions. In 2021, they further researched lithium brine extraction as part of their diversifying supply chain efforts. As part of their recycling research, they conducted a project focused on recovering lithium and cobalt from end-of-life lithium-ion batteries.[93]

CMI also conducts joint research with interested companies operating in the lithium-ion battery value chain who have subcontracts with CMI. Some of these companies include: All American Lithium, American Manganese, Electra Battery Metals and mining giant Rio Tinto. CMI has affiliate relationships with a number of companies (they receive priority communications on technology breakthroughs) that include American Battery Metals, Piedmont Lithium Carolinas and South Star Battery Metals.[94]

I think it is a smart move by companies in the lithium-ion battery space to partner with world class research facilities like Ames. New ideas and emerging technology are the ultimate origins of the upstream value chain. When assessing a company's ability to maximize the lithium-ion battery value chain, one must take into account their R&D efforts, human capital and how they create new ideas. We can do the same with assessing countries and regions as well. Those that don't have robust R&D efforts in this space can't unlock lithium's tremendous value (i.e. Bolivia).

Senate Committee on Energy and Natural Resources

This Committee was officially formed in 1977, although it was really just renamed from previously being the *Committee on Interior and Insular Affairs*. The Committee was originally the *Committee on Public Lands*, which was formed in 1816. Over the years, its title changed several times as did its responsibilities. The committee is a bipartisan enterprise with 20 members: ten Democrats and ten Republicans.

---

[92] https://www.ameslab.gov/cmi/about-critical-materials-institute

[93] Critical Materials Institute Annual Report – 2021.

[94] Critical Materials Institute Annual Report – 2021.

Traditionally, the senior ranking member of the majority party sits as the Committee Chairman.

The Committee has four subcommittees one of which is Energy that has legislative oversight and responsibility that focuses mainly on oil, gas and coal. However, they do cover the topics of DOE National Laboratories (like Ames National Laboratory) and global climate change (although I am unsure as to the political acrobatics required to reconcile that topic with the global warming caused by the fossil fuel industry). Another area of interest to us is the Subcommittee on Public Lands, Forests and Mining.

Importantly, this subcommittee is responsible for "national mining and minerals policy and general mining laws; surface mining, reclamation and enforcement; mining education and research; Federal mineral leasing; ...and deep seabed mining."[95] It is this subcommittee that would sponsor legislation to be proposed for law reference a national critical mineral strategy. Also, we would expect them to address outdated laws (i.e. Mining Law of 1872), the current onerous permitting process and prioritizing lithium production.

House Committee on Natural Resources

The sister committee to the Senate Committee on Energy and Natural Resources is the House Committee on Natural Resources. The Committee is composed of 45 members, 26 being Republican and 20 Democrat. Whoever is the majority party at the time chairs the committee and has a majority of its members filling the committee. These dynamics switch whenever the other party gains majority of the House which could be every two years.

The Committee has a variety of oversight and legislative duties, but chief priorities include advancing the interests of Indigenous People and overseeing federal conservation and species protection programs.[96] Subcommittees are broken down into Energy and Mineral (EMR) Resources; National Parks, Forests and Public Lands; Indigenous Peoples; Water, Oceans and Wildlife; Oversight and Investigations; and Full

---

[95] https://www.energy.senate.gov/sub-public-lands-forests-mining

[96] https://naturalresources.house.gov/about/the-committee

Committee Insular Affairs. Energy and Mineral Resources is the subcommittee where we would expect mining reform to come out of if anywhere.

The Committee and Subcommittee can influence national policy in several ways. One way is by introducing legislation addressing mining laws which must pass the House and then the Senate before being signed into law by the President. Another way to influence policy is by weighing in on legislation that is introduced by a different committee but is then referred to the EMR Subcommittee. The Committee can and does hold public hearings on mining laws with testimony by expert witnesses.

National Science and Technology Council (NSTC)

The mission of the NSTC is to facilitate the policy making process involving science and technology topics of national concern. The Council was established in 1993 by President Clinton and is located within the Executive Branch. NSTC provides an advisory function to the President, informing on matters of interest with input from its 21 participating member agencies. Several of these agencies have an ongoing role in critical mineral management such as the Department of the Interior, the Department of Agriculture, the Department of Defense and the Environmental Protection Agency.

In 2016, the NSTC's Subcommittee on Critical and Strategic Mineral Supply Chains published a report outlining U.S. Geological Survey's early warning screening tool to identify potentially critical minerals and their associated supply chain vulnerabilities. USGS' tool assesses three areas: Supply Risk, Production Growth, and Market Dynamics. Apparently, the bureaucracy wasn't listening because the recognition of battery minerals as a national economic and security concern didn't get any traction that year or the next. But this was an example of the U.S. government enterprise slowly coming to the realization that they had no effective critical mineral strategy and their associated supply chains were in fact very insecure.

In 2018, the Subcommittee published the report *Assessment of Critical Minerals: Updated Application of Screening Methodology*. This six-page report recognized the U.S.' continuing critical mineral insecurity and that its associated supply chains were prone to disruption and dominated by competitors. The main thrust of this report was informational, providing an update on Subcommittee activities and the evolution of collaborating with various involved agencies. Essentially, as this report illustrates, the Subcommittee is a tool to coordinate and move the bureaucracy in the right direction.

Mine Safety and Health Administration (MSHA)

The *Federal Coal Mine Health and Safety Act of 1969* was enacted to protect miners who suffered from occupationally induced disease (i.e. black lung) and on the job accidents (i.e. cave-ins, methane gas explosions). The Secretary of the Interior and the Secretary Health, Education, and Welfare were directed to establish much improved health and safety standards. They were also responsible for ensuring mining companies and the States complied with these standards (i.e. mining company violators faced jail time).[97]

Initially, DOI tasked the Bureau of Mines with inspections and enforcements of the Act. Later, in 1973, DOI stood up the Mine Enforcement and Safety Administration in order to avoid conflicts of interest. In 1977, the original Act of 1969 was revised with the 33-page *Federal Mine Safety and Health Act of 1977 (FMSHA)*. The Act of 1977 expanded the safety standards regime from covering just coal mines to addressing all mines.[98]

With the Act of 1977, the responsibility of the Secretary of the Interior was amended and transferred to the Secretary of Labor. The Department of Labor created an organization called the Mine Safety and Health Administration to enforce the safety provisions of the Act of 1977. This Act also stood up the Federal Mine Safety and Health Review Commission which was appointed by the President who would in turn help review and enforce the provisions of the Act.

The Act of 1977 was further amended by the *Mine Improvement and New Emergency Response (MINER) Act of 2006*. The Act of 2006 enhanced miner safety even more, requiring mining companies to have established emergency response plans, teams and communications in place. Also, mines in violation the Act faced increased civil and criminal penalties and could be closed due to non-payment of fines.[99]

---

[97] Federal Coal Mine Health and Safety Act of 1969. This is a 63-page document that goes into detail as to how miner safety will be improved and establishes a system of accountability. This is not a vague document.

[98] https://www.msha.gov/about/history

[99] https://www.msha.gov/miner-act

Federal Mine Safety and Health Review Commission (FMSHRC)

The Commission is an independent entity created by the *FMSHA of 1977* with the mission of adjudicating disputes reference violations of the FMHSA. Their headquarters is in Washington, DC with regional offices positioned in Pittsburgh, PA and Denver, CO. The Commission gets involved when a mining company disputes penalties issued by inspectors from MSHA who are enforcing the FMHSA of 1977. The Commission's specific role is the penalty phase of the process, not enforcement of the FMSHA. Commission actions are regulated by the 41-page *Procedural Rules 29 CFR Part 2700*.[100]

United States Army Corps of Engineers (USACE)

The Corps was officially formed as a permanent military formation in 1802, although engineering officers served in the Revolutionary War as early as 1775. From its very beginning, the Corps has conducted activity of a civil nature, meaning its mission went beyond just purely military operations. With the rise of environmental awareness at the national level in the 1960's, the Corps became involved with preserving and regulating American wetlands and water resources.[101]

Today, the Corps is a large organization with 37,000 military and civilian employees. Corps headquarters is in Washington, DC while the geographic U.S. is divided into eight separate divisions. As most hard rock mining takes place in the west, like Nevada, Arizona and California, that area is covered by the South Pacific Division. The Corps has past and current engineering operations of many types in all 50 states.

Of interest to us, the Corps has regulatory responsibilities according to *Section 404* of the *Federal Water Pollution Act Amendments of 1972*.[102] This amended version became commonly known as the *Clean Water Act*. This section specifically regulates discharge of material into waters and wetlands from projects to include mining. If a

---

[100] https://www.fmshrc.gov/about

[101] https://www.usace.army.mil/About/History/Brief-History-of-the-Corps/Introduction/

[102] https://www.usace.army.mil/About/History/Brief-History-of-the-Corps/Environmental-Activities/

mining operation potentially impact a water system, the mine will have to apply either for an individual or a general permit through the Corps.[103]

Once a permit application has been submitted to the Corps, as part of the permitting approval process, the EPA will review it. If the mining company submitting the permit cannot mitigate all potential water system issues in accordance with Section 404, their permit will be denied. We will discuss these dynamics more in depth in a subsequent chapter on the permitting process.

U.S. Bureau of Mines (BOM)

The BOM is a defunct agency that was created in 1910 under the Department of the Interior but was abolished in 1996. BOM headquarters was located in Washington DC. Its primary mission was the conduct of scientific research and educating the public on all aspects of mineral resources. Despite having a small budget, USBM consistently won awards for its scientific research, analysis and accomplishments despite much better funded competition in the field.

In 1969, Congress determined that the U.S. required a national mine map repository and assigned this function to the DOI, BOM. The collection of tens of thousands of maps pertaining to closed and abandoned mines dating back to the 1790's was divided among two BOM offices: Pittsburgh and Wilkes-Barre, PA. In 1982, the responsibility for the repository of maps was removed from BOM and given to the Office of Surface Mining, Reclamation and Enforcement (OSMRE).[104]

As we see with the above example, over time, the Bureau of Mines lost its functions to other agencies. When the Bureau was eventually terminated in 1996, all its duties were transferred throughout the federal government. Agencies picking up the BOM's missions included the Department of Energy, U.S. Geological Survey, Bureau of Land Management, National Mine Map Repository, Mine Safety and Health Administration and the Office of Surface Mining. As researchers, we can still find high quality BOM products today relating to the mining sector which have been saved from their time as a functioning office.

---

[103] https://www.epa.gov/cwa-404/overview-cwa-section-404-regulatory-authority-factsheet

[104] https://www.osmre.gov/programs/national-mine-map-repository

Looking Ahead

As we can see, there are many players in the mining space that a prospective mining enterprise will confront if they want to establish an operation in the continental U.S. While we briefly described just 16 of the most prevalent ones they will encounter, these are just the biggest players at the federal level. There are more federal agencies that indirectly shape the mining space like Department of Commerce, Department of Defense, Director National Intelligence, etc....

As we get into subsequent chapters covering mining politics, the permitting process and actual active mining operations in the U.S., we will become familiar with even more players in our space. Some of these include specific political personalities, various Tribal Nations, State regulators, local communities, wildlife species and even plants. We will also encounter more laws that regulate the mining space, adding more layers to an already complicated enterprise.

Importantly, if a lithium mining company is going be successful, it needs to develop a comprehensive strategy to address every issue at every level. The company needs to understand which laws are relevant to their operations and which ones have faded away. They need to understand what regulations each agency plays by and have a corresponding plan to meet their expectations. This assessment of the regulatory space can determine if mining in Nevada is more advantageous that mining in Minnesota. Or maybe it's better to go to Quebec or to the Lithium Triangle.

1. How do we change this bureaucratic gridlock to get something done in the critical mineral space? Maybe, an administration just needs enough political muscle on a specific topic during a narrow window of time. The Presidency of Lyndon Johnson and his ability to pass the Civil Rights Act of 1964 comes to mind. One also thinks of the Cold War consensus as the Reagan Administration confronted the Soviet Union until its collapse in 1989. It remains to be seen if the *Inflation Reduction Act* passed in 2022 when the Democrats held the Executive Branch, Senate and the House has the incentives to move the lithium value chain in the right direction.

2. Where we do see consistent, disciplined critical mineral strategy is in China. However, as a de facto dictatorship, their leadership can enact a national strategy promoting mineral security, battery and EV production and push it forward with little concern for public opinion. Thus, we have seen China

implement consistent policies from multiple chairmen, starting with Jiang Zemin (1989-2002) to Hu Jintao (2002-2012) to current leader Xi Jinping (2012-2022). Xi Jinping has personally pushed forward China's investment in the extended lithium value chain, underpinning it with his Belt and Road Initiative that has global reach.

3. Another means for change is that a creative genius comes along and single-handedly changes the entire BEV market and associated lithium value chain through sheer force of personality. This person would have to be a certified fucking madman. Someone equally comfortable with achieving incredible success as they are with enduring crushing failure. Someone whose unyielding vision creates an unavoidable wake behind them, sucking in multiple supporting industries in an inescapable vortex of change. (By the way, this person received a loan from DOE in 2010.)

4. Also, change can come from the bottom up, by societal consensus, from a growing idea that cuts equally across political, geographic and economic lines. An idea that a low carbon future is not only feasible but absolutely critical. We see elements of this in Western Europe today, where governments, courts and the public are willing to combat global carbon emissions. As an example of this, the European Union voted in 2022 to outlaw the sale of most internal combustion engine vehicles by 2035 – a far more progressive track than anything seen in the U.S.

5. Or we accept the bureaucratic status quo and continue to maneuver within it. We accept a ten-year process and act accordingly. Mining companies create strategies that involve decade long timelines, pursue multiple operations globally and search for technology that could change traditional mining dynamics (like Direct Lithium Extraction). Lithium mining interests continue to play the old game. They hire environmental attorneys, pay for industry lobbyists, grease political palms, partner with industry allies and create jobs in local communities to build grassroots support to minimize the damage from their inevitable lawsuits. We already know what this looks like.

Above, a portrait of Antonio de Mendoza. As Viceroy of Spain's newly acquired empire in what is South America, Mendoza became an early expert in bureaucratic warfare. None has done it better.

CHAPTER 4

Mining Politics of the House

"Americans want mining in America, but Democrats don't." – Pete Stauber, Ranking Member, Energy & Mineral Resource Subcommittee

The Politics of Mining

There I was, grinding away, sitting in Starbucks having a conversation with a friend of mine who is a retired environmental attorney. We were discussing all kinds of things: the mining permitting process, EPA regulations and his experience in getting projects approved in California. I mentioned that the key to getting a mining operation going was a good legal team who knew all the laws. He thought so too. But you know what he thought was just as important if not more so? A good lobbyist.

I thought about that for a second and realized he was right. Politics is part of any process involving money with stakeholders who have something to gain and something to lose. Competing resources and competing ideas means politics will be involved. After reviewing the general responsibilities of House and Senate Natural Resources committees in Chapter 3, I quickly realized that the subject demands that we dig in deeper to each of them.

Specifically, we should know what legislative actions these committees and their leadership have enacted since the beginning of 2018. This date is a good marker since it was immediately after the issuance of Executive Order 13817 in December 2017 (*A Federal Strategy to Ensure Secure and Reliable Supplies of Critical Minerals*). As we have seen in *Chapter 2: U.S. Lithium Policy*, there were several subsequent laws, orders and agency studies enacted to further the government's understanding of critical minerals to include lithium. Therefore, it is reasonable to expect the U.S. political system to have at least incrementally increased its awareness of the need for a coherent critical mineral strategy.

As we get into the mining politics of the House, we should understand the general political thinking reference mining as it relates to both Democrats and Republicans. In general, Democrats support strong environmental regulations that govern the mining industry. Republicans, generally, support more relaxed environmental regulations in order to expand economic mining activity.

Importantly, the Democratic Party recognizes that man has warmed our Earth and accepts the science supporting the human causes of global warming. In contrast, the Republican Party minimizes or denies the reality of climate change and its underlying causes. Public surveys/polls, voting records and other open-source data covering both parties reinforce this truth. The Democrats face the need to balance immediate, local environmental mining regulations with the overarching goal of limiting man-made global warming. However, carbon reduction requires greatly increased lithium mining to underpin the growing LIB industry and there is no way around it. This is where Democrats and Republicans should find common ground – the need to increase battery mineral mining activity.

Republicans are considered pro-mining and don't see a need to revise the Mining Law of 1872. Part of their reasoning is that they don't support mining companies paying royalties for using federal lands they make a profit from. Democrats very much want to update the 1872 Law and charge mining companies royalties on their profits. Recently, the National Mining Association (NMA) 'evolved' their position and now agree that an acceptable level or royalties would work for them.

Another continuous sticking point is the permitting process and how long it takes to approve a mining operation – the average runs about ten years. Democrats are okay with the long process as it acts as a brake on mining operations, although they have passed legislation to improve it. Republicans want a much more streamlined process in line with other countries like Canada and Australia (about a three-year process). From a strategic negotiating point between the two parties, the Republicans can agree to a royalty on mining. The Democrats can agree to streamlining the permitting process. Environmental regulations remain in place. And thus, a deal can be struck. However, I won't hold my breath on this.

The House Committee on Natural Resources (HCNR)

In June 2023, the Committee was composed of 45 members (25 Republicans and 20 Democrats). The Committee chairman was Bruce Westerman (R-AK) and Raul M. Grijalva (D-AZ) was the Ranking Member. The committee leadership oversaw half a dozen activities: the full committee on Insular Affairs and the subcommittees on Energy and Mineral Resources (EMR); National Parks, Forests and Public Lands; Water, Oceans, and Wildlife; Indigenous Peoples of the United States; and Oversight and Investigations.

Westerman is a native of Arkansas and an engineer and forester by trade. He graduated from the University of Arkansas with a degree in Biological and Agricultural Engineering and from Yale in 2001 with a Master of Forestry.[105] He is also the Co-Chair and Co-Founder of the Working Forests Caucus. He was first elected as Congressman of the 4th District in 2014. In 2019, he was assigned to the subcommittees on Energy and Mineral Resources (EMR) and National Parks, Forests and Public Lands. He became the committee Chair in 2023 when Republicans became the House majority.

Westerman's district covers the approximate southwest corner of the state, bordering Louisiana, Texas and Oklahoma. The geological Smackover Formation, which is potentially rich in lithium brine, runs through the entire southern border region of Arkansas. Accordingly, Standard Lithium, a Canadian company, is pursuing two different joint lithium brine extraction projects located in Westerman's district.[106] As we would imagine, Westerman was aware of this and spoke at Standard Lithium's commencement event in 2020, publicly giving his support to their lithium extraction efforts.[107]

During his tenure, Westerman raised just over $6 million in campaign contributions from 2013-2022. Almost $518,000 of these contributions were from the Energy & Mineral Resource Sector. The Oil & Gas Industry specifically contributed $329,000.00 to him. Of note, Westerman contributed $2,500.00 to Pete Stauber's (R-MN) campaign over the 2021/22 election cycle. Stauber is the chair of the Energy and Mineral Resources Subcommittee.[108]

---

[105] https://westerman.house.gov/about

[106] https://www.standardlithium.com/projects/arkansas-smackover

[107] https://www.standardlithium.com/investors/news-events/press-releases/detail/81/standard-lithium-marks-commencement-of-operations-at

[108] https://www.opensecrets.org/members-of-congress/bruce-westerman

The National Mining Association (NMA) gave Westerman $7,000.00 in 2021/22.[109] There were no other obvious mining companies in the top 100 contributors to his campaigns. Of note, Standard Lithium is a member of the NMA. Overall, the mining industry focuses the vast majority of its political monetary contributions on the Republican Party. As an example, in 2020, mining interests contributed $6.1 million to Republicans and just $692k to Democrats. The NMA calculates that they can get more influence and return from Republican candidates who are inclined to support the mining industry vice Democrats who largely do not and will not support their agenda.

Westerman sponsored 46 bills over the course of four Congresses. None of these bills addressed mining or critical minerals. Westerman doesn't have any particular expertise in mining as his wheelhouse is forestry and that is what he has focused on legislatively.

Part of the game between Republicans and Democrats is using their official positions to score political points. For example, on the Republican's HCNR webpage, they blasted President Biden with a March 13, 2023, headline pronouncing "Biden Administration Deals Hypocritical Blow to American Energy." Here we see the different parties' agendas on display. Westerman encourages more oil exploration and drilling in Alaska while the Democrats want to limit it. The Republicans continue to pursue high carbon projects that increase global warming while Democrats prioritize renewable energy solutions. The Republicans couch their position in terms of "energy security" when in fact a warming Earth causes incredible long-term insecurity. And thus, the two opposing positions can't bridge the intervening political chasm.

Subcommittee on Energy and Mineral Resources (EMR)

Let's move on to the Subcommittee on Energy and Mineral Resources (EMR) which should in theory have a role in forming a critical mineral strategy. The Subcommittee oversees energy (oil, gas, renewables) and mineral resources (hard rock mining), ensuring they are developed in a safe and equitable manner and that U.S. taxpayers are properly compensated for their use. This oversight necessarily overlaps with responsibilities of the Department of the Interior and the Department of Agriculture as mining activity is located on lands that they manage.

The EMR is presently chaired by the Republicans as they hold the majority in the

---

[109] https://www.opensecrets.org/members-of-congress/bruce-westerman

House. There are 14 Republicans on the EMR, including the Chair, Congressman Peter Stauber (R-MN). Stauber was a star hockey player at Left Wing in college and was good enough to get drafted by the Detroit Red Wings. Later, as a police officer, he survived being shot in the head. He is a legit tough guy. Stauber was elected to Minnesota's 8th District in 2018. The 8th District covers the northeast quarter of the state. Importantly, Minnesota is a mining state, mainly producing iron ore and taconite (a lower grade iron ore). The Mesabi Iron Range (MIR), which has Minnesota's remaining iron ore operations, is located squarely in Stauber's district. In 2021, Minnesota was ranked 5th in the U.S. for mining value, producing some $4 billion of non-fuel minerals, the vast majority of this from iron ore.[110]

Cleveland-Cliffs Inc, an American mining and steel company owns and operates the Minorca Mine in Virginia, MN located in the Mesabi Iron Range. Cliffs also owns Northshore Mining, United Taconite and are in a joint venture with U.S. Steel forming Hibbing Taconite. PolyMet Mining Corporation is another company pursuing business in Stauber's district. PolyMet is majority owned by mining giant Glencore and is exploring copper, nickel and cobalt deposits in the MIR – all key elements for EV battery production.

Iron ore is not a critical component of lithium-ion batteries, but nickel is. In 2022, Tesla signed a 75,000 metric ton nickel concentrate offtake agreement with Talon Metals.[111] Talon is a Canadian company pursuing mining operations in nickel, copper and cobalt to support the EV battery value chain. Talon's future battery metal extraction operations have targeted an area just outside of the small town of Tamarack, Minnesota. Tamarack is also in Stauber's 8th District.

Since 2018, Stauber raised just over $2 million in campaign contributions. The NMA gave him $7,500.00 in 2021/2022. Talon Nickel USA LLC (i.e. Talon Metals Corp) and PolyMet are members of the NMA. Cleveland-Cliffs is not an NMA member. Of interest, Stauber gave Yvetter Herrell (R-NM) $2,000.00 in 2021/22 for her election campaign. She was Stauber's Vice Ranking Member on EMR at that time.

Legislatively, Stauber introduced several bills to advance the U.S. critical mineral strategy. To start, he sponsored H.R. 527: *Superior National Forest Land Exchange Act of 2019*. This Act would trade private land from PolyMet Mining Corporation to the

---

[110] https://taconite.org/ima/minnesota-named-a-top-5-mining-state-in-2021/

[111] https://talonmetals.com/tesla-and-talon-metals-enter-into-supply-agreement-for-nickel/

Forest Service who would in kind trade the same amount of federal land to PolyMet. However, part of the federal forest land PolyMet would receive would be used for mining.

Stauber had eight Republicans and one Democratic as co-sponsors. The lone Democrat was Collin Peterson, a fellow congressman from Minnesota who was very conservative for a Democrat and has since left office. The land in question was located in Stauber's congressional district. This bill had no bipartisan support in the HCNR or the EMR subcommittee – it was dead on arrival.

In 2020, he sponsored H.R. 6630: *Securing America's Critical Minerals Supply Chain Act*. This was a straight-forward one-page bill to amend the Internal Revenue Code of 1986. Specifically, the bill requested a 10% tax deduction on the purchase of domestically manufactured ores. The intent was to make the U.S. manufacturing supply chain more secure and competitive with geopolitical rivals like China and Russia.[112]

The Bill was co-sponsored by seven other Republicans to include HCNR Ranking Member Westerman and former EMR Subcommittee Chairman Gosar (R-AZ). As such, it was a Republican Party bill with no bipartisan support. The bill was referred to the House Ways and Means Committee where it has sat ever since. With no bipartisan support in a Democrat majority House, one can assume it was dead on arrival until/ unless the Republican Party regains the majority.

In 2021, Stauber followed up with H.R. 4932: *Manufacturing America's Mineral Security Act*, which was a slight revision of his earlier act. The act now included domestically produced minerals and metals, which would be used to make alloys and magnets, eligible for the 10% tax deduction. Don Bacon (R-NE) was the only co-sponsor. This was another Republican Party bill referred to the House Ways and Means Committee – which is where it sits today.[113]

Stauber introduced H.R. 488: *Saving America's Mines Act* in 2021. Overall, the act barred the President, the Department of the Interior and the Department of Agriculture from declaring a moratorium on mining involving critical minerals. The bill encompassed any territory administered by Bureau of Land Management and Forest Service. The bill had strong support among Republicans with 25 co-sponsors from their party. However, they had no bipartisan support and Democrats weren't

---

[112] https://www.congress.gov/bill/116th-congress/house-bill/6630/actions ?r=2&s=1

[113] https://www.congress.gov/bill/117th-congress/house-bill/4932

about to pass legislation restricting the powers of their own Democratic Party president. The bill was DOA.

Stauber continued that year with H.R. 2604: *Accessing America's Critical Minerals Act of 2021.* The bill addressed the biggest hurdles in the mining industry by establishing and enforcing timelines for regulatory reviews, limiting them to 18-24 months. The bill also transferred EPA regulatory authority to the states and local governments so as to free up environmental reviews from the centralized bottleneck of the EPA. Again, this legislation had 25 Republican co-sponsors and no bipartisan support. DOA.[114]

In March 2023, Stauber and Westerman co-sponsored the *Transparence, Accountability, Permitting and Production American Resources Act* (TAPP). This is primarily a fossil fuel advocacy bill whose intent is "To restart onshore and offshore oil, gas, and coal leasing, streamline permitting for energy infrastructure, ensure transparency in energy development on Federal lands, and for other purposes." We are interested in *Section 302 Minerals Supply Chain and Reliability* where it seeks to amend the existing *Infrastructure Investment and Jobs Act* by changing every reference of "critical minerals" to just "minerals".

There is also some language in the bill to improve the timeliness of the permitting regime, to expand the general mining exploration process and it requests that USGS determine uranium to be a critical mineral. This bill doesn't contribute anything meaningful to a national critical mineral strategy nor does it mention anything about battery metals/minerals. As there were no Democratic co-sponsors, this is a partisan fossil fuel bill that is dead in the water and most likely won't make it to the Senate who would kill it on sight regardless. Thus, this bill was nothing more than political theater which is common for both parties.

It's worth noting that a consistent player for the last decade on the HCNR is Congressman Paul Gosar (R-AZ) who represents Arizona's 4th District. He has served in the House since 2010. His district covers almost the entire western side of the state bordering Nevada and California. His district ends far south, just north of Yuma, sharing a common border with Grijalva's own district. The western part of the Grand Canyon is in the 4th District. Gosar lives outside his district in the northern Arizona town of Flagstaff, although he recently acquired an additional townhouse in Mohave County.

---

[114] https://www.congress.gov/bill/117th-congress/house-bill/2604

Gosar grew up in Wyoming, moving to Arizona in the late 80's to open a dentistry practice. His brother, Peter, is a Democrat who ran for governor of Wyoming. Gosar is considered a far-right politician with many right-wing connections.[115] The League of Conservation Voters, an environmental advocacy group, gave Gosar a 0% rating in 2021 and a 4% lifetime rating.[116] This is unsurprising as Gosar has been continually identified as a climate change denier.[117]

The Congressman served on the EMR subcommittee and the Oversight and Investigations subcommittee for ten years, from 2011-2021. In January 2017, with the Republican Party in the majority, he was selected to be the EMR Chairman. As background, Gosar is a pro-mining advocate, especially uranium mining. In fact, he is the founder and chairman of the Congressional Nuclear Energy Caucus.[118]

Gosar is from the northernmost district of Arizona while Grajilva is from the southernmost district. Just as their two districts are geographic polar opposites, so too are their personal backgrounds and politics. In 2019, Grajilva became the Natural Resources Committee Chairman. Grajilva then appointed Alan Lowenthal (D-CA) to replace Gosar as the EMR Chairman. In 2021, House Democrats censured and removed Gosar from all his committee assignments. This move followed Gosar posting online a spliced anime-Border Patrol video of him attacking and killing Congresswoman Alexandria Ocasio-Cortez (D-NY) with a sword.[119]

Over his career, Gosar has raised $5,367,000.00. During this time, the NMA contributed $21,000.00 to Gosar. Mining company Freeport-McMoRan donated

[115] "Rep. Paul Gosar promotes, then disavows, extremist group's event." R. Hansen. April 7, 2022. https://www.azcentral.com/story/news/politics/ arizona/ 2022/04/07/rep-paul-gosar-denies-involvement-far-right-group-event/9498207002/

[116] https://scorecard.lcv.org/moc/paul-gosar

[117] "These are the 130 current members of Congress who have doubted or denied climate change". By Ellen Cranley. April 29, 2019. https://www.businessinsider.com/climate-change-and-republicans-congress-global-warming-2019-2#alabama-1

[118] https://gosar.house.gov/biography/

[119] 'Absolutely disgraceful': Anger as Paul Gosar shares anime clip showing him killing AOC. John Bowden. Nov 18, 2021. https://www.independent.co.uk/ news/world/americas/us-politics/gosar-anime-aoc-ocasio-cortez-b1953912.html

$50,250.00. Freeport is also a member of the NMA. In total, he received $120,000.00 from the mining industry.[120]

On the minority side, ten Democrats fill the EMR with the Congresswoman Alexandria Ocasio-Cortez (R-NY) being the subcommittee Chair. AOC assumed her position in 2023 when the Republicans assumed the majority in the House. As she represents a rather small district in New York City, which includes the Bronx and Queens, she has no obvious connection to the mining space nor critical mineral strategy. However, she has long been an outspoken proponent for the implementation of a Green New Deal which pushes a wide-reaching, low carbon, clean energy agenda. We can see much of the Green New Deal in the recently passed *Inflation Reduction Act* of 2022. With her, we see the embodiment of the clashing of ideas within the green movement: a low carbon future requires extensive mining of battery minerals.

AOC has received no obvious financial contributions from mining companies. Her top 20 donors from 2017-2022 are largely academic institutions, tech companies and unions. Based on the geography and demographics of her district, I can find no political nexus between her and the mining industry-because there is none. While this means AOC has no official experience dealing with the mining industry in her district, it also means the mining industry, from a political perspective, does not and cannot influence her positions. While the Congresswoman has derived no professional knowledge in mining from her district, she has been prepared on the subject by her staff.

In February 2023, we saw the long-held positions of Democrats and Republicans put on display during a HCNR hearing when AOC had opportunity to question Rich Nolan, President of the National Mining Association (NMA). During the discussion, AOC made clear that she didn't support weakening of the National Environmental Protection Act (NEPA) as only 1% of mining operations require an Environmental Impact Statement. AOC also took the mining industry to task for decades of irresponsible management, leaving 400,000 abandoned mines behind that produce toxic waste and other pollutants that harm local communities. Nolan said he supported some form of royalty on mining operations on federal land to help clean up these mines, but with caveats.

During this hearing, AOC precisely held the Democratic party line reference the mining sector: no relaxation of environmental regulations, streamlining the permitting

---

[120] https://www.opensecrets.org/members-of-congress/paul-gosar

process is okay, royalties for mining companies on federal land is required and abandoned hard rock mines need to be cleaned up with contributions from the mining sector to hold them accountable for their past bad behavior. And now we know why the Congresswoman receives no campaign contributions from the NMA.

Ranking Member Grijalva (D-AZ)

I mentioned Congressman Grijalva earlier in this chapter and I wanted to discuss him more in depth here as there is quite some political ground to cover. Since we will cover some mining activity in his district and other AZ mining politics, I thought it would interrupt the flow of the chapter to go into all this earlier. As some background, Grijalva was the HCNR Chair from 2018-2022 and then transitioned to being the Ranking member when his party became the minority in 2023.

Grijalva represents Arizona's 7th Congressional District located in Southern Arizona. Arizona has nine congressional districts. The 7th District starts at the southwest corner of Arizona, along the border of California, anchored by the Arizonan city of Yuma. The district runs along the Mexico border to the Southeast, encompassing the port city of Nogales and stopping just west of Sierra Vista and Fort Huachuca. The northeastern boundary then zig zags its way up to southwestern Tucson and up to southwestern Phoenix. The northwest border then cuts due west from Phoenix to just outside the town of Centennial, down straight south and then west, back to Yuma.

Demographically, the district has just over 800,000 people with 64% of a Hispanic origin. Almost 25% are white (non-Hispanic), less than 4% are black and about 3% are Native American. The district does encompass the Tohono O-Odham Nation Reservation with 28,000 members and 2.8 million acres of land. The median household income is just above $54,000.00 and 20% of the district lives in poverty.[121, 122]

Environmental policy is a concern since the 7th District has large tracts of land designated as national forests, national wildlife preserves, national wildlife refuges and designated wilderness parks. The district also has a strong agricultural character with more than 3 million acres of farmland selling almost $1.2 billion worth of products

---

[121] https://datausa.io/profile/geo/congressional-district-3-az#economy

[122] http://www.tonation-nsn.gov/about-tohono-oodham-nation/

annually.[123] This is about a third of the total annual agriculture products sold in the state of Arizona.[124]

Additionally, there are three active mines in the district. There are two copper mines, adjacent to one another, just outside of Tucson. Specifically, they are several miles due west of the retirement community of Green Valley. There is a third copper mine located further north in Marana – the Silver Bell Mine. Freeport-McMoRan Inc owns the Sierrita Mine while ASARCO owns the adjacent one and Silver Bell.

From 1998 to 2003, Grijalva served on the Pima County Board of Supervisors. Again, he worked his way up to being the Board Chairman for the last two years. He resigned from his position after running for and winning the 7th District congressional race in 2002. He has since won nine consecutive races heading into the elections of 2022.

From the beginning, Grijalva served on the HCNR, landing a spot on the National Parks, Forests and Public Lands Subcommittee. In 2008, Grijalva was considered a frontrunner for Secretary of the Interior as part of President Obama's cabinet, but Ken Salazar was selected instead.[125] Regardless, he became the Ranking Member in 2015 (he was the senior Democratic Party member on the committee while the Republican Party held the majority). When the Democratic Party became the majority in 2019, he was selected as the Committee Chairman.

Grijalva is a strong and continuing supporter of Native Americans in his district and across the country. He has taken many actions throughout his career to help maintain their sovereignty, protect their lands and improve their lot. For example, in 2021, he moved forward the *Old Pascua Community Land Acquisition Act* to put Pascua Yaqui lands in trust with DOI. The Act passed the House that same year. For geographic reference, the Yaqui reservation is just southwest of Tucson city limits, about ten minutes west of Sunnyside High School, where Grijalva graduated from.[126]

---

[123] 2017 Census of Agriculture. Arizona 3rd District.

[124] Arizona Agricultural Statistics 2020. https://www.nass.usda.gov/Statistics_ by_State/ Arizona/Publications/Annual_Statistical_Bulletin/2020/AZAnnualBulletin2020.pdf

[125] https://www.thenation.com/article/archive/grijalva-interior-secretary/

[126] https://grijalva.house.gov/rep-grijalvas-old-pascua-community-land-acquisition-act-passes-u-s-house-of-representatives/

Grajilva is a staunch conservationist, a true environmental OG. When he was on the Pima County Board of Supervisors, he advocated for the highly acclaimed *Sonoran Desert Conservation Plan*.[127] He later authored the *National Landscape Conservation System Act* and the *Federal Lands Restoration Act*, both of which were signed into law in 2009.[128] Earth Justice applauded his 2021 *Environmental Justice for All Act*.[129] The Sierra Club perpetually endorses him, backing him in his political battles without hesitation. Asking if environmental groups support him is like asking if the sky is blue. When it comes to legislation, Grijalva invariably comes down on the side of the environment.

Sierrita Copper Mine – Green Valley

Freeport-McMoran Inc. is an international mining company with its headquarters in Phoenix, AZ. Freeport trades on the NYSE as FCX and as of March 2023 they had a $53 billion USD market cap. They have mining operations in North America, South America and Indonesia. They have no active lithium operations. They primarily focus on copper, molybdenum and gold.[130] In fact, they are the world's largest producer of molybdenum.

Molybdenum is used to make steel alloys and for applications requiring improved strength at extremely high temperatures. For the month of July 2022, molybdenum was sold for $19.71 a pound, although recently it traded much lower. In 2016, it traded at under $6.00 a pound. In 2016, it traded for nearly $40.00 a pound. A mining company like Freeport can find itself in boom or bust mode depending on its commodities pricing trajectory.[131]

Copper faced a similar run as molybdenum. In 2016, copper prices ran less than $2.00 per pound. In early 2022, it was priced much higher at under $5.00 per pound. That was the highest price copper brought per pound in the last 20 years. A major contributor to these high prices was the global supply chain disruption brought about

---

[127] https://webcms.pima.gov/government/sustainability_and_conservation/conservation_science/the_sonoran_desert_conservation_plan/

[128] https://naturalresources.house.gov/about/chair-grijalva

[129] https://earthjustice.org/news/press/2022/175-environmental-environmental-justice-civil-rights-and-allied-organizations-send-letter-to-house-natural

[130] https://fcx.com/operations/north-america

[131] https://www.dailymetalprice.com/metalpricecharts.php

by COVID and the associated health restrictions.[132] In March 2023, copper prices hovered around $4.00 USD per pound.

Freeport runs the Sierrita Mine, an open pit copper and molybdenum mine operation located a few miles due west of Green Valley, AZ. They bought this mine from the Phelps Dodge Corporation in 2007. Its location puts it in the congressional territory of the 7th District. The mine produced 85,000 tons of copper in 2021.[133] Freeport estimates that this mine directly employs 1,100 people in the 3rd/7th District and led indirectly to the creation of 2,982 jobs in the state of Arizona. They also estimate that they contributed $221 million in 2020 to the 7th District Economy and $311 million to the Arizona State economy.[134]

In 2009, Freeport bought the adjacent Twin Buttes property, which is private property, from the Phelps Dodge Corporation. This property is adjacent to and just east of their main Sierrita operation. The Duval Mine Road that runs east from the Sierrita Mine into Route 19, separates the two mining operations. Twin Buttes is a defunct former copper and uranium mine. To date, Freeport has not brought it back into operation.

In 2013, Freeport bought an additional 765 acres of land which used to be part of the old Ruby Star Ranch property. This property is located very close to its current Sierrita operation and Twin Buttes. The 765-acre parcel was previously donated to the Reid Park Zoological Society who intended to use if for conservation efforts. Freeport ruffled local environmentalists when they bought the property for $3 million, allowing them to expand their operations even further in the surrounding areas. To date, they have not mined this land either.[135]

ASARCO Copper Mines – Green Valley/Silver Bell

ASARCO (American Smelting and Refining Company) is the American subsidiary of Grupo Mexico. ASARCO employs 1,700 people in its North American Operations which are primarily located in the 7th District. Many of these employees are members

---

[132] https://www.dailymetalprice.com/metalpricecharts.php

[133] https://www.mining-technology.com/marketdata/five-largest-copper-mines-the-us-2021/

[134] Sierrita Mine Fact Sheet 2020. https://fcx.com/operations/north-america#sierrita_link

[135] Land donated for conservation sold to mining company. By Tony Davis. January 5, 2014. Arizona Daily Star.

of various unions. ASARCO runs the Mission Complex mine located on 20,000 acres of property. This open-pit copper mine is located west of Green Valley and adjacent to the Twin Buttes inactive mine owned by Freeport.

The Mission Complex has a portion of its mining operation north of its main operations called the San Xavier pit. This is located on the San Xavier Indian Reservation which is a separate area but part of the Tohono O-Odham Nation. To operate on this land, ASARCO went through a competitive bidding process and received approval from the Nation to conduct their mining. The San Xavier pit began operations in 1972.[136]

ASARCO also runs the Silver Bell mine, an open-pit copper operation located on 19,000 acres of land. This mine was opened in 1954 and has been owned (partially or wholly) by ASARCO ever since. One assumes this is a patented, locatable mine on land administered by the Bureau of Land Management. ASARCO would thus own the mining claim as it was in operation prior to 1994, otherwise it would be leased.

As mentioned earlier, ASARCO is the American branch of Grupo Mexico (GM). GM is one of the largest companies in Mexico and is an international conglomerate conducting business in the mining, transportation, construction and oil & gas space. GM has mining operations in Mexico, Peru, Spain and the U.S. Grupo Mexico trades in the U.S. over the counter as GMBXF. In March 2023 it traded at $4.40 USD a share with a market cap of $29 billion USD.

In summary, there are two major mining companies in the 7th District: Freeport and ASARCO. They bring in hundreds of millions of dollars for the community and pay county, state and federal taxes and fees. They provide thousands of jobs to local hardworking union members. They comprise part of the larger Arizonan copper enterprise, providing the majority of copper that is consumed domestically in the U.S. The International Copper Association forecasts that the need for copper by the vehicle industry will grow from 1.55 million tons in 2022 to 1.7 million tons in 2025. They believe 56% of wiring harness needs will be from BEVs and hybrids.[137] We should understand that copper is also used in the lithium-ion batteries themselves, in electric motors and for the cables used by charging stations. It is estimated that Chinese car company BYD used 13,000 tons of copper in its vehicle production in 2016 and 147 tons in its charging cables.[138]

---

[136] https://www.mindat.org/loc-32000.html

[137] https://copperalliance.org/resource/growing-demand-for-copper-in-electric-vehicles/

[138] https://www.copper.org/publications/pub_list/pdf/A6191-ElectricVehicles-Factsheet.pdf

*The ASARCO copper mine located in southwest Tucson. The open pit mine
is in the left of the picture. The mine is located just minutes away from
where Congressman Grijalva grew up as a child. (by Author)*

Grand Canyon Centennial Protection Act (2019)

Uranium prices started to climb in the summer of 2003 after sitting at around just $11.00 a pound. By June 1, 2007, uranium prices had peaked at $140.00 a pound – the highest ever. This skyrocketing valuation drove mining companies to pursue new uranium operations in an area called the Arizona Strip. The Strip is located in the northern half of Mohave County, AZ. The southern boundary of the strip is the northern rim of the Grand Canyon.

Mohave County Supervisor Buster Johnson fully supported uranium mining in his county. Mohave County, some 13,000+ square miles in size, covers the northwest corner of Arizona, bordering Utah, Nevada and California. The Grand Canyon, running East to West, cuts the county in half. Almost all of Mohave County falls in Paul Gosar's district. This is Republican territory – 75% of voters cast their ballots for Trump in 2020.[139] The county also has a long history of mining to include uranium mining. This is reflected in the name of Kingman's daily newspaper called *The Miner* (Kingman is the County Seat).

In 2011, Buster Johnson helped form the Arizona/Utah Local Economic Union with the intent of pursuing uranium mining in their districts. The Union was comprised of Mohave and Fredonia County in Arizona and several Utah Counties across the border to

---

[139] https://abcnews.go.com/Elections/arizona-county-presidential-election-results-2020

include Kane County. Johnson became connected with Kane County resident Pam Hill, who was the Executive Director for ACERT (American Clean Energy Resources Trust).

Hill was a veteran of the uranium mining industry who used to work for Energy Fuels Nuclear, Inc. Energy Fuels previously ran a series of uranium mines in the Arizona Strip. ACERT headquarters was a non-descript office in a small multi-purpose building in Kanab, UT. But they also had a P.O. box across the border in Fredonia, AZ, about a ten-minute drive away. This helped create the impression that ACERT was an Arizona endeavor. However, ACERT wasn't Arizonan or even American. It was really a front for three foreign mining companies: one British, one Canadian and one Russian owned.

Starting in 2008, ACERT retained a lobbyist, Utah native Robert K. Weidner. Weidner got his start as a legislative assistant for Utah Senator Jake Garn who served on the Energy and Natural Resources Committee. During his career, Garn sponsored several bills relating to the mining industry to include uranium mining. After a decade plus of experience on the hill, Weidner created his own lobbying firm. Subsequently, starting in 2008, ACERT paid Weidner at least $548,000.00 to lobby on their behalf to promote uranium mining in the Arizona Strip.

However, at the same time, a broad coalition of opposing interests began to grow to limit uranium mining in and around the Grand Canyon. Groups like the Grand Canyon Trust, the Sierra Club and several adjacent Indian Nations all came out in active opposition to it. Grijalva, who was serving on the HCNR, personally campaigned against opening more mining in the Grand Canyon. Gosar, who was serving on the EMR subcommittee, supported more uranium mining. Unsurprisingly, Johnson and Hill both publicly backed Gosar and published official letters supporting his pro-mining legislation. The opposing sides continued to push their narratives through 2011 as the topic came to a head.

On January 1, 2012, then Secretary of the Interior, Ken Salazar, signed a Public Land Order.[140] The Order withdrew 1 million acres of federal land, both north and south of the Grand Canyon, from mining access for a period of 20 years. Existing approved mines were not affected nor were future mines located outside the area of withdrawal. Despite the 20-year ban, proponents for mining uranium continued their efforts.

That same year, The NMA and Nuclear Energy Institute challenged the constitutionality of the ban. In 2014, the U.S. District Court of Arizona upheld the mining ban.

---

[140] https://www.doi.gov/news/pressreleases/Secretary-Salazar-Announces-Decision-to-Withdraw-Public-Lands-near-Grand-Canyon-from-New-Mining-Claims

Again, in 2017, the U.S. 9th Circuit Court of Appeals District Court in San Francisco, CA upheld the Department of the Interior's 2012 withdrawal order.[141] In 2018, the U.S. Supreme Court refused to hear a challenge from the NMA and the American Exploration and Mining Association who argued that the ban was illegal. This refusal by the court effectively upheld the ban yet again.

Despite the decisions by the U.S. federal courts, Grajilva didn't think the 20-year ban offered the Grand Canyon enough protection. Accordingly, just one month after becoming the HCNR chairman in 2019, he introduced the *Grand Canyon Centennial Protection Act* to the House. The bill permanently banned from mining activity the one million acres withdrawn by the DOI in 2012. Grijalva had 122 co-sponsors – all of them Democrats. Even the Speaker of the House, Nancy Pelosi (D-CA) got in on the action. She provided her public support for Grijlalva and his bill by invoking the memory of the great conservationist Theodore Roosevelt.

The bill passed the House that year and was sent to the Senate where they referred it to their Energy and Natural Resources Committee. In December 2019, Senator Kyrsten Sinema (D-AZ) then introduced the Act in the Senate. Senator Mark Kelly (D-AZ) was her co-sponsor. Kelly sits on the Committee on Energy and Natural Resources as well as the Subcommittee on Public Lands, Forests, and Mining.

In the Senate version, Sinema asked the General Accounting Office (GAO) to conduct a study of the state of domestic uranium production to meet national security needs. GAO was given a one-year deadline to complete the study and provide a brief (December 2020). At the time, the Senate bill had no chance of passing until January 2021 when the Democrats gained 50 seats and the Vice President could cast the 51st vote to pass a bill. As of publication, and despite their majority, the Senate version of the bill still had not been passed.

The revised *Grand Canyon Protection Act* was introduced to the House in February 2021 with 23 co-sponsors, all of them Democrats. A a portion of the territory addressed by the bill is located in Congressman Gosar's district. Naturally he expressed his opinion of the legislation as it affected his constituents. "This legislation imposes a massive land grab of more than 1 million acres and permanently bans mining and other multiple-use activities in an area nearly the size of President Biden's home state of Delaware. While

---

[141] Court upholds Obama-era ban on uranium mining near Grand Canyon. By J. Bowling. Dec 12, 2017. The Republic.

the sponsors say this is about protecting the Grand Canyon, the reality is the Grand Canyon, like all of our National Parks, are some of the most protected lands in our nation. Rather, this bill is about destroying jobs and layering some of the most intrusive federal limitations on a million acres of lands."[142] As the reader may have garnered from his statement, Gosar was less than supportive of the legislation. The bill was later referred to the Subcommittee on National Parks, Forests, and Public Lands where it didn't go anywhere.

The Grand Canyon/uranium mining case study is instructive in understanding the politics of mining. Here, we see the opposing sides line up and the variety of players involved. We see the tactics used. Now, take out the word "uranium" and insert "lithium". Do we think the story would have changed in any way? Do we think lithium would get a free pass and lithium mines would be dotting the Grand Canyon?

As a national treasure and a globally recognized natural wonder of the world, the Grand Canyon is a different animal. Not much attention would be given if we were talking about the Mesabi Iron Range. People don't travel from all over the world to tour northern Minnesota (no offense). Any mining strategy that relies on operating in or near the Grand Canyon is probably built on quicksand. You will never get past the sound bite: "Mining Company Plans to Destroy Grand Canyon". If you are a mining company and have other places you can mine, from a risk-based decision perspective, I would choose somewhere else.

Defense Production Act of 1950 (DPA) – Invocation (2022)

Let's remember from *Chapter 2: U.S. Lithium Policy*, that President Biden invoked the DPA through a Presidential Determination (PD) on March 31, 2022. The President's intent was to encourage the mining of critical and strategic minerals to support the U.S. domestic EV battery supply chain. So, what did Westerman (R-AK) think of this PD, from his position as the HCNR Ranking Member?

Westerman was critical of Biden, taking the President to task for only just now realizing that U.S. needed domestic production of critical minerals. Westerman also pointed out the contradiction that Democrats had done nothing to improve the permitting process. In a prepared statement, Westerman said, *"It's patently obvious that we need a dramatic increase in domestic critical minerals production to support a growing technological demand. Unfortunately, both this administration and congressional*

---

[142] Gosar, Paul. "Doing Russia's Work". The Miner, March 26, 2021.

Democrats have been content since day one to say 'not in my backyard' and allow China to develop a stranglehold on mines around the world."[143]

Westerman succinctly laid out the Republican position. Yet, Westerman, himself, had never sponsored any mining or critical mineral legislation during his eight years in Congress. He sponsored nothing during the 115th Congress of 2017-2019 when Republicans had the majority in the House and Senate. Ironically, this PD by President Biden was very similar to President Trump's own Executive Order 13953 issued in September 2020. But Westerman is a Republican. We can expect him to play inter-party politics and to push Republican legislation while disparaging the Democrat's. It's called politics.

In contrast, the reader can rest assured that HCNR Chairman Grijalva was supportive of the President. And EMR Subcommittee Chairman (at the time) Lowenthal too. Both were Democrats. Right? Well, the opposite was true. Instead, Grijalva and Lowenthal both authored a letter in opposition to the President's attempt to increase critical mineral production using the DPA. "While we share the administration's goal of improving sustainable sources of materials needed for our clean energy future, that does not mean we can risk permanent damage to sacred places, wilderness, recreation access, public health, and more".[144]

Girjalva remained focused on reforming the Mining Act of 1872 and refused to accept any increased mining activity that didn't maintain strict environmental oversights. Lowenthal wasn't running for reelection in November 2022 so he could voice opposition to the President. It didn't affect him politically as he was retiring in eight months. For Grijalva, he had the political capital to publicly oppose the President and stick to his values. Importantly, Grijalva had placed his opposition on the official record which he could show his base.

We should remember, Grijalva had won three elections during the Bush presidency and then two more under Trump. For the last ten years, Grijalva had continuously pummeled his Republican opponents in the elections. It wasn't even close. In 2016, Republicans didn't even bother to run anyone against him (after all, why waste all the time, money and effort just to get your ass publicly handed to you again?).

But let's also be aware, since Biden had been elected, Grijlava voted with the

---

[143] https://republicans-naturalresources.house.gov/newsroom/ documentsingle.aspx?Document ID=410896

[144] Official HNRC letter to President Biden from Raul Grijalva, Alan Lowenthal, dated March 29, 2022.

President's key legislation 100% of the time. If we use that as an indicator, when push came to shove, and the President needed support for a critical mineral strategy, Grijalva would get in line. Afterall, he was running for reelection in November 2022. He would rather have the Speaker of the House and the President supporting him than opposing him. As expected, Grijalva was re-elected.

Clean Energy Minerals Reform Act of 2022

In April 2022, just a month after Biden's PD, Grijalva introduced the *Clean Energy Minerals Reform Act of 2022*. This must have been a new bill that was in line with the President's published critical mineral strategy, right? Wrong. This 128-page bill had absolutely nothing to do with clean energy and had nothing to do with a critical mineral strategy. However, it was an effort to amend all aspects of the Mining Law of 1872 that the Democrats didn't like and wanted changed for decades.

First, the bill closed all federal lands to any new mining claims and all mines would be leased by the federal government – the mining company would not own them. All existing mines would come into compliance with this Act within a 10-year period. Most importantly, existing hard rock mines would pay an 8% royalty rate while new ones would pay 12.5%. Everyone in the mining company value chain would retain detailed records of their operations and provide them to the SOI whenever requested. Anyone refusing to participate in an audit would forfeit their mining claim.

National Park Systems and National Monuments would receive strong environmental protections. Of note, Indian Tribes would be consulted prior to any mining if the operations had any direct/indirect impacts on them. The bill provided a detailed permitting process dependent on operational and reclamation plans and the ability to show the funding to execute environmental protections. Under the bill, individual States could add more restrictive measures to the Act and work in conjunction with the SOI.

While this Act updated many aspects of the antiquated Mining Law of 1872, it did not address the modern issues of critical mineral supply chain security. There was nothing about improving the timeliness of the permitting process so new mines didn't take ten years to come online. There was nothing about streamlining critical mineral production reference minerals identified by USGS as being key to national security. It made one think the bill was a bait and switch, a reflection of Grijalva's own agenda as it did not jive with the Administration's published policy.

Stauber (R-MN), the EMR Subcommittee Ranking Member at the time, responded a month later during public mining hearings about the Act. He identified that this act made it harder to mine in America and would undermine domestic mineral supply chains. Stauber mentioned the PolyMet mining operation in his own district, which had been working through the approval process for almost 20 years. This was in spite of PolyMet pursuing three key battery metals needed for electric vehicles (nickel, copper, cobalt).[145] Overall, Republicans used this public platform to highlight Democrat obstructionist policies that ran counter to their own critical mineral strategy published by their own president.

Did Republicans do any better when they were the majority? Rob Bishop (R-UT) was the HCNR chair from 2015-2018, serving one term under President Obama and the next under President Trump. He was replaced by Grijalva in 2019. However, under Trump, Republicans held majorities in both the House and Senate from 2017-2019. This was the time to move President Trump's critical mineral strategy forward. So, it is a fair to ask the question: what critical mineral legislation did Bishop advance during his tenure as chairman?

During those four years, he sponsored 42 pieces of legislation – none of them addressed mining or critical minerals. During that same period, he co-sponsored 364 more. Of these 364 bills, he co-sponsored one House Resolution reference the impact of coal mining. He did not co-sponsor any legislation relating to critical minerals or non-fuel hard rock mining. While the Democrats' contradictions between published strategy and actual legislation deserves criticism, Republicans fared no better when they had the chance to move legislation forward.

Mining Politics of the House: A Legislative Post-Mortem

So, what do we make of this mess? Looking forward, I think there is less than a zero chance of bipartisan legislation on mining policy coming out of the HCNR and the EMR Subcommittee. The two sides are too far apart. The topic of environmentalism, for one, keeps the two sides distant. For example, the League of Conservation Voters (LCV) an environmental advocacy group, gives Grijalva a lifetime rating of 96% based on his environmental voting record.[146] In contrast, LCV gives his Republican counterpart, Westerman, a lowly 4% rating.[147]

---

[145] https://stauber.house.gov/media/press-releases/remarks-energy-and-mineral-resources-subcommittee-ranking-member-pete-stauber

[146] https://scorecard.lcv.org/moc/raul-grijalva

[147] https://scorecard.lcv.org/moc/bruce-westerman

Also, Grijalva is considered far left based on the topics of the bills he has either sponsored or co-sponsored from 2017-2022.[148] Only six other Democratic congressman consistently voted in a manner considered more to the left than Grijalva. Based on the same official and public voting criteria, Westerman is considered center-right.[149]

According to the Bipartisan Index developed by the Lugar Center and Georgetown University, Grijalva was ranked #293 out of 437 congressmen. His score of -0.2 meant that, based on the bills he sponsored or co-sponsored, he was not considered a bipartisan legislator. Westerman was ranked much higher with a score of 0.3, making him #157 of all congressmen. He is considered a bipartisan legislator.[150]

Stauber, the EMR Subcommittee Chair, received a lifetime score of 18% by LCV.[151] Ideologically, Stauber is a Republican centrist – square in the middle when compared to his peers' voting records.[152] His bipartisan mark of 1.05 makes him a strong bipartisan legislator, coming in at #55 out of all congressmen (top 13%).[153]

AOC (D-NY), the EMR Ranking Member, received a perfect rating by the LCV in 2022 and a lifetime score of 97%. She is considered a strong environmental supporter as her sponsoring of the Green New Deal would indicate. Based on her legislative record, she is left of center on the political spectrum. Out of 378 bills that she co-sponsored during the 117th Congress, she only supported eight that were sponsored by a Republican.[154] AOC's bipartisan score was predictably very low, placing her #401 out of 435 representatives.

Looking Ahead

1. Based on this data and the current personalities, new bipartisan mining legislation would have to come from outside the HCNR and EMR Subcommittee. A different legislator on a different committee would have to introduce such a bill. Or, the respective parties, in this case the Democratic Party, would have

---

[148] https://www.govtrack.us/congress/members/raul_grijalva/400162

[149] https://www.govtrack.us/congress/members/bruce_westerman/412610

[150] https://www.thelugarcenter.org/ourwork-Bipartisan-Index.html

[151] https://scorecard.lcv.org/moc/pete-stauber

[152] https://www.govtrack.us/congress/members/pete_stauber/412792

[153] https://www.thelugarcenter.org/ourwork-Bipartisan-Index.html

[154] https://www.govtrack.us/congress/members/alexandria_ocasio_cortez

to move in different leadership on the HCNR and EMR with more centrist political views (at least on mining legislation). Personally, I don't see lithium getting a free pass or any special carve-out legislation to advance the industry. Of course, this could change.

2. On the topic of critical mineral strategy, there is a political disconnect between the HCNR, the Executive Branch and the Senate. When Congressman Grijalva was the Chair of the HCNR, he didn't advance legislation that supported President Biden's critical mineral strategy. In fact, he publicly opposed it. He advanced mining legislation that didn't have strong support among Democrats in the Senate, highlighting a disconnect between the House and the Senate. With the Republicans now chairing the HCNR, there is equally unlikely a chance that they will propose any legislation in line with the Executive Branch.

3. I spoke to an acquaintance who used to work on the National Security Council staff assigned to the critical mineral policy desk. I picked his brain for over an hour as I tried to understand how the system worked in reference to the relevant natural resources committees and legislation. I told him it didn't seem like critical minerals legislation was formulated in a manner of how I thought it should. He agreed and opined that the system "was broken". I told him that I came to the same conclusion. But then we need to ask ourselves, what better system would we create?

4. If Winston Churchill had the opportunity to experience the U.S. legislative mining process, surely, he would have uttered his famous observation. "Indeed it has been said that democracy is the worst form of Government except for all those other forms that have been tried from time to time."[155] But the peoples' House is messy. With its two-year election cycles, it's a continual political knife fight. It was designed to be that way. The Senate, on the other hand, with its six-year terms and only 100 members, is a far more elegant institution. When it comes to mining legislation, in comparison to the House, it must run like a Swiss watch. Would the reader care to take a bet on that statement?

[155] https://winstonchurchill.org/resources/quotes/the-worst-form-of-government/

A miner stands in front of the Hull-Rust-Mahoning mine as he looks at the camera. This is an open pit iron ore operation that is still in operation today. The mine is part of the Mesabi Iron Range located in the state of Minnesota. This is in Congressman Stauber's district. Picture taken in 1941. *(from the Library of Congress)*

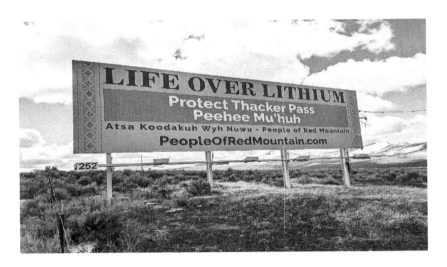

A billboard on Route 95 just south of Orovada, NV, which is the closest town to the proposed Thacker Pass lithium mine. Local communities, farmers, and native tribes have come out in opposition to Lithium Americas' proposed mine. Lithium is required for widespread electrification to halt manmade global warming that will increasingly devastate our societies and wildlife. However, local communities often prioritize their immediate circumstances over global concerns regardless of research and data. *(by Author)*

Congresswoman Ocasio-Cortez is the new Ranking Member of the Subcommittee on Energy and Mineral Resources (EMR) as of January 2023. Obviously, with her congressional district encompassing parts of both the Bronx and Queens in New York City, she has no constituent related interests in the mining space. However, she is a quick study, is well prepared by her staff, and understands the details of the Democratic Party's position on the mining industry. *(Official Website)*.

CHAPTER 5

Mining Politics of the Senate

"I've tried everything humanly possible, I can't get there." – Senator Joe Manchin (D-WV),
December 2021, on why he couldn't support President Biden's Build Back Better Act

Senate Committee on Energy & Natural Resources (CENR)

The Committee is chaired by Senator Joe Manchin (D-WV) and across the aisle is Ranking Member Senator John Barrasso (R-WY). The Full Committee has jurisdiction over national energy policy, nuclear waste policy, the territorial integrity of Antarctica and Native Hawaiian issues. They oversee several subcommittees on: Energy, National Parks, Public Lands, Forests and Mining (PFM) and Water & Power.

Joe Manchin, born in 1947, is from a small coal town in West Virginia. He attended the University of West Virginia on a football scholarship, graduating with a degree in business. Manchin founded Enersystems Inc. in 1988, which sells waste coal to power plants. His company mainly supplies the Grant Town Power Plant, the only plant in the state burning waste coal. Waste coal is low energy leftovers of coal mining that contains toxic pollutants like mercury and cause significantly more damage to the environment (e.g. acid leaching into water systems). Manchin has been pilloried in the press for manipulating state legislation to support his business which is now run by his son.[156]

---

[156] https://www.eenews.net/articles/joe-manchin-connected-power-plant-hasnt-paid-rent-in-a-decade/

To be accurate, Enersystems is just one cog in a much larger coal enterprise that dominates West Virginia's energy industry. In 2019, almost 27,000 West Virginians owed their jobs to the coal industry. Coal mining generated some $9 billion USD in economic activity while contributing $514 million to the State's tax base. Around 90% of the State's energy still comes from burning coal despite the continuing advances in renewable energy technology. Because of his personal ties to the coal industry and his state's overreliance on coal, Manchin has been consistently criticized as unwilling and incapable of advancing nationwide clean energy legislation.[157]

Manchin has deep political roots in his home state. He served in the West Virginia House of Delegates from 1982-1986 and then in their senate from 1986-1996. He was elected as West Virginia Secretary of State in 2001, serving in that role through 2005. He ran for governor for West Virginia in 2004 and won, taking office from 2005-2010. Manchin won his state's open senate seat in 2010 and has retained it ever since. Manchin knows the U.S. political system inside and out. He's good at it.

Since joining the Senate in 2010, Manchin has served on the CENR. From 2019-2021, he was the Ranking Member of the committee and in 2021 he was selected as the Chairman. Out of 420 pieces of legislation he sponsored over his career, only one addressed the topic of critical minerals. Of the 53 bills that he co-sponsored and became law, none of them addressed critical minerals.

In 2017, Manchin introduced the *Rare Earth Element Advanced Coal Technologies Act 2017*. The bill authorized DOE $160 million USD in the pursuit of technology to extract rare earth elements (REE) from coal. While there are trace REE in coal ash, they are in such small concentrations, it's not economical to extract them. This bill had no co-sponsors (in a Congress with a Republican majority), offered no means of funding and is quite clearly an attempt to prolong the life of the coal industry. This bill was dead on arrival and never went anywhere.

Manchin sponsored the *Energy Infrastructure Act 2021* six months after becoming the CENR Chairman, with the Democrats in the majority. To date, this was the only legislation he sponsored that addressed the topic of critical minerals and LIBs. This 578-page beauty was extensive and detailed. Overall, it authorized funding for various

---

[157] The data is clear: Coal remains vital to West Virginia and the U.S., for now. July 1, 2021. https://www.wvnews.com

bills that had already been enacted into law. It had bipartisan support including that of the CENR Ranking Member. Let's review the key points.

TITLE I—GRID INFRASTRUCTURE AND RESILIENCY, Section 1013 amends the *Energy Act of 2020* and provides guidance for the re-use of EV batteries to be incorporated into the grid.

TITLE II – Supply Chains for Clean Energy Technologies, Section 2001, Earth Mapping Resource Initiative, provides USGS $320 million to conduct mineral mapping of the U.S.

Section 2001, National Cooperative Geologic Mapping Program, amends the *National Geologic Mapping Act of 1992*, directing USGS to map abandoned mines and mine waste.

Section 2003, National Geologic and Geophysical Data Preservation Program, amended the *Energy Policy Act of 2005* to better track critical minerals.

Section 2004, USGS Energy and Minerals Resource Facility, $167 million is provided for the facility.

Section 2005, Rare Earth Elements Research Facility, amends the *Energy Act of 2020*, providing the facility with $140 million.

Section 2006, Critical Minerals Supply Chains and Reliability, directs that critical minerals be produced to the greatest extent possible in the U.S. and the mining permitting process needs to be improved through streamlining.

Section 2007, Battery Processing and Manufacturing, establishes the "Battery Material Processing Grants Program", providing DOE $3 billion to execute the program. It provides $10 million for the LIB Recycling Prize Competition of the *Stevenson-Wydler Technology Innovation Act of 1980*. Provides grants of $60 million for battery recycling programs. Provides the States $50 million in grants to state battery recycling programs. Private retailers providing battery recycling services are authorized $15 million in grants. DOE is to create a battery Recycling Task Force.

Section 2008, Electric Drive Vehicle Battery Recycling and Second-Life Applications Programs, amends the *Energy Independence and Security Act of 2007*. DOE is funded $200 million to develop an EV battery recycling and second-use program.

Section 2009, Advanced Energy Manufacturing and Recycling Grant Program, is provided $750 million.

Section 2010, Critical Minerals Mining and Recycling Research, provides $400 million for this program.

Section 2011, 21st Century Energy Workforce Advisory Board, will be established by DOE.

TITLE X—AUTHORIZATION OF APPROPRIATIONS FOR ENERGY ACT OF 2020

Section 10001, Energy Storage Demonstration Projects, are provided $35 million in grants in support of the *Energy Act of 2020*. The Long-Duration Demonstration Initiative and Joint Program is funded $150 million.

Section 10003, Mineral Security Projects, is provided $13.6 million in support of the *Energy Policy Act of 2005*. In support of Rare Earth Mineral Security under the *Energy Act of 2020*, $127 million is provided. In support of Critical Material Innovation, Efficiency, and Alternatives under the *Energy Act of 2020*, $465 million is authorized. To fund a Critical Material Supply Chain Research Facility under the *Energy Act of 2020*, $75 million is authorized.

This bill showed Manchin's (and his staff's) comprehensive understanding of the many aspects of renewable energy, the battery supply chain and critical minerals. This Act was perhaps an indicator that a critical mineral consensus was beginning to develop in the U.S. government. His office had to reach out to many different agencies, committees and subcommittees to construct such a complex bill. Officially, Manchin was the only sponsor of the bill and after introducing it to the Senate, it hasn't gone anywhere. This is because many of these topics were absorbed under the *Inflation Reduction Act of 2022*.

Inflation Reduction Act 2022

It can be argued Senator Manchin really isn't in a Democrat. Based on his state and its constituents, he votes more like a Republican. There is only one other Democratic Senator more to the right than him, which is Kyrsten Sinema, formerly a Democrat and now an Independent. Based on the bills he sponsored and co-sponsored from 2017-2023, he is more to the right than all other democratic senators. So, from a legislation perspective, he could be described as either a right-leaning Democrat or a left-leaning Republican.[158]

In January 2021, the Democratic Party held 50 seats in the Senate, up from their previous 48. With 50 seats, for any legislation requiring a simple majority, the Democrats could get what they wanted with the Vice-President casting the 51st vote.

---

[158] https://www.govtrack.us/congress/members/joe_manchin/412391

This Vice-Presidential vote was key for breaking any 50-50 stand-off in the Senate. But this only worked if the Democrats had every single Senator on board for their agenda. They had no wiggle room for one or two Senators going astray. Thus, Joe Manchin could be a problem.

The signature piece of legislation President Biden and the Democratic Party wanted since claiming the White House in 2021 was the *Build Back Better Act (B3A)*. B3A provided $2.4 trillion of spending on programs through 2031 with $2.2 trillion in offsets, meaning, the Act would trigger $200 billion of deficit spending.[159] B3A hit the Democrats' key pillars: Family Benefits, Climate & Infrastructure, Individual Tax Credits, Health Care, Affordable Housing, Education, and Immigration Reform. The House passed the bill in November 2021. Now it was off to smooth sailing in the Democrat majority Senate.

Unfortunately for the Biden Administration, Manchin didn't see it that way. Specifically, Manchin was concerned with the U.S. national debt and believed B3A would cost far more than the advertised $2.4 trillion – more like $4.5 trillion. He also believed the Act tried to propel the transition to a clean energy infrastructure faster than was technologically possible. While both were major concerns for him, the problem with the U.S. deficit weighed on his mind most. B3A would have to get smaller if he were going to support it.[160]

B3A was dead and there was no reviving it. Manchin stuck to his guns over the winter of 2021/22 and into the following summer. The right-leaning Democrat was really a left-leaning Republican; this was the final nail in that discussion. Clean energy proponents gnashed their teeth, there was Joe "Coal" Manchin at it again! More articles rained down with renewed vigor, detailing how Manchin was terminally tied to the West Virginia coal industry. Rolling Stone ran the article, "Manchin's Coal Corruption is So Much Worse Than You Know." Climate activists targeted Manchin as Public Enemy #1. Vox declared, "Joe Manchin May Have Doomed America's Climate Policy." Even the United Mine Workers of America weighed in. They wanted B3A passed to fund health expenses for black lung, to support incentives for manufactures

---

[159] https://www.crfb.org/blogs/whats-houses-build-back-better-act

[160] https://www.manchin.senate.gov/newsroom/press-releases/manchin-statement-on-build-back-better-act

to help coal workers transition to clean energy jobs and to penalize coal companies that denied coal workers from unionizing.[161]

Then, on July 27, 2022, Manchin announced a bombshell: he had worked out an agreement with Senate Majority Leader Chuck Schumer (D-NY) for a revised version of B3A. The new and evolved bill was the *Inflation Reduction Act of 2022 (IRA)*. However, the numbers attached to the bill were much different. Instead of increasing the national debt by $200 billion through 2031, it reduced it by $300 billion. This revenue increase would come from a 15% minimum corporate tax rate, prescription drug pricing reform, increased tax enforcement by the IRS, and closing the carried interest loophole.[162]

In the Act there was continued funding to treat black lung, which was key for Manchin to retain the support that he could with coal miners. Also, there was a great deal of funding provided to the Departments of Energy and the Interior to update, modernize, and improve environmental reviews for the permitting process. Funds were also provided to the EPA to do the same. The EPA had long been vilified for its drawn out, inefficient review and authorization process that often appeared to be nothing more than an obvious form of anti-mining guerrilla warfare.

Manchin supported the IRA because it had provisions to pay down the national debt, which was important to him, especially in the context of continuing inflation. The debt reduction provisions in the IRA took the form of increasing taxes on large corporations. He also reiterated the need to advance clean energy solutions in a manner supporting the technology available to keep energy prices low. In his official statement, Manchin also emphasized the need to reduce critical minerals supplied by China and to improve the mining permitting process.[163]

After Manchin's announcement, he had to weather some blowback. For example, Chris Hamilton, the president of the West Virginia Coal Association, went on Fox News for a brief segment to express his disappointment in Manchin's decision. Also, a group of eight separate coal mining associations published a letter criticizing

---

[161] https://umwa.org/news-media/press/umwa-statement-on-build-back-better-legislation/

[162] https://www.democrats.senate.gov/imo/media/doc/inflation_reduction_act_one_page_summary.pdf

[163] https://www.manchin.senate.gov/newsroom/press-releases/manchin-supports-inflation-reduction-act-of-2022

Manchin's decision as threatening America's coal industry because it doubled the tax on coal. They couldn't wrap their heads around the idea that America was transitioning to clean energy. However, the United Mine Workers of America maintained their public support of Manchin, coming out in support of the IRA and praising his decision.[164]

As the evolution of his position with the IRA showed, Manchin had to walk a political razor's edge. In the 2020 presidential elections, West Virginia voted 68% for the Republican candidate and just 29% for the Democrat candidate. Now we understand why Manchin is a right-wing Democrat – because he couldn't survive any other way. Based on his State's recent voting history, he couldn't approve the $2 trillion Build Back Better Act. But he might get away with backing the smaller *Inflation Reduction Act*. Manchin was up for re-election in 2024. We'll see how his political balancing act turns out.

CENR Ranking Member – John Barrasso (R-WY)

Senator Barrasso was born in 1952 in Reading, PA. He went to Georgetown University and earned an undergraduate degree in Biology and an M.D. He conducted his medical residency at Yale University and then moved to Wyoming to open an orthopedics practice. He served as a state senator for Wyoming from 2003-2007. He was appointed to the U.S. senate in 2007 and has been reelected twice since. While he is the CENR Ranking Member, he also sits on the Senate Finance Committee, the Senate Foreign Relations Committee and is the Republican Conference Chair. He is up for reelection in 2025. Of note, he previously chaired the CENR subcommittee on mining from 2013-2014.

Over his career, Barrasso introduced 164 bills. Of these, one addressed the topic of BEVs and three the topics of mining. To start, Barrasso introduced the *Abandoned Mine Land Reclamation Fee Reauthorization Act of 2020* that amended certain aspects of the *Surface Mining Control and Reclamation Act of 1977*. It had nothing to do with critical minerals or mining reform. The bill had one co-sponsor, Senator Enzi (R-WY). It never went anywhere and died in Congress.

He followed up the next year with the *Abandoned Mine Land Reclamation Fee Reauthorization Act of 2021*. This bill reduced the fees that coal mining companies

---

[164] https://umwa.org/news-media/press/umwa-applauds-inflation-reduction-act/

would pay for reclamation efforts. There were two other Republican co-sponsors, one from Wyoming and one from North Dakota. The bill hasn't gone anywhere since.

In 2021, Barrasso introduced *ELITE Vehicles Act* that amended the Internal Revenue Code of 1986 to end the $7,500.00 tax credit for new qualified electric vehicles. Barrasso's reasoning for the bill was that only the wealthy used the tax-credit and they didn't need the financial assistance to begin with.[165] With a Democratic majority in the House and Senate that was determined to promote zero emission vehicles, the bill had zero chance for survival. It didn't go anywhere.

Lastly, he sponsored the *Mining Schools Act of 2022*. This was a bipartisan bill with eight co-sponsors including five Democrats. The bill required DOE to provide $80 million in competitive grants to mining schools. One of the areas the grants would be put towards was the study of the extraction of critical minerals and rare earth elements (REE). The bill was sent to Congress in March 2022 to be considered by the House Committee on Natural Resources. It was sent back to the CENR at the end of 2022 for review.

From 2017 to 2022, Barrasso raised $7.8 million in campaign contributions. The Oil & Gas industry contributed the most to his campaign with $600,000.00. Of note, Iberdrola SA gave him $15,000.00 in contributions. Iberdrola is a multi-national power company that has a growing renewable energy portfolio. 65% of its campaign contributions target Democrats. As Barrasso sits on the Energy Committee, Iberdrola targets both Democrats and Republicans. In the time when the Republicans had the Executive Branch, House, and Senate, Barrasso advanced no critical mineral legislation.[166] Of the 16 Republican CENR press releases published under his leadership through March 2023, none of them addressed a critical mineral strategy. Most were focused on promoting the fossil fuel industry.

Subcommittee on Public Lands, Forests and Mining

The Subcommittee on Public Lands, Forests and Mining (PLFM) is the Senate equivalent to the House Subcommittee on Energy & Mineral Resources for the topic of

---

[165] https://www.barrasso.senate.gov/public/index.cfm/2021/6/barrasso-rep-smith-introduce-legislation-to-end-electric-vehicle-tax-credits

[166] https://www.opensecrets.org/members-of-congress/john-a-barrasso/summary?cid=N00006236&cycle=2022

mining. PLFM provides oversight of public lands administered by BLM and the Forest Service, national mining and mineral policy, general mining laws and federal mining leasing just to name the ones we are most interested in. The Chair is Senator Catherine Cortez Masto (D-NV) while the Ranking Member is Senator Mike Lee (R-UT).

Senator Cortez Masto was born in 1964 in Las Vegas, Nevada. She attended the University of Nevada-Reno and graduated with an M.S. in Finance. She then went to law school at the University of Gonzaga. From 2007-2015, she was elected and served as the Attorney General of Nevada. She was subsequently elected as a U.S. Senator in 2017 with a re-election race coming in November 2022. Cortez Masto supported President Biden's critical mineral and electrification goals and her legislation showed it.

Cortez Masto introduced the *GREEN Vehicles at Airports Act* in September 2018, which amended U.S. Code Title 49. The intent of the bill was to incentivize the use of zero-emission vehicles at public airports. The Department of Transportation (DOT) was the lead for the program that included the build-out of charging infrastructure for BEVs. The federal government would shoulder 80% of the costs. Ultimately, the provisions of this bill were incorporated into the *FAA Reauthorization Act of 2018* and signed into law by the President that same year.[167]

At this time, the Republicans were the majority in both the House and the Senate. While the government was still trying to figure out their BEV strategy, Tesla was already on the march, with over 1,100 supercharger stations already in place at the start of the year. They were taking their profits from their charging fees to build out their network at an increasingly fierce pace.[168] As we will discuss later in Chapter 18, the Biden Administration would later ask Tesla to open their charging network to all BEVs in order to advance the U.S. national charging network.

Cortez Masto introduced four separate bills promoting the adoption of BEVs. They included the *Electric Transportation Commission and National Strategy Act* in 2019 and *A bill to establish a working group on electric vehicles* in 2021. Both directed the creation of a BEV working group under the direction of DOT and DOE. She followed up with the *Electric Vehicles for Underserved Communities Act of 2021* and then the *Clean School Bus Act of 2021*, both pushing for EV adoption.

---

[167] https://www.govtrack.us/congress/bills/115/s3514

[168] https://electrek.co/2018/05/12/tesla-supercharger-2018-growth/

Also, Cortez Masto introduced more substantive legislation with the *NEXT in Transportation Act* in the summer of 2021 as the House simultaneously moved forward with their *Infrastructure Investment and Jobs Act (IIJA)*. The provisions from her bill were incorporated into the IIJA which was signed into law November 2021. Since the programs in NEXT were considered redundant to the much larger IIJA, the IIJA took precedent. Let's look at some of NEXT's more important provisions.

NEXT provided $500 million to build out an intelligent transportation architecture that included automated and connected vehicles (think robotaxis) functioning as part of a SMART community. The Secretary of Transportation, in cooperation with the Secretary of Energy, would establish and chair the EV Working Group to move the enterprise forward. Finally, $5 billion was provided for a nationwide BEV charging infrastructure which included working with the individual States. For context, by the end of 2021, Tesla had installed 31,000+ chargers at 3,400 different locations.[169] They were building out the BEV charging infrastructure that the government had yet to figure out.

In October 2021, as the IIJA was heading towards Presidential signature, Cortez Masto introduced the *Battery Material Processing and Component Manufacturing Act of 2021*. Similar to the NEXT bill, this too was incorporated into the larger IIJA. The bill required the Department of Energy (DOE) to establish a grant program to encourage the production of battery metals, batteries for EVs and an associated battery recycling program. $600 million a year for five years was provided to develop a secure U.S. and North American battery supply chain. In comparison, Chinese battery giant CATL's net profit alone for 2021 was $2.47 billion USD and growing fast.[170] A single Chinese battery company was far outpacing the entire U.S. government effort.

It made sense that Cortez Masto sat on the PLFM subcommittee as Nevada is an historic mining state, producing large quantities of gold, silver, and copper. It is also home to the only active lithium mine in the country: Albemarle's Silver Peak brine operation. Although, lithium mining is still very much underdeveloped as an industry in both the U.S. as well as Nevada. Out of the 28 different mining categories the state of Nevada tracks in their annual report, lithium isn't even mentioned.[171] Overall, mining

[169] https://www.benzinga.com/news/22/02/25441617/tesla-updates-supercharger-map-with-new-upcoming-stations-35-growth-in-2021

[170] https://cnevpost.com/2022/04/21/catls-net-profit-grows-185-to-about-2-47-billion-in-2021/

[171] https://goed.nv.gov/wp-content/uploads/2023/01/mining.pdf

provided 15,000 jobs and $13.5 billion of economic activity for the State of Nevada in 2020. To keep this in perspective, mining only contributed to 1.9% of Nevada's GDP.[172]

From 2017-2002, Cortez Masto raised a lot of money: $26 million. From 2020-2022, as one might imagine, Cortez Masto received the second highest amount of campaign contributions from the mining industry. By receiving $55,450.00 she was right behind Joe Manchin who received $55,900.00. She also received $59,000.00 from NextEra Energy, a Florida-based company with a growing renewable energy portfolio. NextEra primarily targets Democratic legislators at a rate of 62% Democrat to 37% Republican.[173]

Also, General Motors gave her $37,000.00 from 2017-2022. GM more evenly split their campaign contributions at 54% Democrat to 45% Republican.[174] In 2022, GM sold only two BEV lines: the Chevy Bolt and Hummer. Importantly, GM had much larger plans to go 100% electric in the future which included their Cadillac and pick-up truck lines. I expect GM to increasingly direct their lobbying efforts towards key legislators in the electrification enterprise.

Senator Mike Lee (R-UT).

Senator Mike Lee was born in in 1971 in Mesa, AZ. His family moved to Utah when he was a child with his father becoming the founding Dean of Brigham Young University's (BYU) law school. His father later served as the president of BYU. Lee himself went on to study at BYU, earning a B.A. in Political Science and a J.D. from the law school his father helped stand up. After graduation from law school, from 1997 to 2010, Lee held a variety of public (both state and federal) and private attorney positions.

Lee was elected as Utah's representative to the U.S. Senate in 2010 and has held the position ever since, winning reelection in 2022. He has served on the CENR since his election in 2010. He has been on the PLFM subcommittee since 2013. He has had a decade in the trenches, long enough to understand the key topics reference critical minerals and mining reform.

Lee was a prolific legislator, sponsoring 304 separate bills, but only one was re-lated to critical minerals or mining and then only tangentially. In October 2021, he

---

[172] Nevada Mining Association.

[173] www.opensecrets.org

[174] www.opensecrets.org

introduced *To amend the Energy Policy Act of 2005 and the Geothermal Steam Act of 1970 to describe the scope of activities subject to a presumption of the applicability of an exclusion under the National Environmental Policy Act of 1969.* This bill was a simple one-page amendment that facilitated the transition of oil and gas wells to geothermal use. This might be useful if it led to lithium brine extraction, but to date it hasn't. The bill was referred to the Committee on Environment and Public Works.

One of the issues for the Republican Party is nuclear energy. In general, Republicans and their base support nuclear energy programs while Democrats and their base are less supportive, getting behind renewable energy programs like solar, wind and hydro. So, when Republicans hear "critical minerals" they don't necessarily move to support lithium mining, they move to support uranium mining. We saw this in the previous chapter with Paul Gosar (R-AZ) in the House and the political battle over uranium mining in the Grand Canyon. Similarly, Lee came out in support of adding uranium to the USGS critical minerals list and of mining in the Grand Canyon. It should also be remembered that Utah has the last active uranium extraction operation in the country.[175, 176]

Lee raised $7.9 million from 2017-2022. He was heavily targeted by the fossil fuel industry like Energy Transfer LP, Walter Oil & Gas, Sinclair Oil and Chevron. He also received donations from DEPCOM Power, a utility scale solar energy company. However, DEPCOM exclusively targets Republicans, giving them 100% of their contributions. DEPCOM is owned by Koch Industries, who also contributed to Lee's campaign and who mainly targets Republicans 93% to just 7% for Democrats.

Lee sits on 15 different committees and subcommittees, with the Subcommittee on Public Lands, Forests and Mining, obviously, being just one of them. Because the Senate is less than one quarter the size of the House, members must sit on a large number of committees and subcommittees. It's impossible to have expertise on all the topics of their various committees. Lee, for one, has not shown an interest in critical minerals, the BEV battery supply chain nor associated mining topics as highlighted by his legislative history. His own homepage, under the sections "Natural Resources" and

[175] Utah's Vital Role in American Uranium Supply. https://www.youtube.com/watch?v=fSSOhL3X7LI

[176] https://www.eenews.net/articles/mike-lee-holds-up-action-on-energy-package/

"National Security", don't mention any of these topics as issues that are of concern to him.[177]

Committee on Energy and Natural Resources: Comparisons

Senator Manchin received a lifetime score of 58% by the League of Conservation Voters, although they scored him at 70% in 2022 for his pro-environmental voting record.[178] Previously, Manchin came out against the 2015 Paris Climate Agreement, insisting that the Senate needed to approve it, not just the President. But his position has "evolved" as we saw with him being the key vote enacting the most sweeping climate legislation the U.S. government has ever passed with the *Inflation Reduction Act of 2022*. The LCV rating reflects Manchin's record as a maybe Democrat, maybe Republican as we have discussed.

While Manchin is a far-right Democrat, he did vote 100% of the time with the Biden Administration on key legislative issues. As a maybe Democrat, maybe Republican, Manchin scored a 1.3 on the Lugar Center Bipartisan Index, making him the #7 most aisle friendly member of the Senate. Of the ten most collaborative Senators in the Bipartisan Index, seven of them were Democrats.

In contrast to Manchin, Senator Barrasso received a 0% rating from the LCV in 2022 and lifetime rating of just 8%.[179] He is on the record as recognizing that man has contributed to climate change. However, he maintains the U.S. must continue using oil, gas, and coal for power generation as well as renewables.[180] Wyoming produces 40% of the coal consumed in the United States and Wyoming itself depends largely on coal for electricity production despite making significant advances in onshore wind production.[181] As we have seen, Barrasso's voting record does not reflect any desire to pursue a clean energy enterprise. And in line with the Republican Party, he supported pulling out of the 2015 Paris Climate Agreement.

Barrasso is a center-right Republican based on his legislative record. He is

---

[177] https://www.lee.senate.gov/NaturalResources

[178] https://scorecard.lcv.org/moc/joe-manchin-iii

[179] https://scorecard.lcv.org/moc/john-barrasso

[180] https://www.c-span.org/video/?c4983779/senator-barrasso-republicans-climate-change-man-made

[181] https://www.eia.gov/state/?sid=WY#tabs-4

more to the right than 80% of his Republican peers. But he did vote with the Biden Administration's key legislation 25% of the time. Barrasso scored a -1.0 on the Bipartisan Index, ranking him #82 out of 100 Senators, meaning he is not likely to support bipartisan legislation.

Public Lands, Forests and Minerals Subcommittee: Comparison

Senator Cortez Masto received a 96% score in 2022 and a lifetime score of 97% from the LCV.[182] In step with the Democrat Party, she is on the record supporting the 2015 Paris Climate Agreement. As one would expect with the 97% rating, the Sierra Club has endorsed Cortez Masto throughout her career. To further her environmental credentials even more, in 2021, the Senator introduced legislation to create a Climate Service Corps.

Based on her legislative record, Cortez Masto is a center of the road Democrat, right down the middle. Accordingly, she voted for the Biden Administration 100% of the time. Cortez Masto received a 0.2 on the Bipartisan Index, putting her in the top third of the Senate at #34, meaning she is willing to sponsor and support bipartisan legislation.

In contrast, Senator Lee had a 5% score in 2022 and a lifetime score of just 8% by the LCV, the same as Barrasso. Like Barrasso, Lee supported the Trump Administration's withdrawal from the 2015 Paris Climate Agreement. Unsurprisingly, Lee has repeatedly questioned the impact of manmade fossil fuel emissions on our warming Earth.[183] This is in line with the Republican Party that questions man's role in global warming and supports the continued burning of fossil fuels, much more so than Democrats.[184] Lee's climate "skepticism" was in line with his non-existent legislative solutions relating to critical minerals and the lithium value chain.

Based on his legislative record, Lee is a centrist Republican, leaning slightly to the left. However, he voted with the Biden Administration 0% of the time on key legislation,

[182] https://scorecard.lcv.org/moc/catherine-cortez-masto

[183] https://newrepublic.com/article/145615/republican-senator-nasa-disputes-climate-consensus-nasa-no-dont

[184] https://www.pewresearch.org/science/2019/11/25/u-s-public-views-on-climate-and-energy/

no matter the topic. He did not support the *Inflation Reduction Act*. Accordingly, Lee received a -1.3 from the Bipartisan Index, making him even less collaborative than Barrasso, dropping him to #89. Of note, the 11 least collaborative Senators are all Republicans (89-100). Of the 20 least collaborative Senators, 17 are Republicans.[185]

Post-Mortem

We see in this snapshot of the Senate, on the actual committees that should be leading critical mineral strategy and mining reform, more partisan politics. There is an environmental divide where the two Democrat senators have much higher ratings for environmental polices than the Republicans who earned dismal scores. This is clearly reflected by the party who supported the 2015 Paris Climate Agreement (Democrat) and the party that opposed it (Republican).

Manchin's record since 2018 was a mixed bag. The one piece of legislation he sponsored pertaining to critical mineral strategy or mining reform, the *Energy Infrastructure Act 2021*, amended previous enacted laws and provided funding for them. This wasn't blazing new territory, but it was a step in the right direction. As we saw, he was the key swing vote for the *Inflation Reduction Act of 2022*, a much smaller version of the *Build Back Better Act* that was fiscally more responsible. This act does stand out as the most sweeping climate change mitigation legislation to ever have been passed by any U.S. administration.

Although he is a far-right Democrat, Manchin covered down on President Biden's agenda every single time when it counted. Because Manchin straddled both parties, he had the highest bipartisan rating of our sampling. The negotiations between Manchin and Schumer resulting in the *Inflation Reduction Act* also revealed the strategy necessary to get battery value chain legislation passed. Although Trump and Biden both published executive orders pushing a national critical mineral strategy, it didn't get them far. In this instance, the Executive Branch had to maneuver a large, many-faceted bill that gave enough room to negotiate with the varied Democratic stakeholders. A small, narrow bill wouldn't have made it through the complex political system because it didn't give the sponsors the political room they needed to maneuver and negotiate a final deal.

We see with Barrasso the typical Republican profile of a dismal environmental

---

rating reinforced with his opposition to the Paris Climate Agreement. This is also not surprising considering Wyoming's overdependence on coal, much like that of West Virginia. Two of Barrasso's bills focused on the coal industry, one repealed the BEV tax credit and one, the *Mining Schools Act*, pushed forward a small but vital part of an overall critical mineral strategy. Education was one of the few areas both parties could cooperate on without confronting their own core party issues.

Barrasso, as a center-right Republican, was unlikely to pursue bipartisan legislation even though he occasionally voted with the Biden Administration. He didn't back the *Inflation Reduction Act*, a key piece of legislation that moved critical mineral supply chain resiliency forward. While Manchin and Barrasso co-sponsored some "safe" legislation (*Outdoor Recreation Act, America's Revegetation and Carbon Sequestration Act*), that's where it ended. Barrasso and Manchin were far enough apart on core party issues that they never co-sponsored critical mineral or mining reform legislation.

On the PLFM Subcommittee, Senator Cortez Masto was a Democratic centrist willing to work across the aisle and had pushed forward critical mineral and BEV value chain legislation in line with President Biden's guidance. In fact, she was one of the most assertive and consistent legislators on those topics.

Senator Lee is quite the opposite. However, the two collaborated on safe legislation (*REDUCE Government Waste Act*) just like Manchin and Barrasso did. But when it came to moving critical mineral legislation forward, either under Trump or Biden, Lee revealed a complete lack of interest. This was despite him being the Ranking Member on the Subcommittee responsible for overseeing mining. This is one of the political contradictions we often must live with: the lawmakers responsible for critical mineral legislation and strategy may never actually do anything in that space.

We have observed that the dynamics of the committees overseeing critical mineral legislation in the Senate were like the dynamics of the House. There was a partisan divide in both sides of the Congress with no bipartisan critical mineral or mining reform came from either committee. When the Republicans had the majority in the House and the Senate from 2017-2019, they moved forward no significant critical mineral legislation. And to be fair, even though a coherent critical mineral strategy was long overdue, it was still an immature idea within the massive U.S. federal bureaucracy. It would take years to build policy momentum on the topic.

The Democrats were able to get their policies through with simple majorities in

Congress, cutting deals on big bills and muscling legislation through the system. The *Infrastructure Investment and Jobs Act* was bipartisan because both Republicans and Democrats got what they needed out if it. In contrast, the *Inflation Reduction Act* was a straight party vote and the deal cutting was internal to the Democrat Party.

Now that the various legislation we have seen was signed into law, it was up to the U.S. bureaucracy to execute it. By 2022, significant laws were in place to advance critical mineral extraction, to speed up the mining permitting process and to promote EV and battery production. But it didn't matter that all this was public record. Merely reading these laws didn't get actually get anything done. The administration and its accompanying bureaucracy had to move out on it and move out fast. As we take stock of the various battery manufacturing companies moving to the U.S. in 2023, it looks like the IRA will be one of the few laws incentivizing the overall lithium value chain that has its intended impact.

Hope for the Lithium Value Chain

So, where did all this Congressional drama leave the lithium value chain? For the time being, it was trapped out in a political no-man's land, stuck in a crossfire between both Republicans and Democrats. The Republicans supported mining in general, but the transition to a green economy undermined their political dependencies on the fossil fuel industry. This, combined with their climate change denial, restrained them from embracing the lithium value chain. They were further conflicted by their desire to constrain China while needing to develop a domestic critical mineral supply chain. But in this process, they would necessarily have to build an EV and battery value chain that would transition the country off fossil fuels, putting them, ideologically, back at square one.

The Democrats were not fully on board with the lithium value chain either, because increased lithium extraction equaled mining, which they disliked from an environmental standpoint. But if they wanted to halt manmade global warming with its even more dire environmental consequences, they had to develop a domestic lithium supply chain that equated to more mining. And now the Democrats found themselves, logically, back at square one.

But the reality was, reducing carbon emissions meant increased battery metals mining and there was no way around it. You did one to achieve the other and that was the bill that must get paid. Consequently, some Democrats preferred a North

American critical mineral value chain where Canada and Mexico would do the dirty work of mining for the U.S. Our allies would dig the giant holes in the Earth, they would pollute their local water supplies, and they would fight the pitched political battles with their local communities. The U.S. would just sit back and watch the lithium roll in across the border without even breaking a sweat. Problem solved.

But there was hope, maybe even bipartisan hope. Congressman Lance Gooden (R-TX5) and Vicente Gonzalez (D-T15) co-sponsored legislation *To amend the Internal Revenue Code of 1986 to permanently allow a tax deduction for the mining, reclaiming, or recycling of critical minerals and metals from the United States* in April 2021. The bill defined cobalt, graphite, lithium, and manganese (all materials that are required for LIBs) as critical minerals and metals. Entities buying these materials would be provided a 200% tax credit based on their expenditures for said materials. The bill also provided a $200 million grant program to DOI to advance the critical mineral and mining enterprise.[186]

Curiously, neither Gooden nor Gonzalez sat on the mining subcommittee. Gooden was a Republican centrist and Gonzalez a right-leaning Democrat (only eight other congressmen are as to the right or more so than he). The bill had three Republican and three Democrats co-sponsors. Importantly, the younger generation of Republicans increasingly recognized the reality of climate change and the need to pursue low carbon solutions. Gooden was born in 1982, putting him in a generation more supportive of green energy measures, much different than previous generations of GOP leaders saddled with their antiquated ideas and political dependencies.[187]

This bill was referred to House Ways and Means and the House Committee on Natural Resources, specifically to the Energy and Mineral Resources Subcommittee, where Stauber (R-MN) sat as Chairman and Ocasio-Cortez (D-NY) as the Ranking Member. Although this bill may not become law, most never do, the U.S. political system needed a constant drumbeat of bipartisan critical mineral support to move the enterprise forward. This was part of the process of developing political inertia throughout the U.S. government in support of a critical mineral strategy and battery value chain. In hindsight, looking back now from the perspective of 2023, the *Inflation*

---

[186] https://www.govtrack.us/congress/bills/117/hr2688/text

[187] https://www.pewresearch.org/science/2022/07/14/americans-divided-over-direction-of-bidens-climate-change-policies/ps_2022-07-14_climate-change-policies_00-015/

Reduction Act took these Congressmen's ideas into account and incorporated them in some form into the final bill.

Looking Ahead

1. Is the present U.S. political system with lawmakers from the older generation capable of sponsoring legislation with the modern ideas required to move a critical mineral strategy forward? Is the U.S. political system capable of identifying and selecting the right lawmakers with the education and experience required to make intelligent critical mineral legislation? Or do we need elected officials with desire to promote a critical mineral strategy and just the willingness to be informed by expert members of their staff to inform their decisions?

2. What will it take to get bipartisan legislation out of the natural resource committees that positively impact the critical mineral value chain? Will it take new, younger members from a different generation with fresh ideas that are free from the old ideas of their predecessors? Or are these core party issues that have nothing to do with generational thinking and business as usual will continue?

3. Or, maybe the natural resource committees will never figure it out as they continue to use their platforms to appease their respective bases. Maybe we saw with the *Inflation Reduction Act* what it takes to muscle change through the political system and is has nothing to do with the committees. The committees serve a purpose, but passing critical mineral legislation isn't one of them. Perhaps the model for legislative change on the critical minerals topic is already known because we already saw it with the IRA.

4. A question remains for me, and perhaps the reader can answer it, then what is the purpose of the committees responsible for critical mineral legislation? Is it merely an educational purpose? To hold hearings with industry experts in order to air different views to the public? Is their purpose to test the political temperature in the room to see where public sentiment lies? What is your opinion on the below statement.

5. What is the role of committees in the legislative process?
   "Committees are essential to the effective operation of legislative bodies.

Committee membership enables members to develop specialized knowledge of the matters under their jurisdiction. Committees monitor on-going governmental operations, identify issues suitable for legislative review, gather and evaluate information, and recommend courses of action to the Senate."[188]

---

[188] https://www.senate.gov/committees/committees_faq.htm

CHAPTER 6

The U.S. Mining Permitting Process

"This document is an honest attempt to present all the permits that may be required by a mining operator in Arizona. Despite our best efforts, it is probably not complete." – Bureau of Land Management, Arizona Mining Permitting Guide, 195 pages long

A Declining Industry

As we discussed many times in previous chapters, one of the central obstacles for moving a mining operation forward in the U.S. is the multi-layered permitting process. Every senior manager in the lithium industry has confirmed this. It's not a secret. A ten-year process is the norm, although, depending on the specific characteristics of the mine, it could be even longer. Much longer. Like 20 years.

So why is this? How is this even possible? To an outside observer, this sounds completely ludicrous. There are many reasons (political, social, legal, environmental), but the biggest one is bureaucratic. There are so many layers of laws and regulations involved in the permitting process, it takes years to navigate them. Also, many of the approving agencies are understaffed and under-resourced. Any new mining application is just one more in an already overwhelming pile of other applications. Heaven forbids if a company makes a mistake on their Mine Plan of Operation (MPO) paperwork, causing the application to get kicked back. They just ate another year.

Over time, mining lost importance as an industry in America. In 2009, there were 20 active uranium mines in the U.S. while in 2023 there was just one – in Senator Mike Lee's State of Utah. The U.S. imported 95% of its uranium from a variety of countries, some being allies like Australia and Canada. Others were not so friendly like Russia.

From a free market perspective, other countries had richer sources of uranium and could sell them at a lower price. U.S. uranium mining companies simply couldn't compete, especially when supply outstripped demand and the price of uranium dropped.[189]

In the Rare Earth Elements (REE) space, China dominated the global market by mining and processing the majority of the World's REE supply. This fact was a direct result of China steadfastly executing a multi-decade REE strategy. Despite transitioning through several different leaders since the 1990's, China remained on track and steadily grew its control of the REE value stream. Today, by some estimates, China has captured 90% of downstream REE products. This included the REE used to make magnets for BEV motors. In contrast, the U.S. has only one REE mining operation owned by MP Materials located in Mountain Pass, California, but they ship out all their extracted minerals for processing.[190] Any guess where they send it? China.

We have seen the same dynamics play out with lithium. The U.S. was caught flatfooted with lithium, showing no ability to forecast global trends and act accordingly despite a decade of detailed market intelligence. The U.S. had no inkling of even a very basic critical mineral strategy until 2018 and then it came in fits and starts. As of today, one could even argue, this strategy exists more on paper than it does in reality. The U.S. let everyone else do the mining with little to no thought to its national economic and security implications. This is illustrated by the U.S. having only a single lithium mine in the entire country, despite having significant lithium resources.

With U.S. mining declining in several critical areas, it may not have really mattered that the mining permitting process was so painful. Afterall, there wasn't a whole lot of mining going on in these critical areas. As the U.S. government enterprise gradually became aware of its very weak position in context to the global EV battery value chain, it realized the permitting process was a problem. Accordingly, the *Inflation Reduction Act of 2022* had very specific language and significant funds designated to improve the process.

Let's better understand the beast we are dealing with. For the purposes of this chapter, we will dig into the specifics of getting a hard rock mine approved in the state of Arizona. I chose Arizona because it is the second most active mining state in the country after Nevada. Secondly, there are several proposed lithium projects on the

---

[189] https://www.eia.gov/energyexplained/nuclear/where-our-uranium-comes-from.php

[190] https://www.mining-technology.com/analysis/china-rare-earths-dominance-mining/

horizon in Arizona, both hard rock and brine. Also, if you could find it in your heart to allow me just this one small privilege, I live in Tucson.

To start, the mineral a company is looking to mine matters as the characteristics of uranium are much different than lithium. The process a company uses to mine matters as well since hard rock mining is much different from brine extraction. The immediate physical location of the proposed mine also matters – try putting an open pit mine in the Grand Canyon and get back to me. The communities near the mine matters, as does wildlife, plants, and water systems.

The associated political geography overlaying the physical mining location matters a great deal. A company will have local, county, state, federal and tribal offices, and regulations to deal with depending on the location of the mine. Also, personalities can be crucial. Try starting a poorly thought out mine operation in Congressman Grijalva's county and let me know how it goes. Everything and anything near a proposed mining operation matter. A successful mining plan takes into consideration and reflects all these elements. If not, a company will pay a price, counted in years.

Fixing America's Surface Transportation (FAST) Act

The U.S. federal government has recognized the permitting process problem for quite some time and has tried to speed it up through legislation. For example, President Obama signed the 491-page FAST Act into law in December 2015, mainly involving the Department of Transportation (DOT). While FAST focused on federal highways, rail, and public transportation, they did address the permitting process under *Acceleration of Project Delivery*.

Section 1301-1318 offered 30 pages of guidance on how to streamline the project permitting process which often involved navigating environmental regulations. Section 1304 *Efficient Environmental Reviews for project Decisionmaking* offered nine pages of suggestions that included some deadlines and ways to reduce redundancies. Overall, I think it missed the mark and didn't recognize how complex the overall permitting process was.

Section 1305 *Integration of Planning and Environmental Review* offered four pages directing that products used in planning be used in the environmental review process to save time. Section 1309 *Program for Eliminating Duplication of Environmental Reviews* had six pages directing an experimental program. With this model, States reviewed environmental regulations and approved related permits instead of the federal government. Section 1311 *Accelerated Decisionmaking in Environmental Reviews* directed federal agencies to minimize unnecessary draft revisions of key documents like the Environmental Impact Statement (EIS).

Section 1313 *Aligning Federal Environmental Reviews* directed DOT and other relevant agencies to develop a process to coordinate their mutual actions reference the National Environmental Protection Act. This included developing a joint checklist for action that all agencies could review. Of interest, FAST stood up the Federal Permitting Improvement Steering Council (FPISC) consisting of 15 major federal agencies to include key mining players like BLM, USFS, USFWS, EPA, and USACE.

The Council, which is a permitting Task Force consisting of the key members of the bureaucracy, were responsible for overseeing large-scale critical infrastructure projects. Their mission statement is to "improve the outcomes" of the associated environmental review and authorization process.[191] Projects qualifying for their interagency assistance fell under the FAST-41 program. Until 2021, mining didn't qualify for FAST-41; a vote of the FPISC members in 2020 changed that.

Ironically, the FPISC are the lead players of a complex bureaucracy who are supposed to cut through the complex bureaucracy that they themselves comprise to make it work faster. I searched their Permitting Dashboard for any mining project, both completed and ongoing, in any state initiated by any agency. The search results came up blank. FPISC confirmed that they have not assisted any mining projects since January of 2021 when it was added to their list of sectors covered.

Importantly, a complex mining operation would most likely never be covered under FAST-41 as they must meet several requirements. These included a $200 million project value which should be met easily with, say, a lithium mine. However, within 60 days of submission to FAST-41, the mining operation must show a complete timetable of all necessary permits that the Council can coordinate on (this is an impossible standard to meet). Consequently, only 3-4 projects a year of any kind from all sectors qualify for FAST-41. The Council themselves estimated that much less than ten mines would qualify. Hence, the Council and their FAST-41 program is no solution to the challenges of the mining industry nor advancing a critical minerals strategy.[192]

[191] https://www.permits.performance.gov/fpisc-content/federal-permitting-improvement-steering-council

[192] https://www.federalregister.gov/documents/2021/01/08/2021-00088/adding-mining-as-a-sector-of-projects-eligible-for-coverage-under-title-41-of-the-fixing-americas

Of note, Alexander Herrgott was the Executive director of FPISC under the Trump administration from 2018-2021. When the Biden administration came in, he departed and formed The Permitting Institute (TPI). TPI is a non-profit advocating for the transformation of the permitting process through participation by non-partisan actors. TPI seeks to streamline the complex bureaucracy while being good stewards of the environment. In other words, TPI took the federal FPISC model and privatized it. Mining companies can join TPI and/or pay for their strategic permitting advice.[193]

Biden-Harris Permitting Action Plan (BHPAP)

The BHPAP of 2022 was intended to "strengthen and accelerate federal permitting and environmental reviews" by leveraging the recently passed *Infrastructure Investment and Jobs Act* of 2021.[194] To provide meaningful improvements to the complex bureaucracy that oversees the permitting process, the Plan would have to provide something much different than what was already being done. If one merely exhorted the complex bureaucracy to work faster, do we think it would immediately start working faster? Let's dig in.

A pillar of the Plan is early interagency coordination that would be facilitated through the FPISC and their FAST-41 program (which we have already determined is not useful to the mining industry). Of the 24 projects nationwide being tracked in FAST-41 as of Q12022, none were mining operations.[195] The criteria to meet FAST-41 was so restrictive, only a score of projects could ever be addressed.

The Plan also relied on the Department of the Interior's (DOI) Interagency Working Group (IWG) to come up with legislative suggestions to reform the *Mining Law of 1872*. The IWG was guided by the *Biden-Harris Administration Fundamental Principles for Domestic Mining Reform* published in February 2022. They were directed to present their suggestions to Congress by November 2022. We will see if these suggestions were anything different than what the respective House and Senate committees overseeing mining policy had already reviewed.

The Plan also directed that project timelines and milestones be published on the Federal Permitting Dashboard to increase transparency. FPISC was now authorized to list

---

[193] https://www.permittinginstitute.org/toolsandservices

[194] The Biden-Harris Permitting Action Plan, May 2022.

[195] Federal Permitting Improvement Steering Council, Quarterly Agency Performance Report, Q12022.

even non-FAST-41 covered projects on their public online dashboard if they were deemed important enough. This sounded good on paper, but the volume of projects that could be effectively tracked was probably still quite small. Also, what happened to a mining company's schedule when the Sierra Club dropped repeat lawsuits on an extraction operation like a low-level bomber, blowing up their timeline and sending it into the next decade?

Furthermore, agencies were to engage in early outreach to Tribes, State, local and community stakeholders. This was essentially repackaging what the *FAST Act* of 2015 had already mandated for DOT. Agencies were also told to improve their responsiveness and assistance to those involved in the permitting process to help them navigate the bureaucracy. This echoed President Trump's previous *Executive Order 13953* from September 2020 that directed agencies to streamline their permitting processes. Finally, agency CERPOs (Chief Environmental Review & Permitting Officers) were instructed to prepare their respective plans to implement these directives.

This plan was another effort to improve and streamline the administrative processes that the government itself could control (sort of). However, there were many elements outside of its control which this plan did not and could not touch. For example, the lawsuits filed by environmental groups against both mining companies and federal agencies were fought over in federal courts. And there was a myriad of laws from the *Clean Water Act* to the *Endangered Species Act to* contend with. These necessitated a steady stream of very complicated operational plans and follow up reports by both mining companies and federal agencies. Many of them required review and comments by the public. A single document could take two years and $10 million to complete.

Mine Plan of Operations (MPO)

This is a critical document in the permitting regime that kicks off the whole thing. I've seen them run to hundreds of pages and more. It is sufficiently technical and dependent on the local conditions that a mining company will most likely hire a local business specializing in MPOs to write it up for submission. The MPO lays out how the mine will be established to include actual mine dimensions, roads required, the work force and new construction. Pollution considerations are a major topic to be addressed involving sound, light, water, air, and soil. Detailed environmental considerations required for approval involve animals, plants, insects, habitats, and nearby communities.

Over time, MOPs became more comprehensive because they had to. Mining companies must stay abreast of new laws, regulations, and guidance from the bureaucracy

(DOI, EPA, Executive Branch). New concerns have come to the forefront such as carbon emissions, environmental justice, and Tribal consultations. An effective document required a platoon of experts working on it for months so the reviewing agencies wouldn't shoot holes in it. The final document could easily qualify as someone's PhD dissertation.

A MOP is designed from the start to address all permitting concerns to get the mine approved for operation. Consequently, it is an extremely optimistic document because the authors need to show their project is feasible. Since the MOP is a screenshot in time, up until the point of submission, it can eventually become a work of fiction as the project progresses. Also, MOPs are generally dominated by engineers and academics and the document reflects their thought processes. As a result, there can be holes in an MOP large enough for Raul Grijalva to drive his RV through.

While the MOP is for public consumption, a mining company must have a realistic internal plan as well. To start, a company must be sober about the price of their mineral and how it trends as a commodity. Their market intelligence must be forward looking as they seek to understand global trends. If they submit an MOP for a lithium mine while LCE sells at $50,000 USD a ton, their mine is viable. If the lithium market becomes flooded with Chinese processed LCE and crashes the market to $10,000 USD a ton, the company could now go bankrupt. Market prices can halt a mine as surely as a denied permit.

As we saw in Chapters four and five, local and national politics must be considered. A company must understand the specific political positions and personalities of the relevant, local, county, state, and tribal officials – knowing their legislative record is key. If a company wants to mine in Paul Gosar's (R-AZ) district, he will support it. If a company wants to mine in Raul Grijalva's (D-AZ) district, he's going to fight you tooth and nail. At the national level, key personalities change with the election cycle. If Raul Grijalva (D-AZ) is the chair of the House Natural Resources Committee, that might not be helpful. However, if the Republican Party becomes the majority and Pete Stauber (R-MN) goes from Ranking Member to Chairman, that's a different story.

It helps to understand the environmental groups who will most likely come out in opposition to a specific mining operation (they will, it is just a matter of which ones). This will help to inform a mining company's legal team as they prepare their strategy. For example, if a company wants to mine uranium in the Grand Canyon, they might want to understand who the Grand Canyon Trust and the Sierra Club (Grand Canyon Chapter) are. They both have the public support base and money to continuously drop lawsuits on mining operations. Literally, it's their job.

Understanding public opinion about mining issues and how they are trending can be critical because it affects the overall operational environment. For instance, most Americans support carbon neutrality and pursuing clean energy alternatives.[196] Also, Americans largely support government incentives for BEVs, with the younger generation more likely to purchase them.[197] This could buttress a mine's environmental narrative: that they are in pursuit of battery minerals like lithium or manganese.

Equally, Americans strongly support conservation and believe the government should be involved in these efforts.[198] Because a mine permitting process could evolve over a multi-decadal time continuum, circumstances could change. For instance, in 2012, the U.S. Fish and Wildlife Service designated as "critical habitat" some 1,200 square miles of land that included the Santa Rita Mountains south of Tucson, AZ.[199] Thus, five years after submitting their MOP, the Rosemont mine now overlapped protected jaguar lands. That was a problem for them.

Beyond just the wildlife problem, there are many environmental contradictions with any open pit mine. For example, Hudbay touted their Rosemont copper mine as supporting a green economy and reducing greenhouse gases.[200] Yet, their proposed open pit mine was an environmental abomination, leaving a hole in the Earth one mile wide and half a mile deep. It would be just as if a nuclear bomb struck there, and if this was a uranium mine, opponents would argue there was no difference.

A mine's carbon footprint is problematic, especially if a company advertised their operation as reducing greenhouse gas emissions. The Rosemont MOP had two 100,000-gallon diesel storage tanks on site, numerous diesel-powered generators and the mine's truck force would burn some 9 million gallons of diesel fuel a year.[201] Tell us again how exactly did

---

[196] https://www.pewresearch.org/science/2022/03/01/americans-largely-favor-u-s-taking-steps-to-become-carbon-neutral-by-2050/

[197] https://www.pewresearch.org/fact-tank/2022/08/01/americans-support-incentives-for-electric-vehicles-but-are-divided-over-buying-one-themselves/

[198] https://conservationtools.org/library_items/1205

[199] https://www.tucsonsentinel.com/local/report/081712_jaguars/feds-propose-1200-sq-miles-jaguar-habitat-s-az/

[200] https://hudbayminerals.com/united-states/default.aspx

[201] Rosemont Project, Mine Plan of Operations, July 11, 2007.

the mine contribute to reduced carbon emissions? Where was the on-site integrated solar farm, electric battery energy storage system (BESS) and electric vehicle fleet? Rosemont's greenwashing couldn't hide the reality of their carbon intensive procedures.

Waste was an obstacle that couldn't be overcome satisfactorily. Rosemont Mine would produce an estimated 1.2 billion tons of waste rock and 660 million tons of tailings (more physical waste). These mountains of discarded earth would stand 700 feet tall and cover 2,400 acres of land.[202] Additionally, an open pit mine used millions of gallons of water a year. In Southwestern U.S., which has suffered from decades of drought, how did a company justify giving all this water to a mining operation at the expense of agriculture, local wildlife, and the surrounding ecosystem?

Hence, mining operations found themselves in the crossfire of two sides: national public support for reduced carbon emissions and local public support for protecting wildlife and scenic lands. This created the conditions that were ripe for legal warfare. The ensuing court battles, that directly impacted the permitting process, could drag out for years, even decades.

Accordingly, mining companies had to be cautious and detailed in their application process. Approving agencies had to be equally thorough in their own reviews and analysis that would result in an approved permit. If either side made even a minor mistake in the process or a new legal precedent was set somewhere in the country at a different mining operation, the lawsuits from environmental groups and Tribal Nations soon followed. The litigation would play out typically for years until a decision was made. Then another round of litigation would begin based on that earlier decision and the process would repeat itself.

Many times, the permitting process wasn't the chief culprit, it was the legal process associated with the permitting process. Consequently, an MPO had to cover every single aspect that might end up in litigation. As an example of how complex MPOs became, Rosemont Mine's "final" MPO submitted in 2018 was 165 pages in length. But the associated attachments were another 4,137 pages. The NMA estimated that the overall permitting process had cost $100 million which meant the overall document cost more than $23,000.00 a page.

---

[202] https://www.azmirror.com/2022/06/01/hudbay-wins-latest-court-battle-over-the-rosemont-mine-as-heavy-equipment-continues-to-roll-in-the-santa-rita-mountains/

A **Record of Decision (ROD)** is a published document issued by the relevant authority approving the MPO. The ROD enables actual mining to legally begin. The ROD summarizes the thinking behind the decision and references the previously completed Environmental Impact Statement (EIS). A variety of alternatives are considered and the one with the least environmental impact is chosen.

As an example, the Canyon Uranium Mine ROD issued by the U.S. Forest Service in 1986 was 15 pages in length. It approved a modified MPO based on the previously completed EIS. The final EIS was part of the published ROD. Although the ROD is "final" it can be challenged in court. Also, the modified MPO approved in the ROD must be followed or the mining company will face legal jeopardy by regulators. In another example, Energy Fuels Nuclear Inc. submitted it's 27-page MOP in October 1984 and received an ROD only two years later.

In comparison, the 2021 Thacker Pass Lithium Mine Project ROD and Plan of Operations Approval was 32 pages in length. This document was prepared by BLM in cooperation with several other federal, state and county agencies. Under *Conditions of Approval*, the Lithium Nevada Corporation was bound by 41 separate environmental protection measures such as undertaking an Eagle Conservation Plan and installing cattle guards to keep out open range livestock.

An **Environmental Impact Statement (EIS)** is required under the National Environmental Policy Act of 1969 (NEPA) when a mining operation constitutes a major federal action. The EIS is extensive and must address all direct, indirect, and cumulative environmental concerns. First, the lead agency announces a Notice of Intent to prepare an EIS in the Federal Register (the official daily publication for all federal agencies where notices are posted). A draft EIS is developed. Next, public scoping meetings are held in nearby towns where the mining operation is located. Then, a 45-day public comment period is held with virtual information sessions. The input from these invents are then incorporated into a draft EIS.

The Forest Service's EIS for the Canyon Uranium Mine in 1986 was 233 pages. The EIS referred to five existing laws including the *Mining Law of 1872*. Five different plans of action were considered. Ten main sets of Issues & Concerns were identified that the EIS addressed. The mining company, Energy Fuels, had to get 17 different permits and approvals at the federal, state and county levels. Six separate environmental Acts were addressed (Clean Water Act, etc....) as well as a reclamation plan. Over 900 separate agencies, offices and individuals were provided a copy of the EIS.

For comparison, the Thacker Pass Lithium Mine Project EIS was conducted by

BLM in coordination with the U.S. Fish & Wildlife Service. This document, published in 2020, was actually shorter in length at only 196 pages. Would we care to guess what the cost of preparing this EIS was? $8.9 million or $45,000.00 a page.[203]

National Environmental Policy Act (NEPA) of 1969

While NEPA is only six pages long (just like the *Mining Law of 1872*), no other law has had such profound impact on the mining permitting process. Part of the purpose of the Act is to "…encourage productive and enjoyable harmony between man and his environment…" Section 102, paragraph C, provides the framework that we see in an EIS. An EIS will be initiated whenever "major Federal actions significantly affecting the quality of the human environment…" occur, such as mining on federal land. The responsible federal agency will provide a statement on the action that addresses its: environmental impact, unavoidable adverse environmental effects, alternatives to the proposed action, the relationship between short-term and long-term activity and the commitment of resources. Combined, these five requirements make up what we know as an EIS.[204]

Furthermore, before issuing a detailed EIS, the lead agency responsible for the major federal action will solicit comments from other agencies that may have jurisdiction as well, hence where we get a draft EIS from. Comments made by federal, state, and local agencies will also be made available to the public. A state agency may provide an EIS as long as the lead federal agency was consulted and provided input.

Generally, an agency will conduct an overview of a project. If they determine that the project does not have any readily identifiable environmental impact, they will conduct an Environmental Assessment (EA) to gather more data. If upon further analysis there is no significant environmental impact, a determination of Finding of No Significant Impact (FONSI) is applied and there is no requirement for an EIS. If analysis does reveal significant impact, then an EIS is required. NEPA does not provide an agency the authority to render a decision on a mining operation. It provides the legal requirement to disclose to the public the impact of the action on the environment.[205]

Over time, the NEPA review process became slow and costly, mainly due to the

---

[203] Thacker Pass Final EIS, Dec 4, 2020. BLM and USFWS.

[204] The National Environmental Policy Act of 1969, as amended.

[205] Arizona Mining Permitting Guide, 2017, Bureau of Land Management

complex bureaucracy that needed to manage it but couldn't do so effectively. In a sampling of DOE projects requiring an EIS in 2015, the average cost of preparing the report was $4.19 million. The average time to complete the EIS was just over four years. The DOE recognized that the NEPA bureaucracy functioned so poorly that they even published quarterly "Lessons Learned" to identify the associated problems and find solutions. In 2017, they stopped publishing these – I guess they gave up.[206]

Federal Water Pollution Control Act (FWPCA) of 1972

This law is commonly referred to as the *Clean Water Act*. The Act regulates the discharge of pollutants into water sources. Any discharge of any pollutants into water sources not covered by this Act is illegal. The EPA administers this Act. Persons knowingly violating this act face up to $250,000.00 in fines and not more than 15 years in prison.

Section 401: a mining company will provide a certification from the State showing that they are in compliance with this Act before applying for a federal permit (p.185).

Section 402: The EPA issues this permit, or a State agency that is in compliance with the FWPCA; a National Pollutant Discharge Elimination System (NPDES) permit is required for any point source discharge. This regulates stormwater runoff. This must be renewed every five years.

Section 404: Regulates the "discharge of dredged or fill material into the navigable waters at specified disposal site." The Army Corps of Engineers is responsible for ensuring Section 404 is met by mining companies and issuing the associated permit. EPA also reviews the application before permit issuance.

In 2019, students from the University of Irvine conducted a study of the Section 404 permitting process to determine its timeliness. They studied a variety of projects (285 total) that were issued permits by the U.S. Army Corps of Engineers (USACE) in the Southwest U.S.: California, Arizona, Nevada, New Mexico, Colorado, Utah, Texas. The study covered a period of 3.5 years from 2013-2016. The average time duration from submission to approval for a Section 404 permit was 1.2 years. For projects that were approved during the period studied, the average time was just under ten months. For those projects still under review, the time was closer to three years.[207]

---

[206] Department of Energy, Lessons Learned Quarterly Report, Mar. 2016, available at http://energy.gov/nepa/downloads/lessons-learned-quarterly-report-march-2016.

[207] Evaluating Environmental Permitting Process Duration: The Case of Clean Water Act Section 404 Permits, N. Ulibarri, J. Tao. 2019.

The above study also found that Arizona, of all the states in the data sample, had the longest permitting time. Today, the Arizona Department of Environmental Quality (ADEQ) offers a mining specific Multi-Sector General Permit (MSGP). The ADEQ Water Quality Division has an 81-page packet with Subpart G pertaining to Metal Mining specifically. There are 11 pages of specific instructions that must be met to comply with the Arizona Pollution Discharge Elimination System (AZPDES). Stormwater Pollution Prevention Plan (SWPPP) guidance is provided for ores like copper, gold, silver, lead, zinc, nickel, manganese, and uranium. There is no mention of lithium.

The applicant must submit a completed SWPPP along with a Notice of Intent to ADEQ along with the application fee. Once ADEQ has received these, they will provide a Notice of Intent Certificate within 30 calendar days. However, if there are questions about the SWPPP (e.g., incomplete information, inaccurate data, non-compliance with existing regulations) then the process gets held up until the applicant resolves the identified issues.

ADEQ has a 23-page SWPPP template which is much longer once it is filled out. The applicant provides all the necessary attachments, appendices, and graphics like detailed maps of the mine and all the stormwater runoff measures to be implemented. The SWPPP is sufficiently technical a document that the EPA offers a 50-page guide on how to complete one.

As an example, I reviewed a SWPPP for a DOT construction project in Pima County, AZ that ran 269 pages. The SWPPP for the utility corridor to support Rosemont's proposed mine, also in Pima County, was 150 pages long and might have taken two years to complete, based on the several revision dates included in the document.[208] Hudbay Minerals' name is on the SWPPP, but they most likely hired a local Tucson environmental engineering firm specializing in SWPPPs to prepare the document.

Clean Air Act (CAA) of 1970

This law was enacted to protect human health and the environment from the effects of emissions that pollute the air. It requires the EPA to establish minimum national air quality standards and directs the individual States to enforce compliance. The Act also established a comprehensive permitting system. There are 27 different acts and amendments that together make up *U.S. Code 42* that regulates air pollution in the U.S.

---

[208] SWPPP, June 2017, Rosemont Copper Company

There are 141 separate state, county and local agencies involved in the issuance of air quality permits in the U.S. Timeliness of the permitting process depends on the unique personalities, workloads, and processes of each office. The length of time from submission to approval depends on, among other things, the class of air permit one is requesting. Does the permit require a public hearing? Did the company make a mistake on the permit submission and get it kicked back?

The Arizona Department of Environmental Quality (ADEQ) has a 41-page application packet for a Class I Air Quality Permit. ADEQ has a self-imposed timeline of ten calendar days to review the submission and determine if it is complete or requires corrections and additional information. Once ADEQ has received a complete air permit packet, they "strive" to provide a final decision back to the applicant within 365 calendar days.[209]

A company can try to ensure a faster process if they schedule an appointment to sit down in person with an ADEQ Air Quality Permit Liaison to go over the details of their packet prior to submission. A company would want to do this if they had a complex and valuable long-term operation like a lithium mine. One could also get their respective application put at the top of the submissions pile if they paid an "Accelerated Permit Deposit" of an additional $15,000.00. Personally, If I was in the business of selling lithium carbonate equivalent (LCE) at $60,000.00 USD/ton, I would kick in the extra 15k to get my packet at the top of the pile.

Federal Land Policy Management Act (FLPMA) of 1976

This Act serves as the basis for the Bureau of Land Management (BLM) surface management regulations for lands under their purview.

The purpose of the Act included that "the public lands be managed in a manner that will protect the quality of scientific, scenic, historical, ecological, environmental, air and atmospheric, water resource, and archeological values". Section 314 provides guidance reference filing requirements for unpatented mine owners. Section 317 addresses mineral revenues and payment guidance for leased BLM lands.[210]

However, the FLPMA does not address mining on BLM lands in any significant way, so the topic remained open to regulation by other existing laws like the *Mining Law of 1872*. As such, BLM officials operated under the idea that domestic and foreign

---

[209] https://azdeq.gov/node/446

[210] The Federal Land and Policy Management Act of 1976, as amended.

mining companies had a right to mine on BLM administered land. BLM was there merely to regulate the activity according to the various relevant laws.

BLM will initiate environmental reviews as required under NEPA and conduct Environmental Assessments (EAs) and Environmental Impact statements (EIS). EA's can be very detailed depending on the nature of the project. In 2020, BLM published a 22-page EA for the Cape Yakataga Placer Mine in Alaska. The EA was conducted in context of the *Mining Law of 1872*, the *FLPMA of 1976* and BLM Surface Management Regulations. The EA recognized that the Northern Aurora Gold Company would have to receive an Alaska Pollutant Discharge Elimination System Permit. Aurora would also have to comply with Clean Water Act Section 404 guidance in coordination with the U.S. Army Corps of Engineers.[211] In comparison to other EAs that can run into the hundreds of pages, this one was rather precise.

When appropriate, BLM will prepare a Finding of No Significant Impact (FONSI), meaning that an Environmental Impact Statement is not required. The Keystone Gold Mine near Death Valley California submitted a modified MPO in 2018 to conduct more exploratory drilling. Since the drilling was within the existing operational footprint already approved in the original MPO, the impact was most likely minimal. A subsequent EA performed by BLM determined the environmental impact was the same as previously assessed. Hence, BLM issued a 4-page FONSI.[212]

For projects that are already on the record and have been addressed previously with an EIS, BLM can issue a Determination of NEPA Adequacy (DNA). A DNA can be more detailed than a FONSI as it shows that BLM has addressed all applicable laws and regulations and why the DNA is appropriate. For instance, BLM's published DNA for the Desert Hawk Gold–Kiewit Mine Expansion in Utah was 18 pages long.

If a proposed activity is assessed to have no significant impact on the human environment, BLM can make a Categorical Exclusion (CE). This means an EA or EIS is not required. The Council on Environmental Quality (CEQ) issued a memorandum in 2010 providing guidance on when and how to execute a CE.[213] They advised that the documentation supporting a CE decision should be retained and/or published. In practice, a mining operation on BLM land would not qualify for a CE, but subsequent modifications to their MPO could.

---

[211] Environmental Assessment, BLM (Glennallen Field Office), 2020.

[212] Finding of No Significant Impact, BLM (Ridgecrest Field Office), November 29, 2018

[213] CEQ, Categorical Exclusion memorandum, Nov 23, 2010.

Endangered Species Act (ESA) of 1973

The ESA protects endangered animals and plants as well as the ecosystems that support them from economic development like mining activity. The ESA is administered by the U.S. Fish and Wildlife Service (FWS) and the National Marine Fisheries Service (NMFS) although all federal agencies must enforce its provisions and consult with FWS and NMFS. In 2013, the U.S. Supreme Court let stand a 9th Circuit Court of Appeals decision involving mining (dredging the Klamath River in Northern California) on U.S. Forest Service administered land. Importantly, the court determined that the ESA superseded the *Mining Law of 1872*.[214]

About 1,100 miles southeast of the Klamath River, Hudbay Minerals Inc, an international Canadian mining company, purchased private land in the Santa Rita Mountains in Vail, AZ for its Rosemont copper mine. We mentioned this mine earlier in the chapter. They also intended to mine on the adjacent U.S. Forest Service administered land. They submitted their first mining plan in 2007 that kicks of the permitting process (187 pages long). However, they had some problems.

First, their proposed mining operation overlapped critical habitat for an endangered jaguar population. Second, the mine put at risk the threatened Bartram's stonecrop, a succulent requiring water sources the mine would disrupt. Third, local politicians didn't support the mine because nearby communities didn't want a giant hole dug in the scenic mountains that were the backdrop to their neighborhoods. At the time, we lived in Vail, AZ and my family didn't want the mine there either.

The Rosemont mine sits just due East of Raul Grijalva's congressional district. He can't touch it. However, the mine was in Ann Kirkpatrick's District, a fellow Democrat who came out in opposition to the mine. (Kirkpatrick vacated her seat in January 2023 and Republican Eli Crane subsequently won her seat). As the mine was in Pima County, the Pima County Board of Supervisors weighed in and they came out in opposition to the mine. Guess who sits on the Pima County board? Raul Grijalva's daughter, Adelita. Several environmental groups filed a lawsuit challenging the legality of the permitting process, but the mine was cleared to move forward in May 2022.[215] Presently, Hudbay

---

[214] https://earthworks.org/blog/court_rules_endangered_species_act_trumps_1872_mining_law/

[215] https://www.tucsonsentinel.com/local/report/052422_rosemont_challenges_dismissed/judge-challenges-new-arizona-copper-mine-moot-after-hudbay-abandons-rosemont-water-permit/

is building access roads and preparing the overall site for mining as they wait for a new Air Quality Permit and an amended Aquifer Protection Permit which is anticipated to be issued in summer 2023.[216]

National Historic Preservation Act (NHPA) of 1966

The NHPA provides protection to prehistoric and historic archeological sites and areas of religious or cultural significance. National agencies must conduct a review process of any activity that may impact places that meet the NHPA protection requirements. Of note, relevant Indian Tribes will be consulted for any activity that may impact their associated historic interests as defined in the NHPA. If not, a mining operation would place itself in regulatory jeopardy.

Trilogy Metals Inc, a Canadian mining company, would have been aware of the NHPA provisions. Trilogy and their local subsidiary, Ambler Metals LLC, intended to mine copper and cobalt in the Ambler Mining District (AMD) in Alaska.[217] In turn, the Alaska Industrial Development and Export Authority (AIDEA) proposed the Ambler Access Road to connect Dalton Highway with the AMD in Northern Alaska. The road would cut through a patchwork of private land, state land, Native American land, and federal National Preserve. Even a quick review of this jurisdictional patchwork revealed a complicated permitting minefield. After looking at the map of where the proposed road would go, my best estimate was a 15-year process if things went even reasonably well.

At the ten-year mark, in 2020, things were going pretty good for Trilogy-Ambler. BLM had issued their Final Environmental Impact Statement and BLM and the U.S. Army Corps of Engineers had issued their Joint Record of Decision under the National Environmental Policy Act.[218] However, this was under the Trump Administration which looked to fast-track mining operations in Alaska. In 2021, a new sheriff was in town.

Under the Biden Administration, the Department of the Interior relooked the approval process (they were prompted by a lawsuit) and determined that the road approval process violated the NHPA, Section 106. Section 106 stated that local Native Alaskans must be consulted during the process. A native consortium of 37 different Alaskan tribes

---

[216] Abbot, David. "Hudbay ramps up excavation for Copper World Complex as local resistance continues and expands." AZ Mirror, Jan 06, 2023.

[217] https://trilogymetals.com/ Trilogy had no published plans to mine lithium.

[218] https://ambleraccess.org/About/History

stated that they were in fact not properly consulted during the process.[219] Hence, the road permitting process came to an immediate halt, subject to further legal review.

In 2021, Senator Murkowski (R-AK) personally interviewed then future Secretary of the Interior, Deb Haaland, during her nomination hearings.[220] Murkowski tried to determine Haaland's intention regarding mining in Alaska. She was satisfied enough to support her nomination. Now that Haaland had put the project on hold, Murkowski's political rivals jumped on her. They blamed her for supporting Haaland and thus harming Alaska mining interests.[221] Murkowski was re-elected in January 2023.

Case Study: Rosemont Mine

Now that we have a better understanding of the permitting process, let's look at permitting timelines and other key events for the Rosemont Copper Mine. As mentioned previously, this mine is in southern Arizona and was cleared for operations that most likely won't occur until 2024. This is a relevant case study because it is current and there is a lot of publicly available information about it. Keep an eye out for what is dragging the process out: permitting or other factors?

2005: Augusta Resources Corp purchases private land in the Santa Rita Mountains, Vail, AZ

2007: Augusta submits 187-page MPO for Rosemont Mine

2008: Groundwater withdrawal permit is issued by Arizona Department of Water Resources

2011: A game camera photographs "El Jefe" an adult male jaguar in the Whetstone Mountains of southern Arizona; jaguars were listed as an endangered species in 1997

2012 (Apr): Aquifer Protection Permit is issued by AZ Department of Environmental Quality

[219] https://www.tananachiefs.org/about/

[220] https://www.murkowski.senate.gov/press/release/murkowski-questions-interior-secretary-nominee-haaland-on-alaska-priorities

[221] https://www.kellyforak.com/post/murkowski-approved-haaland-again-targets-alaska-from-4-000-miles-away

2012 (Aug): Augusta Resource Corp presents Pima County with a 328-page Technical Feasibility Study for the Rosemont Mine written by M3 Engineering & Technology

2012: Certificate of Environmental Compatibility is issued by Arizona Corporation Committee (to set up power lines)

2013: Right of Way Encroachment License Agreement from Town of Sahuarita for construction of a water pipeline

2013: USFS publishes their 212-page FEIS and draft ROD for the Rosemont Mine

2014: Pima County issues Flood Control District Permit (Floodplain Use Permit-FUP) for constructing a new water line

2014: (Sep): Hudbay Minerals acquires Augusta Resource Corp

2014: USFWS designates areas in the Santa Rita mountains affected by the Rosemont Mine as critical habitat for jaguars

2015: El Jefe is captured on an automated game camera in the Santa Rita Mountains[222]

2015: USFS publishes 813-page Supplemental Information Report (SIR) based on 101 objections to their previous FEIS; they hold 30 separate interagency co-ordination meetings over the course of a year and find no significant changes to their original analysis

2016: USFS publishes a 66-page Second SIR which largely defends the 2015 SIR resulting in no changes to their previous Biological Opinion or Biological Evaluation; they conclude that they don't require a revision of the previous Rosemont EIS

2017 (Jun): U.S. Forest Service Issues 142-page Record of Decision approving Rosemont Mine, provides comments for MPO revisions[223]

2017 (Jun): Rosemont Mine submits 150-page Stormwater Pollution Prevention Plan (SWPPP)

2017 (Sep): The Center for Biological Diversity sues USFWS over their biological opinion that the Rosemont Mine doesn't negatively impact jaguar habitat[224]

---

[222] https://news.azpm.org/p/news-splash/2021/9/3/199914-us-fish-and-wildlife-rejects-rosemont-copper-petition-to-shrink-critical-jaguar-habitat/

[223] Rosemont Copper Company, MPO Volume I, October 2018

[224] https://www.biologicaldiversity.org/news/press_releases/2017/rosemont-copper-mine-09-25-2017.php

2018 (Mar): Rosemont publishes revised MPO based on USFS comments

2018 (Apr): Class II Air Quality Control Permit is issued by AZ Department of Environmental Quality

2018 (Jun): Rosemont publishes revised MPO based on USFS comments

2018 (Oct): Rosemont publishes revised MPO (165 pages long)

2019 (Mar): U.S. Army Corps of Engineers (USACE) issues Rosemont a Section 404 permit under the Clean Water Act; environmental groups file lawsuit against the USACE for violating Section 404

2019 (Jul): U.S. District Court of Arizona rules that the 2013 USFS EIS and ROD were deficient and vacates them, ruling in favor of Ctr. for Biological Diversity[225]; National Mining Association says $100 million has been spent on the Rosemont permitting process[226]

2019 (Aug): USACE suspends Rosemont's Section 404 permit

2020 (Feb): U.S. District Court of Arizona overturns USFWS decision that Rosemont mine did not impact jaguar critical habitat, ruling in favor of Center for Biological Diversity

2021: Hudbay buys an additional 2,400 acres of private land near Rosemont; this is for an expanded and renamed Copper World Complex mining operation

2021 (Mar): Rosemont Mine receives Approved Jurisdictional Determination (AJD) that affected waters were outside of the Navigable Waters Protection Rule (NWPR) meaning they are not considered Waters of the U.S. (WOTUS); a win for Rosemont

2021 (Sep): USFWS rejects Rosemont Mine petition to reclassify and shrink identified jaguar habitat[227]

2021 (Oct): Arizona Mined Land Reclamation Plan is authorized by the State of Arizona

2022 (Apr): Center for Biological Diversity initiates lawsuit against Rosemont

---

[225] Ctr. For Biological Diversity vs U.S. Fish & Wildlife Service

[226] https://www.azmirror.com/2022/06/01/hudbay-wins-latest-court-battle-over-the-rosemont-mine-as-heavy-equipment-continues-to-roll-in-the-santa-rita-mountains/

[227] https://news.azpm.org/p/news-splash/2021/9/3/199914-us-fish-and-wildlife-rejects-rosemont-copper-petition-to-shrink-critical-jaguar-habitat/

Mine for violating Section 404 of the Clean Water Act[228]; Rosemont surrenders their Section 404 permit rendering moot all applicable lawsuits[229]

2022 (May): U.S. District Court of Arizona upholds previous decision that the USFS improperly applied Section 612 of the *Surface Resources and Multiple Use Act of 1955* to approve Rosemont's MPO.[230]

2022 (June): Assistant Secretary of the Army (Civil Works) sends memorandum to the Commanding General USACE rescinding Rosemont Mine's AJD; affected waters are now considered WOTUS[231]

2022 (June): Pima County Board of Supervisors publishes memorandum officially opposing Hudbay's Copper World Complex

2022 (Jun): Hudbay develops a strategy to mine on private land, requiring only local and state permits; this Phase I will last 16 years, giving it time to develop a federal land solution

2022 (Aug): El Jefe is captured on a game camera in Sonora State; the 12-year-old male appears muscled and healthy and most likely has staked claim to his territory[232]

Permitting Roll Up

The U.S. government is composed of an overlapping web of complex federal, state and county bureaucracies that attempt to manage an already complex society. The mining permitting process is a direct reflection of these complex bureaucracies which in turn are a product of our complex society. To say the chief problem with the mining industry is the permitting process is a gross over-simplification of the topic. It is and it isn't.

The permitting process is tied to 150 years of various mining and environmental laws that overlap one another. Over time, the mining environment has become

---

[228] Center for Biological Diversity letter dated April 14, 2022

[229] https://news.azpm.org/p/news-splash/2022/5/4/209841-rosemont-returns-clean-water-permit/

[230] Ctr. For Biological Diversity vs USFWS, US Court of Appeals for the Ninth District, No. 19-17585, May 12, 2022.

[231] Memorandum for Commanding General, USACE, June 3, 2022, by M. L. Connor.

[232] https://www.azcentral.com/story/news/local/arizona-environment/2022/08/05/rare-jaguar-el-jefe-roamed-arizona-spotted-across-border/10251057002/

more complex, not less so. This trend will continue. Just to refresh your memory, the Canyon Uranium Mine submitted its MPO and received an ROD in two years (1984-1986). Now, it takes two years or longer just to write an MPO, an EIS or a SIR.

Competition by different societal stakeholders over a mining operation is an enduring characteristic of the permitting process. They can't be separated from one another. If we look at the Rosemont Copper Mine, the permitting process as administered by the County or State is relatively straight forward. Their requirements and timelines are published. However, this means nothing if an associated lawsuit drags a company into court for several years. That's not the County or the Forest Service's fault, that's society's stakeholders using the established legal system to pursue and defend their interests.

Of course, politics play a role. The Trump administration tried to fast track mining during their tenure and was criticized for rolling back environmental protections. Despite this, a new lithium mining operation was never brought on board during that four-year period spanning 2017-2020. The Biden administration then reinstated stricter environmental regulation as the pendulum swung back. As we discussed in this chapter, the Biden administration also tried to streamline the permitting process. They never did get to the heart of the matter and mainly recycled bureaucratic measures that had already been tried.

In my opinion, both administrations were unable to make any significant headway in the permitting space. The interlocking wall of complex bureaucracy, competing stakeholders, an accessible legal system and a laundry list of related laws stood firm. Repeat volleys of executive orders and mandates for interagency coordination to improve the permitting process merely bounced off it. It remains to be seen what effect the Biden administration's numerous enacted laws and directives have on this space. If they are effective, we should see much different statistics from 2021-2024 with respect to lithium mining operations coming on board.

While we have gone quite far down the permitting mineshaft as it were, understanding the process informs us on other areas of the value chain as well. Any construction process from BEV manufacturing and battery plants to geothermal brine and evaporation pond operations all must go through a permitting process. I remember having several heart attacks every time I read that Tesla's Giga Berlin plant was delayed another month because of opposition from an environmental group. It took two years for Giga Berlin to become operational. When we compare that to the Rosemont Mine timeline, Giga Berlin was practically slapped up overnight.

Looking Ahead

1. U.S. society has collectively determined that they accept the complex permitting process based on the goals of competing stakeholders. Should we weaken existing environmental regulations to speed up the process? Do we accept polluted streams, dead wildlife, and other toxic wastes to streamline mining production? Do we ignore local, tribal and community concerns and promote mining regardless?

2. From an investing perspective, would the reader go all in on a lithium mine based on a simple press release? Recognizing where a mining operation is in its timeline is important. Understanding the complexity of the operation and the regulatory environment is critical. If an investor puts money into a mining company that hasn't even broken ground yet and hasn't delivered a product, they are assuming a lot of risk. The first thing I would ask a mining company is where are they at in the permitting process.

3. What does the reader think about the Rosemont Copper Mine permitting process? What do you think are the chief causes for its continuing delay? Is it the permitting process, the legal process or both combined? How much do we value the North American jaguar? Should we delay, modify, or halt a battery metal mining operation to protect its habitat?

4. What does the reader think of the *National Environmental Protection Act of 1969?* This law has had the most impact on mining operations since the *Mining Act of 1872* itself. The NEPA corrected all the environmental wrongs of the 1872 Act and finally provided a tool to hold irresponsible mining companies accountable for their actions. But did the NEPA go too far or not far enough? What would the reader have done differently if they were given the opportunity to craft a new NEPA? Would you come down on the side of our environment or the mining companies?

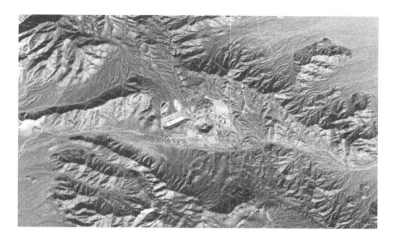

An aerial view of the remote Mountain Pass, CA rare earth elements (REE) mining operation run by MP Materials. This is the only mine in the U.S. extracting REE. China controls upwards of 85% of the global refined REE space and even 100% of some specific elements. Can the reader guess where MP Materials ships its minerals for processing? You guessed it, China. *(by NASA)*

Senator Manchin walks a political tightrope in West Virginia as a conservative Democrat in a state with strong Republican leanings. He was the key vote in getting the *Inflation Reduction Act* passed into law. He was vilified by his opponents as he held up passage of the IRA.

(Official Portrait)

⊗EPA *Wetland Regulatory Authority*

Regulatory Requirements

Section 404 of the Clean Water Act (CWA) establishes a program to regulate the discharge of dredged or fill material into waters of the United States, including wetlands. Activities in waters of the United States regulated under this program include fill for development, water resource projects (such as dams and levees), infrastructure development (such as highways and airports) and mining projects. Section 404 requires a permit before dredged or fill material may be discharged into waters of the United States, unless the activity is exempt from Section 404 regulation (e.g. certain farming and forestry activities).

Wetlands subject to Clean Water Act Section 404 are defined as "areas that are inundated or saturated by surface or ground water at a frequency and duration sufficient to support, and that under normal circumstances do support, a prevalence of vegetation typically adapted for life in saturated soil conditions. Wetlands generally include swamps, marshes, bogs, and similar areas."

The basic premise of the program is that no discharge of dredged or fill material may be permitted if: (1) a practicable alternative exists that is less damaging to the aquatic environment or (2) the nation's waters would be significantly degraded. In other words, when you apply for a permit, you must show that you have, to the extent practicable:

- Taken steps to avoid wetland impacts;
- Minimized potential impacts on wetlands; and
- Provided compensation for any remaining unavoidable impacts.

Proposed activities are regulated through a permit review process. An *individual permit* is required for potentially significant impacts. Individual permits are reviewed by the U.S. Army Corps of Engineers, which evaluates applications under a public interest review, as well as the environmental criteria set forth in the CWA Section 404(b)(1) Guidelines. However, for most discharges that will have only minimal adverse effects, a *general permit* may be suitable. General permits are issued on a nationwide, regional, or State basis for particular categories of activities. The general permit process eliminates individual review and allows certain activities to proceed with little or no delay, provided that the general or specific conditions for the general permit are met. For example,

minor road activities, utility line backfill, and bedding are activities that can be considered for a general permit. States also have a role in Section 404 decisions, through State program general permits, water quality certification, or program assumption.

Agency Roles and Responsibilities

The roles and responsibilities of the Federal resource agencies differ in scope.

U.S. Army Corps of Engineers:

- Administers day-to-day program, including individual and general permit decisions;
- Conducts or verifies jurisdictional determinations;
- Develops policy and guidance; and
- Enforces Section 404 provisions.

U.S. Environmental Protection Agency:

- Develops and interprets policy, guidance and environmental criteria used in evaluating permit applications;
- Determines scope of geographic jurisdiction and applicability of exemptions;
- Approves and oversees State and Tribal assumption;
- Reviews and comments on individual permit applications;
- Has authority to prohibit, deny, or restrict the use of any defined area as a disposal site (Section 404(c));
- Can elevate specific cases (Section 404(q));
- Enforces Section 404 provisions.

Striped bass

The front page of a two-page pamphlet published by the Environmental Protection Agency (EPA) providing an overview of Section 404 of the *Clean Water Act (CWA)*. Any mining activity affecting WOTUS (waters of the United States) will meet Section 404 requirements. The U.S. Army Corps of Engineers issues Section 404 permits in accordance with published regulations. Private entities can challenge 404 permits in federal court if they can establish violation of the CWA. *(by EPA)*.

CHAPTER 7

Lithium Mining in America

"The first recorded production of lithium in the United States consisted of an estimated 30 tons of lithium minerals mined in 1889, but the source of this material is not recorded."
– Lithium Resources of North America, Geological Survey Bulletin, 1955

A Brief History of Lithium Mining in America

The U.S. has a history of lithium mining, although that seems to be forgotten. Prior to World War I, lithium had a variety of uses such as in mineral waters and lithia citrate tablets. Lithia tablets were indicated as a diuretic and an antacid. They were also used to treat rheumatism, gout, lithaemia, and gravel (concentrations of uric acid, calcium oxalate or phosphate that forms in the kidneys).[233]

There was an increase in lithium production during WWI, although the LIB wasn't here yet. Submarines did use banks of lead-acid batteries, which let them cruise silently below the water, undetected. But they had to come to the surface to recharge their batteries using their diesel-powered main engines. In the last year of the war in 1918, U.S. lithium extraction reached 5,894 tons. The vast majority of this was mined out of California and a small amount from South Dakota. In the future, both of these mining sources would dry up as lithium extraction operations shifted elsewhere.[234]

---

[233] https://americanhistory.si.edu/collections/search/object/nmah_714679

[234] "Lithium Resources of North America", Geological Survey Bulletin, 1955, by J. Norton & D. Schlegel.

Post-WWI, lithium found increasing use in ceramics to reduce thermal expansion and enhance glazing. Other early industrial uses for lithium chloride capitalized on its hygroscopic properties (attracts water) for desiccation purposes (dehumidifying, inducing dryness).[235] Also, lithium hydroxide was used in alkaline batteries; they never took off like cheaper lead-acid batteries.[236] More than 11,000 tons of lithium were mined in 1920, reaching peak production that year. However, this dropped quickly to just 2,000 tons by 1940.[237] Up until WWII, the U.S. was a net exporter of lithium with most of that going to Germany.

In WWII, lithium production increased again, largely due to the use of lithium hydride pellets for life preservers, life rafts and inflatable balloons for the military. With this, lithium was merely a transport system for the hydrogen that would expand greatly when put in contact with water.[238] Again, lead-acid batteries were used throughout the war by competing submarine forces and for powering torpedoes. This combination of lead batteries with diesel engines remained the norm for submarine propulsion until the transition to nuclear powered models in the 1950's.[239] Lithium peak production during the war was in 1944 when 13,000 tons were extracted.[240]

After WWII, lithium use expanded into greases as it offered good mechanical stability at high temperatures. Lithium was used widely in multi-purpose greases and owned the majority of market share for that sector. It was popular not just for its superior lubricity, but for keeping down costs as it could be used for many different applications and environments. Ultimately, it was cheaper for a company to buy just one grease product in bulk. It also simplified the overall acquisition process for company logisticians.[241]

Lithium was also used in the manufacturing of aluminum alloys. The introduction of lithium improved strength and rigidity characteristics as well as resistance to

---

[235] *Ullmann's Encyclopedia of Industrial Chemistry*, by Fritz Ullmann, 1914

[236] https://ethw.org/Edison%27s_Alkaline_Battery

[237] Lithium Resources of North America.

[238] https://inf.news/ne/tech/d4e044562561d098e93ef9e62b15d888.html

[239] https://www.batterytechonline.com/materials/role-submarine-batteries-undersea-warfare-technology

[240] Lithium Resources of North America.

[241] https://www.machinerylubrication.com/Read/29658/multi-purpose-grease

fatigue, corrosion, and damage. Lithium aluminum products thus had application in the aerospace industry where lightweight, high-performance metals were required. Post-War extraction continued to increase, reaching 28,000 tons in 1953 with much of this coming out of South Dakota.[242] Once again, Germany became a chief recipient of U.S. lithium.

U.S. lithium production peaked in 1974 at around 26,000 tons of LCE and remained near these levels until 1986. Of interest, up until this time, the U.S. was the world leader in lithium production.[243] Similar to the U.S. drop off in mining of rare earth elements and uranium, lithium dwindled to nothing with the last American hard rock lithium mine closing in 1998. This left the U.S. with only a single lithium brine operation in Nevada. Nevertheless, the rest of the world picked up the slack as the U.S. became a net importer of the soft white metal. By the year 2000, the U.S. imported 96% of its needed lithium from just two countries in the Lithium Triangle: Chile and Argentina.[244]

Just as the U.S. wound down its own lithium production, a new use for lithium was taking off, the lithium-ion battery (LIB). At the time, the LIB was becoming increasingly popular for powering small electronic devices like watches, calculators, watches, cell phones, and eventually laptops. In the year 2000, global lithium extraction soared to meet this new demand with 74,000 tons of LCE being mined. However, not only did the U.S. have little lithium extraction capability, but it also had no battery production capability either. The LIB industry was about to take off and the U.S. was not positioned to compete.

In 2010, the lithium apathy continued in the U.S. with Chile and Argentina providing 97% of its imported lithium needs.[245] Chile, Australia, China, and Argentina combined to produce 97% of the world's lithium production. Total global lithium mined in 2010 was almost double that of 2000 production volumes at 148,900 tons of LCE. Let's remember, in that same year, Tesla received a loan from DOE to expand their BEV production in Fremont, CA. In 2015, the U.S. lithium production and import stats

[242] Lithium Resources of North America.

[243] The Rise and Fall of American Lithium, A. Miatto et al, Yale University.

[244] U.S. Geological Survey, Mineral Commodity Summaries (Lithium), Jan 2001, by J. Ober.

[245] U.S. Geological Survey, Mineral Commodity Summaries (Lithium), Jan 2011, by B. Jaskula.

remained virtually unchanged. However, about 35% of all lithium end products world-wide were batteries.[246] The trend was clear.

In 2020, as the global BEV revolution was in full swing in every major market, the U.S. still only had Albemarle's brine evaporation operation running in Nevada. The U.S. now imported 91% of its lithium needs from the Lithium Triangle, plus 5% from China. Australia, Chile, and China now dominated the world upstream lithium market, extracting 87% of global needs (not counting the U.S.' own estimated 1% contribution). World lithium production had exploded from 172,500 tons LCE in 2015 to 435,000 tons LCE in 2020 – an increase of 256%.[247] The numbers would only increase from there.

We must ask the question: how did the U.S. find itself in such a disadvantaged position? There are several reasons. First, most U.S. lithium extraction was historically from hard rock open pit mining. This type of mining was more expensive to run as compared to evaporative brine operations in the Lithium Triangle. Open pit mines required heavy equipment, thousands of employees, and an increasingly complex permitting process. Lithium end users could get a cheaper product elsewhere, which was outside the U.S. This is where the ridiculously inefficient and inherently insecure lithium supply chains started, they were all based on lower costing.

Also, in 2000, the U.S. had no LIB industry to speak off. The global industry was dominated by Asia and specifically Japan, South Korea, and China. This dominance only grew over time as the U.S. did not invest in the technology nor the human capital to build out its own battery industrial base. From the U.S. perspective, there was no sense in producing a mineral for a battery industry that didn't exist on American soil. Even though market intelligence clearly showed that the LIB industry was blowing up, U.S. industry collectively made the decision to import both lithium and LIBs. Both industries relied on far-flung supply chains prone to disruption.

As China rapidly grew to dominate the lithium processing space, it was cheaper for them, as it shortened their supply chain, to source their lithium as close to home as possible, and this meant Australia. It made no sense to ship a product from the other side of the planet if they could avoid it, especially considering any number of supply chain disruptions that could and did occur. In other words, they weren't going to import it from the U.S.

---

[246] U.S. Geological Survey, Mineral Commodity Summaries (Lithium), Jan 2016, by B. Jaskula.

[247] U.S. Geological Survey, Mineral Commodity Summaries (Lithium), Jan 2021, by B. Jaskula.

Additionally, the U.S. placed no strategic value on developing its battery industry nor its associated supply chains until 2018, much like with rare earth elements, uranium, and microchips. To be clear, when we say 2018, that's just when serious discussions began on the topic. Conceptually, the U.S. government hadn't pursued evolving its global supply chains so that they were shorter, domestically based and thus inherently more secure. Instead, they doubled down on the status quo and focused on securing their existing supply chain paradigm through enhanced security measures like protecting key global maritime chokepoints with the U.S. Navy. Consequently, as you read this in 2023, the U.S. is still far behind and trying to play catch up with the global lithium value chain that they studiously ignored for the last 20 years.

Foote Mineral Company

There may be no better way to understand the history of lithium mining in the U.S, with all its twists and turns, than to understand the journey of the Foote Mineral Company. If we don't understand the lithium past, then we can hardly understand its present circumstances. Foote was an early bulk lithium mining company and an industry leader for many decades. Importantly, Foote laid the foundation for much of today's lithium enterprise in the U.S. They also became the nucleus for America's biggest lithium mining company as of the writing of this book. However, Foote Mineral Company had very humble beginnings.

Albert Edward Foote (A.E. Foote) lived from 1846-1895. He was a certified Medical Doctor and a professor of Chemistry and Mineralogy at the Iowa State Agricultural College. As a young man in his 20's, he developed an interest in mineralogy and began collecting a wide variety of samples. He became quite good at it, leading him to open a minerals trade business out of Philadelphia. Foote's collection became world renown, leading him to publish his 42-page *The Naturalists' Agency Catalogue* in cloth binding. His catalogue was both educational and comprehensive, enabling other mineralogists to order any one of some 1,600 different mineral specimens by mail.[248] [249]

In 1876, in the aftermath of the American Civil War, the Foote Mineral Company was founded in Philadelphia. Foote and his wife, Augusta Matthews, had three children with the oldest being Warren Matthews Foote. Warren was born in 1872, just four

---

[248] https://mineralogicalrecord.com/new_biobibliography/foote-albert-edward/

[249] "The Naturalists' Agency Catalogue", A.E. Foote, 1876.

years before his father's company would take off. He later earned a B.S. in Chemistry from the University of Pennsylvania. When his father died in 1895, Warren took over the family business.

Warren improved on his father's catalogue, expanding it with even more mineral offerings. The company's hardcover illustrated publication in 1904 was now 216 pages long and cost 50 cents (about $16.00 in 2023 money).[250] Warren eventually became the president and general manager of the company and remained so until his death in 1936.[251] Towards the end of his tenure, the company pivoted away from selling individual rock specimens to collectors and moved into the bulk mineral sales business. One of their primary business lines became lithium processing and extraction where they later marketed themselves as the world's leading lithium producer. While lithium was their wheelhouse, they also diversified their business as illustrated by their acquisition of the Vanadium Corporation of America in 1967.

The Foote lithium enterprise would eventually consist of two lithium extraction sites consisting of a hard rock mine in North Carolina and a brine operation in Nevada. They also had several processing and distribution sites located in Pennsylvania, North Carolina, Virginia, and Tennessee. In their time, from the 1950's through 1980's, Foote was a leader in the lithium space. Afterwards, they went through a series of corporate acquisitions that essentially laundered their name and identity, relegating them to the history books.

As early as 1941, Foote ran a lithium processing operation on a 79-acre site in East Whiteland Township, PA. They eventually closed the location in 1991, which became notorious for revelations of extensive pollution and later designation as an EPA superfund site. Foote conducted a variety of operations there to include lithium processing and ore crushing and resizing. The site had two quarries and about 50 buildings. This location made geographical sense in that it was only 30 miles west of Philadelphia where Foote Mineral Co. originally began. The site was also about 2.5 miles east of Exton, PA where their corporate HQs was later located.

In 1943, the Solvay Process Company (SPC) established a lithium mining operation and processing plant near Kings Mountain, NC.[252] The larger area in Gaston

---

[250] "Complete Mineral Catalog", by Warren Foote, Foote Mineral Company

[251] https://mineralogicalrecord.com/new_biobibliography/foote-warren-mathews/

[252] Britt, Bloys." Wartime Boom in Minerals Work in Cleveland County Will Extend Into Postwar". The Burlington Daily Times-News, Feb 12, 1944.

County eventually became known as the Kings Mountain Mining District with 60 separate mining operations that included lithium, manganese, tin, and barite.[253] SPC was the U.S. branch of an international chemical company based out of Belgium that had expanded into the U.S. They manufactured a variety of lithium-based products and entered the mining business to secure their upstream resources. Solvay is still in business today and provides a variety of products for the EV battery industry as well as improved lithium brine extraction processes.[254]

Foote was aware of Solvay's King's Mountain operation and wanted it to expand their own growing lithium business. In 1951, Foote Mineral bought Solvay's 881-acre lithium operation for $350,000.00 USD. That is equivalent to just shy of $4 million in 2022 dollars after adjustment for inflation. Prior to the purchase, Foote had 100 men working on site, a number they intended to double as they increased production volume.[255] Thirty-five years later, Foote closed its onsite hard rock extraction operations in 1986, although they continued to process imported lithium concentrate and brine LCE at that location long afterwards.

In the 1950's, Foote mined spodumene at King's Mountain and then sent some of the concentrate to a different processing plant in Sunbright, VA. The Sunbright operation was up and running as of 1952 with an onsite limestone quarry operation. The closest town to the Foote mining operation was Duffield, which was three miles down the road. A 1950 census showed that Duffield had just 176 residents.[256] I am unsure how Foote thought they were going to get the skilled human capital to work their operations there.

Lithium and Nuclear Weapons

Logistically and from a cost efficiency perspective, why send lithium from King's Mountain to be processed elsewhere? Duffield was a small, isolated town in southwest Virginia near the Tennessee border. This made no supply chain distribution sense whatsoever. It was 200 miles and four hours by truck from Kings Mountain to Duffield. Foote Mineral could ship bulk lithium by rail also, not that it was any faster. Foote

[253] https://www.mindat.org/loc-102619.html

[254] https://www.solvay.com/en/solutions-market/batteries/battery-cell

[255] "Ore Firm leases Cleveland Tract". The News and Observer, Oct 1, 1951.

[256] Number of Inhabitants – Virginia. 1950;https://www2.census.gov/library/publications/decennial/1950/population-volume-1/vol-01-49.pdf

Mineral Company had to be bleeding money from shipping their product to the middle of nowhere and back. Maybe, economics had nothing to do with it.

In 1957, it became public that Foote Mineral had classified contracts supporting the Atomic Energy Commission (AEC), but it wasn't known how lithium fit into the equation.[257, 258] However, people who moved in the right circles knew the connection between lithium and lime. A Soviet report, written by two of their nuclear scientists in 1958, revealed the importance of lithium mining for making thermonuclear weapons. The weaponization process required lithium hydride and the isotopes lithium-6 and lithium-7. How did one separate the lithium from the ore it was mined from? The Russian scientists knew it could be done by fusing the lithium with lime, creating caustic lithia or what is called lithium hydroxide (LiOH). Importantly, this lime fusion method was both simple and cheap.[259]

Foote was taking lithium from King's Mountain and shipping it to Duffield and using the high purity lime from its onsite quarry to separate the lithium. The processed lithium hydroxide was then shipped across the state border, either by truck or rail, to Tennessee and onwards to Oak Ridge National Laboratory. Southern Railway owned a rail line running adjacent to the Foote facility. Oak Ridge National Laboratory, located west of Knoxville, was about 120 miles away from Duffield, VA. Foote Mineral didn't employ nuclear scientists, but Oak Ridge did. The scientists at Oak Ridge worked on the original atomic bomb during WWII as part of the Manhattan Project and then continued to work on the hydrogen bomb during the Cold War.

In a hydrogen bomb, lithium deuteride is used in the secondary bomb and is bombarded by neutrons from the primary bomb. The lithium reacts with neutrons to produce tritium which fuses with the deuterium. The yield of the bomb is determined, in part, by how much lithium deuteride is used in the device.[260] Foote Mineral provided the lithium and Oak Ridge provided the nuclear know-how for America's hydrogen bomb project.

That explains why Foote had a lithium and lime operation collocated at a single

[257] "AEC's Contract with Foote ads Lithium Mystery", by J.A. Daly, The Charlotte News, April 19, 1957.

[258] Foote Mineral@Sunbright (Horton's Summit), Nov 18, 2017, L. Fleenor, Jr.

[259] Thermonuclear Weapons, by N. B. Neyman and K. M. Sadilenko

[260] https://www.atomicarchive.com/science/fusion/index.html

place. This also explains why they were in such an isolated location – for security reasons. If you weren't from Duffield or working at the mine, you had no business being there. Outsiders trying to conduct surveillance and collect intelligence on the Sunbright operation would most likely be detected. Years after Sunbright closed, every building and structure, thirty in all, was eventually disassembled and removed. Except for a decades old tailings pond and an underground lime tunnel, there is hardly any evidence indicating the Sunbright facility ever existed.

Foote Mineral wasn't the only lithium company at the time in the nuclear weapons business. Both Lithium Corporation of America (LCA) and American Potash and Chemical Corporation (AMPOT) also contributed lithium to the AEC. In fact, in 1956, the three formed a consortium called the American Lithium Institute, Inc. (ALI) located in Princeton, NJ. This was an easy drive, maybe 90 minutes depending on traffic, from Foote's corporate headquarters in Exton, PA. While ALI was ostensibly created to pursue technical research on the topic of lithium, there are no records of its activity. Although there were 16 news articles mentioning the institute from 1956-1957, there were no public records in print newspaper mentioning ALI after February 1958.

Marshall Sittig, a well-known chemist and prolific publisher on many chemistry topics including lithium, was the first (and only) president of ALI. Sittig passed away in 2006 at the age of 87. His obituary revealed that he worked for the Ethyl Corporation from 1948 to 1956. Then, in 1959, he joined the Office of Research Administration at Princeton University. Despite the many newspaper stories and technical conferences at the time mentioning Sittig as the President of ALI from 1957-1958, this period was omitted from his obituary.[261]

When Sittig was the president of ALI in 1957, he hired celebrated Princeton alumni and Chemistry Professor Arthur V. Tolbosky to conduct a research project. Specifically, Tolbosky would oversee graduate research on lithium compounds and how they reacted with polymers. On the face of it, ALI was funding the Princeton chemistry department to research a topic that was of interest to both parties. However, just like we never heard anything about ALI after 1958, we never heard anything more about Tobolsky and his research for ALI after 1957.

As far as one can tell, ALI was defunct as of 1958 with no public record of it

---

[261] https://www.legacy.com/us/obituaries/dailyprogress/name/marshall-sittig-obituary?id=29379327

actually producing anything. During WWII, Princeton's physics and chemistry departments were actively involved in the Manhattan Project, as were many other U.S. universities. Tobolsky, as a young and talented chemist, personally participated in the project and received an award for doing so. At the time, all three corporate members founding the ALI had classified government contracts supporting nuclear weapons programs. One is left with the question, was this research really about lithium polymers or for an ongoing weapons program?

LCA, one of the other founding members of ALI, was formed in 1941 to develop lithium products in bulk for the U.S. military during WWII. While originally founded in Minneapolis, LCA eventually relocated its corporate headquarters to New York City. LCA ran several hard rock lithium mining operations, primarily in Black Hills, SD and Bessemer City, NC. By 1960, LCA had concentrated all its manufacturing and research facilities at its Bessemer City location.[262] Then, LCA merged with Gulf Sulfur in 1967 becoming the Lithium Corporation Division of Gulf Resources and Chemicals.[263]

In 1985, FMC Corporation bought the rebranded LCA and renamed their newly acquired lithium division FMC Lithium Corporation. During their tenure, FMC Lithium closed its Bessemer City hard rock lithium mine in 1998. It was cheaper for them to run their brine operation in Chile and focus on processing imported lithium.[264] This also meant there was no longer an active hard rock lithium mine on U.S. territory. In 2018, FMC Lithium Corp. was spun off to form its own independent entity called Livent Corporation.

The third originating member of the now-forgotten ALI was AMPOT. They had a lithium extraction operation at Searles Lake near Trona, CA – an absolutely desolate place. As early as 1921, AMPOT specialized in extracting borax and potash from brine. By 1938, they were extracting lithium. Specifically, they produced dilithium sodium phosphate, which is only slightly different from the dilithium crystals used in fleet starships to achieve warp speed. The Kerr-McGee Corporation purchased AMPOT in 1967 and renamed AMPOT the Kerr-McGee Chemical Company. This company was then spun off as Tronox in 2006. As Tronox did not work in the lithium space, AMPOT's previous lithium identity was effectively dead.

[262] Lithium Corporation of America Inc. circular. Date unknown.

[263] Senate Commerce Committee joint hearings on Automobile Steam Engine and Other External Combustion Engines, May 1968.

[264] "New growth for old company", by Kirsten Valle, The Charlotte Observer, May 15, 2010.

A New Lithium Business Model

Now that we covered the original American Lithium Institute members, let's get back to Foote Mineral. In 1966, Foote began lithium brine operations in Silver Peak, NV which is 170 miles northwest of Las Vegas. That first year they had almost 1,000 acres of brine-filled evaporation ponds. Up to that point, Foote had invested $2 million into brine operations. Part of their goal was to develop more economical brine extraction methods as compared to King's Mountain. The President of Foote at that time, L.G. Bliss, recognized that it was cheaper to run the Silver Peak brine operation than the Kings Mountain hard rock operation.[265]

Foote was at the height of its industry influence in 1968 when L.G. Bliss presented testimony at the Senate Commerce Committee joint hearings on Automobile Steam Engine and Other External Combustion Engines. At the hearings, Foote revealed that it had been working on electric vehicle drivetrains for the past five years and was pursuing lithium battery development as well. Foote used the hearings as a platform to voice their commitment to reducing pollution, although there is no evidence of their EV and battery projects ever coming to fruition.[266]

Foote believed a BEV would require from 7-15 pounds of lithium metal per car. Hence, the lithium industry would have to produce between 60 million to 120 million pounds of lithium a year to sustain a manufacturing rate of 8 million cars annually. Foote revealed that their King's Mountain mine had proven reserves of 500 million pounds of lithium (a generous estimate for sure). However, Foote would not let their Silver Peak brine operation be outdone which he concluded had anywhere from 5 billion to 10 billion pounds of lithium reserves. Thus, Foote Mineral Company itself could support the impending BEV revolution for several decades through their own steadfast efforts.[267]

Foote signaled the changing dynamics of the U.S. lithium industry in 1984 when they began brine operations in Chile. There, they established evaporation pond extraction systems much like their Silver Peak location. They also constructed a lithium carbonate processing plant nearby on the coast in Antofagasta. From an operational cost perspective, it was cheaper to extract the lithium in Chile and ship it 4,000 miles

---

[265] Nevada State Journal, Aug 13, 1966, by Cheri Cross.

[266] Senate Commerce Committee joint hearings on Automobile Steam Engine and Other External Combustion Engines, May 1968.

[267] Ibid.

across land and sea to the U.S. This is where the ridiculous high carbon and high-risk supply chain that is prone to disruption comes into existence.[268]

Once the lithium was removed from the evaporation ponds, it was shipped by truck (there was no rail) from the Salar to the Port of Antofagasta. This initial ground route was 130 miles as the crow flies but closer to 200 miles by main roads. Most likely, they would ship it from Antofagasta through the Panama Canal, between Cuba and Haiti, past the Bahamas and on to the port of Charleston. This was only 4,400 miles. Then, it was about 220 miles by truck to King's Mountain. If they couldn't go through the Panama Canal, they were stuck with a 5,200-mile trip by sea to the port of Los Angeles. This was followed by another 2,200-mile leg by rail to King's Mountain for processing and distribution.

Just imagine that the operational costs of hard rock lithium mining in the U.S. was such that the above supply chain was still a better option financially. Workers had to load drums of lithium onto trucks, unload them at the port and then load them onto a ship. Then, they had to reverse the process and truck it to King's Mountain. This supply chain involved dealing with truck driver unions, longshoreman associations, shipping contracts, fuel prices and any number of disruptions like weather, politics, and the global price of lithium as a commodity. And with all that factored in, it was still cheaper.

As mentioned earlier in this chapter, 1986 was the year when the U.S. reached peak lithium production. It declined and then peaked again in 1990 but then fell off a cliff in 1998 and never recovered. In 1986, Foote stopped extracting lithium from its King's Mountain hard rock mine as operations costs were too high as compared to the alternatives. After 1986, Foote focused on its Silver Peak brine operation and importing its LCE from its Lithium Triangle operation. Thus, Foote had divested itself of all its hard rock mining operations and focused solely on brine.

The End of Foote Mineral Company

In 1989, Cyprus Minerals Company bought an 82% interest in the Foote Mineral Company, who at the time marketed themselves as the world's largest producer of lithium.[269] This was probably true as their Chile operations picked up their slack after closing King's Mountain. The newly created Cyprus Foote Mineral Company had a

---

[268] USGS, 1997 Minerals Yearbook – Lithium, by J. Ober.

[269] https://www.encyclopedia.com/books/politics-and-business-magazines/cyprus-minerals-company

ten-year run. During this time, Cyprus streamlined their operational footprint, closing Foote's former headquarters offices in Exton, PA. They also shut down the ore processing plant down the road in East Whiteland in 1991. However, the Sunbright lithium processing and lime quarry was still carried on their books as they had never sold the property even though it closed some 20 years earlier in 1972.

In 1995, Cyprus Foote became embroiled in a trade secrets lawsuit when FMC Lithium alleged that Cyprus poached one of their employees to gain an industry advantage. Joseph D. Fickling worked at FMC's Bessemer City mine for 14 years as a lithium metallurgist pursuing lithium battery projects.[270] He was later hired by Cyprus Foote at their King's Mountain facility, thus triggering the lawsuit. Cyprus and Fickling denied all allegations. As FMC's and Cyprus Foote's offices were only five miles apart from each other, Fickling's commute probably remained about the same.

More important than Fickling's commute, was this confirmation that Cyprus Foote was working on a lithium battery project as L. G. Bliss told the Senate committee in 1968? Was accomplished polymer expert Arthur V. Tobolsky really hired by ALI in 1957 to advance Lithium polymer batteries despite his classified weapons background? There is no public record of Foote Mineral or Cyprus Foote ever actually producing lithium batteries for the BEV industry other than Bliss' 1968 statement. Perhaps it was a long-standing research project that never took off due to a lack of human capital, immature technology and an industry that never gained traction due to fossil fuel and political dependencies.

In 1998, Chemetall Group acquired Cyprus Foote Mineral for $305 million USD. In the deal, they acquired Cyprus Foote's Silver Peak brine operation along with its collocated lithium carbonate and lithium hydroxide processing plants. They took over the old Foote infrastructure located at King's Mountain which still had downstream production capability. The deal included Foote's New Johnsonville, TN butyllithium plant located near Oak Ridge National Laboratory.

They also received Foote's entire Chile operation. Chemetall inherited a brine-only enterprise in the same year that FMC closed its hard rock mine in Bessemer City, which was also the last remaining hard rock lithium mine in America. FMC, too, had moved into the Lithium Triangle brine business for the same reasons Foote Minerals had. That year, Chile was the largest lithium carbonate producer in the world.[271]

---

[270] "Firm says worker hired for secrets", Sept 1, 1995, by Chip Wilson.

[271] USGS, 1998 Minerals Yearbook – Lithium, by J. Ober.

Only six years later, in 2004, Chemetall Group was acquired by Rockwood Holdings Inc. Rockwood, an advanced chemical and materials company headquartered in Princeton, NJ. However, Rockwood would continue to use the Chemetall Foote name (and two others) for its lithium business for eight more years. In that year of acquisition, Chile was the largest producer of lithium in the world and LIBs were still a sideshow at best. The U.S. was importing 95% of its lithium from both Chile and Argentina.[272]

In 2009, it became public that Chemetall Foote would receive a $24.8 million USD grant from the Department of Energy (DOE) to expand their lithium operations in King's Mountain.[273] This amount was 45% of the estimated $55 million required. Specifically, they would build a new plant capable of processing another 5,000 metric tons per year of lithium hydroxide.[274] Additionally, Chemetall intended to refurbish and double the size of the Silver Peak operations using the same DOE grant to help with the expenses.[275] However, they never actually got around to this expansion in Nevada.

In 2010, DOE published their Final Environmental Assessment (FEA, 165 pages) for both Chemetall's King's Mountain and Silver Peak locations. For King's Mountain, they would expand an existing building and construct six new aboveground storage tanks to produce the increased 5,000 tons annually of lithium hydroxide. Lithium carbonate feedstock would be imported from Chemetall's operations in Chile and Nevada. As this construction was located on previously disturbed ground, there weren't any significant new environmental considerations.[276]

In Nevada, Chemetall planned to refurbish its existing lithium carbonate plant. It would also refurbish and upgrade its existing evaporation pond system. Improvement of the ponds would consist of deepening them, meaning there would be no increased physical footprint. As Silver Peak was a remote location and there was no significant new construction, as with King's Mountain, new environmental impacts were minimal.[277]

---

[272] USGS 2005 Lithium Report, by J. Ober.

[273] "Chu announces grant for energy innovation" by B. Henderson, Aug 6, 2009, The Charlotte Observer.

[274] "Final Environmental Assessment for Chemetall Foote Corporation", DOE, Sep 2010.

[275] "Nevada could be lithium hotspot", by S. Timko, Feb 7, 2011, Reno-Gazette Journal.

[276] "Final Environmental Assessment for Chemetall Foote Corporation", DOE, Sep 2010.

[277] Ibid.

It is interesting to note that the Silver Peak Final Environmental Assessment discussed the reality of greenhouse gas (GHG) emissions and pending legislation that may require GHG permitting. The assessment also discussed in some detail CO_2 emissions and reporting requirements. There was even an overview of the two sites' carbon footprints as well as the carbon footprints of the states of NV and NC.[278]

It was ironic that Chemetall's expansion was due to the increased lithium demand for BEVs that in turn was driven by the need to reduce transportation sector CO_2 emissions. However, Chemetall made no effort to decarbonize its own operations. The Silver Peak site could easily be powered by solar with battery backup as could King's Mountain. Apparently, Chemetall thought carbon emissions was someone else's problem, not theirs. Chemetall's cognitive disconnect between larger industry goals driving their own business model and their lack of commitment to these same goals at the tactical level was stark.

In early 2012, Rockwood had three different lithium businesses: Chemetall – the lithium company, Chemetall Foote, and Sociedad Chilena de Litio. To consolidate operations and remove any confusion, the three were merged into Rockwood Lithium Inc.[279] Rockwood CEO Seifi Ghasemi recognized the growth of the LIB industry and intended to position Rockwood as an industry leader.[280] Later that year, Rockwood split Chemetall into Chemetall GmbH and broke off their lithium and specialty metals business. The latter was now named Rockwood Lithium GmbH.[281] After 137 years of being a recognized leader in the lithium industry, the Foote name was dead.

Two years later, in 2014, Rockwood showed how serious they were about competing in the lithium space when they acquired a major position in Talison Lithium. Talison was a joint venture (JV) with Tianqi Lithium Corporation holding a 51% position and Rockwood Lithium with a 49% position.[282] Talison managed the Greenbushes Mine in Western Australia, the single largest hard rock lithium mine in the world. With

---

[278] Ibid.

[279] https://www.businesswire.com/news/home/20120401005068/en/Rockwood-Holdings-Inc.-Rebrands-Global-Lithium-Business-as-Rockwood-Lithium

[280] https://www.businesswire.com/news/home/20120401005068/en/Rockwood-Holdings-Inc.-Rebrands-Global-Lithium-Business-as-Rockwood-Lithium

[281] https://www.chemeurope.com/en/news/139597/rockwood-completes-split-of-chemetall-gmbh-into-two-separate-legal-entities.html

[282] https://www.talisonlithium.com/

this acquisition, we continued to see U.S. companies looking outside of American territory to expand their lithium capabilities.

Just a year after making their move on Talison Lithium, Rockwood Holdings itself was bought by Albemarle Corporation. Overall, Rockwood did very well for itself after acquiring Chemetall Foote. In January 2006, their stock (NYSE: ROC) traded at $22.61 a share. Nine years later, in January 2015, their stock traded at $79.20 a share – a 350% increase in value for shareholders.[283] The Albemarle buyout was worth $6.2 billion USD, with payouts and stock options putting the value of each Rockwood share at $85.53.[284]

Albemarle, a large, international specialty chemicals company, had its headquarters in Charlotte, NC. Albemarle made a variety of products with lithium being just one. With their acquisition of Rockwood, Albemarle instantly made themselves one of the major players in the U.S. and global lithium value chain. After acquiring Rockwood, Albemarle continued to expand aggressively in the lithium space. As an example of this, Albemarle acquired a 60% interest in the Wodgina spodumene mine in Western Australia in 2019 for $1.3 billion USD.[285]

In January 2021, Albemarle announced plans to double its Silver Peak production from 5,000 tons per annum to 10,000 tons. Albemarle intended to expand its existing pond footprint and to diversify into lithium extraction from clay deposits. Albemarle anticipated the expansion taking until 2025 to complete.[286] Although this was a relatively modest goal, it did seek to maximize production from the Nevada site. Large volume extraction operations would continue to come from outside the U.S. in Australia and the Lithium Triangle.

In 2022, Albemarle revealed even more ambitious plans to expand their lithium processing capability in the U.S. Specifically, Albemarle intended to build another lithium processing plant with a 100,000 metric ton annual capacity. This capacity would almost be one-fifth the amount of lithium mined globally in 2021. The President of Albemarle Lithium, Eric Norris, said they would put the plant somewhere in

[283] https://www.investing.com/equities/rockwood-holdings-inc-historical-data

[284] https://www.inddist.com/mergers-acquisitions/news/13765344/albemarle-to-buy-rockwood-in-62b-deal

[285] https://www.albemarle.com/news/albemarle-announces-completion-of-lithium-joint-venture-with-mineral-resources-limited

[286] https://www.mining.com/albemarle-to-double-lithium-production-in-nevada/

Southeastern U.S. with access to rail lines and a major port as they would be shipping in the unprocessed lithium from abroad.[287] Albemarle eventually ended up choosing a location in Chester Country, South Carolina.

However, Norris wasn't satisfied with just a 100,000 ton per annum increased lithium processing capacity. By 2030, Albemarle intended to have a 500,000 ton per annum processing capacity.[288] The additional 400,000 tons of capacity would most likely be outside the U.S. with likely candidates including Germany and China. If we calculate lithium hydroxide costing $77,000.00 USD per ton (the price fluctuates of course) that comes to a theoretical $38.5 billion annual return. This is more than what Albemarle is valued at today. In July 2022, Albemarle's market cap was estimated at $34 billion USD.

Lithium Mining Today

It is interesting to note, that despite the offshoring of U.S. lithium extraction operations starting in the 1980's, the U.S. is still an attractive location to start a new mining operation. Fraser Institute's Annual Mining Survey compiled responses from 290 mining companies on their perceptions towards the mining business for 2021. Mining companies based their operational decisions on a variety of factors, not just the qualities of the potential mineral deposit, but also policy considerations. Western Australia, where Albemarle has their Greenbushes and Wodgina lithium hard rock mines, was ranked as the #1 place to mine in the world. Saskatchewan, Canada was ranked #2; Nevada #3, where Silver Peak is; Alaska #4 and Arizona was #5. China was ranked #80 out of 84 jurisdictions.[289]

While the permitting process in the U.S. can be drawn out and expensive, depending on your mining location and strategy, the current sky-high pricing of lithium per ton makes it worth it. There are many potential mining operations on the horizon, both hard rock and brine, although brine has lower operating costs and thus higher returns. In the future, if and when direct lithium extraction (DLE) matures as a technology and is employed at scale, DLE will be superior in every way to the current evaporation pond model. Let's look at some of the more prominent pending lithium operations in the U.S. below.

---

[287] https://www.reuters.com/business/energy/albemarle-plans-major-us-lithium-processing-plant-2022-06-27/

[288] Ibid.

[289] Fraser Institute Annual Survey of Mining Companies 2021, by J. Yunis and E. Aliakbari.

Nevada Lithium Projects

- Thacker Pass, open pit hard rock/clay operation, timeline: production begins 2023, Lithium Americas Corp (Canadian), NYSE: LAC
- Bonnie Claire Project, open pit or borehole operation, timeline: exploratory drilling, Nevada Lithium Resources Inc (Canadian-50% ownership), CSE: NVLH, Iconic Minerals Ltd (Canadian- 50% ownership) TSXV: ICM
- Clayton Valley Lithium Project, open pit hard rock operation, timeline: pilot stage, Cypress Development Corp. (Canadian), OTC: CYDVF
- Rhyolite Ridge Lithium-Boron Project, open pit hard rock operation, timeline: production begins 2023, Ioneer Ltd (Australian – 50% ownership), OTC: GSCCF, Sibanye-Stillwater (South African – 50% ownership), NYSE:SBSW

California Lithium Projects (Salton Sea – Imperial Valley)

- Hell's Kitchen Lithium-Geothermal Project, brine extraction/DLE, timeline: production begins 2024, Controlled Thermal Resources (Australian), public unlisted
- Project ATLiS, lithium-geothermal brine extraction/DLE, timeline: production starts 2024, EnergySource Minerals (American), private unlisted
- Salton Sea, geothermal-lithium brine extraction/DLE, timeline: production begins 2025, Berkshire Hathaway (American), NYSE: BRK.A

North Carolina Lithium Projects

- Piedmont Mine, open pit hard rock operation, timeline: production begins 2026, Piedmont Lithium (Australian), NASDAQ: PLL
- King's Mountain, open hard rock operation, timeline: production begins 2027, Albemarle Corp. (American), NYSE: ALB

Arkansas Lithium Project

- Smackover Lithium Project, brine extraction/DLE, timeline: production begins 2025, Standard Lithium Inc. (Canadian-51% ownership), NYSE: SLI, LANXESS AG (German-49% ownership), OTC: LNXSF

Utah Lithium Project

- Ogden Lithium Salt Project, brine extraction/DLE, timeline: production begins 2025, Compass Minerals International Inc (American), NYSE: CMP

Arizona Lithium Projects

- Big Sandy, open pit hard rock operation, timeline: exploration, Hawkstone Mining/Arizona Lithium (Australian), ASX: HWK/ASX: AZL

When it comes to the type of lithium mining projects being planned, there was a seven to five split with seven operations pursuing hard rock open pit operations and the other five investing in brine ones. Even though brine operations were more cost efficient, lithium prices per ton were still so high that even hard rock operations were profitable. However, when lithium prices drop, the hard rock operations will find themselves in a difficult financial position which is exactly why King's Mountain and Bessemer City hard rock mines were closed.

Of the five brine operations, all of them pursued DLE operations. DLE was deemed a much better option than the antiquated evaporation ponds with a large land footprint and using millions of gallons of water. In contrast, DLE has a very small footprint and uses little water as their operational model returned the water back where it came from. This was a closed loop system. Companies that pursued DLE lithium brine operations would enjoy significant advantages over both hard rock and evaporation pond operations and would realize more profits.

Eight of these twelve projects were run by foreign companies: five different Canadian companies, four Australian, one South African and one German. Thus, the U.S. allowed two-thirds of their potential lithium projects to be captured by other countries, although they were allies. If we assumed these companies sold their products first to U.S. battery and EV companies in the continental U.S., America still achieved a higher degree of lithium supply chain security than previously. However, the U.S. will miss a chunk of the value chain as corporate profits flow away to the originating companies in Canada, Australia, and the like.

In 2017, Chinese mining company Ganfeng Lithium Co. bought a 19.9% stake in Lithium Americas Corp.[290] The intent of the investment was to facilitate Lithium

---

[290] https://www.lithiumamericas.com/news/lithium-americas-announces-us174-million-strategic-investment-by-ganfeng-lithium

Americas' Argentine brine project. The deal also allowed Ganfeng to add a member to Lithium Americas' board of directors. But the agreement also provided Ganfeng access to Lithium America's future offtake from their proposed lithium hard rock mine at Thacker Pass, NV. Consequently, almost 20% of the profits taken by the Thacker Pass lithium operation will go to Ganfeng's bottom line. Every day, Nevada miners will work hard to provide added value to China's global lithium supply chain, the U.S.' chief competitor.

The author stands on the shoulder of the road (Route 293) that cuts through Thacker Pass. This pictures shows the north side of the pass where extraction operations will eventually take place. This area is administered by the Bureau of Land Management. Ganfeng owns 20% of this mining operation. Of note, this pristine and scenic land will be devastated by the coming hard rock open pit mining. Picture taken in April 2023.

Looking Ahead

1. How will the *Inflation Reduction Act* affect the pace of lithium mining exploration in the U.S., considering their operations now qualify for a 10% subsidy?

The same can be asked of other battery mineral mining operations as well. Will we see an increase in other associated U.S. mining operations like a resuscitation of the cobalt mining belt in Idaho? Will we see momentum to develop a domestic natural flake graphite mining industry? If the IRA is in fact effective, we should see an increase in mining permitting applications, exploration activity and mining.

2. Will hard rock or brine operations become the dominate form of lithium extraction methodology in the U.S.? Will we see mining companies try to bring old hard rock lithium operations back to life in North Carolina and South Dakota to meet growing demand? Also, has there been enough technological innovation in the hard rock industry to make their operations more economical than back in the 1980's? How is that the Greenbushes hard rock mine in Australia can operate at a cost of $250.00 a ton? Especially when the price of lithium softens and no longer commands maximum pricing, will hard rock mines be competitive? We've been down this road already.

3. What will the DLE (Direct Lithium Extraction) industry look like in the U.S. as we move forward? Will the industry develop the technology to make DLE a reality and instantly render evaporation pond operations uneconomic? Will the Smackover Formation become a lithium goldmine? Or, is there such demand for lithium products that DLE extraction operations will merely run in parallel to existing hard rock and evaporation operations?

4. Since only 18% of the continental U.S. land mass has been geologically surveyed, will geologists discover previously unknown lithium deposits somewhere in the U.S. that we are unaware of? Will these newly discovered deposits be hard rock or brine? But are we even asking the right questions here. Has the U.S. government provided the effective leadership, guidance, and funding necessary to expand geological survey operations? Is the U.S. even capable of finding new battery mineral deposits using its current system? More importantly, is the U.S. committed to employing the U.S. Geological Survey office to its full capability? When is USGS going to be fully integrated into the critical mineral policy process in order to maximize the effectiveness of future U.S. policy?

5. Two final questions for the reader: will foreign mining companies dominate the U.S.' domestic lithium extraction industry or will U.S. companies come online to compete effectively in this space? What do you think of Chinese mining companies moving into the U.S. lithium space in the context of a critical minerals strategy? China already owns a portion of the future Thacker Pass hard rock lithium mine in Nevada. How does that fact strengthen the U.S. critical mineral supply chain?

CHAPTER 8

American Lithium Mining Companies

"We believe that growth in EV sales will drive significant growth in demand for performance lithium compounds." – Livent Annual Report, 2018

Introduction

As we have seen, U.S. domestic lithium mining production peaked around 1986, had a resurgence for a decade and then dropped off a cliff in the late 1990's. By then, the original big American lithium producers, Foote Mineral, Lithium Corp. of America, American Potash, had all been bought out and rebranded. The trend in the American lithium industry was to offshore lithium production to the Lithium Triangle in South America. Consequently, the U.S. lithium industry had a stronger domestic lithium processing capability vice actual production.

Two of the early U.S. lithium giants were bought out, rebranded and continue to this day as major lithium players. As we read in Chapter 7, the original Foote Mineral Company enterprise was absorbed by the modern-day Albemarle Corporation. Lithium Corp. of America was in turn absorbed by FMC Corporation and spun-off as the modern day Livent Corporation. Both Albemarle and Livent continue to grow their operations in the lithium space, and we will examine both of their business models in this chapter.

There are several other smaller American lithium players trying to get into the business with strong potential. BHE Renewables is getting into the brine business and has deep pockets as a division of Berkshire Hathaway. Compass Minerals already has a large established brine extraction salt operation and is working to pivot toward lithium extraction. EnergySource is also focused on brine operations and have developed their own proprietary DLE technology. Significantly, these three entrants are all focused on DLE brine operations that have the highest potential return on the lithium value chain.

Albemarle Corporation

In 1924, the Ethyl Gasoline Corporation (EGC) was incorporated in the State of Delaware. EGC was a joint effort between General Motors Corp. and the Standard Oil Company of New Jersey. Standing up EGC took a $5 million USD investment, equivalent to $86.6 million today, and was owned 50/50 by GM and Standard Oil. GM focused on marketing ethyl, which was designed to stop engine "knock", while Standard Oil focused on its distribution.[291]

As early as 1924, EGC officers recognized that tetraethyl lead (TEL) used in their ethyl additive was considered poisonous to humans. However, EGC maintained that their ethylized fuel was safe for general use and that it was considered crucial for conserving the world oil supply.[292] In fact, EGC posted large ads in multiple newspapers across the country announcing that their product was safe for continued use by the average person.

As a side note, Marshall Sittig worked at Ethyl from 1949 -1956 until he was hired as president of the American Lithium Institute (ALI). In 1948, Sittig gave a presentation on "Atomic Energy for Laymen", where he was described as a chemical engineer with the Eastern Corporation.[293] In 1954, Sittig wrote an article detailing the specifics of the use of lithium in hydrogen bombs that included previously unknown data.[294] Sittig wrote the article as an individual expert in the field and not as representative for Ethyl.

While Sittig was several years removed from ALI and in his new job at Princeton, the Albemarle Paper Manufacturing Company (APM) was on the move. In 1962, APM

---

[291] "General Motors and Standard Oil in Great Combine", The News Journal, Aug 24, 1924.

[292] "Ethylized Gasoline", by Ethyl Gasoline Corp, Nov 20, 1924, San Angelo Daily Standard.

[293] "Kiwanians Hear Talk on Atomic Energy" The Bangor Daily News, May 7, 1948.

[294] "Importance of Defense to Lithium is Related" by. J.A. Daley, July 7, 1954, The Charlotte News.

purchased Ethyl Corporation who had changed their name in 1942, dropping the "Gasoline" from their title. Ethyl represented a completely different industry and the move perplexed the business world at the time. Also, Ethyl was ten times bigger than APM by market cap, meaning APM had to come up with $200 million for the buy-out. GM and Standard Oil both voiced their support for the deal indicating they were willing to accept the offer.[295] Close observers of the transaction suspected both companies wanted to get out of the TEL business due to its pollution and poisoning liability. After APM completed the merger, they changed their name to Ethyl Corporation.

After the Albemarle/Ethyl merger, the new Ethyl went on a corporate buying binge, snapping up a variety of new businesses in new markets with no apparent pattern. In the 1960's, Ethyl expanded into plastic films, polyvinyl chloride (PVC), aluminum, bromine and opened an office in Europe. In the 1970's, Ethyl expanded their aluminum and plastic operations, bought into lubricants, got into coal, expanded into Belgium, and sold off their paper business. In the 1980's, they expanded their aluminum and bromine businesses, sold off their PVC, packaging and plastics/aluminums operations while moving into the life insurance, semiconductor, and pharmaceutical space. In the early 1990's, Ethyl spun off its life insurance business and then their specialty chemicals business.

In 1994, Ethyl's newly independent specialty chemicals division was named Albemarle Corporation in recognition of the original company that bought Ethyl in 1962. From 1994 to 2015, Albemarle aggressively expanded their chemical business overseas. Over that time, they acquired companies, formed joint ventures, or opened offices in: Japan, Jordan, England, China, France, Germany, Austria, Korea, Netherlands, Singapore, Brazil, Saudi Arabia, Dubai, and Hungary. In 2011, Albemarle announced a new lithium brine extraction process, but it never went anywhere. At no point were they involved in the actual lithium mining or processing business.[296]

As we discussed in Chapter 7, Albemarle instantly became a major lithium player when they acquired Rockwood Holdings in 2015. From 1962, when they were Albemarle Paper Manufacturing and bought Ethyl Corporation, until now, Ethyl exhibited an aggressive, expansive corporate culture. Ethyl leadership had a willingness to pivot into completely new industries and then expand rapidly in that space. More

---

[295] "Giant Ethyl Dwarfs Buyer", Associated Press, Sep 19, 1962, The Courier-Journal.
[296] https://www.albemarle.com/about/history

than fifty years later, Albemarle showed the same mindset, acquiring a lithium company and then expanding rapidly in that space.

With the acquisition of Rockwood, Albemarle gained the Silver Peak lithium brine operation, the Chile brine operation, the Greenbushes hard rock mine and the old lithium processing capability at King's Mountain. This was a good base to start from, but Albemarle wanted to expand both its extraction capability and its processing capacity. They also made the strategic decision to move into the biggest battery and EV market in the world: China.

In 2017, Albemarle bought Jiangxi Jiangli New Materials Science and Technology Co. Ltd., a Chinese company specializing in lithium salts. The acquisition gave Albemarle new assets producing both battery grade lithium carbonate and lithium hydroxide at 15,000 tons per annum.[297] The locations included Chengdu/Sichuan and Jiangxi, both landlocked inland provinces. This enabled Albemarle to further secure its Asian lithium supply chain. They could now ship their lithium concentrate from their Greenbushes Mine in Western Australia to their own lithium processing plants in China. From there, it was an easy process to supply any number of domestic Chinese battery companies like CATL and BYD.[298]

Next, Albemarle started a Joint Venture with Australian mining company Mineral Resources Limited (MRL) in 2019. In this $1.3 billion USD deal, Albemarle gained a 60% ownership in the Wodgina hard rock lithium mine. The open pit operation was named the MARBL Lithium Joint Venture. Also, MRL would get a 40% stake in Albermarle's Kemerton lithium processing operation near their Greenbushes Mine. MARBL, of which Albermarle was the 60% owner and MRL was the 40% owner, would manage both the Wodgina and Kemerton operations. Importantly, Albemarle would manage 100% of the related marketing operations.[299, 300]

To be sure, Albemarle buying into MRL and Wodgina was a strategic move. To

[297] https://www.spglobal.com/marketintelligence/en/news-insights/blog/watch-nickel-market-outlook-complex-demand-supply-fundamentals

[298] "Albemarle signs definitive agreement to acquire lithium salts production assets in Asia". PR Newswire, Aug 23, 2016.

[299] https://www.mineralresources.com.au/about-us/joint-ventures/

[300] https://www.albemarle.com/news/albemarle-announces-completion-of-lithium-joint-venture-with-mineral-resources-limited

start, Wodgina is located on the northwestern coast of Australia, some 1,400 miles north of the Greenbushes Mine. This moves Albemarle's lithium concentrate much closer to their Asian customers. The Wodgina mine itself is positioned 75 miles south of Port Hedland. From Port Hedland to the Port of Qinzhou in Southern China, passing through the Sunda Straight near Jakarta, is 3,480 miles. Also, it is 4,300 miles by sea to the Port of Pusan, South Korea and 4,400 miles to Tokyo Bay.

Thus, Wodgina could service three of the largest battery companies in the world: CATL in China, LG Chem in South Korea, and Panasonic in Japan. In comparison, it is 10,700 miles to Tokyo Bay from the Port of Antofagasta, Chile where LCE from the Lithium Triangle is shipped. It is 6,000 miles from the Port of Long Beach, USA to Tokyo Bay – the route that lithium exported from the Salton Sea brine operations might one day take. If Albermarle had a lithium mine near Darwin on the north-central coast of Australia, it is "only" 3,500 miles to Tokyo Bay. This would save 900 miles of sea travel as compared to shipping lithium from the Port of Hedland.

Albemarle astutely recognized their need to construct a lithium hydroxide plant near their Wodgina operation at the end of 2018 as they were finalizing the deal.[301] Without this plant, they still had to ship their lithium concentrate to their processing plants in Jiangxi and Chengdu/Sichuan, which we determined was a 3,480-mile trip by sea just to Qinzhou Port. This was fine if the finished product was staying in China to feed their battery industry. However, it added thousands of miles and months of delay if they wanted to sell the processed lithium elsewhere. To date, this processing plant has only been discussed and not actually built.

In 2021, Albemarle acquired Guangxi Tianyuan New Energy Materials Co., Ltd. for $200 million. Tianyuan has a 25,000 metric tons per annum lithium conversion plant that can produce lithium carbonate and lithium hydroxide. The facility is in the Port of Qinzhou in Guangxi Province. It is about a 4,200-mile trip by sea from the Port of Bunbury (which is a 47-mile drive from the Greenbushes Mine) to Qinzhou.[302]

In 2022, Albemarle broke ground on a new lithium conversion facility at the Pengshan Economic Development Park in Sichuan Province. They anticipated the facility coming online in 2024 with an annual capacity of 50,000 metric tons. The

---

[301] Albemarle Corporation, Form 10-k, SEC, for calendar year 2018

[302] Albemarle Corporation, press release. Oct 25, 2022.

facility will produce lithium hydroxide for cathodes in batteries for the Chinese EV industry.[303] They will get their lithium concentrate feedstock from both Albemarle's Wodgina and Greenbushes mines if the Kemerton processing facility is not up and running.

Finally, Albemarle had been working on their Kemerton lithium processing plant for several years but got it up and running in 2022. The plant is in the Kemerton Industrial Park, about a 60-mile drive from their Greenbushes mine in Southwest Australia. From the plant to Bunbury Port is only a 15-mile drive. Albemarle initially planned for the plant to produce 50,000 tons of lithium hydroxide annually but already have intentions to double this to 100,000.[304] The only drawback to the Kemerton/ Greenbushes operation is its remote location on the southwestern coast of Australia. This location necessarily means a many thousands of miles supply chain to wherever the finished lithium product is being shipped.

Albemarle runs two bromine extraction operations in Magnolia, Arkansas, located in the southwest part of the state. They get bromine from the large Smackover brine formation that runs through much of southeast U.S. However, not only is bromine present in the brine, but there is also lithium. As we mentioned in the previous chapter, Standard Lithium and LANXESS are already pursuing lithium brine operations about 30 mile east of Magnolia. However, Standard Lithium is also eyeing territory in Magnolia, adjacent to Albemarle's own operations. Albemarle has yet to conduct DLE operations from their Magnolia site.

As of 2022, Albemarle's lithium business came to dominate its three corporate pillars. Some 45% of Albemarle's net annual revenue now came from lithium while 34% came from bromine and 21% came from catalysts. With these identified projects, Albemarle anticipated being able to produce and sell 200 ktpa (kilotons per annum) of both lithium carbonate and lithium hydroxide. However, Albemarle was pursuing other projects beyond 2025 that could bring their total annual production to 500,000 tons a year.[305]

[303] https://www.albemarle.com/blog/albemarle-breaks-ground-in-china-to-support-the-expansion-of-lithium-conversion-capacity

[304] https://www.albemarle.com/news/albemarle-announces-completion-of-lithium-joint-venture-with-mineral-resources-limited

[305] Albemarle Investor Presentation, May 2022.

My strategic advice to Albemarle would be to build out a lithium processing plant for the Wodgina mine near the Port of Hedland to shorten their export supply chain. This will eliminate the step of having to process the lithium concentrate elsewhere like the rather remote Chengdu/Sichuan location which is 680 miles north of the Port of Qinzhou. This also means Albemarle can ship battery grade ready lithium anywhere in Asia like South Korea and Japan. This would give them strategic flexibility, shorten their supply chain, and save them on operational costs.

Second, treat DLE technology efforts like the Manhattan Project – it's time to go all in on the human capital and resources to make this happen. Obviously, Albemarle's previously announced DLE technology is not ready, but they need to get their fast because a dozen other companies are almost there. With that in mind, they should prepare their lithium brine infrastructure at their Magnolia project for DLE operations. Once they get that DLE brine project perfected, Albemarle will have a competitive operational advantage over everyone else in the U.S. who does not.

On the heels of that, Albemarle should then convert its Silver Peak and Atacama evaporation pond operations to the much better DLE model. I would deconstruct the old methods and reap the benefits of operations with much lower operational, social, environmental and carbon footprints and I would advertise this. Then, I would pursue other DLE brine operations wherever it makes supply chain sense. Since, ideally, they want to have their brine extraction and battery grade processing plants collocated to one another and near their end customer who is a battery manufacturer.

I would not pursue hard rock mining operations in the U.S. except under certain conditions. Specifically, I would not try and resuscitate the King's Mountain hard rock operation. It was closed for a reason and that's because brine operations were and are much cheaper. When lithium prices correct and decline once again, Kings Mountain will become a stranded asset again. I might buy into a successful hard rock operation somewhere as a junior partner, such as Thacker Pass. But I would let Lithium Americas run the day-to-day operations and I wouldn't make it the main effort.

Presently, Albemarle is focused on China as that is where the preponderance of their lithium assets is arrayed. This makes sense as China has the largest EV battery market in the world. But the BEV market isn't static and other regional battery players are coming on board like Europe and North America. Albemarle must look to the future and array their lithium assets accordingly to get ahead of the wave. I would also keep a close eye on Japan and work towards a strategic partnership with Toyota, the largest car manufacturer in the world. Although Toyota has been a BEV laggard to date, they are starting to get on board, mostly because they have to.

Livent Corporation

Livent is the other major U.S. lithium player, although they are a much smaller operation compared to Albemarle. For instance, Albemarle employed 6,000 people as of 2021 and Livent only 1,100. As we noted in the previous chapter, Livent was built on the original Lithium Corporation of America enterprise until it was bought by FMC and then spun off as Livent in 2018. Livent and Albemarle have similarities because Foote Mineral and LCA both moved in the same circles such as the American Lithium Institute and providing bulk high purity lithium to the hydrogen bomb program. Both had hard rock mines in North Carolina and evaporation operations in the Lithium Triangle.

In 2018, Livent's sole lithium extraction operation was the Salar del Hombre Muerto in Argentina. They had a lithium carbonate plant collocated with the brine operations at the Salar of which produced 17,000 tons of lithium carbonate in 2018. However, they had plans to triple this production to 60,000 tons by 2025.[306] Livent also had a lithium chloride plant located to the east of their brine operations in Guemes. Livent's local subsidiary, Minera del Altiplano SA (MdA), managed the onsite operations.

The Salar de Hombre Muerto site is a remote desolate location in northwestern Argentina that comprises the area making up the overall Lithium Triangle. As the brine operation is positioned in the Andes Mountains, there are no nearby east-west roads from Livent's evaporation pond. Consequently, Livent trucks must travel a 265-mile torturous rout going north and then east to get to their lithium chloride processing plant in Guemes. If they bypassed Guemes and went straight to the Port of Buenos Aries, the distance is 1,100 miles easy. Or, if they went north and west to ship the lithium through Chile, they could hit the Port of Antofagasta with a much shorter 450-mile trip.

As we saw with the Chemetall brine operations in Silver Peak, Nevada, Livent didn't make the connection that their business model was largely driven by the need for decarbonization of our economies. The reality was, they produced lithium for an

---

[306] Livent Corporation, Form 10-K, 2018.

exploding BEV industry to reduce transportation sector carbon emissions. However, Livent powered their Salar operations with diesel generators and natural gas.[307] This was in spite of the fact that their relatively small operations could be powered by solar panels and onsite battery back-up. Livent, like Chemetall, thought that carbon emissions were someone else's problem to deal with, not theirs.

It is important to note that the geography for Chile brine operations, like Albemarle and SQM, was much kinder to them than to Livent. While Albemarle's operations were only located 150 miles to the northwest of Livent's, their supply chains were much different. Albemarle and SQM (whose operations were adjacent to one another) only had a 200-mile trip from their brine ponds to the Port of Antofagasta. In contrast, Livent had to navigate five times that distance to get to their closest port of Buenos Aires. Then, if they wanted to feed the U.S. BEV industry, it was a 6,700-mile ocean trip to the Port of Charleston. To Tokyo Bay, going past the tip of Tierra del Fuego, it was 12,500 miles. To Pusan, South Korea it was 13,100 miles and to the Port of Shanghai it was 13,300 miles. Just getting around Tierra del Fuego added 1,700 miles.

For 2018, Livent earned revenues of $442 million. 50.3% of this was earned on sales of lithium hydroxide and another 13.2% on lithium carbonate and lithium chloride. By application, 41.8% of this revenue was for energy storage (i.e., lithium for EV batteries). 63.6% of this revenue came from buyers in Asia, 19.1% form North America and then 16.8% from Europe/Middle East. From this, one could assess the global market and devise a strategy: sell large quantities of lithium hydroxide to Asian battery makers. Then, prepare for emerging markets in North America and Europe.[308]

A year later, in 2019, Livent's revenues declined substantially – by 12%. They manufactured just under 17,000 tons of lithium carbonate and just over 21,000 tons of lithium hydroxide. In 2019, they had only $388 million of revenues with 55% from lithium hydroxide, 46% for batteries and 65% from Asian buyers. However, this data confirms our previous identified strategy: sell more lithium hydroxide to Asian battery makers. We can even add to this: construct a more resilient lithium supply chain that more effectively supports your Asian customers. And by this, I think Livent should acquire lithium extraction operations in the Asia market.[309]

---

[307] Livent Corporation, Form 10-K, 2018.

[308] Livent Corporation, 10-K, SEC, 2018.

[309] Livent Corporation, Form 10-k, 2019.

Although revenues were down that year, Livent partnered with Canadian company E3 Metals whose business model centered on lithium extraction from the Leduc brine field in Alberta. However, E3 pursued DLE operations as opposed to evaporation ponds, which was Livent's operational blueprint in Argentina. E3 partnered specifically with Livent for their expertise in lithium-ion exchange technology. Up until that time and even until the writing of this book, Livent has not actually used their DLE technology in a live brine operation. Obviously, Livent has some proprietary technology that they are testing out and it remains to be seen what it results in.[310]

Livent doubled down on its disconnect for the need to decarbonize their operations and continued to not understand what was driving their business model. In their annual report, they revealed their need for more natural gas supply to support their intended expansion in the Salar. They also revealed that their Guemes plant was powered by natural gas and diesel generators. Once again, they didn't understand that they could power their operations in a zero-carbon manner with solar panels and battery storage systems.

In 2020, Livent's revenue dropped like a rock, bringing in only $288 million for the year – a 26% difference. However, the trend remained with 55% of revenue coming from lithium hydroxide sales, 49% for energy storage systems and 64% of business came from Asia. Lithium carbonate production dropped to 15,400 tons and lithium hydroxide to 14,600 tons.[311]

In 2021, Livent bounced back strong with $420 million in revenue. 49% came from sales of lithium hydroxide, 57% was for energy storage systems and 70% of business was from Asia. This revenue was earned on selling 19,600 tons of lithium hydroxide and 15,500 tons of lithium carbonate. Livent confirmed that they were building out 5,000 tons of additional lithium hydroxide capacity per year at their Bessemer City facility which would be ready in 2022. Also, they were building out an additional 20,000 tons of lithium carbonate capacity at the Salar in Chile that would come online in 2023. Their stated goal was achieving 60,000 tons of capacity in Chile by 2025.

In their annual report, Livent discussed the various aspects of climate change that could negatively impact their operations like severe weather and drought. They also had a section dedicated to identifying the various political, legal, and social aspects

[310] https://e3lithium.ca/our-assets/operations/
[311] Livent Corporation, Form 10-K, SEC, 2020.

of climate change that could impact the lithium sector. Livent also revealed that they had a 2040 net zero carbon reduction commitment. Additionally, they began the process for implementing the framework of the Task Force for Climate-Related Financial Disclosures (TCFD). And after printing all this ink about carbon induced risks, they continued to power their operations with heat trapping fossil fuels although they could transition easily and quickly to renewable energy sources.[312]

In May 2022, Livent expanded its operations by buying into Nemaska Lithium Inc., a Canadian mining company. Livent already owned 25% of the company, but the new purchase moved them up to 50% ownership. In doing so, Livent bought a 100% share in Quebec Lithium Partners (QLP) which became a wholly owned subsidiary of Livent. In turn, QLP would manage Livent's 50% stake in Nemaska.[313]

Nemaska's primary asset was the Whabouchi open pit hard rock lithium mine. The mine was in a remote location in the central western part of Quebec Province, 440 miles northwest of Montreal. Operationally, crushed spodumene concentrate from the mine would be trucked to the Quebec Societe-Parc Industriel located 80 miles northeast of Montreal on the St. Lawrence River. The park is located less than two miles from Becancour Port. In January 2023, Nemaska bought land at the park where it would build its lithium hydroxide conversion plant with a 30,000 tpa capacity. Importantly, from Becancour Port to downtown Detroit is only 700 miles by ship.[314]

Livent was expanding its operations to meet growing demand forecasted to continue through at least 2030. For example, Tesla extended its current lithium offtake contract with Livent through at least 2021. The details of the existing contract or the new extension was not publicly disclosed. However, it was understood that Livent would provide larger quantities of battery grade lithium. Since Tesla planned to manufacture 20 million BEVs annually by 2030, they would need continuing long-term offtake contracts with just about every North American lithium company in business.

Then, BMW and Livent signed a $334 million lithium offtake agreement in 2021, taking effect the following year.[315] Livent would provide BWM battery cell manufac-

---

[312] Livent Corporation, Form 10-K, SEC, 2021.

[313] "Livent Announces Agreement to Double its Ownership Stake in Nemaska Lithium to 50 Percent ". PR Newswire, May 02, 2022.

[314] https://www.nemaskalithium.com/en/

[315] "BMW signs Eur285 million lithium supply deal with Livent". S&P Global, March 30, 2021.

turers with both lithium carbonate and lithium hydroxide. Part of BWM's decision for the deal was the fact that Livent used a sustainable methodology in their lithium evaporation ponds that used less water than their competitors. As of this deal, Samsung SDI (S. Korea) and CATL (China) were BMW's battery cell suppliers. Later, Northvolt (Sweden) became another BMW supplier.[316]

In 2022, Livent signed a six-year binding lithium hydroxide offtake agreement with General Motors. The six-year offtake period would begin in 2025 and run through 2030. GM will use the battery-grade lithium hydroxide for the cathodes in their Ultium batteries used in a variety of models like the GMC Hummer and Cadillac Lyriq. While most of this lithium would obviously be sourced from their Chile operations, Livent agreed that they would ultimately move the downstream processing of it to their North America facility in Bessemer City. This was important, because the *Inflation Reduction Act of 2022* only provided cash incentives for vehicles and batteries that progressively had to be made in North America.[317]

I know exactly what it is about Livent that maddens me: they remind of me of how Panasonic operates in the battery space – too conservative. They don't attack their space. I would like to see Livent diversify from the remote location that is the Lithium Triangle. South America has no BEV industry nor a battery industry, meaning they must ship their lithium ridiculously long distances to sell it. I do like that Livent bought into Nemaska Lithium in Canada, but the Whabouchi mine is still many years away before production commences – even estimates of 2025 are very generous.

I would explore, start, and buy into lithium extraction operations in the three big markets: Asia, Europe, and North America. As we saw, Albemarle bought into two lithium operations on the Australia continent close to China and Livent should do the same. Regionally, Livent should explore mining operations in Australia, China, and Mongolia. They should pursue the principle of getting their product from as close to the market that it will be consumed in.

Also, there are multiple locations in Europe from where lithium can be sourced.

[316] https://www.electrive.com/2020/07/16/northvolt-becomes-3rd-battery-cell-supplier-to-bmw/

[317] https://www.prnewswire.com/news-releases/general-motors-and-livent-enter-long-term-lithium-hydroxide-supply-agreement-301593251.html

For example, Vulcan Zero Carbon Lithium is pursuing geothermal brines in Germany's Rhine Valley. Emerging battery companies in Europe like Sweden's Northvolt, Norway's Freyr and England's Britishvolt (bought by Australian company Recharge Industries in February 2023 after Britishvolt declared bankruptcy) all want European-sourced lithium. Any locally sourced lithium company will sell every ounce of lithium they can extract to the score of battery plants presently being built from England, across Scandinavia, and all the way to Poland.

Also, Livent could benefit from expanding into the U.S. and focusing on DLE brine extraction operations. For instance, as we have mentioned previously, the Smackover brine formation runs from Texas to Florida. Livent could explore and secure DLE operations somewhere along that nexus like Standard Lithium to get its product closer to the market that consumes it. A company will never produce cheaper lithium products than those developed and delivered to their nearby market using the most efficient processes.

Finally, Livent could use their overall battery materials expertise to get into an associated industry like graphite. Specifically, there is growing demand for graphite manufactured in a zero-carbon manner and powered by 100% renewable energy. Graphite is the often-overlooked material needed in every anode of every battery. Livent could pursue flake graphite mining in Canada or Mexico and they could produce synthetic graphite on their own. Imagine Livent producing synthetic graphite in Reno, NV, powered 100% by solar energy, and selling all of it to Tesla's gigafactory right down the road. They would sell every ounce they make.

BHE (Berkshire Hathaway Energy) Renewables

BHE Renewables operates mostly in the renewable energy generation space owning associated solar, hydro, geothermal, and wind projects. Their title is partially deceiving as they still own and operate four separate natural gas power generation plants. So, they are clearly guilty of greenwashing as natural gas is a polluting, heat trapping fossil fuel. Organizationally, BHER placed their natural gas operations in the same bucket as their geothermal ones. BHER's ten geothermal plants operate as CalEnergy Operations.

We are specifically interested in these ten separate geothermal operations located in Imperial Valley, CA. When we hear the words Imperial Valley, we should immediately think of the Salton Sea located in Imperial County. Significantly, the Salton Sea has been identified as holding large potential reserves of brine with lithium, although, to date, none has been recovered from there at scale. Presently, there are three companies developing lithium brine extraction operations near the Salton Sea: BHE, EnergySource and Controlled Thermal Resources (an Australian company).

BHER is aware of the potential for lithium extraction from their geothermal brine operations and are pursuing two different projects. First, BHER received a $6 million grant from the California Energy Commission in 2020 to pursue the extraction of lithium chloride from their ongoing geothermal brine operations. Lithium Chloride (LiCl) is mainly used as a desiccant for dehumidifying and making metals. BHER used the grant to construct a demonstration plant forecasted to be operational by 2022.[318]

BHER further received a $14.9 million grant from the Department of Energy (DOE) in 2021 to match BHER's own investment in a conversion plant. This plant would convert the previously mentioned lithium chloride into battery-grade lithium hydroxide. This second demonstration plant was anticipated to be completed by 2023 and actual production of lithium hydroxide to take place in 2024.[319]

However, BHER was plagued by continuing technical problems and couldn't make its DLE technology work, resulting in DOE pulling its grant in 2022. For the project, BHER partnered with U.S. company AquaMin Lithium and Water Recovery Inc, using their DLE technology. It is believed that the geothermal brine near the Salton Sea was so acidic that it corroded BHER's equipment and fouled the piping which made extraction operations impossible. Additionally, BHER changed its plans to produce lithium hydroxide to pursuing LCE production instead. It remains to be seen if BHER's Salton Sea geothermal brine project can acquire the technology required to become viable.[320]

As background, Berkshire Hathaway Energy Company was incorporated in 1999 with its headquarters in Des Moines, Iowa. They are not listed on the NYSE so one can't buy into them directly as a retail investor. For more context, BHE Renewables is just one of eight separate entities that fall under the overarching corporate umbrella of BHE. Consequently, BHER's Salton Sea lithium brine project is a just a minor

---

[318] BHE Renewables – Lithium, Fact Sheet, April 2022.

[319] https://www.thinkgeoenergy.com/bhe-renewables-receives-15m-in-u-s-doe-grant-funding-for-geothermal-lithium-demonstration-project/

[320] Scheyder, Ernest. "U.S. steps away from flagship lithium project with Berkshire." Economic Times: Auto.com, Oct 05, 2022.

sideshow and is in no way a priority for the larger organization. For instance, in BHE's 2021 annual 10-K report to the SEC, there is no mention of the word "lithium", "brine" nor even "Salton Sea" anywhere in the document.[321]

This picture was taken in February 2023, about one half of a mile east of the Salton Sea. You can't see it, but the Salton Sea is directly ahead. This is the area where several geothermal energy operations take place to include BHE's. The El Centro area is dominated by agro-business and the specific locations with geothermal brine activity are remote with access provided only by dirt roads. The terrain in this area consists of low-lying wetlands. When I was there, the roads were muddy as was the surrounding area. On the side of most roads are deep earthen canals that channel runoff from the nearby farmland. If a vehicle accidentally falls into one, it will take a crane to get it out. The geothermal brine activity is not related to the nearby Salton Sea. In other words, the Salton Sea itself has nothing to do with the nearby lithium deposits.

EnergySource Minerals (ESM)

EnergySource Minerals LLC is an American company located in San Diego. In 2012, they built the John L. Featherstone geothermal brine energy plant located in Imperial Valley. The geothermal plant itself is named after ESM's Chief Technology Officer who

---

[321] Berkshire Hathaway Energy Company, SEC, 10-K, 2021.

holds the patent on the plant. Featherstone is in the Salton Sea Known Geothermal Resource Area (KGRA). Presently, the plant is used to provide geothermal generated electricity to the Salt River Project in Arizona on a 30-year contract.[322]

In 2016, ESM began their Project ATLiS which is an operational subset to extract lithium from their existing geothermal energy operation. Specifically, ATLiS is a lithium hydroxide conversion plant located near their geothermal plant which is bureaucratically referred to as HR1 (Hudson Ranch Power 1 Geothermal Plant). In 2021, ESM submitted a 1,388-page Draft Environmental Impact Report (DEIR) to Imperial County for review and comments. In the DEIR, ESM reveals that they intend to produce lithium hydroxide, manganese, and zinc for commercial sale. Also, ESM highlighted the importance of collocating their ATLiS plant close to HR1 for purposes of operational efficiency. ESM plans to have ATLiS up and running some time in 2023 with actual production occurring in 2024.[323]

Constructing their ATLiS lithium hydroxide conversion plant was one thing, but it was based on the premise that they could extract the necessary lithium from the brine itself. In 2017, ESM began developing their proprietary ILiAD DLE technology. ILiAD (Integrated Lithium Adsorption Desorption) is a closed loop system that extracts lithium from the geothermal brine pumped to the surface for steam energy generation. After the heated brine passes through the generator, it then passes through the ILiAD extraction system and back down to the underground aquifer where it came from.

As of May 2022, ESM claimed that its ILiAD DLE technology was commercially viable and production ready. That month they inked a deal with Schlumberger New Energy (SNE) to deploy the ILiAD system with NeoLith Energy's brine operation in Nevada. For background, Schlumberger is a French oil services company with headquarters in Paris. SNE is a subordinate organization within Schlumberger and NeoLith is in turn a subcomponent of SNE. (Author's note: at time publication, ESM had provided no new updates to its ATLiS project or its ILiAD technology indicating they may not be on track to meet their published timeline.)

NeoLith Energy's brine operation will be in Clayton Valley, NV, adjacent to Albemarle's ongoing evaporation pond operations. While a SNE press release claimed NeoLith Energy's DLE brine operation pilot plant would be up and running by 2021,

[322] https://www.energysource.us.com/john-l-feathertsone-plant

[323] "DEIR for Energy Source Mineral ATLIS Project". Chambers Group Inc, June 2021.

this never happened. SNE claims they have their own DLE technology and wouldn't be using EnergySource's system if it was commercially viable. In other words, they are hedging their bets. To date, NeoLith Energy hasn't gone beyond securing a permit for their Clayton Valley Pilot Plant. Also, they don't have a website or domain name secured. I suspect they won't be commercially viable until around 2028 at the earliest.

Compass Minerals International Inc.

Compass is an American company with an international footprint, selling salts and plant nutrition products. They are headquartered in Kansas, with a workforce of over 1,900 people and strong revenues in 2022 of $1.2 billion with EBIDTA of $188 million. Their salt operations comprise 82% of their business. While they have several surface and underground salt operations, their primary location is their salt evaporation effort on the Great Salt Lake near Ogden UT.[324]

What is interesting to us, is that the brine Compass uses to extract salt, potassium, and potash from also holds lithium. Compass estimates that some 25 mg/L to 51 mg/L of lithium is present in the Great Salt Lake. In their evaporation ponds, there is anywhere from 205 mg/L to 221 mg/L of lithium. Compass is serious enough about expanding into lithium that they sold two plant nutrition operations, one in North America and one in South America, to lower their debt and give them room to expand.[325]

On the topic of lithium extraction, Compass made the operational decision to pursue DLE technology instead of more evaporation ponds. In this effort they partnered with Veolia Water Technologies (VWT), one of the many subsidiaries under French company Veolia Environnement S.A., headquartered in Paris. VWT's U.S. office is in Plainfield, IL where they manufacture and sell their registered HPD Evaporation and Crystallization technology. Veolia advertises their ability to make both lithium carbonate and lithium hydroxide from either spodumene or brine.

However, while Compass partnered with Veolia to determine the feasibility of converting their exiting brine fields to useable battery-grade lithium, they chose EnergySource Mineral's actual DLE system. As mentioned before, ESM's ILiAD DLE technology is designed for closed-loop lithium brine extraction. Compass worked with

[324] Compass Minerals, 2022 Annual Report.
[325] Compass Minerals, 10-K, SEC, 2021 Annual Report.

ESM for three years, testing their ILiAD system and anticipates starting LCE production in 2025 with a 11,000 tpa capacity.[326] Compass already has non-binding battery-grade lithium offtake agreements with Ford and LG Chem that would begin in 2025.[327]

Looking Ahead

1. Albemarle and Livent inherited their present successful enterprises from two historic lithium companies: Foote Mineral and Lithium Corporation of America. The foundation was already built for them and they have improved on it. With that in mind, how will the differing approaches of Albemarle and Livent look moving forward? Will Albemarle's more aggressive approach enable them to capture more of the lithium value chain or will softening lithium prices expose them to overreach? How will Livent's more cautious, incremental approach play out over the next several years? Every company has their own culture – what is the reader's opinion of Albemarle's and Livent's cultures?

2. BHE Renewables is just one part of their larger energy enterprise focused on fossil fuels with a large carbon footprint. When it comes to their Salton Sea project, they could hit or miss, and it wouldn't affect the big picture. Consequently, will they put the intellectual capital and technological expertise towards making their DLE operation work? Or will they cut their losses, sell what they have and move on?

3. Compass is established in the salt industry and their lithium project won't make or break them either. However, I assess their effort as being low-risk with a high probability of success. Their existing brine evaporation operations means they just need to secure DLE technology that works. Everything else is already in place. But that is obviously harder said than done as no company to date has DLE that works at scale.

---

[326] https://investors.compassminerals.com/investors-relations/investor-news/press-release-details/2022/Compass-Minerals-Announces-Selection-of-Direct-Lithium-Extraction-DLE-Technology-Provider

[327] https://www.compassminerals.com/info/news/compass-minerals-and-ford-motor-company-sign-non-binding-agreement-for-the-supply-of-battery-grade-lithium/

4. What is the reader's opinion on the viability of the Salton Sea area to provide lithium from geothermal brine? We have been hearing about the potential of lithium from that area for almost fifteen years yet there is still nothing of value coming from there. Is the KGRA just too tough a nut to crack? When might we see the DLE technology mature that can handle the specific nature of the brine found there and then extract LCE at scale?

5. Overall, what will the U.S. lithium industry look like in 2025? 2030? Will the industry grow expansively or incrementally? Will a new player come into the picture out of nowhere like Albemarle did to alter the landscape? How much market cap will American companies have compared to the growing Chinese and European lithium enterprises?

An ariel view of Albemarle's lithium brine evaporative ponds in Silver Peak, NV, about a two-hour drive from Las Vegas. For many decades, this has been the lone lithium extraction operation in the United States and North America. The Foote Mineral company first started production here in the 1960's, shipping their end-product across the country to their original hard rock operation in Kings Mountain, NC for refinement. *(by NASA)*

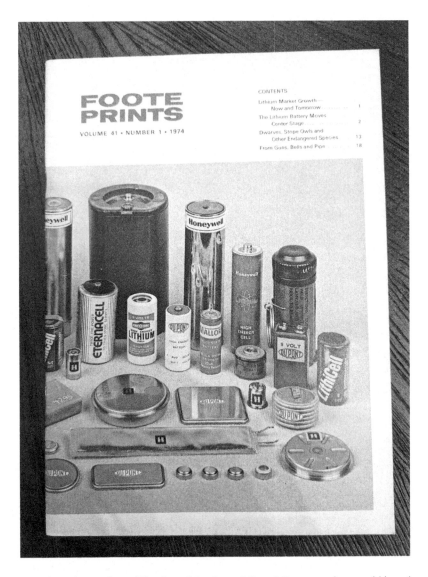

Foote Prints, the regular publication of the Foote Mineral Company that would later be owned by Albemarle. The lead article by Dr. Harold R. Grady was "The Lithium Battery Moves Center Stage". The 12-page article provided an overview of the history, present status, and future uses of the lithium-ion battery in modern society. While Dr. Grady states in the article that Albemarle had no intentions of entering the battery manufacturing space, he himself was General Manager of Albemarle's Lithium Battery Department. My question is, why hasn't Albemarle entered this space long ago like Ganfeng has? *(by Author)*.

CHAPTER 9

The Canadian Lithium Value Chain

"Canada is a global mining powerhouse. Our geological endowment and reputation are the envy of the world.Canadian leadership and expertise can be found at virtually every link along the mining value chain." – *Canadian Minerals and Metals Plan, November 2019*

Canada's Critical Mineral Strategy

Canada has been working with the U.S. to coordinate a North American critical mineral and supply chain strategy since 2019. The official title for this effort is the *Canada – U.S. Joint Action Plan on Critical Minerals Strategy*. A driving force for this cooperation was recognition of China's continuing dominance in certain areas like Rare Earth Elements (REE) and battery metals like lithium. The Plan looks for ways to maximize cooperation with not just the U.S. but also the EU, Australia, and Japan. Implicit in their strategy is recognizing the significant mining potential of Canada that includes the ability to produce mineral extraction in support of a low-carbon energy future.

Senator Joe Manchin recognized the importance of Canadian-U.S. cooperation in the critical minerals space during a full hearing of the Senate Energy and Natural Resources Committee in May 2022. Specifically, Senator Manchin recognized China's dominance in battery minerals: "Unfortunately, China controls 80% of the world's battery material processing, 60% of the world's cathode production, 80% of the world's anode production, and 75% of the world's lithium-ion battery cell production. They've cornered the market." During the hearing, Senator Manchin explicitly recognized the need for the U.S. and Canada to source battery minerals from North America as a supply chain security imperative.[328]

In doing so, Senator Manchin raised the persistent idea that Canada can provide the U.S. with the minerals that it cannot or does not produce itself. Just as Australia evolved into China's lithium mine, Canada could evolve into the U.S.' battery minerals mine. As we saw in previous chapters, environmentalists in the U.S. would prefer mining to occur outside the U.S. and for American industry to simply import needed materials from abroad. That would conveniently solve the problem posed by years of legal battles mining companies routinely fight with entrenched environmental groups in the U.S.

For instance, the Sierra Club has provided detailed guidance to its local chapters on the topic of mining in general and lithium mining specifically. Guidance includes: "Battery production will require an increased use of lithium, an essential stock for lithium-ion batteries, which have high energy-storage capacity, among other desirable features. We should, however, resist the broad narrative of inadequate supplies of these minerals, from which it follows that we must mine them where possible without regard to impacts."[329] Overall, the Sierra Club recognizes the need for lower-carbon economies, but the mining piece of this transition should not be done recklessly. In other words. lithium doesn't get a free pass.

Beyond partnering with the U.S., Canada seeks to strengthen its relations with Japan through the *Canada-Japan Energy Policy Dialogue*. With this forum, Canada looks for new ways to secure the critical mineral supply chain of mutual interest between the two. A key element of this relationship is ensuring free and open trade in the Indo-Pacific region. Although it is not stated explicitly, it is clear that a strong Japan is important as a counterweight to China's pervasive economic power in the Asia markets.[330]

Japan itself has no battery minerals of significance on its territory and, unsurprisingly, has a very small domestic mining industry. In contrast, Canada has vast mineral

[328] https://www.energy.senate.gov/2022/5/manchin-calls-for-stronger-u-s-canada-energy-and-mineral-partnership-to-ensure-free-world-s-energy-security-and-address-climate-change

[329] "Guidance on Lithium Mining and Extraction". The Sierra Club, November 13, 2021.

[330] Japan-Canada Action Plan for contributing to a free and open Indo-Pacific region, 2022.

resources and a well-developed mining industry. One could expect a future relationship to develop with Canada providing Japan with the battery minerals Japan doesn't have. It is logical that Japan would also develop a robust midstream conversion capability, although, to date, they haven't. Currently, Japan imports 100% of its battery grade lithium, with most of it coming from nearby China. In return, Japan could provide Canada with battery manufacturing expertise just like Panasonic does with Tesla at their gigafactory in Nevada. What would make the most sense is for Japanese battery technology companies to set up shop in Canada to use locally sourced battery minerals and then sell them to the adjacent U.S. market.

While partnerships with allies are a central part of their strategy, Canada also must get its own house in order, something that has been long overdue. To this end, Natural Resources Canada published a Critical Mineral List that includes 31 different minerals. Some of these include REEs and uranium, which is important for supporting the U.S. national defense industry. Presently, the U.S. imports these elements from its chief competitors in the global system to include China (REE) and Russia (uranium). Importantly, Canada also recognizes the importance of minerals critical for the battery supply chain to include lithium, cobalt, copper, manganese, and nickel.

In 2019, Natural Resources Canada published *The Canadian Minerals and Metals Plan* (CMMP), where Canada sets the bar high for becoming the world's leading mining nation. In many ways, the CMMP is the start of a national discussion that will lead to "A new, pan-Canadian, collaborative public geoscience strategy for mineral exploration" by 2022.[331] Part of the plan is to create a more favorable tax and investing environment as investing in Canadian mining has declined over the last several years. To achieve this, Canada can leverage the Toronto Stock Exchange (TSX) and the TSX Venture Exchange (TSXV) where 40% of all publicly traded mining companies are listed, although 50% were listed in 2017. In 2022, the TSX raised $7.6 billion in mining equity capital (down from $10 billion in 2021) and held $521 billion in mining market capitalization (down from $558 billion in 2021).[332]

While the CMMP provided a general direction in which the national enterprise should move, more details and updates were provided in annual Action Plans (published every October) as the strategy evolved. CMMP action Plan 2021 revealed that

---

[331] https://www.nrcan.gc.ca/sites/www.nrcan.gc.ca/files/CMMP/CMMP_The_Plan-EN.pdf

[332] https://www.tsx.com/listings/listing-with-us/sector-and-product-profiles/mining

$47 million was granted by the federal government to advance R&D for critical mineral processing like feedstock conversion facilities and battery precursors required for battery manufacturing. From a knowledge generation perspective, $9.6 million was provided for establishing a Critical Mineral Center of Excellence, like the initiative by the U.S. And to create an attractive environment for industry, there was a 50% reduction in the corporate tax for manufacturers of zero-emission technologies.[333]

In step with their national mining strategy, the Trudeau administration's 2022 budget offered $3 billion USD in incentives to advance related mineral, battery, and BEV manufacturing industries. The funds will be spent over the next eight years and will target specific sectors of the value chain. To start, $1.5 billion CAD was allocated for critical mineral supply chain development, $79.2 million CAD for improved data related to mineral exploration (a similar problem the U.S. suffers from) and a 30% tax credit for mining companies exploring and developing critical minerals on the published national list. The tax credit applies to all the major battery materials to include lithium, graphite, nickel, cobalt, and copper.[334]

Another key initiative is the Incentives for Zero-Emissions Vehicles (iZEV) program, that offers tax credits for businesses and individuals buying battery electric vehicles (BEVs), plug-in hybrid electric vehicles (PHEVs) and fuel-cell electric vehicles (FCEVs). There are 141 different makes/models that qualify for the $2,500.00-$5,000.00 CAD incentive by meeting published pricing requirements. Eligible BEVs receive the maximum incentive of $5,000.00 and there are 65 makes/models listed that qualify for the iZEV program.

Ontario's Critical Mineral Strategy

While the Canadian national government has its own critical mineral vision and associated incentives, its provinces have the freedom to act both in concert with the federal government and independently as they see fit. The dynamics are the same in the U.S. where the federal government is slow to act, for example, on setting national policy for the transition to BEV's. However, that doesn't stop California from already announcing its ban on new ICE vehicles starting in 2035. Correspondingly, Ontario

---

[333] https://www.minescanada.ca/sites/minescanada/files/CMMP-ActionPlan2021_May27-ACC.pdf

[334] https://www.greencarcongress.com/2022/04/20220408-canada-cm.html

is already moving out after publishing its five-year blueprint entitled *Critical Mineral Strategy 2022-2027*.

Ontario, its capital is Ottawa, has a robust and established mining industry, contributing $11 billion annually to Ontario's GDP and employing 75,000 people.[335, 336] Ontario has large deposits of battery metals to include lithium, nickel, cobalt, and graphite (not a metal). As an example, in 2020, Ontario's nickel production was valued at $1 billion. Also, Canada's provinces are massive compared to the U.S.' own states – Texas fits into Ontario twice. Just as the U.S. looks to its northern partner to supply its own mineral needs, Ottawa recognizes that it can tap into the mineral resources of its comparatively remote north to feed its lithium value chain in its southern industrial base.

Ottawa's leaders envision Ontario leading Canada's critical mineral enterprise through progressive mining policies. To this end, Ottawa is providing $24 million to the Ontario Junior Exploration Program which offers grants to mining companies specifically to explore new mineral resources. Of this, $12 million is dedicated to critical mineral discovery. Plus, they are giving $5 million to a critical minerals innovation fund to advance new ideas in mining extraction techniques.

According to data from the Ontario Mining Association (OMA), the province has 41 active mining operations. 21 of these 41 mines are gold operations that produce the most value by mineral in the province. On the battery metals front, by production volume, Ontario produces 38% of Canada's nickel, 26% of its copper and 24% of its cobalt. Nickel and cobalt are used in conjunction with many forms of current LIBs, although there is a move in the wider battery industry to move away from the products – but that is many years down the road. Copper has many uses but most noticeably in the wire harnesses paired with completed LIBs. While they have not reached the production stage yet, there are three different lithium mining and two graphite extraction operations ongoing in the province.[337]

To start, Avalon Advanced Materials Inc. is pursuing their open pit hard rock Separation Rapids Lithium Project located in Kenora in western Ontario, only 30

---

[335] https://www.ontario.ca/files/2022-03/ndmnrf-ontario-critical-minerals-strategy-2022-2027-en-2022-03-22.pdf

[336] https://www.investontario.ca/mining#intro

[337] https://oma.on.ca/en/ontario-mining/2022_OMA_Economic_Research_Report.pdf

miles from the border with Manitoba. Avalon originally pursued lithium production in the late 1990's but they couldn't secure the spodumene concentrate offtake agreements to justify going into operation. Today, Avalon anticipates producing 475,000 tpa of concentrate that when converted using a 6.3:1 ratio equals 75,000 tpa of LCE. Avalon is presently coordinating with Rock Tech Lithium Inc. to build a concentrate processing plant to produce lithium sulphate which is a precursor for lithium hydroxide. However, Avalon is still many years away from being operational. They still must complete a Definitive Feasibility Study, secure financing, and get offtake agreements.

Rock Tech Lithium Inc. is a joint Canadian-German mining company in the early stages of developing their open pit hard rock lithium mine in Ontario. Their project is located just north of Thunder Bay, a major port located on the northern shore of Lake Superior. In August 2022, it was reported that Mercedes was securing an offtake agreement with Rock Tech for 10,000 tpa of lithium hydroxide starting in 2026. To accomplish this, Rock Tech is working on construction of a spodumene concentrate to lithium hydroxide midstream conversion plant in Guben, Germany. This conversion plant will have a 24,000 tpa capacity with deliveries anticipated to start in 2024.[338]

While Mercedes touted the deal as a step towards building supply chain "resilience", the chain itself is still ridiculous. Let's have a look at it. It is only 115 miles by road from Rock Tech's proposed mine located southeast of Lake Nipigon to Thunder Bay. Their trucks can get on Route 11, a major road that runs near their lithium project, take it south to Route 17, that goes right to Thunder Bay, where their proposed joint lithium sulphate conversion facility will be. Keep in mind, in the winter, roads must be plowed, and the port kept free of ice. Also, when considering Thunder Bay for the supply chain, icebreaker ships must clear shipping lanes through the Great Lakes.

Then, it's 2,350 miles through Lake Superior, Lake Huron, Lake Erie, Lake Ontario, up the Saint Lawrence River, through Montreal and Quebec and past the last land mass of Newfoundland. Next, it's across the Atlantic, through the English Channel and on to the port of Bremerhaven – that is 5,350 miles traveled via sea. The last land leg is 330 miles across Germany's excellent road system, taking the southern route from Bremerhaven to Guben, avoiding the Hamburg and Berlin traffic hubs.

A 6,000-mile supply chain sounds like a supply chain prone to disruption.

---

[338] https://www.electrive.com/2022/02/02/rock-tech-lithium-considers-second-plant-in-germany/

A "resilient" supply chain is a short supply chain. Obviously, since Rock Tech has a German owner, they are bringing their feedstock and conversion plant to German customers like Mercedes. Rock Tech and Mercedes would be better suited pursuing a lithium feedstock source in Germany or Europe. Similarly, their lithium mine in Ontario should feed to the battery supply chain in North America and specifically the Big Three in Detroit. In comparison, the water route from Thunder Bay to the mouth of the Rouge River in Detroit is just 640 miles.

Now, let's get back to Ontario's mining industry and Frontier Lithium Inc., a Canadian company advancing their open pit PAK (Pakeagama Lake) lithium project. Frontier has been pursuing their 100% owned PAK project since 1999, located in the northwestern part of the province. Frontier intends to develop a lithium hydroxide conversion facility to serve the growing EV battery industry located in southern Ontario and north central U.S. This EV/battery corridor is centered along Detroit-Toronto-Ottawa. However, frontier is many years away still with a proposed 2027 spodumene concentrate production date.

The D-T-O EV/battery corridor bears some investigation. Ideally, lithium mined in Ontario should feed the immediate North American EV/battery value chain as envisioned by both the U.S. and Canadian federal governments' critical mineral supply chain strategies. As we saw, shipping lithium feedstock 6,000 miles to eastern Germany isn't what a critical mineral strategy envisions and doesn't make good business sense. Mining, shipping, and using lithium feedstock locally and regionally is what both sides of the border should be working towards.

Unsurprisingly, with Ontario's territory being so close to Detroit, the historic U.S. auto manufacturing hub, Ontario itself has a strong auto manufacturing base with more than 100,000 people employed in the industry. However, since the year 2000, many new North American auto manufacturing projects moved south of Ontario and Detroit. Just think of Tesla in Texas, Lucid in Arizona, Rivian in Illinois/Georgia, and Ford making its Mach-E in Mexico. In the U.S., Detroit is no longer the hub for automotive innovation. To stop their increasing marginalization in the industry, Ontario should move aggressively into the lithium value chain space, and this means: mining, batteries and BEVs.

To understand the totality of the topic, we must explore the basics of the *U.S.-Mexico-Canada Agreement* (USMCA) signed July 1st, 2020, which updated the North American Free Trade Agreement (NAFTA) signed in 1994. NAFTA was the most comprehensive trade agreement the U.S. had participated in up to that time and was significant in that it removed all tariffs and most non-tariff barriers on merchandise traded between the three countries. Importantly, from 1994 until 2020, Mexico's GDP doubled and Canada's and the U.S.' GDPs almost tripled. The USMCA kept most of the NAFTA rules in effect while modernizing topics like digital trade, intellectual property rights, labor laws and North American motor vehicle requirements.

As background, one year before the NAFTA agreement, in 1993, the U.S. ran a $10 billion a year deficit in auto parts, meaning the U.S. imported more parts than it exported. By 2020, this imbalance skyrocketed with the U.S. running an $80 billion trade deficit, importing far more car parts than it exported. This was one of the reasons why NAFTA was ostensibly modernized with USMCA, to address glaring trade imbalances. This was important taken in the light of the Detroit based auto makers' declining market influence with the rise of BEV companies like Tesla and a legion of other companies in China.

Consequently, USMCA required, to avoid tariffs, that imported vehicles and auto parts have 75% of their content originate in North America (up from 62.5% and 60% respectively under NAFTA). Also, 70% of the steel and aluminum used in these vehicles must originate from North America and upwards of 45% of imported auto content must be made by workers earning $16 an hour or more (average Mexican auto workers make $2.60 USD an hour). To enforce these provisions, origin certification requirements were strengthened. Thus, cars or auto parts imported to the U.S can't just be put together in Canada or Mexico, the origin of the parts must be North American. If importers can't meet these requirements, they are subject to a 2.5% tariff. However, a secure North American auto supply chain means these products must come from North America.

But, not so fast, there is a loophole in the USMCA reference vehicles in what's called the Section 232 side letter. The letter stipulates that 2.6 million passenger vehicles a year from both Canada and Mexico are exempt from the USMCA. All light trucks imported from Canada and Mexico are exempt as are $32.4 billion of auto parts from Canada and $108 billion worth from Mexico a year. However, Mexico only exports 2 million autos of all types a year to the U.S., so USMCA really has no effect on them. And in 2020, Canada only exported 1.2 million light vehicles into the U.S. and $31 billion in auto parts, so the USMCA clearly has no effect on them either.[339]

---

[339] https://www.cvma.ca/industry/facts/

Ultimately, in the realm of the auto industry, the USMCA had no teeth as it accepted the status quo of an $80 billion U.S. trade deficit.

Absent from the USMCA was any provision reference EV batteries and their originating composition. This is, perhaps, unsurprising as the trade agreement discussions began in 2017 when Canada and Mexico had no BEV industry and the only game in town for the U.S. was Tesla. In contrast, the *Inflation Reduction Act of 2022* addressed BEV's in depth to include tax credits for purchasers and battery component sourcing requirements. The IRA provided American buyers a $7,500.00 tax credit on new BEV purchases and $4,500.00 on used BEV purchases. However, for a BEV to qualify for these tax credits, there were increasingly stringent requirements for battery minerals and components to be sourced from North America.

This had a positive impact on Ontario's developing lithium value chain because it showed how serious the U.S. government was incentivizing the transition to BEVs. This meant that Ontario would have a strong market to sell its BEV related products to, confirming the logic of its *Critical Mineral Strategy 2022-2027*. Importantly, Ontario had no existing domestic BEV, battery nor lithium mining industry in 2022. They were moving forward with a blank slate and had no supply chain or domestic political dependencies holding them back. Thus, moving forward, they could build these industries from the ground up with the necessary local and North American sourcing requirements.

We mentioned before Ontario's efforts to develop the Detroit-Toronto-Ottawa EV/battery corridor. Is this actually becoming a reality or is this just a fantasy by some detached provincial planners who don't know what's happening on the ground? Based on the evidence, it appears that it's happening and, in fact, by 2022 the business was pouring in. In 2022, Stellantis announced that it was investing $2.8 billion USD to retool its two auto factories in Windsor and Brampton in pursuit of its electrification strategy. In support of these BEV retooling efforts, the Trudeau Administration granted Stellantis an additional $410 million USD, while Ottawa contributed $398 million USD. This was an example of the federal administration, provincial government and industry operating in concert.[340]

Additionally, Stellantis partnered with South Korean battery giant LG Energy

---

[340] https://techcrunch.com/2022/05/02/stellantis-trudeau-invest-2-8-billion-to-boost-ev-production-in-canada/

Solutions (spun off from LG Chem), investing $3.65 billion USD in an EV battery man-ufacturing plant to be built in Windsor. Windsor is located south of Detroit, with the two cities separated by the Detroit River. The Ambassador Bridge connects the two cities. For context, the bridge is the most important crossing point between the U.S. and Canada with $390 million worth of trade occurring every day. 26% of Canada's exports cross the Ambassador annually, meaning most of its auto parts are shipped there to feed the Detroit auto industry. Consequently, from a North American sup-ply chain security perspective, Windsor is the ideal location to position a new bat-tery factory. If this future factory secures its lithium feedstock from Ontario mining companies, they would be the shining example of how to maximize the lithium value chain.[341]

In another example of Ontario's growing BEV industry, GM is in the process of retooling its Ingersoll CAMI plant that will build GM's BrightDrop electric vans. BrightDrop, who has contracts with FedEx, specializes in last-mile delivery solutions, a market ripe for electric disruption as the space consists of short distances, in defined areas, with overnight charging. GM has a production target date of Q42022-Q12023.[342] GM is investing an estimated $800 million in their CAMI facility while the Canadian federal government and Ottawa administration are each granting $259 million to the CAMI plant and another GM plant in Oshawa.[343]

Quebec's Critical & Strategic Minerals Plan

Like Ontario, even though they do not have a developed auto manufacturing sec-tor, Quebec has been moving forward in the critical mineral space. In 2019, Quebec's Legault administration began studying and devising a provincial strategy resulting in the *Quebec Plan for the Development of Critical and Strategic Minerals 2020-2025*. In the plan, Quebec recognizes 22 minerals as critical to their circular green economy (nine less than Natural Resources Canada), that include the usual battery mineral sus-pects: copper, cobalt, lithium, nickel, and graphite. Furthermore, the plan recognizes

---

[341] https://tc.canada.ca/en/binder/16-economic-impact-blockades

[342] https://media.gm.ca/media/ca/en/gm/news.detail.html/content/Pages/ news/ca/en/2022/ apr/0429_cami-plant-in-ingersoll.html

[343] https://www.cbc.ca/news/canada/london/gm-plants-government-funding-1.6407621

the need of capturing the value of the entire critical mineral value chain from mining to BEV production.[344]

Quebec has a robust mining industry with various sectors at different stages of maturity, depending on the mineral in question. To start, Quebec is home to nine separate projects resourcing nickel, copper, and cobalt with two of these mines active. Then, there are ten graphite projects in the province with one active and another one about to come online. On the topic of lithium, there are six projects with one operational and the other five in the developmental stages. However, the status of the one operational lithium mine is like dating Kim Kardashian – it's complicated.[345]

In 1955, the Quebec Lithium Corporation (QLC) opened the first active open pit lithium mine at scale in the country. By the time of opening, QLC already had a five-year offtake agreement with Lithium Corporation of America (LCA). The contract stipulated $11.00 for each 1% of spodumene concentrate per ton delivered with a minimum of 4.5% lithium oxide per ton. QLC calculated that it would have to process 800 tons of ore a day (they had 1,000 tons/day capability) to produce 165 tons of spodumene concentrate a day with the minimum required lithium content. At the time, QLC President Pierre Beauchemin also discussed their intent to build a lithium carbonate conversion plant.[346]

Importantly, the lithium bought by LCA was being shipped to the Atomic Energy Commission (AEC) to build hydrogen bombs. In fact, 50% of all LCA's sales at the time were through classified supply contracts with the AEC. LCA lithium sales to the AEC went from $3.1 million in 1954 to $12.1 million in 1956. LCA received so much lithium from Quebec, that they shut down their own mining operations in North Carolina and focused solely on processing the lithium imported from QLC. As 90% of QLC's lithium was going to LCA, they too were almost solely dependent on U.S. classified weapons programs to keep them in business. LCA assumed the hydrogen bomb boom would last. They were wrong.[347]

---

[344] Quebec's plan is modern, progressive and comprehensive. If anyone has a need for a critical minerals strategy, just copy theirs.

[345] https://cdn-contenu.quebec.ca/cdn-contenu/ressources-naturelles/Documents/PL_critical_strategic_minerals.pdf?1604003187

[346] National Post, Dec 1955, "Quebec Lithium Now Producing".

[347] The Charlotte Observer, Jan 5, 1964, by J. Demott, "For LCA, Lithium Came First".

In early 1959, LCA signed QLC to another three-year offtake agreement that ended in 1962. They needed to keep the avalanche of lithium coming to feed the AEC's weapons program. However, this assumed that the AEC required a continuing influx of fresh lithium. What they didn't know was that the AEC had been stockpiling lithium from LCA, Foote Mineral and American Potash for many years. Now, the AEC had hoarded far more lithium than they could ever use, enough to continue their secret weapons programs for many decades into the future. It was time to turn the contracts off.

In 1959, to LCA's surprise, the AEC let their existing lithium contracts with them expire and did not resume them as anticipated. But now LCA had a problem, they had already inked QLC to a three-year contract for a continuing supply of lithium that they couldn't sell. However, business is business, so LCA unceremoniously terminated their contract with QLC. In response, QLC filed a lawsuit against LCA for $4,477,924.00 for breach of contract. The amount was based on the stipulated 17,000 units of lithium a month for 36 months. QLC President P. Beauchemin insisted that the existing offtake agreement had no escape clause and LCA was committed to completing the contract or paying the difference. This breach of contract was devastating for QLC as their off-take sales to LCA was practically their entire business.[348]

The two sides settled later that year for $1.9 million. Publicly, LCA stated that the reason for termination of the contract with QLC was that they were standing up their own mining operations in North Carolina and no longer needed Quebec's lithium. That was partially true, but we know the real reason. For many years after terminating their contract with QLC, LCA bought what lithium they needed from nearby competitor Foote Mineral who had their own mining operation only 15 minutes down the road. With terminating the Quebec contract, LCA simply did the math and calculated that paying a settlement was still cheaper than being stuck with tens of thousands of tons of lithium they couldn't offload. The termination of the AEC contracts almost bankrupted both companies that year. LCA would survive to become Livent Corporation while Quebec would struggle on life support until 1966.[349]

By 1961, QLC appeared to have weathered the LCA storm and was diversifying its lithium capabilities to hit different sectors of a very uncertain market. QLC had

348 The Gazette, Sep. 10, 1959, "Quebec Lithium Sues for Contract Losses".
349 The Bridgeport Post, Dec 31, 1959, "Lithium Settles Suit with Quebec Ore Firm".

already built a lithium carbonate conversion facility, the one Beauchemin had mentioned back in 1955. They were also in the process of completing their lithium hydroxide monohydrate conversion plant scheduled to be operational that December. Furthermore, QLC began developing a new facility to produce sodium chloride and lithium metal. Sadly, QLC was on track to produce full-spectrum lithium products for a market that wouldn't take off until fifty years later.[350]

By the mid-1960's, there was a global lithium oversupply and prices were so low that it wasn't profitable for QLC to continue hard rock lithium operations. For QLC's financial year ending in 1965, they only had a net profit of $1.2 million. At that time, QLC was reliant on its investments in other mining operations to keep the lights on. Moreover, QLC was suffering from striking employees which meant their lithium production had effectively come to a standstill. The end was near.[351]

As background, QLC was just one of nine mining businesses owned by the Sullivan Mining Group. Pierre Beauchemin, the former president of QLC, later became the president of Sullivan. Thus, it was Beauchemin who had to pull the plug on their only lithium mine in 1966, putting it in cold storage for the foreseeable future. For 1966 (Sullivan's financial years ran from September 1st through August 31st), QLC's net profits were only $107,122.00. Their diversification into various lithium products couldn't beat depressed prices as well as entrenched competitors like LCA. That year, Foote Mineral started lithium brine operations in Nevada because the operation costs were much lower.[352]

A decade later, Sullivan considered reopening their Quebec mine. In 1977, they estimated it would cost $21.5 million to bring the mine back into production by 1979.[353] This time, J. Jacques Beauchemin was pushing the idea. He had followed his father steps in becoming president of Sullivan. Pierre Beauchemin, who died in 1968 after an illustrious career, was inducted into Canada's Mining Hall of Fame in 1989 and is known as "Mr. Lithium".

However, the idea of reopening the mine would never be realized for two reasons that plagued the Quebec Lithium Mine until the present day. First, the market price of

---

[350] The Montreal Star, Aug 29, 1961,"Quebec Lithium to Widen Scope of Operations".

[351] National Post, Mar 5,1966, "Quebec Lithium".

[352] National Post, March 4, 1967, "The Sullivan Mining Group".

[353] The Gazette, Feb 19, 1977, "Sullivan Mining".

lithium remained low, meaning it was impossible to run mining operations at a profit. Second, the mine's aging facilities and equipment were exposed to very harsh environmental conditions for decades and no longer worked. This meant anyone starting up the mine again would have to invest a great deal of money to bring it up to date and make it functional. Only favorable market conditions and pile of cash could bring the mine back to life.

In 1987, Cambior Incorporated, a Canadian mining company, bought Sullivan Mining for $44.7 million, acquired the Quebec Lithium Mine along with it. Cambior had a pile of cash, but they weren't interested in lithium mining and didn't mine an ounce of it over the ensuing 20 years. The name of the game for Cambior was gold mining. Consequently, Cambior assessed that the Quebec Lithium Mine's aged facilities weren't recoverable, so they sold off all the individual pieces of equipment and disassembled and removed all existing structures. By 1991, the mine no longer existed and had been returned to its original state. Subsequent annual reports by Cambior don't even mention the mine as an asset. Canada no longer had the capability to produce lithium.[354]

Then, the revolving door game began in 2006 when IAMGOLD Corporation bought Cambior for a whopping $3 billion. IAMGOLD is a Canadian based international mining company that is still in business today. As their name indicates, they are focused on the gold industry with major mining projects in Africa. They obviously had no interest in the lithium business and only acquired the Quebec Lithium Mine by accident as a collateral asset. If anyone from IAMGOLD bothered to do a drive-by of their remote "lithium mine", all they would have seen is a flat piece of ground surrounded by trees.

Two years later, the Canada Lithium Corporation (CLC) thought they would give the lithium game a shot and bought the mine in 2008; IAMGOLD dumped it for a mere $350,000.00. CLC bit off quite a lot as they had to treat the opening of the mine as if it was brand new, meaning they had to go through the entire permitting process. After buying the QLM, CLC backed out on two other deals to explore a lithium brine operation in Nevada and a lithium project in Manitoba. They rolled the dice and put all their money on QLM. Until they could sell battery-grade lithium at scale, they would be burning piles of cash and operating in the red.

[354] Independent Technical Report, by Caracle Creek International Consulting Inc, Dec 16, 2009.

CLC moved forward over the next several years, constructing an open pit hard rock mine with plans to build a spodumene processing and conversion plant capable of producing 99.5% pure battery-grade lithium carbonate. By 2012, they had secured a three-year contract with Japanese company Marubeni who would distribute CLC's lithium carbonate to various Japanese customers. Marubeni agreed to buy an initial 2,000 tons of lithium carbonate starting in 2013 with options to buy up to 5,000 tons through 2015. CLC also secured a five-year offtake agreement with Chinese company Tewoo ERDC for a minimum of 12,000 tons of lithium carbonate a year with options up to 14,400 ton a year.[355] However, the conversion facilities were never built, and the subsequent battery-grade lithium profits were never realized.

In early 2014, CLC formally bought out and merged with Sirocco Mining Incorporated, renaming their new enterprise RB (Red Back) Energy Incorporated. Sirocco was a small company with mining interests in Africa and an iodine operation in the Atacama Desert, Chile. Perhaps this would be the bridge CLC needed to get in into the Lithium Triangle brine business. With concurrent hard rock and brine operations cemented to existing offtake agreements, RB Energy could blow up the Asia market and start competing with FMC and Rockwood.

But this was not to be as only months later, in October of the same year, RB Energy declared bankruptcy and entered into the provisions of the CCAA – *Companies' Creditors Arrangement Act*. They ran out of money before they could reach capacity production and no investors wanted to back their play. As part of the proceedings, RB Energy received $13 million USD under the DIP – *Debtor in Possession* loan program. This money would pay for the care and maintenance of the now idle mine, that had modern spodumene processing and conversion equipment, to maintain and protect it from the elements. RB Energy looked for buyers interested in their modernized hard rock mine, but there were no takers.[356]

North American Lithium: China's Foothold in Quebec

In the summer of 2016, North American Lithium (NAL) bought the Quebec Lithium Mine. However, NAL was just the name of the locally incorporated company created to run the mine. NAL was owned 75% by "9554548 Canada Inc" (to supposedly give

---

[355] Canada Lithium Corp., "Management's Discussion & Analysis", December 2012.

[356] News Release, RB Energy Inc, May 8, 2015.

the company a Canadian persona) which itself was a wholly owned subsidiary of Chinese company Jien International Investment Limited, a wholly owned subsidiary of Chinese Jilin Jien Nickel Industry Company Limited. The other minority 25% of NAL was owned by Ressources Quebec, a division of Investissement Quebec.

Let's discuss Investissement Quebec (IQ) briefly as it is relevant to supporting Quebec's critical and strategic mineral plan. IQ was created by an act of law in 2010 as a state-owned joint stock company. IQ's mission is to promote Quebec's economic development in line with provincial government policies which include electrification and fighting climate change. Ressources Quebec (RQ) is a division of IQ that provides investing capital to private companies pursuing projects specific to the energy and natural resources sector.[357]

RQ manages the Natural Resources and Energy Capital Fund which is resourced to the tune of $1 billion. The published fund guidelines (Section 35.1) allow money to be provided to enterprises developing resources in Quebec for the purpose of low carbon energy projects. Section 35.1 is both broad and specific enough that a lithium mine project with a midstream conversion facility producing battery-grade lithium carbonate and lithium hydroxide for EV battery manufacturing is exactly what the fund was created for. There are no published restrictions as to investor company origination and outside foreign capital is explicitly encouraged. Consequently, IQ/RQ providing seed capital with Jilin Jien to promote lithium production was 100% in line with IQ's publicly mandated mission.

However, the existing laws regulating IQ also allowed foreign companies, like Jilin Jien, to come in and extract critical minerals from Canada for their own use abroad. There was no end use requirement for the fund requiring that the resources being produced be used in Canada. And there was no majority ownership requirement so that Quebec could direct how the mined lithium was ultimately used. As mentioned previously, all Canadian Lithium Corporation's previous offtake agreements went to either Japan (an ally) or China (a competitor), of which both arrangements did nothing to secure a North American supply chain.

Regardless, NAL brought their new lithium mine into production, mining some 1,689,000 tons of ore with an average grade of 1.11% Li_2O from 2017 through

[357] https://www.legisquebec.gouv.qc.ca/en/document/cs/I-16.0.1?langCont=en#ga:l_ii-gb:l_iii-gc:l_3-h1

February 2019. Of that amount, NAL milled 1,356,000 tons with an average grade of 1.18% Li_2O.[358] In 2018, the actual amount of spodumene concentrate produced was 114,000 tons.[359] If we use a 6.3:1 conversion factor for lithium carbonate, NAL had 18,000 tons of lithium carbonate to sell. If they sold this carbonate at a price of $15,000.00 USD per ton, that's revenues of $270 million USD. However, NAL wasn't selling battery-grade processed lithium, they were selling straight spodumene concentrate feedstock. Thus, 114,000 tons sold at $650.00 USD a ton would net them only $72.1 million USD.

Despite the steady production, NAL was in deep financial trouble, owing debtors some $1.1 billion in 2018. This deteriorating financial situation let open the door for battery giant CATL who whaled in and bought 43% of NAL which further diluted shares of IQ to just 5%. Now, the only active lithium mine in all of Canada, and only the second one in North America, was 95% majority owned by Chinese companies.[360] As there were no end use requirements for the spodumene, the mine's offtake was shipped overseas to CATL's midstream conversion facilities and Transamine Holdings and Investments Ltd, a Chinese company headquartered in the Bank of America building in Hong Kong.

While the ore production numbers were promising and CATL had the deepest pockets in the industry, NAL had been accumulating debt since day one of their purchase. In May 2019, in all too familiar story, NAL filed for debtor protection under provisions of the CCAA. Lithium mining stopped earlier in the year, in February.

In 2020, Sayona Mining Limited, an Australian company, bought the Quebec Lithium Mine out of bankruptcy as they tried their hand at beating the curse. They named their Canadian based subsidiary Sayona Quebec Incorporated (SQI). A year later, in 2021, Piedmont Lithium Incorporated, an American company, bought a 19.9% share of parent company Sayona and a 25% ownership of SQI which then became a JV. SQI estimated, in 2022, that they needed to invest $80 million to upgrade the QLM facilities. This was a key part of their business strategy because NAL went bankrupt, in part, because their operations costs were so high. It cost them $1,000.00

---

[358] Sayona Mining Ltd., ASX Announcement, Sep 13, 2021.

[359] www.mining.com, Sayona bids for North American Lithium, Feb 24, 2020, by J. Chen

[360] Yicai Global, "China's Biggest Battery Maker Doubles Down on Canadian Lithium Mine Buy-In", by T. Shihua, Mar 12, 2018.

USD to make one ton of spodumene concentrate, when the market price ranged only $600.00-$700.00 USD a ton. Compare this to Greenbushes mine in Australia who has operating costs below $250.00 USD a ton. SQI needed to get their operating costs per ton way down and they need a conversion facility.[361, 362] Their future success depends on how well the company leadership can develop and execute an intelligent business plan.

Canada's Critical Mineral Strategy Revisited

On November 02, 2022, Canada made a decisive move to secure its national battery minerals supply chain when it directed three Chinese companies to divest of their Canadian lithium operations. One of these companies was Sinomine (Hong Kong) Rare Metals Resources Company Limited, a subsidiary of Sinomine Resource Group (SRG) Limited. SRG is an international mining company with interests globally, to include Canada and the U.S., with their headquarters in Beijing. They are publicly traded with a $5.6 billion USD market cap – from 2020 through 2023, their shares increased from $1.40 USD a share to $12.44 USD a share.

Sinomine was directed to divest of Power Metals Corporation, a Canadian company located in Vancouver. Power Metals is a much smaller company exploring three different hard rock mining projects with potential for cesium, tantalum, and lithium. The Canadian government's directive specifically referred to the Case Lake hard rock project of which its lithium offtake would go to Sinomine. Power Metals is many years away from any of their hard rock mines becoming operational. Sinomine had invested a relatively small amount of only $1.1 million USD, that was a little more than 5% of the company.[363]

Chengze Lithium International Limited, based in Hong Kong, was also directed to divest of Lithium Chile Incorporated. Chengze was only incorporated in the fall of 2021 and is owned by Chengtun Mining Group Company Limited. Chengtun is a much larger international mining business with projects positioned globally and has a

[361] ASX Release, "Piedmont Lithium Announces Strategic Investment In Quebec Hard-Rock Lithium Developer Sayona Mining", Piedmont Lithium, Jan 11, 2021.

[362] https://piedmontlithium.com/projects/quebec-projects/

[363] https://powermetalscorp.com/news/2022/power-metals-provides-comment-on-recent-national-headlines/

$2.6 billion USD market cap. When taking an overall look at their enterprise (copper, tin, tungsten), much of their business is not in the battery minerals space.

Lithium Chile is a small company with headquarters in Calgary that explores for gold, silver, copper, and lithium. They have two brine projects in Chile (Salar de Laguna Blanca, Salar de Coipasa) and one brine project in Argentina (Salar de Arizaro). None of these projects are operational. In 2022, Chengxin Lithium Group bought 29,380,000 shares at $0.95 a share for $27,911,000.00 giving them a 19.86% ownership stake.[364] Chengxin Lithium Group is Chengze's parent company. With considerable irony, Lithium Chile appointed two officers from Chengxin Lithium to their board of directors on the very same day the Canadian government directed them to divest.

Lastly, Zangge Mining Investment (Chengdu) Co. Ltd., was ordered to divest from Ultra Lithium Incorporated. Zangge is headquartered in Qinghai province and focuses on potassium chloride and lithium carbonate and has a $266 million USD market cap. Recently, Zangge had been experiencing 300% and 400% YoY quarterly growth.

Ultra Lithium is headquartered in Vancouver and is pursuing four lithium projects. To start, they are invested in two hard rock lithium projects in Ontario and a lithium brine project in Nevada, none of which are operational. However, the project in question is the Laguna Verde I and II brine operations in Argentina, which also isn't operational. However, in 2022, Zangge bought a 65% stake in the Argentine operations for $50 million.

So, what do we make of this? The Canadian government conducts a national security review with input from its intelligence services and directs three Chinese companies to divest of three small lithium companies. But these three companies aren't operational, make no lithium and don't make a profit and won't for many years to come – if they survive. Additionally, it doesn't look like the Canadian government coordinated their public announcement with the Chinese companies in question, which isn't surprising, but they also didn't tell the Canadian companies either as they expressed their own surprise at the announcements.

The first sanctioned company, Sinomine, had a very small minority stake of only 5% in Power Metals, who can recover from the loss of this small divestment. But how

---

[364] https://lithiumchile.ca/wp-content/uploads/2022/07/April-5-2022-Chengxin-Lithium-Increases-Stake-in-Lithium-Chile-To-19.86.pdf

exactly was a 5% stake in a company that didn't make lithium yet a threat to Canada's national lithium supply chain? We could ask the same of Chengxin and Lithium Chile, although Chengxin had an almost 20% stake at $27.9 million. This raises the question: is the Canadian government going to buy the $27.9 million stake that Chengxin must now divest? Another question is, which won't be answered for several years, could this divestment negatively impact Lithium Chile and contribute materially to their future bankruptcy?

A more complicated situation is the last one, where Zangge bought a majority ownership of Ultra Lithium's Argentine brine operation. At a 65% ownership, this deal most likely gave Zangge offtake rights to most of the future brine processed there, which would go to China to feed their insatiable battery market. Now, who fills the $50 million divestment hole blown in Ultra's financial plan for their projects? The Canadian government? Also, can Ultra finish their project or are they bankruptcy bound? Two days after the Canadian government's announcement, Ultra's stock slid 22% from $0.06 to $0.047 a share.

What could be important is that Lithium Chile and Ultra Lithium's projects aren't in Canada. The lithium that may one day be recovered from the brine is actually Chile's and Argentina's national resources, not Canada's. To start, Canada and Chile have had a free trade agreement since 1997 that was updated in 2017. Annex 1 of the *Canada – Chile Free Trade Agreement*, third section, paragraph 1, cites the need for non-Canadian investors to comply with the *Investment Canada Act* dated 1985. Based on the wording in the annex, it doesn't appear that Chengxin's purchase of a 20% in Lithium Chile stake met that threshold. There is also a section on mining, but it refers to the nuclear energy industry and lithium is mentioned only in that context.[365]

However, the *Investment Canada Act* was amended in October 2022 to specifically address the investment in Canadian critical mineral companies by foreign State-Owned Entities (SOEs). As we mentioned earlier in this chapter, lithium is defined as a critical mineral. Under the Act, Canada will conduct a "Net Benefit Assessment" of an SOE investment in a critical mineral company doing business in lithium. One of the guidelines that could force a divestment is...*the degree of competition that exists in the sector, and the potential for significant concentration of foreign ownership in the sector as a result of the transaction.*

---

[365] http://www.sice.oas.org/Trade/chican_e/chcatoc.asp

As Canada employed its intelligence services to investigate Sinomine, Chengze and Zangge, they determined these three were front companies working to secure lithium for the Chinese government. Using calculations from their Net Benefit Assessment, they assessed that Beijing was using their involvement in Canadian mining companies to unfairly compete in and expand their ownership in the lithium space. However, the directive to divest was largely semantics with no real impact on the overall Chinese lithium enterprise.

For example, let's look at the contradictions offered by the Tantalum Mining Corporation (TMC) in Manitoba, Canada. TMC runs their TANCO mine which extracts tantalum, cesium, and lithium. In 1984, TANCO began mining spodumene concentrate for the ceramics market. From 1984 to 2009, TANCO extracted 1,836,243 tons of ore. As they were running about a 7.1:1 conversion rate, this equaled 258,625 tons of spodumene concentrate and with a 6.3:1 conversion rate, this equaled 41,000 tons of battery-grade lithium carbonate over the course of 25 years.[366]

In 2019, Sinomine bought the TANCO mine outright and owns it 100%. Sinomine then got TANCO's defunct lithium operations up and running, producing spodumene concentrate again in December 2021. Sinomine has already shipped this new flow of concentrate to its sister company in China, Jiangxi Donpeng New Materials. But Canada is okay with this arrangement? They are okay with it because the Canadian government has publicly stated they are and have no divestiture directive for this mining operation.[367]

It appears that the Canadian strategic minerals strategy is being applied inconsistently. How does it make sense that Ottawa directs Sinomine to divest of a 5% holding in Power Metals, but is okay with them owning 100% of TANCO and then shipping their lithium directly to China? This also raises interesting questions if we look back at U.S. and Canada's previous lithium business with the U.S. government. In the mid-1950's, the majority of Foote Mineral, Lithium Corporation of America and American Potash lithium sales went to the Atomic Energy Commission. In fact, 90% of Quebec Lithium Mine production went to U.S. government warehouses for stockpiling. Could

---

[366] TANCO Mine Description, by Tetra Tech, 2013.

[367] Canadian Mining Journal, by N. Karim, April 29, 2022, "Historic Tanco mine in Manitoba producing lithium again – but this time under China's Sinomine.

these companies be considered SOE's and thus be sanctioned in return by other countries like China?

One can argue that, no, of course not, they aren't SOE's, they just had long term classified contracts with the U.S. government to stockpile lithium for its strategic reserve – even though this was most of their business. But then, there is nothing stopping Sinomine, Tianqi Lithium or Ganfeng Lithium from having the same relationship with Beijing. They aren't SOE's, but they can provide Beijing with lithium, for whatever purpose, through any number of mechanisms. Which is why I assess Canada's divestment directive as having no significant impact on the overall Chinese lithium enterprise.

Maybe Ottawa's divestment directive was a bureaucratic driven decision based on internal agency dynamics and not a consistent, coherent policy. Or, it could be a form of strategic messaging, signaling to both the U.S. and China that it takes its joint critical mineral strategy seriously. It is most definitely a form of strategic messaging to Beijing, signaling that Canada will act when necessary to secure its critical minerals. Their divestment directive can also serve to condition Beijing to the idea that there may be future similar decisions, so China should look elsewhere to secure its lithium supply chain.

Canada should be very sober to the reality that Beijing will respond in some way to this divestiture directive in the critical mineral space. Presently, Canada is immune to a tit for tat Chinese divestiture directive as there are no Canadian mining companies operating in China. Also, no Canadian mining companies hold major shares in Chinese companies like Tianqi Lithium and Ganfeng Lithium. Because it has virtually no lithium enterprise of its own at present, Canada suffers no immediate consequences in return. However, in the future, as Canada develops it LIB and associated BEV industries, they may experience a similar response.

In March 2023, Canada's Minister of Natural Resources, Jonathan Wilkinson, stated that he would not direct Chinese companies to divest of three Canadian mining companies. These three companies were Teck Resources, Ivanhoe Mines Limited and First Quantum Metals. Teck Resources' single largest shareholder was the China Investment Corporation with 10% ownership. Teck did not have a battery minerals portfolio although they did have a large copper line of effort. Ivanhoe Mines Limited was owned 26% by CITIC Metal Group which is a Chinese SOE. Ivanhoe is primarily a copper mining enterprise focused on its projects in Africa. And First Quantum

Metals, who is largely a copper mining company, sold an 18% stake to Jiangxi Copper. Wilkinson's decision was based on the need to remove uncertainty from investing in the Canadian mining industry.[368]

Looking Ahead

1. Is Canada's strategy to promote BEV adoption strong enough to incentivize the level of changes needed? What will future incentives look like to get to 100% BEV adoption? How will their national strategy change going forward to ensure their goals are met? What happens when President Trudeau's term expires in 2025 – will a Conservative Party candidate be elected? What will their stance be on Canada's present low carbon policies?

2. How will the *Inflation Reduction Act of 2022* affect Canada? Will the Canadian mining industry have the necessary incentive to promote more associated battery mineral extraction operations like graphite and nickel? Will Canada develop its own independent battery industry or will it continue to support the much larger U.S. industry as it currently does in the automotive space? Will it draw business away from Canada to the U.S. or will it encourage more business both in Canada and North America?

3. What does the reader think of the idea of Canada being the U.S.' battery mine because the permitting process is so burdensome in America? Would this be a good North American division of labor where Canada provides the needed resources and the U.S. provides the technological know-how (through foreign companies positioned on U.S soil, of course) and the consumer market? Is this idea offensive or is it merely practical? For context, some Canadian's themselves think they should mine in the remote north of their own provinces to feed their industrial sectors in the south.

4. How will Canada's critical mineral strategy evolve to protect its battery metals supply chain? Will it get tough on foreign SOEs, or will its talk and action remain out of touch with one another? What will an amended *Investment Canada Act* look like? How will Canada and China's relationship evolve in

---

[368] Rajagopal, Divya. "Exclusive: Canada will not force Chinese state investors to divest stakes in Teck, First Quantum." Reuters, March 08, 2023.

the mining space, especially as it pertains to battery minerals? When might we see Canadian mining companies operate in mainland China? Why or why not? What does China think about North American mining companies buying into domestic Chinese lithium operations in Tibet?

5. The Quebec Lithium Mine was up and running by the end of March 2023. Piedmont Lithium, a partial owner of the mine, already had SC6 offtake agreements with both Tesla (in partnership with Panasonic) and LGES, two of the biggest battery manufacturers in North America. How much spodumene a year will this mine be able to produce? How much will it cost per ton once operations reach peak capacity? Sayona Mining, the JV running the actual mine, has a competitive advantage over other offshore SC6 producers because they are physically located in North America, meaning their product and the batteries subsequently made from it qualify for the *Inflation Reduction Act.*

CHAPTER 10

Mexico and Lithium

"Lithium already belongs to the nation." – Mexican President Obrador referencing the nationalization of lithium deposits in his country

In Search of a Critical Minerals Strategy

Mexico has been criticized as a climate laggard, failing to develop a national climate action plan that would realistically put it on a path to net zero carbon emissions by 2050.[369] While Mexico has taken action to reduce its national carbon emissions, it's not nearly aggressive enough. In 2012, Mexico passed the *General Law on Climate Change* (GLCC), which established the federal structures necessary to pursue a reduction of greenhouse gases by 50% in 2050 as compared to the year 2000. The GLCC is a working document and has been amended several times in attempts to lower Mexico's carbon emissions. Furthermore, the Mexican senate ratified the Paris Agreement in 2016 under the Nieto Administration. But these are largely symbolic measures.

A necessary part of an effective climate action plan is a critical minerals strategy, which the Mexican government has yet to develop. It's not mentioned at all in their GLCC. They have not identified minerals crucial to the Mexican economy and its national security and thus have no methodology to secure them and their associated supply chains. While Mexico has identified lithium as a "strategic mineral", this is more an attempt to capture the value from the current distorted pricing rather than

---

[369] https://climateactiontracker.org/countries/mexico/targets/

a disciplined strategic plan. Until Mexico develops a critical mineral strategy, they will be out of step with U.S. efforts to create a North American critical mineral enterprise requiring Canada's and Mexico's coordination and participation.

Mexico's inadequate carbon emissions reduction efforts go hand in hand with a lack of strategic appreciation for battery minerals. If Mexico is serious about reducing its national emissions, then it would have to be serious about pursuing a LIB economy as well. They go hand in hand. Until the Mexican government can articulate an effective carbon reduction plan tied to a clear national minerals policy, their potential battery minerals value chain will suffer accordingly. In addition to a published strategy, the Mexican government must develop incentives at the federal level that enable them to achieve their policy. The U.S., Canada, the EU and China offer examples to model their own policy on or at least to learn from.

The current state of Mexico's BEV industry reflects its inadequate incentives at the national level to achieve electrification. For example, one incentive is waiving semi-annual emission inspections for BEVs, hardly a motivation for owners of cars that don't have any emissions. While almost 1.1 million light vehicles were sold in Mexico in 2022, only 5,600 were BEVs or about 0.05% of total cars. However, the Mexican car industry manufactured a total of 142,000 BEVs that same year that were mainly shipped out as exports.[370] Furthermore, Mexico has made the strategic error of thinking hybrid vehicles reduce carbon emissions the same as BEVs – they don't. While President Obrador stated 50% of all cars produced by 2030 will be zero emission vehicles (ZEV), their current path doesn't get them there.

With virtually no BEV adoption in the country, it is not surprising that there is an equally anemic BEV charging network. One estimate puts the number of charging stations in Mexico at 1,189 with most stations concentrated in major urban areas like Mexico City.[371] To be sure, there are rural areas in Arizona where I live that don't have Tesla charging stations. However, there are enough to make road trips possible from Tucson to San Diego and from Tucson to Las Vegas, it's not a problem. However, if I were to cross the border at Nogales into Sonora state, the charging options get slim.

---

[370] Edelstein, Stephen. "Why Mexico builds many US-bound EVs but buys few of them". Green Car Congress, March 22, 2023.

[371] Mexico Now, "Auto parts production generates US$52.4 billion in the first half of 2022", Sep 28, 2022.

When I do a search for "Tesla destination charger" on google maps for the state of Sonora, only six locations come up: Nogales, Santa Ana, Playa Hermosa, Hermosilla, Obregon and Alamos. That's it.

Mexico's Lagging BEV Industry

Mexico has a large automotive manufacturing industry, ranked number six in the world, but it is composed almost entirely of foreign companies looking to benefit from Mexico's much lower inherent operational costs. In 2022, 13 different auto manufacturers produced 3.3 million vehicles of all types.[372] Of these, 2.65 million were light trucks, meaning pickup trucks or SUVs – 80% of the total. Presently, Ford, GM and Rivian make low-production runs of BEV pickup trucks in the U.S., but none in Mexico. For electric SUVs in North America, only Tesla makes their Model X in their Freemont factory. Several Chinese companies make electric SUVs as well, but not in Mexico.[373]

The only Chinese company in Mexico, JAC (Anhui Jianghua Automotive Group), has had a factory in Mexico City since 2018. JAC is a contract manufacturer that makes both its own line of ICE and BEV cars as well as models for other companies. Case in point, JAC produces Nio's line of BEVs that include both passenger vehicles and SUVs. In 2021, JAC produced 134,118 BEVs of all types, including contract vehicles.[374] In 2022, JAC made a very modest 17,704 vehicles in their Mexico City plant – none of them were BEVs.[375] And to highlight the absurd inefficiency of the global supply chain, JAC imported its first batch of 225 electric SUVs to Mexico in June 2022.[376]

On the topic of passenger vehicles, 658,001 total were produced in Mexico in 2022.[377] By far the largest producer of BEVs in Mexico is Ford who manufactures their

---

[372] https://www.trade.gov/country-commercial-guides/mexico-automotive-industry

[373] https://www.marklines.com/en/statistics/flash_prod/automotive-production-in-mexico-by-month-2022

[374] CNEVPOST, By P. Zhang, "JAC posts 18,126 EV sales in June, up 27% from May", Jul 7, 2022.

[375] https://www.marklines.com/en/statistics/flash_prod/automotive-production-in-mexico-by-month-2022

[376] Princewell, Hillary. "JAC Exports 225 Units Of The E-JS4 EV SUV To Mexico". Cr news China, June 18, 2022.

[377] https://www.marklines.com/en/statistics/flash_prod/automotive-production-in-mexico-by-month-2022

Mach-E BEV at its Cuautitlan plant. In 2022, Ford manufactured 77,959 Mach-E's in Mexico.[378] However, here we see more global supply chain insanity since Ford buys the batteries for the Mach-E from LG Energy Solution. LGES makes these batteries in their Wroclaw, Poland plant, which are then shipped overseas to North America to be paired with the Mach-E. There are no other BEV passenger sedans of any significant volumes manufactured in Mexico. The ongoing global transition to BEVs has largely passed Mexico by.

While Mexico manufactures a significant number of automobiles, they are largely for export to North America, not for domestic consumption. Of all the vehicles manufactured in 2022, 86% were exported, including 71% of passenger vehicles, and 90% of all light trucks. The manufacturers did the math and saw that it was still cheaper to make their vehicles in Mexico, put them on the back of long-haul trucks and then drive them thousands of miles to dealers in the U.S.

All these foreign automakers are in Mexico due to low labor wages for the workers who assemble their cars. As of 2021, the average wage for Mexican assembly line workers was $2.60 USD an hour.[379] Compare this to the average wage of a Detroit United Auto Worker union employee pulling in $22.46 an hour.[380] This means a manufacturer with 1,000 employees working in a Detroit plant has an annual payroll of $47 million USD. This same company in Mexico has an annual payroll of just $5.64 million USD. Over ten years, that payrolls balloon to $470 million USD in the U.S. compared to just $56 million USD south of the border. That is why auto companies are in Mexico.

Mexico has some homegrown BEV companies, but they are microscopic with no industry impact. Probably the biggest name is Zacua, a local company manufacturing mini-EVs with a 100-mile range and a $30,000 USD price tag. This is a two-door micro-car that would appeal only to urbanites on a tight budget. Zacua opened their only manufacturing plant in 2018 and sold 100 cars by mid-2022. Since they make them in-house and by hand, they can make about ten a month. If BEV production to scale is

[378] **Ford Motor Company, 2022 Production & Sales Press Release**

[379] Market Prospects, "The Labor Cost Advantage of the Mexican Manufacturing Industry", Jun 04, 2021.

[380] https://www.ziprecruiter.com/Salaries/UAW-Salary-in-Detroit,MI

going to take place in Mexico in the near future, it won't be from their own domestic production.[381]

Since labor costs are so low, there is real opportunity to expand the BEV industry in Mexico because most OEMs (Original Equipment Manufacturers, i.e. traditional automakers) can't make BEVs at a profit in the U.S. For example, Ford loses money on every Mach-E it makes just like GM loses money on every eHummer it makes. Mexico's low-cost environment might be the only way North American OEMs (not including Tesla) have a chance at being profitable in the BEV game. That is precisely why Ford manufactures its Mach-E in Mexico.

In support of this idea, GM is building their new Chevy Equinox BEV at their Ramos Arzipe manufacturing plant, located in the southeastern part of the state of Coahuila. Coahuila borders Texas. The most direct route from the plant to the U.S. is straight up Route 85 to the port of Nuevo Laredo – about a 180-mile trip. However, this plant was built in 1981 and runs outdated ICE manufacturing lines. One of the reasons Tesla runs the highest profit margins in the world with its BEV lines is that they have the most modern, efficient manufacturing plants in the industry.

In preparation of the Equinox BEV's planned roll-out in late 2023, GM committed $1 billion USD to upgrade their antiquated facility. In 2022, they shut the plant down for six weeks while they configured it for BEV production.[382] For GM to compete with Tesla's ultra-modern gigaplants, they need high levels of automation, the latest equipment and a revamped mentality that simplifies the production process. The most important part in a highly efficient manufacturing process is the one never made. Tesla kills their competition, in part, because of the degree that they relentlessly simplify their manufacturing process.

In a sign that a larger BEV enterprise may finally take hold in the country, LG Magna e-Powertrain began construction in 2022 of a new 260,000 square foot BEV components manufacturing facility in Ramos Arzipe as well.[383] Their business model is making critical BEV powertrain components like electric motors for GM's revamped plant next door. The company is a joint venture between LG Electronics and

---

[381] Dialogo Chino, by A. Cuellar, "Meet Zacua, Mexico's first electric car brand", Jun 8, 2022.

[382] GM Authority, by J. Lopez, "LG Magna e-Powertrain To Provide GM With EV Components In Mexico", Apr 19, 2022.

[383] Ibid.

well-known contract auto manufacturer Magna International (they have been hired by Fisker to make their European BEVs). GM and LG Magna make a powerful team being two companies with deep pockets, but they are missing one central component – batteries.

GM says they will equip the Equinox BEVs with their proprietary Ultium Cells battery platform, a joint venture between South Korean LG Energy Solution and GM. Three Ultium battery plants are already under construction in Ohio, Tennessee, and Michigan. But what does that have to do with making BEV's in Mexico? One can assume GM will make the Equinox batteries in Tennessee and then ship them down to Mexico, creating obvious supply chain inefficiencies. And where will these Ultium plants get their lithium supply? From SQM in Chile, whom LG Energy Solution already signed a binding eight-year offtake agreement with in 2020. That adds another couple of thousand miles to their supply chain. If GM can't turn a profit on their Mexican BEVs, we can see why.

As the LG Magna JV reveals, Mexico has a very large and well- developed automotive parts industry, producing some $94 billion USD in parts a year.[384] This makes them the fourth largest automotive parts manufacturer in the world. There is a real opportunity for the overall BEV value chain if the Mexican parts enterprise can evolve to support the growing BEV industry. As foreign OEMs build out their BEV efforts in the country, like Ford and GM, the Mexican parts supply chain will increasingly adapt to fill their needs. In fact, we already see this occurring with Tesla.

Tesla's gigafactory in Austin is the largest U.S. BEV manufacturing plant closest to the border with Mexico. It is only 240 miles from their gigafactory to the major border port at Nuevo Laredo. This puts them in the best position to benefit from Mexico's auto parts enterprise. Already, Tesla has deals with several auto parts companies positioned in the border state of Nuevo Leon.

Although Nuevo Leon has only a short nine-mile border with Texas, just north of Nuevo Laredo, the state provided Tesla with its own access lane across their border into Texas. Whenever trucks with auto parts destined for Tesla's Austin gigafactory reach the border, they pull over to the second-most left lane which is dedicated for them. The overhead lane sign simply says "TESLA". This ensures they have no wait time, although the border crossing there in general isn't that busy. What this does show, is

---

[384] https://www.trade.gov/country-commercial-guides/mexico-automotive-industry

Tesla's political muscle in Nuevo Leon and the State's extra effort to do business with Tesla's growing BEV enterprise. It's good for business.

Tesla developed such a good relationship with the state of Nuevo Leon that they announced in March 2023 their plans to build Gigafactory Mexico outside the capital of Monterrey. This $5 billion USD factory would eventually employ 7,000 local workers to build Tesla's new $25,000.00 USD BEV. For Tesla to get costs down low enough for the project, they needed to improve their manufacturing processes and supply chains. Importantly, they also needed workers who only make $2.60 an hour. [385]

Mexico's Battery Industry

Because Mexico never developed a BEV industry, and the two factories being built are still in their very early stages, they never built a battery industry either. As we have seen with both Ford and GM, they prefer to build their cars in Mexico and import their batteries from afar. With the Austin gigafactory example, Tesla built a battery factory on-site to reduce supply chain inefficiencies. They preferred to make their batteries right next to their cars, no need to import them from across the border. However, there is potential for this to change, although it is complicated.

China's leading battery company, CATL (Contemporary Amperage Technology Limited) has been considering building a battery plant in Mexico for quite some time, with plans getting more definitive in 2022. The idea was to supply batteries for Ford's Mach-E, GM's Equinox, Tesla's Model Y across the border and other models that might by developed in the future. While CATL planned to build the batteries in Mexico, they had no workable plan to source the necessary battery minerals locally. Most likely, they would take spodumene concentrate sourced from Australia, transfer it to their conversion facilities in China and then ship the refined lithium carbonate/hydroxide across the Pacific Ocean to the west coast of Mexico. Another far flung supply chain prone to disruption.

Then, the Biden Administration passed *the Inflation Reduction Act of 2022 (IRA)* that required BEVs and their batteries sold in the U.S. to be majority sourced from North America. If the BEVs and their batteries didn't meet these sourcing requirements, they didn't qualify for the $7,500.00 USD in tax credits. Hence, the IRA blew

[385] Lambert, Fred. "Tesla Gigafactory Mexico, more details are coming in." Elektrek, March 06, 2023.

up CATL's plans because their battery minerals shipped in from Australia, China and Africa didn't meet the published requirements. This meant that every battery manufacturer that did source its material from North America had a significant competitive advantage over CATL. Their business model in Mexico was rendered untenable overnight.

What the IRA meant was that to be competitive in the U.S. car market and take advantage of cheap Mexican labor, then a company had to source its battery minerals from Mexico and/or somewhere else in North America. Consequently, a company like CATL had to secure offtake agreements with domestic mining companies instead of shipping them in from across the world. Depending on the battery chemistry used in the BEV, this meant securing lithium, nickel, cobalt, manganese, and graphite. But could Mexico provide these resources?

Nationalization of Lithium

Litio para Mexico (LitioMx) was stood up as Mexico's national lithium mining company on August 23, 2022, after several years of political debate. The Mexican Congress voted to change their national mining law on April 20, 2022, paving the way for the creation of a national lithium body. Lithium was now considered a strategic mineral, a national resource that would be extracted and sold by the Mexican government and not by private parties like foreign mining companies. Part of the mission of LitioMx was to: "Promote sustainable use of lithium for the energy transition, for the benefit of the population in general." LitioMx was further directed to begin managing the Mexican national lithium value chain no later than January 30, 2023.[386]

Also, it was clear that Mexico's nationalization of lithium violated the *U.S.-Mexico-Canada-Mexico Act (USMCA)* of 2020. Specifically, it violated *Chapter 14, Article 14.4: National Treatment, Article 14.5: Most-Favored-Nation Treatment, Article 14.6: Minimum Standard of Treatment and Article 14.8: Expropriation and Compensation.* Overall, these articles ensured fair business treatment between all signatories of which nationalization of the lithium mining industry violated. This meant Mexico mining companies could extract lithium from Canada and the U.S., but in return Canadian and American companies were shut out from the Mexican lithium industry.

---

[386] By A. Paras, Formation of the Decentralized Public Entity "Litio para México", Sep 22, 2022, https://www.ccn-law.com

However, this debate served to illustrate the weakness in the USCMA in that it did not address a North American critical mineral strategy at all. We are left to refer to Chapter 14 from an investment perspective and Chapter 22, *State-Owned Enterprises (SOEs) and Designated Monopolies*, because the signatories didn't write a chapter on critical minerals. If the signatories want to address the development and trade of critical battery minerals across country boundaries in the USCMA, then they need to re-negotiate the topic and insert a new chapter or an annex. This would serve to remove confusion and uncertainty by putting all players on the same page conceptually and diplomatically. This also implies each signatory has thought through and developed a national critical minerals strategy, but Mexico hasn't.

Beyond the issues raised by the USCMA, Mexico had another problem: it didn't have a state mining company experienced in lithium extraction. Until lithium prices went through the roof in 2021, Mexico showed little interest in the lithium industry. Now they were trying to play catch-up. Another reason Mexico nationalized lithium was pre-emptive, to stop the rush of foreign companies coming in to extract lithium. Mexico would have to either grant exceptions to existing lithium operations or compensate foreign companies for the loss of their lithium exploration efforts, future profits and associated sunk costs. The sooner they shut off uncontrolled foreign exploration, the less they would have to pay out.

A challenge LitioMx faced was that Mexico had only one proven lithium deposit in the country. That was the Sonora Lithium Project (SLP), which was owned by Chinese lithium giant Ganfeng. Buying the mine back from Ganfeng would cost the Mexican government $400 million USD at least. And that's if Ganfeng agreed to the buyback and didn't take them to court and run the price up even higher. Also, the SLP was located near the very remote town of Bacadehauchi, meaning initial operating costs from infrastructure development would be high.

And to add to the list of hurdles for LitioMx, the SLP is a clay deposit. There are only two major lithium clay deposits in the world under development: Thacker Pass and SLP. Importantly, there is no proven economic way at scale to separate lithium from the clay. That's why every major successful operation is either hard rock or brine. LitioMx's own assessment of the SLP calculated that extracting lithium from the clay would run $4,000.00 USD a ton.[387]

---

[387] Mexico Business News, By Z. Mares, "Bacadehuachi Lithium Deposit Is Economically Feasible: LitioMx", Nov 11, 2022.

Compare this to Albemarle's Greenbushes hard rock mine in Australia running at only $250.00 USD a ton. The most surprising thing wasn't that Mexico nationalized lithium, but that LitioMx concluded that SLP was still a viable operation at that cost. They could only reach this conclusion if they had been following Pilbara's spodumene concentrate auctions where they achieved $6,000.00 USD a ton in May 2022 on the China market. (See *Chapter 14: Pricing Lithium*) This may be feasible with current sky-high lithium prices, but when supply meets demand sometime in the future, $4,000.00 USD a ton in operating costs equals bankruptcy.

I don't think LitioMx can make the SLP work anytime soon, and they know that. This is why they left an escape clause in the nationalization decree stating LitoMx could: "Manage and control the necessary activities for the production, transformation and distribution of lithium derivative products for which it may associate with other public and private parties." This sounds like they have the space to cut a deal with Ganfeng, who has the expertise to make the SLP viable.

After months of discussions, Mexico "evolved" its definition of nationalization to mean existing foreign lithium mining projects could continue their operations. However, for new operations, a foreign company would have to partner with LitioMx. With this relationship, LitioMx would be the senior partner and own 51% of the operation while the foreign partner would only own 49%. Furthermore, only Canadian, American, or Mexican private mining companies could partner with LitioMx. This policy opened the door for foreign investment, encouraged a North American approach to lithium extraction and enabled Mexico to have the final say on how their lithium was used. Also, the language probably satisfies the USMCA.[388]

Mexico is still very much conceptually working out its nationalization of lithium. A 51/49 JV model is a common one in the industry as we saw with the Tianqi/Albemarle deal with their Greenbushes mine in Australia. It allows companies to split risk and expenses. However, there is an advantage to a wholly owned mine as a company doesn't have to negotiate over offtake deals or the strategic direction of the operation. For example, President Obrador stated that lithium mined in Sonora would be used only in batteries made in Sonora and used in BEVs driven in the state of Sonora. That makes no sense as there are no BEV or battery plants in Sonora and there are no plans for

[388] Mexico News Daily, "US, Canadian companies can mine Mexico's lithium' but as minority partners: AMLO", Nov 16,2022.

any. I assume Obrador's statements are just political platitudes because no company is going to sign up for an unworkable plan such as that.

Time will tell if Mexico's 51/49 plan is effective in bringing in enough private mining investments to move the industry forward. If it isn't, they may have to modify their policy. For example, they could allow 100% foreign ownership of an operation but charge them royalties on the tonnage extracted. Or they could mandate a percentage of offtake agreements with battery and BEV manufacturers located in Mexico. Another option is having mining companies partner with local universities to pursue battery chemistry R&D (a form of a JV to show partnering). The point is, Mexico might have to take a flexible approach to bring in the necessary investment while still maintaining a sense of national control.

Mexico's Battery Minerals

Mexico has no historic or current lithium mining operations although there are several potential ones being pursued. Let's discuss the most prominent project, the Sonora Lithium Project (SLP), a wholly owned operation by Ganfeng International Trade (Shanghai) Company, Limited. Ganfeng bought the mine from Bacanora Minerals Limited, headquartered in Calgary, in December 2021 for $391 million USD.[389] Sonora is in northwestern Mexico and borders Arizona and New Mexico. The closest U.S. port is that of Nogales on the border with Arizona. Bacanora is a small rural town located in central-eastern Sonora, although the proposed mine is a considerable distance north of the town.

The SLP is being developed for open pit hard rock extraction in an area with lithium clay deposits. As is common in the hard rock mining industry, the SLP has been under development for more than a decade already, beginning in 2010. Bacanora planned to build a battery-grade lithium carbonate conversion facility onsite with a production capacity of 17,500 tons per annum. Upon completion of this first facility, Bacanora envisioned a second stage facility with another 17,500 LCE tpa capacity for a total capacity of 35,000 LCE tpa.[390]

---

[389] Mining.com, by C. Jamasmie, "Bacanora Lithium accepts Ganfeng's $391 million takeover offer", Aug 27, 2001

[390] By Ausenco Engineering Canada Inc, "Sonora Lithium Project PFS Technical Report", April 2016.

The mining plan of operation forecasts a 20-year production life. If we do backwards math on the project, 35,000 tpa of LCE requires 220,500 tpa of spodumene concentrate feedstock, using a 6.3:1 conversion factor. As we move upstream and use a 7:1 conversion factor from ore to concentrate, Ganfeng will have to mine 1,543,500 tpa of ore to reach their second stage 35,000 tpa LCE goal. Over a period of 20 years, that's 30.9 million tons of ore mined, converted into 4.4 million tons of spodumene concentrate, which is further converted into 700,000 tons of LCE. While we don't know what LCE prices will look like in the future, if they average $40,000.00 USD a ton over the 20 years, that's $28 billion USD of revenue. For Ganfeng, that is a respectable return on their $391 million USD buy-out of Bacanora.

But let's throw some reality onto this potentially rosy outlook. The SLP might be production ready in 2025 if all milestones are reached and everything goes according to plan. But we could just as easily see this timeline slipping several years to 2030, depending on how the lithium nationalization issue proceeds with the Mexican government. Regardless of potential hurdles, Ganfeng has the deep financial resources to absorb ongoing operational costs and the strategic patience to see this project across the finish line. If I had to make a bet on who has the overall ability to pull this off, I would bet on Ganfeng.

When this project does get off the ground, a future Mexican CATL battery plant would be an obvious choice for an LCE offtake agreement. Additionally, Tesla already has offtake agreements with Ganfeng, so we can assume battery grade LCE would be trucked through the port of Nogales and onto Austin. Importantly, because this lithium is sourced from Mexico, Ganfeng could sell their LCE product to any BEV or battery manufacturer in North America and the final sale would qualify for the $7,500.00 USD tax credit in the U.S.

Let's talk graphite, the key material for the negative terminal anode for a BEV's battery. Presently, graphite, both natural and synthetic, is the dominant anode resource and there is no indication that this will change any time soon. Mexico has a modest yet established graphite mining industry, producing some 1,900 metric tons of natural flake graphite in 2022, down from its recent height of 9,160 tons in 2014.[391] [392] Regardless, this is more than what the U.S. produced in 2022, which was zero.

---

[391] https://www.statista.com/statistics/751264/mexico-graphite-production/

[392] USGS, Mineral Commodity Summaries (Graphite), January 2023.

The U.S. doesn't have a graphite industry while Canada produced just 15,000 tons of natural flake graphite in 2022.[393] The U.S. imports 100% of its graphite needs.

This creates problems for the U.S. BEV market since they have an intrinsically insecure graphite supply chain. This also creates problems with the *Inflation Reduction Act* battery minerals sourcing requirements since North America accounted for only 1.3% of global graphite production in 2022. In contrast, China produced 65% of world graphite in 2022.[394] Most likely, the graphite used in batteries of BEVs driving on American roads today is sourced from China. However, in this preposterous supply chain reality there could be a real opportunity for Mexico to be a major graphite player in the North American battery market.

Many graphite mines in Mexico closed over the last ten years as the industry dwindled. Sonora, where Ganfeng's lithium project is located, used to have three active graphite mines that have since closed. Natural flake graphite prices hit $2,500.00 USD a ton in 2012, which drove Mexico's production highs and then prices dropped to $750.00 USD a ton by 2017, that coincided with the shutting down of many now unprofitable graphite operations.[395] In the summer of 2022, large flake graphite hit almost $1,200.00 USD a ton and spherical graphite rose to $3,200.00 USD a ton.[396] Now, as demand for graphite outstrips supply, it is profitable again. Mexico can capitalize on this global surge if they want to be a player in the battery minerals game.

The lithium-nickel-manganese-cobalt (NMC) battery is a chemistry used commonly today by battery and BEV manufacturers to include Tesla. However, just as the U.S. produced not an ounce of graphite in 2022, they also produced no manganese. Canada also produces no manganese. As the sole producer of manganese in North America, this can be another opportunity for Mexico as they produced an estimated 230,000 tons in 2022.[397] Minera Autlan owns and operates their Molango Mine, which produces manganese mainly for the steel industry. The mine is in Hidalgo State, located just north of Mexico City.

---

[393] Ibid.

[394] Ibid.

[395] Seeking Alpha, "Graphite Miners News For The Month Of July 2020", Jul 28, 2020.

[396] Proactive, by E. Jarvie, "Gratomic highlights graphite price increases as demand continues to outstrip supply amid electric vehicle market boom", Jun 23, 2022.

[397] USGS, by E. Schnebele, Manganese Mineral Commodity Summaries, January 2023.

Autlan already produces battery grade manganese dioxide. Their N60 battery grade product has a 65% manganese dioxide content and high oxygen content with peroxidation of at least 93%.[398] Their product is exceptionally dry with a maximum moisture content of 2.5%. Over the last decade, manganese prices have been relatively flat and a metric ton sold for about $4.00 USD in the China market in late 2022. At the same time, battery grade electrolytic manganese dioxide sold at about $1,500.00 USD a metric ton in the China market. Of interest to Autlan, battery grade lithium manganese oxide sold at a much higher price of $21,800.00 USD in the China market in late 2022.

Autlan established its own independent Electrolytic Manganese Dioxide (EMD) division in Spain in 2020. In 2021, they produced 11,150 tons of EMD which they sold to the European market. Their main customers were to alkaline battery manufacturers to include Panasonic Energy (Belgium and Poland) and Varta. Their EMD effort is still very small, perhaps just 5% of total extraction operations, as compared to the rest of Autlan, which is centered squarely on the ferroalloy industry. Autlan is not yet a player in the BEV battery field, but they could be if they were incentivized to do so.[399]

Mexico doesn't mine any cobalt or nickel, but the U.S. and Canada does. This means Mexico won't be able to make their own domestic sourced NMC batteries, but that also might not matter. BEV manufacturers are looking to diversify and get away from the expensive nickel and cobalt content batteries and move towards less expensive lithium manganese oxide (LMO) batteries. As we have seen, manganese provides cheap feedstock and is relatively plentiful. To be clear, LMO batteries still require R&D as they suffer from energy density and lifecycle issues (i.e. Nissan LEAF battery), but manganese is already used to complement and stabilize the cathodes in a variety of battery chemistries.

Like any industry, Mexico can choose to be a leader in the LMO realm and aggressively fill the growing manganese space or be a reactive bit-player who continues to miss most of the value chain. This requires national leadership and vision and associated industry incentives to make the Mexican manganese industry both attractive and competitive. This would also take increased R&D efforts and partnerships with established BEV and battery manufacturers. This means Mexico must be forward

---

[398] https://www.autlan.com.mx/en/business-units/autlan-manganese/manganese-derivatives/
[399] Autlan Annual Report and Audited Financial Statements 2021

looking and identify growing trends based on market intelligence to get out ahead of it. To date, they haven't.

The Cartel Inflation Problem

You don't have to watch *Sicario* to know that Mexico suffers from a widespread drug cartel problem that borders on an insurgency, depending on the state in question. The drug cartel infrastructure has created its own shadow government that is stronger in some states than others, but the associated corruption permeates to national level politics and institutions as well. From 2006, when the Mexican government declared war on the cartels, through 2022, the country suffered more than 360,000 homicides. Additionally, 79,000 people have gone missing who, over time, are presumed dead if no hostage payment is requested. Presently, cartel related deaths average around 30,000 a year.[400]

This cartel-centric violence serves as its own form of country-wide inflation, driving up costs through higher security requirements, paying for "protection", kidnap and ransom (K&R) insurance, hostage payouts and the loss of human capital. The mining industry is also exposed to this cartel inflation. Remote mining operations located in states with a heavy cartel presence are more vulnerable to their influence. If the cartels can clandestinely smuggle thousands of tons of illegal drugs into the U.S., it stands to reason they can smuggle other bulk material as well.

This is exactly what the Knights Templar cartel did from about 2010-2014. The Knights Templar cartel, located in the southwestern state of Michoacan, decided to expand into the mining business. Specifically, they illegally exported iron ore to China; exactly how much is not known. However, in 2014, Mexican authorities seized 119,000 tons of ore on a ship destined to China along with mining equipment like conveyors and crushers. The cartel initially built their China connections through methamphetamine chemicals dealings and later found other uses for their criminal supply chain.[401]

Could this happen elsewhere or was this a unique example? Remember, Mexico's largest proposed lithium project and three cold storage graphite operations all reside

---

[400] Council on Foreign Relations, "Mexico's Long War: Drugs, Crime, and the Cartels", Sep 7, 2022.

[401] Investing News, by T. Matich, "On Iron Ore and Drug Lords: Mexico's Continued Battle With the Knights Templar", May 12, 2014.

in Sonora State, an area where the Sinaloa Cartel operates. If the Knights Templar Cartel can smuggle 119,000 tons of iron ore, couldn't the Sinaloa cartel smuggle a 10,000-ton shipment of lithium carbonate? At $80,000.00 USD a ton, the shipment would be worth $800 million USD. That's worth the risk for a cartel that has many tools of the trade to get the job done: corruption, bribery, document forgery, extortion, inside help, hijacking, hostage taking, etc....

There has been enough criminal activity directed toward Sonoran mining operations that Mexico created the Mining Police in 2020. The first graduating class of 118 officers was assigned to Sonora but the Federal Protection Service envisioned a national force.[402] This initial force couldn't secure all mining in Sonora, but it was a start. It also served as an example of cartel inflation and the associated rising security costs.

However, the owners of the Sonoran Lithium Project seemed to miss this reality. We know this because Bacanora's 261-page feasibility study published in 2018 doesn't mention the need for enhanced security measures. In Mexico, a purely technical study doesn't capture all the dynamics required for a mine to be successful. The cost of mining security must be taken into account and averaged into the operating costs. This includes physical security at the mine itself, transportation security of the extracted product and security of the workforce. If a mine has low profit margins, this additional expense could push them over the line into negative returns.

Some mining companies might not think operating in cartel country is worth the operational risk and will look elsewhere for a more stable environment. We've seen this in Afghanistan already where the country's estimated trillion-dollar mineral deposits remain untouched. Also, BEV and battery manufacturers may look elsewhere for their offtake agreements. No reputable company wants to buy lithium from a mine that pays protection money to a drug cartel. Imagine the headlines: *Tesla Supports Drug Cartel's Lithium Habit.* It's not worth the reputational risk when other options are available. (Authors note: The Sinaloa cartel has already applied the Tesla brand to some if its cocaine to classify its quality as a product. In the past, cartels have also used the Toyota, Lexus, and Nissan car brands to identify their product different products.)[403]

---

[402] Canadian Mining Journal, "Mexico Steps up Security", Dec 1, 2020.

[403] Mexicanist, "Why does the seized cocaine have Prada and Tesla logos?", Jul 28, 2022.

Looking Ahead

1. To date, Mexico has not made a serious effort to identify and capture the lithium value chain in their country. Mexico is just now grappling with the idea of a critical mineral strategy and only in reaction to U.S. prompting. The nationalization of lithium illustrates their growing awareness. But when will we see a published, comprehensive, national strategy that recognizes the importance of battery minerals for the health of their national economy?

2. Mexico has some strong components going for it like a well-developed auto and associated parts industry, low labor rates, established battery mineral mining operations and the huge U.S. car market next door. What incentives does Mexico need to adopt to develop its own BEV industry and accelerate domestic BEV adoption? Canada and U.S. have examples they can follow.

3. When will the Mexican leadership develop a vision for their own domestic battery industry? They have the lithium (potentially), manganese and graphite to develop a robust industry based on LMO chemistry. The longer they wait, the more the miss out. Why are they focused on the alkaline battery industry but not the LIB industry, is the mainly the result of supply chain and relationship dependencies?

4. While Mexico is not a formal member of China's Belt and Road Initiative, it may not matter as trade between the two countries recently reached $100 billion USD annually.[404] Will we see growing cooperation between China and Mexico in the BEV, battery and critical minerals space? Is Mexico the entry point for Chinese companies to penetrate the North American market? Will China provide the technology, intellectual capital, funding and vision that Mexico has lacked to date?

5. What will be the future impact of Tesla's Gigafactory Mexico? Tesla intends for the factory to produce its $25,000.00 BEV at scale, perhaps in volumes never seen before. How much of a magnet will Gigafactory Mexico be to the BEV supply chain? How much can Tesla change the overall BEV environment in Mexico? Will Tesla build a battery factory on site which demands local onshore battery mineral extraction?

---

[404] "Mexico-China trade reaches record $100 billion in 2021." Fundacion Andres Bello, February 15, 2022.

A North American critical mineral strategy means all required battery minerals will only come from this continent. This is all they have to work with. This means increased lithium production in Canada, the U.S., and Mexico. All three need to increase graphite production as well; Mexico would have to open their presently closed graphite flake operations. Mexico also has ongoing manganese operations, but isn't currently focused on the lithium-ion battery industry; they need effective incentives to shift their efforts. Canada does produce low volumes of cobalt, but the U.S. should move away from NCM battery chemistries and enforce a substitution regime. LFP (Lithium-Iron-Phosphate) batteries probably make the most sense for North America. *(by NASA)*

An aerial photo of the Vale Inco nickel mine in Manitoba Canada. 58% of all Canadian nickel production comes from this mine as does 17% of all copper. In 2022, Vale signed a contract with GM to provide the equivalent of 25,000 tons of battery grade nickel sulfate. *(by Getty Images)*.

The electric Ford Mustang Mach-E is built at the Ford plant in Cuautitlan, Mexico. The models built here are shipped to the North American market. Ford claims they will achieve a 270,000 worldwide run rate for its Mach-Es by the end of 2023. Ford will begin outfitting its North American Mach-Es with LFP batteries made by CATL in 2023. Mach-Es are not sold in Mexico and the batteries for them are not made in Mexico. Mexico has missed out on most of the value chain. *(by Vauxford)*

CHAPTER 11

China: Feeding the Beast

"The joint pursuit of the Belt and Road Initiative (BRI) aims to enhance connectivity and practical cooperation. It is about jointly meeting various challenges and risks confronting mankind and delivering win-win outcomes and common development." – President Xi Jinping, The Second Belt and Road Forum, 2019

China's Belt and Road Initiative

What has shaped China's critical minerals strategy the most over the last decade is their ambitious Belt and Road Initiative (BRI), also called the New Silk Road. The BRI was launched by President Xi Jinping in 2013 with the overarching goal to better connect China with the rest of the world. This connection took the form of infrastructure projects built inside and outside China with a multitude of willing partners. Inside China, Beijing develops its own roads, airports, railways, bridges, ports, shipping routes and communications to better connect with the outside world. Outside China, Beijing lends its partnering nations large sums of money at reasonable rates to develop their own infrastructure.

By increasing its physical connections with the world, China increases its two-way flow of trade. Part of this trade is transferring critical minerals (like battery metals) and raw materials to China while exporting finished Chinese products like BEVs and batteries. To be sure, this trade and the loans provided by China creates economic dependencies, giving China influence over their BRI partners' behaviors. More importantly, the increased flow of goods helps grow China's economy which is crucial for providing legitimacy to the Chinese Communist Party.

Ultimately, the BRI is a national strategy to increase the power of the Chinese state. A growing GDP facilitated by enhanced economic cooperation enables China to improve its overall technological sophistication as a society. This, combined with a much larger budget, enables China to upgrade and expand its armed forces which remains the largest military in the world. If we look at China with the DIME model (Diplomatic, Information, Military, Economy) of assessing national power, the BRI addresses every pillar. Without question, the BRI is the most significant political initiative taken by any country this century.

The BRI advances through seven major axes or "economic corridors" in Beijing-speak. The primary goal is connecting China with the Eurasian landmass through multiple parallel efforts. To start, the New Eurasian Land Bridge emanates from western China through Russia and into Europe. This enhances China's access to Russia's many mineral resources that include nickel, graphite, cobalt, and copper. Russia does have domestic lithium resources that they historically accessed when developing their hydrogen bomb program in the 1950's. However, just as with the U.S., Russia found it cheaper to import lithium from abroad like the Lithium Triangle.

Second, there is the China-Mongolia-Russia economic corridor that runs further north and parallel, crossing through much of Kazakhstan. While not a major player, Mongolia has lithium brine resources that companies are now just getting serious about. Russia did some joint explorations in the same geographic area in the 1950's, which I suspect was to support their nuclear weapons program. Similarly, Kazakhstan is believed to have modest lithium resources and the government is beginning to explore them, both independently and jointly with foreign companies.

Next, there is the China-Indochina Peninsula economic corridor running south to Malaysia and Singapore. Since they share a common border, Vietnam offers easy access to nickel, manganese, copper, iron, phosphate, and graphite. Cambodia is different as their lack of geological survey undermines large-scale mining, but companies are pursuing copper and iron deposits there. Next door, Laos offers copper, iron, and silicon. Thailand is not a player in the battery game, but they do have a small manganese industry. In contrast, Malaysia has a well-developed manganese industry and a small iron sector. They also have a very interesting, undeveloped nickel phytomining sector. Finally, Indonesia, another BRI partner, is one of the largest nickel producers in the world with a large copper industry and much smaller manganese and cobalt operations.

In a rather modest effort, the Trans-Himalayan Network will connect China to Nepal and thus India. Nepal has an underdeveloped mining industry and suffers from a lack of comprehensive geological survey. However, mineral exploration has revealed deposits of nickel, cobalt, lithium, copper, iron, and graphite. One would expect mining operations there to be as challenging as nearby Tibet due to high elevation, rough terrain, severe weather, and the lack of fundamental infrastructure. Mining operations would most likely have to receive extensive government backing to make them economic.

The fifth effort is the China-Pakistan economic corridor which connects western China to the port city of Karachi on the Arabian Sea. This puts Chinese goods much closer to the Suez Canal, one of the world's strategic global shipping passages. To start, Pakistan does not have much of a battery mineral industry, producing only small amounts of copper and graphite. Curiously, local government has tried to get Tesla to build one of their giga factories there. This economic corridor does provide improved connectivity with neighboring Afghanistan who reportedly sits on a "trillion-dollar" mineral industry to include lithium. However, Afghanistan's mining industry is underdeveloped to say the least, suffering from a lack of skilled labor, poor infrastructure, and 40 years of continuous war. To sweeten the pot, the Taliban government is enmeshed with a score of extremist and terrorist movements. Good luck doing business there.

A sixth line of effort is the China-Central Asia-West Asia economic corridor cutting through the Caucuses, Iran, Iraq, Turkey and ending in central Europe. This corridor impacts 24 different countries. In one example, Turkey has mature copper and iron mining sectors and already exports these commodities to China. The central connecting mechanism of this corridor is the China-Europe Railway Express which departs western China three days a week. A train with a full container load (FCL) hits Germany in just 12 days. If one wondered how battery mineral tonnage and finished EV battery products at scale reach Europe, search no further. [405]

A final economic line of effort is the 21st Century Maritime Silk Road that connects China's ports to Southeast Asia, India, the Mediterranean, Latin America, the continent of Africa, the Arctic and everywhere else. Africa is a major focus of Chinese mineral extraction efforts and 52 out of 54 African countries have signed

---

[405] www.chinaeuroperailwayexpress.com

agreements with China as part of the BRI. China already extracts large amounts of cobalt from a Chinese wholly owned subsidiary in the DRC, who is a BRI member. Also, Zimbabwe, formerly Rhodesia, has historic lithium deposits and used to be a prominent exporter in the 1960's. Zimbabwe is a BRI member and Chinese mining company Huayou already has bought into a lithium operation there. These are just a very few examples of the many ongoing and developing mining relationships that China cultivates.

Understanding China's lines of economic penetration helps us grasp the enormity of the BRI and its impact. By 2022, 147 countries had signed a Memorandum of Understanding (MoU) with China detailing their respective relationships under the BRI.[406] From a global perspective, Africa, the Middle East, Asia (all of it) and central/eastern Europe were the most heavily penetrated regions by the BRI. Accordingly, two-thirds of our Earth's population and 40% of global GDP is impacted in some way by ongoing Beijing-orchestrated infrastructure projects and related investments.[407] By 2021, China had $2.6 trillion USD tied up in Foreign Direct Investments equaling 6% of the world's total.[408]

From a national critical minerals strategy perspective, China has systematically laid out the political, economic, and interconnecting infrastructure foundations to secure its mineral needs. The seven economic corridors reaching into multiple regions creates redundant operational lines of effort. This ensures that the potential disruption of a single line of economic penetration – or even several – won't shut off the needed flow of minerals, metals, and raw materials. The Belt and Road Initiative's far-reaching influence explains why, as we examine the global lithium industry, the hand of China is everywhere.

China's Lithium Enterprise

China has constructed a lithium devouring beast in a relatively short period of time, beginning around the year 2010. This beast consists of their combined BEV and battery

[406] https://greenfdc.org/countries-of-the-belt-and-road-initiative-bri/

[407] Council on Foreign Relations, by J. McBride et. al., "China's Massive Belt and Road Initiative", Feb 2, 2023.

[408] Congressional Research Service, by K. Sutter et. al., "China's "One Belt, One Road" Initiative: Economic Issues", Dec 22, 2022.

industries that depend on one another for continuing growth. China has the largest BEV fleet in the world which only accelerates faster every year. The same can be said of their battery industry that has to keep the same fierce pace. While Chinese BEV manufacturers are intent on putting millions of asses in zero-emission car seats, Chinese battery companies are equally focused on putting their products in these same cars. None of this can happen without a steady supply of lithium.

Consequently, the Chinese lithium enterprise must grind hard every day to keep the lithium coming in while they simultaneously look for new sources of the powdery white metal. Part of the enterprise consists of Chinese owned lithium mining companies who specialize in the industry. We will take a closer look at two of these in this chapter who are among the biggest in the world by production tonnage as well as market cap. But even they can't secure all the lithium required to feed the beast. Thus, individual Chinese BEV and battery manufacturers reach out to foreign suppliers across the world, like Australia and the Lithium Triangle, to secure long-term lithium contracts.

It is commonly assessed that 65% of the global lithium supply passes through China either for processing, domestic consumption, or resale. This number is regularly thrown about to illustrate China's dominance of the lithium sector and it's not wrong. But it's also a double-edged sword because China imports almost all its lithium needs and must rely on the cooperation of foreign countries to keep its battery mineral supply chains flowing. As we know, the BRI is a mechanism designed to ensure this cooperation and it has been effective in doing so to date. However, China would have improved lithium security if it didn't rely on such an import-heavy model and developed its own domestic lithium industry.

The U.S. Geological Survey estimates that approximately 89 million tons of lithium have been identified worldwide with known reserves of 22 million tons. Of this, China holds 1.5 million tons of lithium reserves. Considering that USGS believes 689,000 tons of LCE was extracted worldwide in 2022, China could easily satisfy its own domestic consumption for the next 20 years. So why don't they? There are several reasons.[409]

While China has significant domestic lithium resources, they have been cursed by its location. To start, most China's total domestic lithium resources are in brine,

___
[409] U.S. Geological Survey, Mineral Commodity Summaries (Lithium), January 2023.

as opposed to hard rock, or some 80%. Of these brine reserves, 78% are in just two provinces: Qinghai and Tibet. Thus, by definition, these deposits are remote, at elevation and in harsh environments. From a hard rock perspective, China's largest active lithium mine is also located in a remote area, at high elevation and exposed to harsh weather conditions. Unfortunately, other discovered hard rock deposits are equally remote or even worse. Once you look at a map, one realizes there is nothing convenient nor economic as to where China's lithium deposits are located.[410]

To start, Ganzizhou Rongda Lithium Company Limited owns and operates the Jiajika lithium mine, an open pit hard rock operation located in the mountains of Sichuan Province. The mine has a relatively low lithia ore grade of 1.2%. While the mine has been operating since at least 2009, it has been closed for significant periods of time because it is an environmental train wreck. For example, toxic spillage from the mine polluted the nearby Liqi River in 2009, killing most of its fish and hundreds of yaks who drink from the river. Additionally, there were reports of local Tibetan residents who drank the water subsequently dying of cancer. Repeated toxic spills forced the government to shut the mine down at different periods from 2013 through 2019.[411]

Furthermore, Chinese efforts at the Jiajika mine have faced persistent local Tibetan popular resistance, not just because of its deadly toxic pollution, but because residents see the mining industry as an affront to their religious beliefs. They believe that God is in the mountains and surrounding land and mining activity destroys this spiritual being. Consequently, local villagers and farmers refuse to support local mining even if they were to receive profit sharing and the mining company returned the land to its natural state after the mine was exhausted. Unsurprisingly, people living in the surrounding area have participated in local protests against the mine, resulting in the mobilization of Chinese soldiers to disperse them.[412]

Beyond these significant issues, the location of the Jiajika mine raises its operating

---

[410] Shanghai Metals Market, "Decryption of China's four major salt lakes, five major refining technical routes! Everything about lithium extraction from the salt lake is here!", Nov 30, 2018.

[411] Santa Fe New Mexican, by S. Denyer, "Chinese mines pollute sacred Tibetan lands", Dec 26, 2016.

[412] Ibid.

costs. It's located at high altitude in the mountains in a remote location. The environment is harsh with cold dry weather and freezing temperatures in the winter, which takes its toll on exposed equipment. The extracted lithium concentrate must then be trucked from the mine along winding roads more than 150 miles to Chengdu. Like many mines, living conditions there are very basic and working there is like being deployed to a warzone firebase.

Youngy Company Limited, Rongda Lithium's parent company, made a move in 2020 to vertically integrate and regionalize its lithium efforts. To do so, they invested $200 million USD in Sichuan Province towards the construction of a lithium processing plant. Youngy agreed with the local government to process at least one million tons of lithium spodumene annually from their Jiajika mine or they would incur penalties. If Youngy and its Jiajika mine can't produce the agreed upon volume, then they would pay fines in taxes and fees to the government to make up the difference. While this is a win-win situation for the local government, it puts Youngy under the gun. [413]

Is this volume production possible? After the Jiajika mine reopened in 2019, some estimated that it would produce 30,000 tons of lithium concentrate that same year and 80,000 tons in 2020.[414] These estimates proved to be overly optimistic as subsequent reporting indicated the mine produced just 40,900 tons of lithium concentrate in 2021.[415] At a 6.3:1 conversion ratio that puts production just shy of 6,500 tons of LCE. I suspect ramping up production will be a slow grind as Jiajika's equipment sat exposed to the elements for the better part of six years. COVID disrupted operations across the global mining industry for most of 2020 and supply chain disruptions ravaged 2021. Accordingly, Youngy's future conversion plant and Jiajika's theoretical max production rate most likely won't come online until 2025 or later.

What about Tianqi's Cuola (also "cuo la") lithium mine? This mine is in Yajiang County near the Jiajika mine in Sichuan with all the same considerations and challenges. Cuola has a 10,000 tpa capacity (presumably lithium concentrate) although

---

[413] Reuters, China's Youngy to build lithium plant as part of $200 million investment in Sichuan", Jan 2, 2020.

[414] Reuters, "China's Ganzizhou Rongda Lithium restarts spodumene mine after five years", June 13, 2019.

[415] Mining Technology, by Carmen, "World's ten largest lithium mines in 2021", June 3, 2022.

there have been discussions of bringing it to a 50,000 tpa capacity.[416] However, the mine has intentionally been idled by Tianqi for several years and was not active as of 2022. This speaks to the challenges we have already identified that Tianqi Lithium, the largest producer of finished lithium products in China, with its headquarters in Chengdu, the capital of Sichuan, doesn't produce an ounce of lithium from what is, essentially, their own back yard.

In 2022, a research team from the Chinese Academy of Sciences (CAS) discovered a new lithium deposit estimated at one million tons. This must be a tremendous windfall and the breakthrough the Chinese lithium world has been waiting for, right? Not so fast. The deposit is located…wait for it…on Qiongjiagang Peak, on a plateau near Mount Everest. The deposit is at the extreme elevation of 5,500 meters or almost 3.5 miles above sea level. I am going to leverage my uncanny expertise on the subject and make the assessment that the costs associated with such an extraction effort in the Himalayan Mountains will never be economic. It's an interesting yet worthless discovery for China's overall lithium enterprise.[417]

We have a general idea about the state of China's hard rock lithium operations, but what is the production capacity of their lithium brine industry? To start, Zhabuye Lithium High Tech Company Limited runs a lithium extraction operation on Zhabuye Lake. The salt lake is just one of hundreds of similar high-altitude land-locked lakes scattered across the lunar landscape of Tibet. It is almost a 1,200-mile direct line distance from the lake to Chengdu. One would be hard pressed to find a more remote, inhospitable, inaccessible location on our planet.

Zhabuye Lithium, a private company founded in 1999, holds exclusive 20-year mining rights at the lake. They are a wholly owned subsidiary of the Tibet Mineral Development Company. They run their extraction operations using traditional solar evaporation ponds, like the operations in the Lithium Triangle. In 2008, Zhabuye Lithium produced some 1,500 tons of LCE. (Authors note: I don't have updated production numbers for the reader as this is the last data I could find from the original source, Highbeam Research, which is now defunct.)

---

[416] Daiwa Capital Markets, "Tianqi Lithium – A", Aug 10, 2020.

[417] Energy Trend, "Himalayan Surprise: Chinese Scientists Find Enormous Lithium Deposit", Feb 17, 2022.

In 2010, Chinese car and battery manufacturer BYD bought an 18% stake in Zhabuye for $30 million USD as they sought to secure their long-term lithium supply chain.[418] Historically, Zhabuye Lithium ran at a loss and it's not hard to imagine why based on its location. One suspects that their production still hovers around 1,500 tpa of LCE although they are reported to have a 5,000 tpa capacity. Until just recently, BYD probably did not see much of a return on their investment. However, if Zhabuye was able to sell their 1,500 tons of LCE at the sky-high rates of 2022, then they are probably in the black. After all, 1,500 tons of LCE sold at an average of $70,000.00 USD would net them $105 million USD for the year.

Qinghai Salt Lake Industry (QSLI) runs a much larger brine extraction operation at Qarhan (or Chaerhan) Lake positioned in Qinghai Province on the Tibetan Plateau. Qarhan, too, is in a remote inhospitable location that is 660 miles direct line distance from Chengdu. Qarhan is an ancient, mostly dried up salt lake covering more than 2,200 square miles of lunar landscape. The lake receives only 1-2 inches of rain a year, meaning it will never truly be a lake again with those rates of precipitation. However, there is much more established extraction activity at Qarhan as opposed the relatively small footprint at Zhabuye. There is a veritable Mos Eisley of an industrial town adjacent to the lake for all the workers from the various chemical, cement, salt and shipping companies located there.

QSLI is a publicly traded, state-owned company listed on the Shenzhen Stock Exchange as 000792.SZ with a $20 billion USD market cap. In 2017, it began making moves to set up lithium extraction operations in Qarhan. By the summer of 2021, QSLI had dropped $483 million USD on the project and was conducting trial operations with the aim of producing 10,000 tpa of industrial grade (i.e., not battery grade) LCE.[419] By June 2022, their Qarhan LCE plant became fully operational, moving past the trial phase and producing 100 tons of LCE a day as they ramped up to a projected 20,000 tpa.[420]

Of interest, QSLI's lithium brine extraction operation in Qarhan has been conducted as a Joint Venture (JV) from the start with Chinese car manufacturer BYD.

---

[418] China Daily, "BYD to buy into Tibet lithium producer", Sep 17, 2010.

[419] Global Times, "China largest lithium extraction project enters trial operation", Aug 17, 2021.

[420] Yicai Global, by T. Shihua, "China's Qinghai Salt Lake Jumps as New Lithium Carbonate Factory Comes Online", June 28, 2022.

QSLI and BYD inked the deal in 2016 with QSLI being the senior partner with 52% ownership and BYD with 48% ownership. At the time, they envisioned the brine extraction operation coming online in 2019 with a production capacity of 30,000 tpa LCE. They were several years off from their calculations which is common in the industry when building such complex projects in remote locations. One assumes their expenses have overrun their own expectations by $100 million USD for every year past schedule. However, both QSLI and BYD have deep pockets and can weather these challenges. [421]

There are far more projects underway than just these as China's national lithium enterprise tries to expand its domestic footprint and achieve improved critical mineral security. For example, Qinghai Dongtai Jinai'er Lithium Resources has a brine extraction operation at Qinghai Dongtai Jinai'er Salt Lake that they use to produce their own lithium end-products. When asked how much it would cost to develop a 10,000 tpa lithium brine operation, they estimated it would cost a mere $88 million USD. Perhaps this is the cost just to add on another 10,000 tpa to their existing operations because, as we saw, QSLI's operation cost them at least $500 million USD to get to that capacity. Regardless, many companies are willing to overcome the financial barrier to entry if lithium prices remain extraordinarily high in line with demand that won't be trending downwards for several decades at least.[422]

Lithium, Human Rights, and the Uyghur Problem

Xinjiang, officially the Xinjiang Uyghur Autonomous Region (XUAR), is China's most northwestern province. It is China's largest province, covering some 620,000 square miles, but is sparsely populated with only 25.8 million inhabitants. XUAR is landlocked, bordering Mongolia, Russia, Kazakhstan, Kyrgyzstan, Tajikistan, Afghanistan, Pakistan, and India. A central geographic feature is the inhospitable Taklamakan Desert that encompasses some 130,000 square miles. XUAR, along with Kashmir, is home to K2, the second highest mountain on Earth. Also, the legendary Silk Road, connecting Asia with Europe, crossed through XUAR two millennia ago. Today, XUAR is the province in which several of Beijing's BIR economic corridors emanate from.

---

[421] China Daily, "BYD joins lithium mining in west China's Salt Lake", June 23, 2016.

[422] SMM, "Exclusive: SMM's lithium battery team Qinghai field trip—Dongtai Jinai'er Lithium Resources", July 25, 2021.

XUAR is a melting pot of many different ethnicities, religions, identities, and cultures. According to China's Seventh National Population Census taken in 2020, the Uyghur people were the largest ethnicity at close to 45%. Uyghurs have their own identity, speak their own language and are predominately Muslim. The Han are the second largest ethnicity in Xinjiang at 42%, who speak Mandarin and practice Confucian, Tao, Buddhist, and Christian religions. The Han are the largest ethnicity in the world, comprising 18% of the global population. In Xinjiang, of course, there are problems.[423]

For the last decade, the PRC (People's Republic of China) have been scrutinized and criticized for its alleged human rights abuses involving the XUAR. Specifically, since 2014, Beijing has been identified as repressing the Uyghurs (and Kazakhs) as they crack down on what the PRC has characterized as Muslim religious extremists, separatists, and terrorists. Based on the description of PRC government actions, one can only conclude that Beijing has implemented a widespread counterinsurgency campaign in Xinjiang. The PRC believes that this "Hard Strike" campaign has been largely successful as there hasn't been a successful terrorist attack since 2016. However, these far-reaching and vaguely defined counterinsurgency measures continue.[424]

The Office of the UN High Commissioner for Human Rights (OHCHR) published a 48-page report in 2022 detailing PRC repressive measures in Xinjiang. Alleged abuses from many independent sources include: extensive pre-trial detention without judicial review; mandated sentences in "Vocational Educational & Training Centers (VETC)" for offenders; expanded rate of incarcerations in established prisons based on discriminatory and criminalized religious factors; physical beatings with batons, torture through electric shocks & stress positions, water boarding, solitary confinement; rape of women, sexual humiliation; suppression of religion and invasive electronic surveillance.[425]

Furthermore, there are allegations that Beijing implemented a widespread involuntary labor program employing Muslim offenders who were forced to attend VETCs.

---

[423] Chinese Consulate, "Main Data of Xinjiang Uygur Autonomous Region from the Seventh National Population Census", June 16, 2021.

[424] "OHCHR Assessment of human rights concerns in the Xinjiang Uyghur Autonomous Region, People's Republic of China", Aug 31, 2022.

[425] Ibid.

This was in tandem with a government sponsored "surplus labor" program, training rural unemployed Xinjiang farmers to become skilled industrial workers. This program began in 2017 and is alleged to be part of the PRC's anti-extremism campaign directed against Muslim minorities, specifically Uyghurs. The OHCHR has determined these work programs to be coercive in nature.[426]

The U.S. government agreed with the evidence leading up to the UN's findings and, consequently, President Biden signed the *Uyghur Forced Labor Prevention Act (UFLPA)* in 2021. The UFLPA strengthened the existing *Tariff Act of 1930* that outlawed the importation of goods made by forced labor. Specifically, the UFLPA prohibits the importation of any "goods mined, produced, or manufactured" by forced labor from the XUAR. This applies to battery metals like lithium and nickel and any downstream product that uses them such as EV batteries.

The U.S.' Forced Labor Enforcement Task Force was directed to establish the means to determine the origin of goods and create transparency of third-party supply chains that might originate in XUAR. Customs and Border Patrol were instructed to develop processes to aid in the identification of supply chains originating in the XUAR. Furthermore, the U.S. would work with its neighbors to ensure the existing *U.S.-Canada-Mexico Agreement* would prohibit the entrance of any forced labor products into North America.

The act specifically identifies the possible use of forced labor by the PRC involving Uyghurs, Tibetans, Kazakhs, Kyrgyz, and other persecuted minorities. The Act calls out any labor scheme as described in the UN report like "pairing assistance" and "poverty alleviation" as falling under its prohibitive authority. The language in the act is broad enough to encompass any and every labor program involving minorities that are considered by the U.S. to be coercive in nature.

From a larger market perspective, the topic of Chinese forced labor isn't just a North American issue, it's a European issue too. The EU already prohibits the importation of certain "conflict minerals" which have been mined in warzones and are the product of human exploitation and suffering. The EU's *Conflict Mineral Regulation*, in force since January 2021, outlaws the importation of tin, tantalum, tungsten and gold which have been produced via forced labor. Furthermore, in 2022, the EU Commission

---

[426] Ibid.

proposed the banning of all goods into the EU that have benefited from forced labor, regardless of the company, industry, or country.

So why are we talking about this? In 2022, it became public that Ganfeng Lithium, one of the largest Chinese lithium companies, was in discussions with the Xianjing government to develop battery minerals extraction operations in the province. While there weren't any productive lithium operations in the XUAR as of 2023, there may be in the future, depending on the results of ongoing geological survey. As we just discussed, there are an estimated one million ethnic minorities working in coercive labor programs as part of their "cultural re-education" in Xinjiang. Looking ahead, some of these forced laborers are likely to end up working on Ganfeng's extraction operations.[427]

To date, Ganfeng has announced battery mineral agreements with Tesla, BMW, and Volkswagen, all of whom sell BEVs in the North American market. In the future, how does the U.S. know that forced labor wasn't used in making the batteries for these vehicles? The U.S. doesn't know as there is no established battery mineral supply chain tracking process. Ganfeng, and any other Chinese mining company for that matter, can tell its customers whatever it wants, and they won't know any different. One suspects Ganfeng will never voluntarily and publicly recognize if and when it benefits from forced labor in its extraction operations. Afterall, Beijing denies that it uses forced labor at all despite the continuing evidence that they do.

Importantly, how would the U.S. ever know a Chinese lithium company used forced labor besides learning this through open-source reporting? What if a lithium company says a certain lot of batteries was sourced from a specific mine that met U.S. labor standards...how does one prove that? One could take a mineral sample of the lithium concentrate and conduct forensic analysis of it to determine its original location.[428] But who is going to do this? Is the U.S. going to fly in teams of forensic mineral analysts to all the Chinese mining and processing sites to enforce this regime? Is Beijing going to acquiesce to this infringement of their sovereignty? Are Chinese

---

[427] Los Angeles Times, by D. Stringer, A. Lee, "Plan to extract lithium from Xinjiang raises forced-labor questions for EV industry", July 22, 2022.

[428] International Union of Geological Sciences, by D. Pirrie, et. al., "Predictive geolocation: forensic soil analysis for provenance determination", March 4, 2017.

mining companies going to forward these samples to the U.S. to prove origination out of compliance? How could the U.S. even confirm the chain of custody?

The world has already seen this battery mineral chain of custody problem play out with the use of child labor in artisanal cobalt mines in the DRC (Democratic Republic of Congo). Responsible battery manufacturers don't want to use cobalt mined from child labor for ethical and reputational reasons. Other companies don't mind, like Chinese miner Huayou Cobalt, who owns Congo Dongfang International Mining (CDM). In the DRC, local children mine cobalt by hand and then their family members sell this to CDM. CDM in turn ships this overseas to Huayou in China. Huayou then sells the cobalt to various LIB manufacturers who ship their products worldwide. Although Amnesty International clearly illuminated the child labor supply chain providing Huayou with cobalt, the company denied any knowledge of unethical practices. Did we think they would admit it even though the entire process was captured on video?[429]

With these deceptive tactics in mind, can't a Chinese mining company simply "launder" its original lithium concentrate, that could be geolocated through forensic analysis, by running it through the midstream conversion process and producing untraceable battery-grade lithium hydroxide? Once this lithium feedstock is converted and distributed through long term and spot contracts across China, the genie is out of the bottle and there is no getting it back in. After the co-mingling of forced labor and "ethical" lithium takes place, how can one prove its place of origination?

As another option, if the U.S. wanted to enforce an ethical lithium labor regime, they could do so through satellite tracking and imaging. The U.S. would essentially have to use its satellite fleet (or contract it out to SpaceX?) to geolocate and conduct mineral origination intelligence on the Chinese lithium industry to determine its supply chain flow. Lithium delivery trucks, trains and ships can be identified, followed, and counted. The downloading and transfer of bags of lithium can be observed and recorded. Any mining operation, conversion plant or battery factory that touches forced labor would then be assessed as "contaminated" according to the UFLPA and prohibited for importation. Is the U.S. going to use its limited satellite resources to do this?

---

[429] Amnesty International, "This is what we die for: Child labour in the DRC cobalt mines", Jan 19, 2016.

I think the reader can rightfully ask, aren't we getting ahead of ourselves here? Afterall, we are merely talking about a hypothetical future problem based on reporting that the XUAR and Ganfeng Lithium are looking to possibly do business somewhere down the road. Actually, the problem is already here. In 2020, the Xinjiang Nonferrous Metal Industry Group (XNMIG) posted pictures of Uyghurs working for them under a suspected forced labor program. XNMIG is an SOE (State Owned Enterprise) mining company that already has contracts for copper, nickel, manganese, and lithium in XUAR – most everything a company needs to produce EV batteries. [430]

Publicly available records show that XNIMG has already shipped its minerals into U.S. and European markets. Also, XNIMG supplies its battery metals to a variety of Chinese EV battery manufacturers, effectively laundering them, who in turn ship their end products into the U.S. and the EU. Theoretically, these shipments should be easily stopped because enforcement of the UFLPA by U.S. agencies began in June 2022. Their interdiction of prohibited goods is assisted by a UFLPA Entity List of known Chinese companies employing forced labor.[431] However, the rather short list, there are only ten companies on it, identified only one mining company, Xinjiang East Hope Nonferrous Metals Co. Ltd. They denied that they engaged in any forced labor program.[432]

As we think about how the UFLPA program might be improved, let's close this section out by leaving some questions for the reader to digest. How does the UFLPA work with U.S. mining companies doing business inside China? As we know, both Albemarle and Livent own midstream conversion operations in China. What are their requirements to ensure originating lithium feedstock doesn't have a nexus with forced labor programs? More importantly, is an American owned lithium operation in China, which was previously bought from a Chinese company, with Chinese employees, going to conduct due diligence reference a human rights problem that Beijing denies even exists? Also, what are the domestic and international economic and political implications of banning large volumes of Chinese originating EV batteries?

---

[430] New York Times, by A. Swanson, C. Buckley, "Red Flags for Forced Labor Found in China's Car Battery Supply Chain", June 20, 2022.

[431] https://www.dhs.gov/uflpa-entity-list

[432] Tianshan Net, "A Solemn Statement from Xinjiang East Hope Nonferrous Metals Co., Ltd. against Unjustifiable Sanctions by the United States", Jul 15, 2021.

As we can see, China has domestic lithium extraction challenges in both the hard rock and brine domains. This is mainly because these deposits are in remote locations, suffering from harsh terrain and severe weather conditions that contribute to tortuous supply chains. The continuing allegations of forced labor abuses doesn't help either. Consequently, the cost of doing business inside China is sufficiently high that it made more economic sense to seek lithium resources externally. Additionally, China needs far more lithium for its BEV and battery industries than is currently available internally, regardless of the costs. Both dynamics pushed China to pursue overseas supply chains which have been aided considerably by the overarching Belt and Road Initiative. BRI wasn't set in motion specifically for the Chinese mining industry, but it was certainly a consideration. Accordingly, in this next part, we will look at the international lithium acquisition efforts of China's two leading lithium companies, Tianqi and Ganfeng.

Tianqi Lithium Corporation

Tianqi Lithium Corporation was founded in 1992 and has its headquarters in Chengdu, Sichuan Province. Tianqi is listed both on the Shenzhen Stock Exchange (SHE: 002466. SZ) and the Hong Kong Stock Exchange (HKG: 9696). They have a market cap of $19.9 billion USD. Of note, Chengdu is an automotive hub, both Toyota and Volkswagen have manufacturing plants there. Chinese battery giant CATL has a manufacturing plant there as well. As Sichuan is a north central province, being in Chengdu puts Tianqi closer to domestic hard rock and brine extraction operations located in Tibet, Qinghai, and Sichuan itself.

Let's look at Tianqi's business model which is heavily focused heavily on midstream conversion to feed the domestic Chinese battery industry. To start, Tianqi runs a full spectrum lithium production plant in Shehong, Sichuan that's been open since 1995. This gives an indication as to how long they have been in the industry for. The plant has a 24,200 tpa capacity capable of producing lithium hydroxide, lithium chloride, lithium carbonate and lithium metal. This plant provides Tianqi a great deal of flexible lithium capability.[433]

In Anju, also in Sichuan, they have another midstream conversion facility with a 20,000 tpa battery-grade LCE capacity. Then, they run an additional midstream

[433] http://en.tianqilithium.com

conversion plant with a 20,000 tpa capacity in Zhangjiagang, Jiangsu, which is a northeastern province. This fully automated facility puts their end-product closer to both the South Korean and Japanese battery markets. Tianqi are part owners of the Kwinana, Australia midstream conversion plant with an overall capacity of 24,000 tpa of LCE, but they can only claim 6,000 tpa of its production.

Finally, in Chongqing, they have an R&D facility that produces a modest 600 tpa of lithium metals.[434]

Adding up all these midstream conversion plant capacities comes out to 70,200 tpa of total production. This is 10% of global LCE production based on USGS' estimate of 689,000 tons of LCE produced worldwide in 2022. If Tianqi sold all 70,200 tons of LCE at an average of $80,000.00 USD, that comes out to the tidy little sum of $5.6 billion USD. If they sell all 600 tons of lithium metal at an average of $420,000.00 USD per ton, add another $252 million USD to their bottom line.

In 2012, Tianqi moved beyond just converting hard rock lithium concentrate and secured its own upstream feedstock source by buying Talison Lithium, who owns and operates the Greenbushes mine in Australia. For a mere $127 million, Tianqi now owned the largest hard rock lithium extraction operation in the world for essentially pocket change.[435] Through this vertical integration, Tianqi could now feed its midstream conversion machine a never-ending supply of lithium concentrate at costs it controlled. But they had problems from the start.

Tianqi had cash flow problems and the global lithium market remained soft – the absolute demand crush for lithium was still ten years away. Consequently, they sold 49% of their Talison holdings in 2014 to Rockwood Holdings for $475 million, more than three times their initial purchase price.[436] Six years later, Tianqi sold another 49% of their remaining shares to Australian company IGO for $1.4 billion that also included 49% of their share in the Kwinana midstream conversion plant.[437] Once again, their reach exceeded their grasp, and they didn't have the strategic patience to hold their

---

[434] Ibid.

[435] PR Newswire, "Chengdu Tianqi agrees to acquire Talison Lithium", Dec 6, 2012.

[436] Businesswire, "Rockwood Completes the Acquisition of 49% Interest in Talison Lithium", May 28, 2014.

[437] Mining.com, by C. Jamasmie, "Tianqi Lithium sells 49% of Australian unit to IGO in $1.4bn deal", Dec 8, 2020.

positions. Tianqi had retrograded from owning the biggest hard rock lithium operation in the world to giving 74% of it away. Although they sold this three-quarters position for thirty times what they originally paid for it, Tianqi weakened their strategic lithium position.

Next, Tianqi targeted and acquired the Zhangjiagang conversion plant in 2015. The plant is in Jiangsu Province and produces battery quality 99.5% pure lithium carbonate with a capacity of 20,000 tpa. Tianqi bought the conversion plant from Australian company Galaxy Resources who originally designed it with a 17,000 tpa capacity. (Galaxy Resources later merged with Orocobre to become Allkem in 2021.) Before the Zhangjiagang plant even came online in 2012, Galaxy had sold 100% of its output in 3-year offtake agreements. 5,000 tons were committed to Mitsubishi Corporation (Japan) and the remaining 12,000 tons were sold to 13 different Chinese cathode manufacturers.[438]

This conversion plant is in the Jiangsu Province Zhangjiagang Economic and Technological Development Zone (ZETDZ). The ZETDZ is an export-oriented enterprise supported by government incentives to draw in increasing economic activity for the benefit of the province. Several government entities at the national and provincial level are involved in advancing the ZETDZ including the Overseas Chinese Affairs Office of the State Council, the Jiangsu Development and Reform Commission and the Department of Foreign Trade and Economic Cooperation. ZETDZ has many ongoing projects like the Zhangjiagang Science & Technology Park, Zhangjiagang Robot Industrial Park, Zhangjiagang Modern Equipment Manufacturing Industrial Park, and the Zhangjiagang International Business Park.

In a very aggressive move that sent shockwaves through the lithium industry, Tianqi purchased 24% of Chilean-based SQM in December 2018 for a whopping $4.1 billion USD. This meant one of the largest midstream lithium conversion powers now owned almost a quarter of the largest lithium brine operation in the world. Importantly, the purchase gave Tianqi the holdings to place three of its own directors on the SQM board. From a strategic perspective, this move diversified Tianqi's holdings geographically, gaining it a foothold in the Western hemisphere. As Chile did not, and does not, have any laws nationalizing lithium like Mexico and Bolivia, there were no concerns from that perspective. But there were monopoly fears.

---

[438] Galaxy Resources Limited, company report.

These were voiced by the state agency CORFO (Production Development Corporation of Chile) whom SQM leases their land from in the Salar de Atacama. CORFO filed a lawsuit through Chilean anti-trust regulators in an attempt to block the Tianqi purchase. The complaint alleged that Tianqi's purchase of such a large block of SQM shares would unite two companies that together would control 70% of the global lithium market. CORFO further maintained that the SQM sale would enable China "to gravely distort market competition".[439]

The Chilean anti-trust regulator FNE (Fiscalia Nacional Economica) conducted an investigation and determined that Tianqi's purchase could indeed result in anti-competitive effects in the lithium market. In response to these findings, Tianqi agreed to legally binding measures to ensure competitiveness in the global lithium space. These measures included prohibitions on Tianqi access to SQM commercially sensitive information, Tianqi employees could not serve on the SQM board of directors, Tianqi and its directors would not take actions that are detrimental to SQM and Tianqi would notify FNE prior to any agreements in the lithium market with either SQM or Albemarle.[440]

We can better understand the outcome of the Tianqi-SQM deal if we know more about the unusually close relations between Chile and China going back a half-century. They began after the election of dedicated Marxist Salvador Allende to the presidency in 1970. Soon after, in 1971, Chile became the first country in South America to recognize the total sovereignty of Peking over Chinese territory.[441] After Allende's death, China still maintained diplomatic relations with Chile during the dictatorship of General Pinochet (1973-1990). More recently, Chile and China signed a Free Trade Agreement in 2005 and then both signed a Memorandum of Agreement in 2018 under the Belt and Road Initiative. By 2021, China was the largest foreign investor in Chile with $8 billion USD spent on various projects.[442]

Let's close out this piece on Tianqi with the unintended consequences of its

---

[439] Reuters, "Chile files complaint to block sale of SQM shares to Chinese companies", March 9, 2018.

[440] Fiscalia Nacional Economica, "TDLC aprueba Acuerdo Extrajudicial entre la FNE y Tianqi sobre la compra del 24% de la propiedad de SQM", April 10, 2018.

[441] New York Times, "Communist China Recognized by Chile", Jan 5, 1971.

[442] Borgen Magazine, "China's Belt and Road Initiative in Chile", Sep 6, 2022.

massive purchase of SQM shares. While CORFO and others recognized the pervasive-ness of China in the global lithium space, the SQM deal served to roll back Tianqi's overall lithium holdings. Because the deal cost so much, and lithium prices remained soft, Tianqi found itself in financial dire straits and confronting possible bankruptcy. Consequently, it sold almost half of its shares in its Greenbushes mine project to IGO (as mentioned) to raise much needed cash. This outcome wasn't surprising to close observers of the industry who have noted Tianqi to be aggressive to the point of reck-less. But this seems to be their corporate personality. When a company's aggressive moves work out, they are "forward looking" and when they don't, they are "reckless". It reminds me of the Aikido proverb, explaining that their art is like a piece of paper: on one side there is life, on the other side there is death. It can be a fine line to walk.

Ganfeng Lithium Company

Ganfeng was founded in 2000 with its headquarters in Xinyu, Jiangji, a southeast-ern landlocked province. Ganfeng trades on the Shenzhen Stock Exchange (002460. SZ), the Hong Kong Stock Exchange (1772.HK) and the New York Stock Exchange (OTCMKTS:GNENF) with a $22 billion USD market cap. Ganfeng is a diversified lith-ium products manufacturing company pursuing several lines of effort to include: bat-tery recycling, EV battery & BESS manufacturing, lithium mining and the production of lithium salt, lithium metal, lithium chloride, LCE and lithium hydroxide. Ganfeng Is well-balanced company with vertical integration up and down the lithium value chain.

Ganfeng is heavily invested in the midstream conversion space and, by their es-timates, they produced 28% of the world's lithium hydroxide in 2021. Their Ma Hong conversion plant in Xinyu City, Jiangxi Province was built in 2012 with a Phase I capac-ity of 11,000 tpa of lithium hydroxide, a Phase II capacity of 20,000 tpa and a Phase III capacity of 50,000 tpa for a total of 81,000 tpa of capacity. The factory is multi-functional, also producing 15,000 tpa of LCE and 12,000 tpa of lithium chloride. If Ganfeng can sell all 81,000 tons of lithium hydroxide at the current ridiculously high prices of $80,000 USD per ton, that equals revenues of $6.48 billion USD. That's some nice cheddar.

Ganfeng is also invested in the LCE midstream conversion flow as well, but much less so. As we saw above, they have a 15,000 tpa capacity at Ma Hong, where they obvi-ously have prioritized their lithium hydroxide line of effort. Additionally, Ganfeng runs a larger lithium carbonate midstream conversion plant in Ningdu, Jiangxi Province which came online in 2018, reaching a capacity of 20,000 tpa LCE in 2021.[443] These two LCE plants convert the lithium concentrate extracted from the Mount Marion and Pilgangoora hard rock mines in Australia. Ganfeng has partnerships with both companies that run these mines.

Ganfeng receives most of its lithium concentrate from the Mount Marion lithium hard rock mine, located in southwestern Australia, east of Perth. The Marion mine is a 50/50 JV owned by Ganfeng and Mineral Resources Limited (MRL). Historically, Marion has had 450,000 tpa of spodumene processing capacity; for example, in 2022 they processed 442,000 tons. In summer of 2022, they began working to double this to 900,000 tpa, with this capacity to be fully installed by 2023. Starting in mid-2022, it was agreed that MRL would take 51% of the offtake and Genfeng would take the remaining 49%. MRL agreed to pay tolling fees and process all its lithium concentrate through Ganfeng's midstream conversion facilities in China. Ganfeng also agreed to find buyers for MRL's battery-grade lithium hydroxide, a logical decision considering their extensive connections in the industry.[444]

Ganfeng's second most import lithium feedstock stream comes from the Pilgangoora hard rock mine, located in northwestern Australia. The mine and its two spodumene processing plants are wholly owned by Pilbara Minerals. In 2022, Pilbara was ramping up its capacity to produce 580,000 tpa of spodumene concentrate.[445] If we use a 6.3:1 conversion rate, their theoretical maximum capacity equals 93,000 tpa of lithium hydroxide. Although Ganfeng is not a joint owner of the mining operation, they do own a 6.16% share of Pilbara itself, meaning they get preference in purchasing bulk lithium from Pilgangoora.[446] Presently, under a Phase I agreement, Pilbara supplies Ganfeng with NMT (No More Than) 160,000 tpa. Under a future Phase II agreement, Pilbara will supply Ganfeng with NMT 150,000 tpa. 160,000 tons of lithium concentrate using a 6.3:1 conversion ratio equals 25,000 tons of lithium hydroxide.

[443] Shanghai Metals Market, "Ganfeng Lithium Industry said that Ningdu Ganfeng has a full production capacity of 20,000 tons of lithium carbonate.", Dec 13, 2021.

[444] Mineral Resources Limited, 2022 Annual Report.

[445] Pilbara Minerals, 2022 Annual Report.

[446] Ganfeng Lithium, 2021 Annual Report.

In 2021, Ganfeng diversified itself from strictly hard rock lithium extraction sources, buying 49% of the Yiliping salt lake lithium brine project located in the northwest province of Qinghai. Ganfeng bought the equity stake from state-owned China Minmetals Corporation for $220 million USD.[447] Minmetals created the Minmetals Salt Lake Company to run the brine extraction operation. By 2021, Minmetals had developed a 10,000 tpa lithium carbonate production train on site.[448] With half ownership of this brine project, Ganfeng will secure itself almost 5,000 tpa of domestically sourced LCE.

To make this slightly more interesting, Minmetals has not been satisfied with the one and a half to two-year evaporative process currently in use there to recover lithium. Consequently, they have pursued a direct lithium extraction (DLE) process with Sunresin New Materials Company since 2019 to set up a large capacity DLE operation. Sunresin developed a 2,000 tpa adsorption process for their existing 10,000 tpa LCE production line. By 2022, they had achieved a 4,000 tpa capacity DLE adsorption process using the Sunresin proprietary Simulated Moving Bed (SMB) methodology. [449]

From an overall cost perspective, we need to keep in mind that this brine extraction operation is in a remote environment on the Tibetan plain. However, moving the final LCE product by truck or rail is still a much shorter supply chain by several thousand miles than shipping in lithium concentrate from the coasts of Australia. Also, LCE production is capped at 10,000 tpa and the current lease for the property expires in 2028, so there is a time consideration as well. These are just a few thoughts regarding if this can be a significant source of lithium for Ganfeng in the future.

Moving forward, Ganfeng is looking to expand its lithium writ across its entire portfolio. They are presently securing potential lithium hard rock resources in Mali, Ireland, and Mexico, where they bought out Bacanora Lithium for $253 million USD.[450]

[447] S&P Global, "Ganfeng Lithium to acquire 49% stake in China Minmetals' Yiliping for 1.47B yuan", March 09, 2021.

[448] Shanghai Metals Market, "The output of lithium salt in Qinghai is close to 100000 tons / year, and the world-class industrial base of extracting lithium from salt lake is ready to be developed.", Aug 05, 2021.

[449] https://www.seplite.com/sunresin-minmetal-s-lithium-carbonate-project-passes-project-acceptance.html

[450] Yicai Global, S. Ning, "Ganfeng Pays USD253 Million for UK's Bacanora to Acquire World's Biggest Lithium Mine Project", Aug 11, 2022.

If Ganfeng can work out the nationalization of lithium by the Mexican government, this could be a significant operation to feed the North American market as incentivized by the *Inflation Reduction Act*. Additionally, they are looking to produce LCE from several lithium brine projects in Argentina. From a midstream conversion perspective, they anticipate bringing on another 25,000 tpa of lithium hydroxide capacity in 2023. Personally, I will be looking to see how Ganfeng expands their lithium metals division, increases their battery recycling capacity, and grow their LIB production capability. These efforts will set them apart from their peers focusing solely on lithium mining and conversion.

Looking Ahead

1. I am curious to see where the Belt and Road initiative goes and if China can continue to grow its influence campaign even more. We should also watch the nexus with the BRI and ongoing mineral extraction to see if China continues to get what it needs reference battery metals. It will be interesting to see if partner countries give China pushback to keep their own minerals and secure more of the associated value chain for themselves as opposed to exporting it to Beijing.

2. We should watch the overall Chinese lithium enterprise to see if they maintain and/or grow their present dominant position. I believe they will continue to grow their enterprise although some regional balancing to North America and Europe will occur. It will be important to see if China can increase its own domestic lithium extraction operations to achieve mineral security. I don't think they can achieve anything close to this earlier than 2035.

3. We need to watch the lithium-human rights nexus to see how it develops and if the U.S. and Europe take any actions to hold China accountable for forced labor programs. An important topic is if the U.S. develops the capability to definitively prove the existence of a battery supply chain that is prohibited by the UFLPA. If the U.S. ever gets serious about the UFLPA, what kind of interaction will the U.S. government have with the major U.S. lithium companies who do business in China and may very well benefit from forced labor programs? Does Washington have the actual appetite to dig into the issue?

4. We can think of Tianqi and Ganfeng as representative of the overall Chinese lithium mining industry. How they go, the industry goes. Hence, it's useful to keep an eye on them and their progress. We should also recognize if they retrograde, like Tianqi has done, and if a new company supplants them. Will we ever see foreign companies buy into domestic Chinese lithium extraction operations or would Beijing ensure they were kept out by law? Any foreign buy-in would have to be approved by the Chinese Ministry of Commerce.

5. China understands that both the U.S. and Europe seek to develop more regionally sourced battery minerals to buttress a fundamentally more secure critical minerals supply chain. Beijing also realizes the pressure is on for both the U.S. and EU to provide incentives to domestic mining companies vice foreign firms. This means Chinese mining companies may be increasingly locked out of the North American and European continents for resources. Because of these reasons and more, China is increasingly looking towards Africa for battery minerals such as graphite and lithium. How does the reader think the competition for battery minerals will play out on the African continent?

CHAPTER 12

Direct Lithium Extraction

"The state sees potential for "Lithium Valley" to be an economic hub (economic ecosystem) centered by clean geothermal power and lithium recovered from geothermal brine, and a lithium battery supply chain." – Lithium Valley Commission, Draft Report, 2022

Lithium Brine Overview

Globally, there are relatively few brine operations working at scale today. As one would expect, there are four brine operations located in the Lithium Triangle. In Chile, Albemarle runs a lithium brine evaporation pond operation and SQM runs two adjacent ones. These are all in the Salar de Atacama with Albemarle's operations being only three miles south of SQM's. They are neighbors. Besides these, there is no other working lithium brine operation in the country.

Just across the border from Chile and southeast of the Salar de Atacama, Livent and Allkem (formerly Orocobre) have the only active lithium brine evaporation pond operations in Argentina. While Livent uses traditional evaporation ponds, they also employ a form of DLE (Direct Lithium Extraction) that uses less water. However, this is not to be confused with modern closed-loop DLE technology that is currently under widespread testing. Significantly, as we learned in Chapter 1, Bolivia has the largest lithium brine deposits in the world. Yet they don't have a robust brine operation in place. Overall, the largest brine resources in the world, in the Lithium Triangle, remain largely untapped.

The only active brine operation in North America is in Clayton Valley, NV. Here, Albemarle has their ongoing evaporation pond operations which they inherited from

Foote Mineral Company. The U.S., too, has neglected to maximize their lithium brine value chain. For example, the massive Smackover brine formation runs from central Texas, up into Arkansas, along the coast and into the Florida panhandle. However, this 300,000 square mile underground brine deposit is untapped and produces not an ounce of lithium. There are several efforts to use DLE technology in the Smackover Formation, but all are pilot plants, and none are viable as commercial scale operations yet.

In the past, lithium mining companies pursued brine operations over hard rock operations for a variety of reasons. First, let's look at the hard rock mining process. After a company has secured an appropriate lithium-rich piece of terrain, they drill a hundred holes, fifty feet down, fill them with explosives and then detonate it. This loosens the earth and the ore within it. Next, giant excavators come in and fill up equally giant dump trucks. The trucks dump the earth into crushers that pulverize the rock.

Conveyor belts take the crushed rock to another machine that grinds it, making it much finer material. The concentrated lithium is then roasted at high temperatures, which involves a great deal of electricity – another expense. The fine particles are then mixed with water (millions of gallons a year) into a slurry. This is put into large flotation tanks, mixed with acid and alcohols, separating the spodumene. The remaining slurry is then dried, removing the water, resulting in dried spodumene concentrate. This concentrate is then shipped to a conversion plant where it is further processed into lithium carbonate or lithium hydroxide.

Let's compare this to a brine evaporation pond operation, which uses a process called chemical precipitation. For this, let's look at SQM's process in the Salar de Atacama in Chile. First, SQM drilled several hundred holes one hundred feet into the earth and pumped brine up from the underground lake (or salar). This brine is then directed to various ponds that have been dug into the ground and lined with plastic to prevent seepage. The ponds are shallow and broad to maximize the evaporation process. The sun does all the work of removing the water while the minerals in the brine remain. With this process, there are several different minerals retrieved for commercial sale, not just lithium. Depending on the company and the kind of brine, these minerals can include salt, magnesium, potassium, iodine, and nitrate.

With lithium evaporation ponds, the remaining concentrated lithium brine is pumped into trucks and driven to a conversion plant. At the plant, the concentrated lithium brine is mixed with sodium carbonate to produce lithium carbonate. This product is then washed and dried resulting in a fine white powder. SQM puts the resulting lithium carbonate into white, heavy duty, square bags that weigh a 1,000 pounds apiece when filled. The bags are square so that they can be stacked and shipped easily either on trucks or in TEUs (Twenty-foot Equivalent Units). A TEU is the standard shipping container used in logistics, measuring twenty feet long, eight feet wide and eight feet tall.

From an operational perspective, evaporative brine operations are preferred to open pit hard rock operations. With brine operations, there is no need for trucks, excavators, conveyor belts or crushing/grinding machines. It is much cheaper to get lithium through simple evaporation and then mixing it with lime or sodium to get a final product. Brine evaporation operations also require much less people to achieve the same volume of lithium produced from hard rock mines. Hence, why over time, companies like Foote Mineral and Lithium Corporation of America closed their hard rock mines in NC and moved to purely brine operations in the Lithium Triangle.

However, brine evaporation operations also have problems involving space, time, and water. To start, the ponds occupy a lot of territory as they must be shallow to speed the evaporation process. This means they cover a lot of ground. The more lithium production a company wants, the shallower ponds they must lay out. SQM's operations in the Atacama Desert already cover 4,000 hectares (or 40 square kilometers) and this is before they announced their plans to double production.[451] This increased land use has impacts on the environment and can be a straight-forward land acquisition problem if operating in a confined area like Clayton Valley, NV.

Evaporation ponds also have a time problem. SQM's lithium chemical precipitation process takes at least a year to execute or even longer, depending on environmental conditions. Consequently, if lithium market prices soar and SQM wants to take advantage of this pricing, they will be waiting a while. They must dig, line, and prepare new evaporation ponds. They may also have to drill new wells and lay more pipe. Once that's done, they will be waiting a year or more for the sun to do its thing. The speed of the overall process is out of their hands. Therefore, it's not responsive and SQM cannot react quickly to a changing market.

---

[451] https://sqmnutrition.com/en/sustainable_agriculture_en/soluciones-de-origen-natural/

Finally, SQM has a water problem. Evaporation ponds are incredibly water in-tensive as they take large amounts of water from underground, moving it to their ponds and letting it evaporate. Since this is not a closed loop operation, the process can have significant environmental impacts over time. This is one of the chief com-plaints environmental groups have with evaporation ponds in areas that suffer from drought and are water stressed. SQM estimates that they use 5,949 gallons of water to produce a single metric ton of LCE.[452] If SQM produces 10,000 tons of lithium carbonate a year, they will go through 59 million gallons of water. That's clearly a problem. Importantly, DLE technology potentially solves these three problems of space, time, and water.

Direct Lithium Extraction – DLE

Based on the historical record, Dr. William C. Bauman can be considered the father of DLE. In the late 1970's, Dr. Bauman founded Dow Chemical Company's Advanced Separations Laboratory which focused on the extraction of minerals from brine. Specifically, Dr. Bauman was interested in the extraction of lithium and he went on to invent an ion exchange resin. Over the subsequent decades, Dr. Bauman filed numerous patents reference the extraction of lithium from brines.[453]

In 1979, Dr. John L. Burba, who earned his PhD in Physical Chemistry from Baylor University, joined Dr. Bauman's Advanced Separations team. Dr. Burba worked with Dr. Bauman for several years with their efforts paying off in 1984 with the development of a DLE pilot plant in Arkansas featuring ion exchange resin. Although their project showed that they could successfully extract lithium chloride (LiCl) from brine, they could not do so in an economic way, so the proj-ect was scrapped.[454]

Undeterred, Dr. Burba later left Dow and joined FMC where he continued his work on DLE technology. In 1994, FMC licensed Dr. Burba's and Dr. Bauman's earlier

[452] https://www.sqmlithium.com/en/nosotros/produccion-sustentable/

[453] https://www.innovationnewsnetwork.com/ibats-direct-lithium-extraction-technology/20994/

[454] https://www.innovationnewsnetwork.com/ibats-direct-lithium-extraction-technology/20994/

DLE patents and put them to use at their Salar del Hombre Muerto brine evaporation project in Argentina. Dr. Burba led FMC's absorbent development program and designed their DLE plant. FMC's DLE commercial operations came online in 1998, the first one of its kind in the lithium extraction industry.[455]

However, FMC's DLE operation was not a completely closed-loop system where brine is pumped up from the underground water source, lithium is extracted, and then the brine is pumped back to its source. With Dr. Burba's and Dr. Bauman's patented technology, FMC pumped brine through the DLE system using Selective Adsorption and sent the initial brine back to its source. They then took the remaining purified lithium chloride brine concentrate and pumped it into nearby evaporation ponds for further chemical precipitation. In 2020, these ponds covered only 45 hectares or 0.45 of a kilometer squared. The solution was then processed into lithium carbonate, trucked across the border into Chile and shipped out to China and the U.S. through the Port of Antofagasta.[456]

This partial closed loop DLE system enabled FMC (and later Livent) to reduce the amount of water it consumed in the processing of its final lithium product. As water sustainability becomes increasingly important in a warming Earth due to man's carbon-based economies, this can be a competitive advantage. As an example of this, BMW signed a multi-year contract in 2021 with Livent worth $273 million USD. In the forefront of BWM's considerations for a lithium offtake agreement was Livent's strong sustainability efforts.[457]

Dr. Burba subsequently left FMC and went on to start Selective Adsorption Lithium Inc (SAL) in 2018, naming his company after his own patented DLE process. SAL specialized in lithium extraction from oilfield brines, which was Dr. Burba's and Dr. Bauman's original DLE pilot plant project in Arkansas in 1984.[458] SAL was probably just Dr. Burba providing consulting services and capitalizing on his many

[455] https://www.innovationnewsnetwork.com/ibats-direct-lithium-extraction-technology/20994/

[456] https://livent.com/wp-content/uploads/2021/06/Livent_2020_Sustainability_Report_ENGLISH.pdf

[457] "BMW Group steps up sustainable sourcing of lithium, March 30, 2021, BMW Group Corporate Communications.

[458] https://www.bloomberg.com/profile/company/1580822D:CN?leadSource =uverify%20wall

decades of unique industry expertise. I say this because Dr. Burba also became the CEO of International Battery Metals Limited (IBAT) in 2018. Then, just two years later, SAL was acquired by IBAT.[459] IBAT is an established company formed in 2010 with headquarters in Vancouver, Canada. Today, IBAT is a public company that trades on the New York Stock Exchange over the counter as IBATF or on the Canadian Stock Exchange as IBAT.

At IBAT, Dr. Burba continued to develop, refine, and perfect his original DLE technology to develop a truly closed loop system. Today, IBAT offers their Modular Direct Lithium Extraction Plant (MDLEP) that is mounted on skids and can be transported by truck. This modular system means there is no requirement for laying concrete. A company just needs an area that is relatively flat to set the system on. This reduces costs and time significantly as the MDLEP can be set up most anywhere in under a week, depending on the size of the work crew.[460]

The basic 35-skid MDLEP system is configured to produce 5,700 tons of lithium chloride (LiCl) annually which is the lithium carbonate equivalent (LCE) of 5,000 tons. The amount of battery grade lithium chloride produced each year can be increased by either deploying multiple MDELP systems or modifying the original base configuration for larger brine volumes. Importantly, IBAT estimates that their modular system recycles 94% of the cycled brine back to the original source.[461]

IBAT is serious about protecting its intellectual property, so its business model is to own and operate their MDLEP so competitors don't acquire its technology. Operationally, this means IBAT has three possible options: 1) IBAT goes into business for itself as a lithium producer from start to finish, 2) IBAT sells the lithium chloride it extracts to another company for conversion (what we call "tolling") or 3) IBAT operates their system onsite for a different mining company and takes an agreed upon percentage of the overall lithium take. Dr. Burba insists that the current MDLEP is not a pilot plant but is ready for commercial scale operations now.[462]

[459] https://pitchbook.com/profiles/company/226929-61#overview

[460] https://www.ibatterymetals.com/direct-lithium-extraction

[461] https://www.ibatterymetals.com/direct-lithium-extraction

[462] https://www.theglobeandmail.com/business/article-battery-metals-lithium-extraction-plants/

Selective Adsorption, Ion Exchange & Solvent Extraction

DLE is different from the chemical precipitation used in evaporation ponds in that it seeks to specifically extract the lithium from a brine while leaving the rest. With a closed loop DLE system, brine is pumped through a container, lithium is extracted, and the brine is pumped back underground where it came from. This system has a very small physical footprint (the seize of a football field or less), extracts the lithium in hours as opposed to a year, and uses very little water – only about 5% of what is currently used. If a company is not using closed-loop DLE methodology, then they have not mitigated the many disadvantages of evaporation pond operations.

There are three major kinds of DLE technology at the more advance stages that companies are pursuing. Let's begin with Selective Adsorption which is the method used by Livent and now IBAT. With Selective Adsorption, a brine solution is passed through a container with a sorbent present. Lithium chloride (LiCL) molecules are then adsorbed and removed from the brine. The brine, that now contains much less lithium, is returned to the original source. The adsorbed lithium is then stripped from the sorbent in a subsequent process resulting in a concentrated lithium chloride (LiCl) solution. This solution is then treated in another step to produce lithium carbonate.

However, the sorbent material (depending on its composition) has a finite life and is only effective for a certain number of cycles before requiring replacement. This is one of the major limiting factors for Selective Adsorption technology as the sorbent material can be very expensive. A few of the companies currently pursuing Selective Adsorption DLE technology include:

- Livent Corporation (American), proprietary partial closed loop Selective Adsorption process, @commercial scale use
- International Battery Metals Corporation Limited (Canadian), proprietary Selective Adsorption process, @ pilot plant stage
- Standard Lithium (Canadian), proprietary LiSTR closed loop Selective Adsorption process, @ pilot plant stage
- Compass Minerals (American), using EnergySource's proprietary ILiAD Selective Adsorption process, @ pilot plant stage

Ion Exchange (IX) DLE technology has a different approach where one uses a porous material, like ceramic beads, to attract lithium ions and trade them with hydrogen ions. In a subsequent step, the lithium is stripped away in an acid solution to produce lithium chloride. The viability of IX technology rests in part on how expensive the material is used to attract the lithium ions and thus how many cycles can it be used before replacement. If the IX technology works only for very few cycles, then the project may simply be uneconomical at scale. Several companies pursuing IX technology to date include:

- Lilac Solutions (Canadian), proprietary closed-loop Ion Exchange technology, @ the pilot plant stage in Kachi, Argentina
- E3 Metals (Canadian), proprietary, closed loop, single stage Ion Exchange technology, @ research and development stage
- Alpha Lithium Corporation (Canadian), testing proprietary sourced Ion Exchange technology with help from Beyond Lithium and Lilac Solutions, @ developmental stage

Lastly, the Solvent Exchange DLE process uses a chemical solution to capture lithium from brine. However, the technology is limited by what kind of brine it is effective with, depending on its composition, and the organic solvents used present environmental problems. Tenova Advanced Technologies, an Italian company, has produced a proprietary Solvent Extraction process called LiSX. They have partnered with Schlumberger New Energy's NeoLith Energy brine project in Clayton Valley, NV.

Tenova's DLE technology centers on their Tenova Pulsed Column (TPC) which they advertise as having superior stripping qualities as well as low operating costs. They also manufacture their proprietary Tenova Settler that is advertised as more efficient with 20% less capital costs. With their process, lithium is captured from the brine in a chemical solvent. This solvent is then scrubbed with another solvent. The resulting purified solvent is then stripped in another solvent, resulting in the creation of lithium chloride (LiCl). The lithium chloride is then precipitated with sodium carbonate (soda ash) resulting in LCE.[463]

The solvent extractant used by Tenova process was developed by Solvay. Solvay's CYANEZ 936P is phosphorous based and marketed as ideal for use with salar brines.

---

[463] Tenova Lithium Recovery Technology – One Process for Any Brine Chemistry, October 2019, by Dr. Jonathan Lipp.

However, CYANEX 936P must be used with a brine that already has magnesium (Mg) and calcium (Ca) removed from it. Solvay believes their product can also be used effectively with geothermal brines, lithium clay and hard rock deposits. However, to date, Tenova and Solvay's joint process is only in the testing phases and has never been used at commercial scale, so it is not known if it is a viable DLE process.[464]

Department of Energy (DOE) – Geothermal Technology Office (GTO)

For the last decade, the U.S. government, through the DOE, has tried to advance DLE technology. For instance, DOE's Geothermal Technologies Office (GTO) provided Simbol Materials assistance under grant DE-EE0002790: Technologies for Extracting Valuable metals and Compounds from geothermal Fluids. Simbol had pursued lithium extraction from geothermal brine from the Salton Sea since 2007. The President and CEO of Simbol from 2013-2015 was Dr. Burba, who we identified earlier as working on Dow's DLE technology in the 1970's and 1980's.[465]

Simbol published a final summary of their DLE project in 2014. In their report, Simbol revealed that they developed DLE technology, proprietary sorbents and produced LCE and lithium hydroxide at both the laboratory and pilot plant scale. Simbol named their three proprietary sorbents: Sorbent-P (2nd generation), Sorbent-S (3rd generation) and Sorbent-A (4th generation). Simbol collected 95% of the lithium in the brine, contributing to their confidence that they could produce battery-grade lithium at scale through their Selective Adsorption DLE technology. Keeping in line with industry security norms, significant portions of the Simbol report covering their methodology for production of lithium hydroxide and LCE was redacted.[466]

In 2014, Simbol was riding high and caught the eye of Tesla who offered $325 million to buy them. Dr. Burba was involved in the negotiations. However, Simbol insisted they were worth $1.6 billion, causing Elon Musk to walk away.[467] Still, Simbol

[464] https://www.solvay.com/en/solutions-market/mining/mineral-processing/lithium-overview/lithium-solvent-extraction

[465] https://www.bloomberg.com/profile/person/16569891

[466] Technologies for Extracting Valuable Metals and Compounds from Geothermal Fluids, April 2014, by Dr. S. Harrison

[467] https://fortune.com/2016/06/08/tesla-lithium-startup-simbol/

estimated that they would build their first commercial production plant in 2016 and be producing 15,000 tons of LCE a year by 2017.[468] However, by the next year, in 2015, Simbol was out of cash, fired all its employees and went bankrupt.

The same year Tesla was negotiating with Simbol, DOE offered up grant DE-FOA-0001016: Low Temperature Geothermal Mineral Recovery Program.[469] With this program, GTO provided $4 million to nine different companies and universities to research different aspects of mineral recovery, including lithium. Specifically, SRI International received $449,00.00 to research advanced ion-exchange resins for lithium and manganese extraction. Southern Research Institute in Alabama was also given almost $500,000.00 to research geothermal power generation system that also extracted lithium from low temperature brine.[470]

SRI published the results of their research in 2016. For their project, SRI used lithium and manganese imprinted polymer beads sorbents in their Selective Adsorption DLE technology. SRI estimated future costs and profits based on their laboratory scale project and determined their DLE technology would be profitable. Their calculations were based on their DLE plant processing 6,000 gallons of brine a minute, with the brine having 400 ppm of lithium, operating 300 days a year, and producing 20,000 tons of LCE. SRI calculated that construction of the DLE plant would cost upwards of $20 million and then would cost $11 million a year to operate. To date, SRI does not have a commercial scale DLE plant in operation.

One way that GTO incentivizes advancing DLE technology is through their "American-Made Geothermal Lithium Extraction Prize". The program, which began in 2021, provided $600,000.00 in awards split among 15 semi-finalists during the Idea & Concept phase. Another $1.4 million was provided to five finalists for the Design & Invent stage. Finally, a $2 million award would be split among three winners for the Fabricate & Test Phase.

In July 2022, five finalists were identified. First, was the George Washington

---

[468] Technologies for Extracting Valuable Metals and Compounds from Geothermal Fluids, April 2014, by Dr. S. Harrison

[469] https://eere-exchange.energy.gov/Default.aspx?foald=3a4d4eec-5a0e-4867-9aaf-799d77cdd464

[470] https://www.energy.gov/eere/geothermal/downloads/low-temperature-mineral-recovery-program-foa-selections

University – Team Ellexco researching "Chemical-Free Extraction of Lithium from Brines". Another was Rice University – Team LiSED pursuing "Lithium Selective ElectroDialysis". Then, University of Illinois Urbana-Champaign – Team SelectPureLi with a project on "A Redox Membrane for LiOH Extraction". Followed by University of Utah – Team University of Utah looking into "Engineered Lithium Ion-Sieve Technology". And, finally, the University of Virginia – Team TELEPORT, focusing on "Targeted Extraction of Lithium with Electroactive Particles for Recovery Technology".

The remaining three winners for the contest will be announced December 1, 2023. The results may provide an indication of technological innovation in the field of DLE, something new perhaps. They should also provide some indication of what is feasible and what can work at commercial scale. The same can be said about the other 12 DLE projects that did not advance in the competition. Perhaps those projects are not mature enough or simply not feasible at scale, either economically or technologically.

The National Renewable Energy Laboratory (NREL) should be helping to advance DLE technology as well. As background, NREL is an office under DOE, overseen by the Office of Energy Efficiency and Renewable Energy (OEERE). NREL has four main offices: Washington DC; Golden, CO; Arvada, CO; and Fairbanks, AK. Their mission is: "to advance the science and engineering of energy efficiency, sustainable transportation, and renewable power technologies and provide the knowledge to integrate and optimize energy systems." The NREL budget for 2022 was $671 million.[471]

While the NREL does have an office that pursues geothermal energy research, it is clearly not a priority. Of the 2022 budget, geothermal projects received just $9 million or 1.5 percent. In comparison, solar projects received $85 million and vehicle research received $42 million. However, BEV's require LIBs for them to work and solar systems need them for energy storage. Therefore, it would make sense to also invest in the upstream supply chain that would help advance DLE technology. So, where does this $9 million go?[472]

Some of it goes towards advanced & enhanced geothermal systems, combining geothermal with existing oil & gas wells and sedimentary geothermal systems. Other funds go toward Advanced Well Technology like high temperature/high pressure

---

[471] https://www.nrel.gov/about/business-volume.html

[472] Ibid.

tools, innovative drilling systems and well construction material. Another area is Geothermal 2.0 focusing on improved well targeting, play fairway analysis, resource management and supercritical geothermal systems. NREL also has a Beyond Electricity program addressing direct use, energy storage, geothermal heat pumps and mineral recovery.

Under the Mineral Recovery topic, NREL recognizes the need for lithium extraction from brines in pursuit of a critical mineral strategy. In support of this idea, NREL pursues new technologies for mineral extraction as well as research into critical mineral supply chains. However, they are focused largely on the desalination of brines to produce drinkable water for a world increasingly suffering from water scarcity. Specifically, NREL is working on technology to remove salt from geothermal brines using zwitterionic ion exchange resin. For this project, NREL is partnered with four different organizations. They include Standard Lithium (who pursues DLE from brines in Arkansas' Smackover Formation), Shell, Colorado School of Mines (they have a mineral supply chain transparency project) and USA Rare Earth LLC (who is pursuing an REE project in Texas).

NREL published the very good 48-page *Techno-Economic Analysis of Lithium Extraction from Geothermal Brines* in 2021. This provides an excellent overview of the lithium brine industry, relevant history, extraction technology and private companies involved in this space. Particularly interesting was the pricing estimates. For their Phase I brine well extraction operations in Arkansas, Standard Lithium estimated it costing $4,020.00 USD per metric ton of LCE. E3 metals estimated that their Canadian oilfield brine project would cost them $3,657.00 USD per metric ton. Lake Resources estimated that their Argentine DLE brine project would cost $4,178.00 per metric ton of LCE. This is useful because it shows that DLE operations in the Lithium Triangle may be more costly than in North America. As compared to present evaporation pond prices per ton, these numbers are uneconomic.

Lithium Valley Commission

There are three primary geographic areas for brine extraction in the U.S. These include the Smackover Formation located in the southeastern part of the U.S., Clayton Valley, NV (where Albemarle has its evaporation pond operations) and the Salton Sea located in southeastern California. To be specific, the Smackover Formation is being targeted as a complementary oil well extraction operation. Albemarle runs a traditional evaporation pond operation in Clayton Valley, NV. In the Salton Sea area, those operations focus on geothermal brines that have their own distinct extraction characteristics and considerations.

In 2020, California estimated that geothermal brine operations in the Salton Sea could produce 600,000 tons of LCE annually. At the price of $70,000.00 a ton of LCE, they were eyeing $42 billion annually in lithium sales. This potential economic windfall motivated the California Energy Commission (CEC) to spur research into DLE technology via grants. However, the work started several years prior. In 2016, the CEC selected SRI international for a DOE grant to advance DLE technology in pursuit of extraction operations from in the Salton Sea. The project fell under California's advanced clean energy technology initiative named EPIC (Electric Program Investment Charge). SRI worked on its project from the Fall of 2016 until Spring of 2020.[473]

In March 2020, the California Energy Commission (CEC) published a 37-page report *Selected Recovery of Lithium from Geothermal Brines* that provided the results of SRI's work. For its hybrid sorbent porous beads process, SRI chose spinel lithium manganese oxide for its inorganic ion sieve. This was then combined with a lithium-imprinted polymer. Afterwards, they used a sorbent regeneration process using CO_2 to form lithium carbonate (Li_2CO_3). They used computer modeling to estimate costs for 20,000 tons of LCE annually with each ton costing $6,885.00, although this would be cost averaged down moving forward.[474]

SRI produced confidential reports detailing each phase of their DLE testing which are not accessible to the public. In 2020, SRI had two patents pending, protecting their proprietary DLE technology. SRI also exclusively licensed its technology to ExSorbtion Inc. meaning SRI shared its intellectual property under a specific agreement. However, soon after, ExSorbtion purchased SRI's DLE patent for $200,000.00 and is the sole owner of SRI's DLE technology. ExSorption's business model is to sell licensing agreements and collect royalties from interested brine extraction companies.[475, 476] To date,

[473] Ventura, Susanna, Srinivas Bhamidi, Marc Hornbostel, Anoop Nagar. 2020. Selective Recovery of Lithium from Geothermal Brines. California Energy Commission. Publication Number: CEC-500-2020-020.

[474] Ibid.

[475] http://exsorbtion.com/

[476] ExSorbtion Investor Presentation, March 2021

SRI's original patent, now owned by ExSorption, has not been used to produce LCE at scale.

Due to the significant amount of interest by various companies in pursuing DLE from geothermal brines in the Salton Sea, the California Energy Commission stood up the Lithium Valley Commission (LVC) in 2021. The purpose of the LVC was to better understand the lithium enterprise in California and devise incentives to advance geothermal DLE projects. Fourteen people sat on the commission to include various local government representatives from the Salton Sea area. There were also corporate representatives like: the CEO of Controlled Thermal Resources U.S. Inc, a FORD EV purchasing representative specializing in raw materials and the Vice President of Legislative & Regulatory Affairs for Berkshire Hathaway Energy Company.

The LVC was directed to produce a final report on the way ahead by October 2022, but they missed their deadline. However, they did publish a 110-page draft in September titled *Report of the Blue Ribbon Commission on Lithium Extraction in California*. As we continue to assess the impact of government direction on the lithium value chain in the U.S., the report cites President Trump's 2017 Executive Order 13817 *A Federal Strategy to Ensure Secure and Reliable Supplies of Critical Minerals*. In the report, the Salton Sea area is referred to as "Lithium Valley" and the "Known Geothermal Resource Area – KGRA".

The LCV had nine key findings. Finding #3 highlighted the belief that that the Salton Sea KGRA had the world's highest concentrations of lithium located in a geothermal brine resource. Finding #4 recognized that hard rock mining and evaporation pond operations were presently the two most common types of lithium extraction and the most environmentally damaging. Finding #5 recognized the benefits of DLE geothermal brine operations as having a minimal environmental impact. Finding #8 recognized that the *Inflation Reduction Act of 2022* and the *Infrastructure Investment and Jobs Act of 2021* would help develop a lithium-based economic hub near the Salton Sea.

The report also provided 44 key recommendations. One of these was for the Imperial Irrigation District to identify overall water needs for DLE geothermal brine projects through 2024. Another was the advancement of a circular lithium economy in California, based in part on environmentally responsible sourcing of raw materials (i.e., lithium extraction through DLE technology). Also, the idea was raised to identify the region around "Lithium Valley" as a defined economic area to incentivize state and federal investment initiatives. Finally, as we can't escape the permitting regime, the LCV advised that California create a centralized permitting coordination system, specifically, for lithium related projects.

Overall, California recognized the importance of lithium extraction for both supporting a national critical mineral strategy and developing a lithium-based circular economy. Their thought process revealed a continuing concern for tribal rights and considerations. This was reflected by the LVC having representatives from the Torres Martinez Desert Cahuilla Indians and the Quechan Indian tribe on the commission. Also, there was a strong commitment to water conservation and environmental impact, meaning large scale evaporation ponds wouldn't get public support. That idea was dead in the water.

Also mentioned was California's lithium tax that would be instituted on January 1, 2023, starting at $400 per metric ton for this first 20,000 tons of LCE. This tax would rise to $600 per metric ton for 20,000-30,000 tons and then go up to $800 per metric ton for an amount past 30,000 tons. Importantly, 80% of the collected tax would go to the counties where the lithium extraction occurred. Imperial County was mandated to provide 30% of the collected tax to its local communities impacted directly by lithium extraction operations.[477]

Lilac Solutions & Lake Resources

Lake Resources N.L. (No Liability) is an Australian mining company trading on the Australian Stock Exchange (ASX) as LKE and on the New York Stock Exchange (NYSE) over the counter as LLKKF. Lake has gone all in on lithium brine extraction as it pursues four separate projects in the Lithium Triangle. Lake's Paso, Olarez, Caucahri and Kachi projects are all located in northern Argentina. Significantly, Lake is only pursuing DLE projects – they are not considering hard rock or evaporation pond business models. With this comes considerable risk. If there is no DLE technology mature enough to support their operations, then their business doesn't exist.

Lake's Paso and Olaroz projects are both positioned adjacent to other proposed brine operations by Ganfeng Lithium and Allkem (created by the merger of Orocobre and Galaxy). In that specific area, it is a crowded field where one company's brine

---

[477] Draft Report of the Blue Ribbon Commission on Lithium Extraction in California, September 21, 2022, by California Energy Commission

claim ends and the other begins. Lake's Cauchari project is positioned on the southern end of this lithium brine claims cluster, just west of Ganfeng's and Advantage Lithium Corporation's projects. Lake's Kachi project is in Catamarca Province, away from the other projects, in the southern part of the Lithium Triangle.

Kachi is Lake's flagship project. Lake's 2020 Pre-Feasibility Study (PFS) for the Kachi site supports the extraction of 25,500 tons of battery grade LCE annually. This production comes from indicated resources of 1 million tons of LCE with a brine concentration of 290 mg of lithium per liter. The PFS calculates a first year EBIDTA of $155 million USD based on LCE selling at $11,000 a ton. The combination of capital costs (CAPEX) and operational costs (OPEX) is expected to be $4,178.00 per ton of LCE.[478]

Importantly, the entire project hinges on Lilac Solutions' Ion Exchange (IX) DLE technology operating at commercial scale in a closed-loop model. To achieve their annual production goals, Lilac must process 23 million cubic meters of brine. The brine that remains after passing through the ion exchange, is further concentrated, and then processed through a traditional lithium carbonate plant. The initial brine that went through the IX process and now has depleted lithium levels, is pumped back down to the underground salar. This is a closed loop system that does not use evaporation ponds.[479]

Lake was confident enough in Lilac's DLE technology that they announced their TARGET 100 Program. The program included doubling their Kachi production output to 50,000 tons of LCE annually and moving out rapidly on their three other projects further north. The expanded production at all sites was intended to reach 100,000 tons of LCE a year in 2030.[480]

Lithium customers were interested in Lake's eventual products and began signing non-binding offtake agreements for its LCE. For instance, Hanwa Company Limited signed a Memorandum of Understanding (MOU) in 2022 for an agreed upon 25,000 tons of LCE a year for ten years.[481] Hanwa, a Japanese company, in turn inked a strategic

---

[478] Lake Resources Pre-Feasibility Study, April 30, 2020.

[479] Ibid.

[480] Lake Resources ASX & OTC Announcement, Feb 14, 2022.

[481] https://www.proactiveinvestors.com/companies/news/978028/lake-resources-at-new-high-on-signing-non-binding-mou-with-japanese-trader-hanwa-for-lithium-carbonate-offtake-978028.html

partnership with Honda in order to supply them with battery metals like lithium to support their BEV production.[482] Several months after the Hanwa deal, Lake signed another non-binding MOU with Ford Motor Company for 25,000 tons of LCE annually for a ten-year length of time.[483] In October 2022, Lake signed a Conditional Framework Agreement with WMC Energy for 25,000 tons annually and a 10% stake in the Kachi lithium project.[484]

In June 2022, Lake suddenly announced that longtime CEO Steve Promnitz was departing the company with no explanation. Critics thought his resignation revealed his lack of confidence in Lake as he immediately cashed out all his stock options. Afterall, why would he depart after signing 50,000 tpa of offtake agreements with two industry giants Hanwa and Ford? Maybe Lilac Solutions had no commercially viable technology after all.

However, some observers thought that there was a strategy dispute within Lake. Specifically, the Lake Board of Directors wanted a North American value chain focus and Promnitz didn't. Maybe he wanted to pursue more business in Asia with Japan, South Korea, and China. If we look at the overall picture, North American businesses were heavily vested in Lake such as Ford (Detroit) and Lilac (Oakland) whose major backers (Bill Gates, Jeff Bezos) were also U.S. based. Perhaps, the dominant thinking in the Lake leadership was to pursue the closest market with the most lithium value chain incentives, which was North America. One can theorize that if Promnitz was not on board with that strategy, he was then asked to resign. Regardless, Lake announced that it would immediately begin looking for a location for its North American offices.[485]

About a week after leaving Lake, Promnitz landed a new job as the Managing Director of QX Resources LTD, an Australian hard rock mining company. QX is in a JV with Zamia Metals Limited who in turn holds exploration licenses for several potential mining operations. One line of effort is the Central Queensland Gold Projects where QX is looking to restart two historic gold mining operations. A second line of effort for

---

[482] https://www.hanwa.co.jp/en/

[483] ASX&OTC Announcement, Lake Resources, April 11, 2022

[484] ASX&OTC Announcement, Lake Resources, Oct 6, 2022

[485] https://www.proactiveinvestors.com/companies/news/985209/lake-resources-new-chair-will-ready-lithium-operations-for-north-america-s-supply-chain-985209.html

QX is exploring potential lithium hard rock mining in the Pilbara region of Australia. Finally, they are looking at pursuing a molybdenum hard rock mining effort as well.[486]

While Lake was all in with Lilac Solutions, Lilac in turn invested significantly in Lake's future. In 2021, both signed an agreement, based on milestones, giving Lilac the potential to acquire 25% ownership of Lake's Kachi operation. To start, Lilac would put in $50 million to fund a proportion of the physical infrastructure for the very remote Kachi high desert site. Remember, there is absolutely nothing at Kachi and everything needs to be built from scratch like roads, building foundations, living quarters, power supply and so forth.[487]

For Lilac to earn a 10% equity in Kachi, they must successfully construct and test their own DLE technology on site at Kachi at their own expense. Lilac will earn a further 10% equity when it meets agreed upon testing criteria with its demonstration plant in accordance with established timelines. Lilac will earn another 5% when it shows that it can produce lithium carbonate of an agreed upon purity level as requested by offtake partners (i.e., Hanwa and Ford). If Lilac doesn't meet this agreed upon criteria, Lake has buyback rights.[488]

Less than a year after agreeing to these terms, conflict arose between Lake and Lilac. One of the milestones agreed upon was that Lilac's onsite DLE plant would have at least 1,000 hours of operations time and produce at least 2,500 kilograms of LCE. Lake asserts that this milestone would be achieved by September 30, 2022, while Lilac said the actual date was December 30, 2022. Obviously, these dates were tied to quarterly investor reporting marks with Lake's date being the end of Q3 2022 and Lilac's at the end of Q4 2022. The two sides agreed that they would figure out this dispute internally or they would send it to arbitration.[489]

Some degree of this conflict must have been stirred up when J Capital Research (JCAP) dropped a short-seller report on both Lake and Lilac in July 2022. JCR claimed that the Kachi project will cost far more to get off the ground than advertised – $1

[486] https://qxresources.com.au/

[487] https://lilacsolutions.com/2021/09/lake-resources-partners-with-lilac-solutions-for-technology-and-funding-to-develop-the-kachi-lithium-brine-project-in-argentina/

[488] Ibid.

[489] https://www.mining.com/web/lake-resources-in-dispute-with-lilac-solutions-over-stake-in-argentina-lithium-project/

billion at least. JCR also stated that Berkshire Hathaway Energy Renewables "parted ways" with Lilac, implying that they lost faith in their DLE technology. Another part of JCR's attack was that Lake/Lilac technology would not decrease water usage as advertised, only cutting its use in half. JCR further pummeled Lake/Lilac for being three years behind schedule and having no Definitive Feasibility Study completed. Furthermore, they concluded that Lilac's DLE technology can't produce the results they say they can.[490]

Lake quickly responded, highlighting that the DLE process described by JCAP wasn't the one being used by Lilac – JCAP didn't know what they were talking about. Lake described the Lilac IX process where proprietary ceramic beads are used to exchange lithium ions with hydrogen ions. The beads are then stripped of their lithium using hydrochloric acid that produces a lithium chloride solution. This solution is then converted to LCE using sodium carbonate, a standard process. Furthermore, these beads were used over 500 cycles in testing and resulted in a total net freshwater loss of zero.[491]

In the rebuttal, Lake showed a picture of construction of the building that would house Lilac's DLE demonstration plant. Lake revealed that the pace of Kachi project construction was slowed considerably by the global COVID pandemic. As a result, previously scheduled testing of the Kachi brine by Lilac had to be conducted in California. Lake also revealed that they had 300 employees in Argentina itself working to further the Kachi project.[492]

However, the short seller report on Lake and Lilac wasn't JCAP's first rodeo. The previous year, they dropped a similar report on Vulcan Energy's Zero Carbon Lithium Project in Germany titled *Vulcan: God of Empty Promises*. Vulcan immediately requested a halt on trading of its stock as it prepared its response.[493] Soon after, Vulcan initiated legal proceedings against JCAP in the federal court of Western Australia. In December 2021, Vulcan won its case, resulting in a public apology by JCAP. Part of

---

[490] JCAP Short-Seller Report, July 11, 2022

[491] ASX & OTC Announcement, July 14, 2022, Lake Resources

[492] Ibid.

[493] https://stockhead.com.au/resources/lithium-darling-vulcan-energy-calls-a-halt-in-the-wake-of-j-capital-short-report/

the settlement included JCAP never publishing anything again about Vulcan or its officers.[494]

Let's update Lake/Lilac efforts before we move on. In January 2023, Lake announced that Lilac had met its milestones by operating its pilot plant for 1,000 hours and producing 40,000 liters of Lithium Chloride.[495] Lake then sent the lithium chloride to Saltworks in Canada for conversion to LCE. 40,000 liters of LiCl weighs 182,400 pounds or about 90 tons of LCE. (LiCl converts to slightly less weight as LCE, a 10% difference). Subsequent tests by Saltworks of the LCE sample in April 2023 revealed a 99.8% purity. Lilac's next milestone is producing 120,000 liters.[496] As that is still an inconsequential amount in the bigger picture, the question remains if Lilac's DLE technology can operate at scale.

DLE & Securing Proprietary Technology

It is hard to invest in many sectors and DLE is no different. Because the technology is proprietary, DLE companies won't talk about their product or where they are their development process. They may be concealing how advanced their technology is from their competitors or they equally may be concealing how far behind they are in contrast with their public statements. When I attended Fastmarkets' Lithium Supply and Battery Raw Materials 2022 conference, nobody in the DLE industry at the conference would talk about their product – it was Top Secret. One of the speakers also brought this up, noting that lithium companies in general don't release their lithium production numbers. Importantly, one can't make an intelligent investment decision if they don't even know what DLE technology a company is using, never mind if it's commercially viable.

For example, Cornish Lithium Limited is pursuing their Trelavour hard rock mining project in Cornwall, England. Cornish is also working with Geothermal Engineering Limited to develop a closed loop lithium brine extraction operation. This joint project is called GeoCubed and is advertised as using "Direct Lithium Extraction". And that's it. There is no indication of what kind of DLE technology they are developing. One

---

[494] https://www.thinkgeoenergy.com/settlement-in-case-of-vulcan-energy-resources-vs-j-capital/

[495] Lake Resources, ASX & OTC Press Release, Jan 10, 2023.

[496] Lake Resources, ASX & OTC Press Release, April 2, 2023.

certainly doesn't know if what they are using is commercially viable at scale. If we don't know that, then we also don't know if their entire geothermal brine operation will work. Cornish replied to an email from me stating that they weren't "currently disclosing that information".

But let's not pick on Cornish Lithium as they are the industry norm when it comes to protecting DLE intellectual property. In another example, Adionics Inc. is a private French company founded in 2012 that originally specialized in removing salt from brine or saltwater. In 2017, they pivoted towards lithium extraction and have spent the last six years investing in DLE R&D efforts. Now, they advertise a proprietary Solvent Extraction capability with the lowest CAPEX and OPEX on the market. Yet, we don't know if they are at the laboratory stage, pilot plant stage or if they can produce at scale.[497]

Let's close this out with a quick look at South Korean steelmaking giant POSCO Group. POSCO has ventured into the lithium business with a brine operation in Argentina at the increasingly crowded Salar del Hombre Muerto (they'll be neighbors with Livent, Alpha Lithium, Orocobre and Lake Resources). Their goal is to produce 25,000 tons of battery-grade lithium hydroxide in 2024 by using their own in-house proprietary DLE technology. While their $830 million investment gets their operation off the ground, they have larger ambitions of producing 100,000 tons by 2028.[498] As with the others, we don't know what DLE technology they developed or what stage it is although POSCO thinks it will be commercial scale ready in a year. What does the reader think?

Looking Ahead

1. Who will be the first company to develop truly closed loop DLE technology that can operate economically and at scale? While it be Lilac Solutions as Lake thinks? How about the CATL led group that won the DLE project in Bolivia. CATL has a 12,000 person R&D division. Does the reader think they

---

[497] https://www.adionics.com/technology/advantages/

[498] https://newsroom.posco.com/en/posco-holdings-begins-construction-of-saltwater-lithium-plant-in-argentina/

have the intellectual capital, money, and technology to crack the DLE code first?

2. If we do see DLE operations in the future, what is the operating cost per ton of LCE produced? If the costs are much lower than evaporation pond operations, the older process will be rendered non-competitive overnight. If the costs are the same or only slightly less, we will most likely see DLE operate in parallel with evaporation ponds due to sunk costs. If DLE remains more expensive per ton as we have seen with these various projects, then evaporative ponds remain king.

3. Also, the industry will need to confirm that DLE uses much less water than evaporation ponds. As we mentioned in the start of the chapter, these ponds have a time, space, and water problem. DLE has the potential of having the least environmental impact of any competing extraction process which will go a long way in minimizing impacts on our environment and moving through the permitting process. All things being equal, will a company buy lithium using less water over a competing product that uses more water? I think an operation using much less water has a competitive advantage, especially considering growing ESG principles.

4. We will need to see how the overall DLE process operates. Can in extract much more lithium in a much faster manner? Will it produce ten times the LCE in half the time as evaporation pond operations? If so, the world won't have a lithium supply problem any longer. Also, will we see DLE technology mature past just brine salars and be able to extract lithium from seawater? If we can achieve this methodology, then lithium supply will always meet demand. Today, we are nowhere near being able to extract lithium from seawater due its relatively low levels.

A satellite image of China's Qarhan Lake complex taken in 2013. These series of lakes are in Qinghai Province, as remote a location as anywhere in the world. The reader can see the rectangular evaporation ponds towards the top of the photograph. Most of China's lithium brine operations are conducted here. Chinese BEV maker BYD has invested in a joint operation at Qarhan as has Ganfeng Lithium. *(by NASA)*

An overview of the Mount Marion lithium extraction operation in Australia. This is a complex, mature operation run as a 50/50 JV between Mineral Resources and Ganfeng Lithium. This mine ensures Ganfeng has an independent source of spodumene for its midstream conversion facilities in China. *(by Ganfeng)*.

This is a 2015 picture of the Allkem (formerly Orocobre) lithium processing plant in Jujuy, Argentina. In the foreground is a lithium brine evaporation pond. This facility is adjacent to numerous competitors like Lake Resources who are pursuing DLE operations that have the potential to render these traditional methods non-competitive. *(by Getty Images)*

CHAPTER 13

Lithium Hard Rock Conversion

"As the world's largest producer of lithium, a key component in batteries for electric vehicles, our minerals sector has an enormous role to play in the success of the energy transition over the coming decades." – Madeleine King, Minister for Resources and Northern Australia

Hard Rock Lithium Conversion in Australia

As I write this, there are only four major operational hard rock lithium mines in the world, and they are all located in Western Australia. These include: 1) Pilbara's Pilgangoora Mine, 2) Albemarle's and Tianqi's Joint Venture at Greenbushes Mine, 3) Albemarle's and Mineral Resources JV Wodgina mine and 4) Mineral Resources and Ganfeng's JV Mount Marion mine. In all these cases, the spodumene concentrate is shipped off to be converted into useable battery grade lithium elsewhere in China. All four used to ship their product overseas for processing until Tianqi/IOG's Kwinana midstream conversion facility came online in 2022.

The business model for the hard rock lithium industry evolved in a way that Australia mined spodumene concentrate and then shipped it to China for midstream conversion processing. Surprisingly, Japan never developed a midstream conversion industry, despite hosting LIB stalwart Panasonic. Likewise, LG Chem (nor its newer battery spinoff LG Energy Solutions) in South Korea doesn't have a conversion plant either. Similarly, the Australian hard rock mining companies did not build their own on-site lithium conversion plants, preferring to ship it to the midstream conversion industry that developed separately in China. These separately evolved industries meant that the companies mining the spodumene concentrate realized much less of the lithium value chain. Although, this is changing today as we will see later in the chapter.

Depending on the cycle of lithium pricing and the region, converted lithium sells at a magnitude of 30 times more than that of the originating spodumene concentrate used as conversion feedstock. Recognizing this, some companies, like Albemarle, moved downstream into the midstream conversion industry, vertically integrating their business model. Also, midstream conversion companies recognized the opposite, that they needed to secure their upstream spodumene concentrate sourcing. Hence, we saw companies like Tianqi Lithium buying into the Greenbushes Mine and Ganfeng Lithium buying into the Mount Marion mine.

Hard Rock Spodumene Concentrate 6%

Spodumene is an ore containing varying percentages of lithium. Spodumene concentrate 6%, or simply SC6, is an ore with a high percentage of lithium. Generally, spodumene requires at least 6% lithium to be economically viable for recovery. In the hard rock mining process, the SC6 is ground up into much smaller pieces (beneficiation) and then baked in a rotary kiln at 1100 degrees Celsius. This heating process, called calcination, changes the original Alpha-spodumene to a new Beta-spodumene crystal structure.

The spodumene concentrate is then roasted in sulfuric acid at 250 degrees Celsius, resulting in soluble lithium sulfate. Lithium sulfate is a white inorganic salt commonly used to treat bipolar disorder. The lithium sulfate is then mixed with water in a process called leaching. This liquid then goes through a filtration process, that can include chemical precipitation, to remove undesired contaminants and minerals. The solution also goes through an ion exchange process to remove more contaminants.

The solution is then mixed with sodium carbonate (soda ash) which converts the lithium sulfate to lithium carbonate (Li_2CO_3). The solution passes through a crystallizer that separates the lithium carbonate, which is now in solid form. To convert the lithium carbonate into battery grade lithium hydroxide, an additional chemical process is required. With this next step, the lithium carbonate is reacted with calcium hydroxide ($Ca(OH)_2$) resulting in lithium hydroxide (LiOH).

This battery-grade lithium carbonate is used in the production of cathodes for lithium-ion batteries. There are different grades of lithium carbonate products, depending on its purity. Standard grade lithium carbonate is 99.5% pure. An enhanced grade is 99.9% pure where the lithium carbonate granularity is finer than the 99.5% product and has less water and impurities. As we would expect, 99.99% pure lithium carbonate has even finer granularity, even less water and impurities. The higher the grade, the better performance characteristics for EV batteries. However, it is also more expensive because it must pass through more purification cycles.

Lithium Carbonate Equivalent or LCE is a widely used industry term. The industry uses this when they are discussing a material, like a brine solution, and what it equates to when compared to and processed into lithium carbonate. Necessarily, the use of the term "LCE" means that the exact amount of lithium carbonate being compared is what is recovered from the material being discussed. This is an easy way to equate, in useful terms, a lithium material or product in a manner that is understood universally in the industry. If someone is using the term LCE, it may mean that they haven't converted their product yet to that form.

Pilbara Minerals Limited

Despite mining companies extracting spodumene from open pit mines, many of them do not actually process this material into a useable battery grade form. Instead, they sell the spodumene concentrate in bulk and let someone else process it. This means the mining company only realizes a small portion of the overall lithium value chain since bulk spodumene sells at a much lower multiple than lithium carbonate and lithium hydroxide. Let's look at these dynamics at play with Pilbara Minerals' operation in Western Australia.

Pilbara Minerals is an Australian company with HQs in Perth, specializing in lithium and tantalite extraction. Tantalite is commonly used in making specialty metal alloys requiring high melting points. Their primary operation is the open pit, hard rock Pilgangoora lithium mine. Pilbara Minerals also runs the on-site Pilgan and Ngungaju processing plants that produce spodumene concentrate. However, these processing plants do not create battery grade lithium products.

Pilbara has a two million tons per annum (tpa) mining and processing capacity of which they can produce 330,000 tons per annum of spodumene concentrate.[499] In October 2021, Pilbara upgraded their Pilgan Plant resulting in an estimated improvement of capacity to 360,000-380,000 tons of both fine and coarse spodumene. Pilbara restarted their Ngungajo Plant in October 2021, with an estimated capacity of 180,000-200,000 dry tpa of coarse spodumene. These production numbers should be attained by the end of 2022.[500]

All of Pilbara's offtake agreements are with the Asia market, which makes geographic sense. Pilbara's operations are ideally located as they are positioned only 55 miles as the crow flies from the Port of Hedland on the northern coast of Western Australia. Practically, Pilbara's trucks must drive due west to Route 95, travel north until they hit Route 1, which then takes them within a mile of the Port of Hedland. This trip is about 75 miles in length. Pilbara's mine is located only 16 miles east and north of Albemarle's own Wodgina Mine, meaning they both have the same logistics considerations.

Once their lithium is at the Port of Hedland, Pilbara has the closest, most direct route to Asia than any other importer – the Lithium Triangle is thousands of miles further away. Unsurprisingly, Pilbara signed its first offtake agreement in 2016 with Chinese company General Lithium Corporation (GLC). This binding agreement guaranteed GLC 140,000 tons of spodumene concentrate for six years from 2018-2024. Also, GLC agreed to purchase up to 5% of Pilbara's shares. Pilbara was already interested in starting a joint venture with GLC to build a midstream spodumene concentration conversion plant as they recognized lithium carbonate was selling at much higher multiples even in 2016.[501, 502]

In 2017, Pilbara continued doing business with Chinese spodumene concentrate conversion companies when they signed a deal with Ganfeng Lithium. With this binding offtake agreement, Pilbara agreed to provide Ganfeng with 160,000 tpa of spodumene concentrate for ten years with plans for additional 5-year incremental commitments. Upon conclusion of this deal, Pilbara locked in 100% of its spodumene

[499] https://www.pilbaraminerals.com.au/our-company/our-projects/ pilgangoora-operation/

[500] https://www.pilbaraminerals.com.au/our-company/our-projects/ pilgangoora-operation/

[501] https://www.spglobal.com/marketintelligence/en/news-insights/trending/-swgmjzidfl-on5gffipmw2

[502] https://www.annualreports.com/HostedData/AnnualReportArchive/p/ ASX_PLS_2016.pdf

sales to both General Lithium and Ganfeng, based on an estimated production volume of 300,000 tpa.[503]

As part of the deal, Ganfeng provided Pilbara with $20 million in financing for its Stage 1 production development. When Pilbara expanded beyond their initial 300,000 tpa capacity, they agreed to sell Ganfeng 25% of this increased capacity. Importantly, Ganfeng would finance 50% of this Stage 2 expansion. If Ganfeng did provide the financing for Stage 2 development, this would trigger an agreement for Pilbara to provide them up to 150,000 tpa of additional spodumene. This would lock Ganfeng in as the biggest recipient by far of Pilbara's lithium.[504]

While Pilbara still wasn't producing any spodumene in 2017, they continued to rack up offtake agreements with major Chinese players like Great Wall Motor Company (GWMC). GWMC was a growing BEV manufacturer looking to secure their upstream battery supply chain and one of the closest geographic sourcing was Pilbara. GWMC agreed to invest $22 million USD in Pilbara for a 3.5% stake of the company and would receive 75,000 tpa of spodumene beginning in 2020. If GWMC agreed to help finance Pilbara's Stage 2 expansion to the tune of $50 million, they could secure another 75,000 tpa.[505]

Pilbara continued their momentum in 2018, inking a binding offtake agreement with South Korean steel giant POSCO for 80,000 tpa of spodumene from their future Stage 2 expansion project. Pilbara again expressed an interest in a midstream conversion capability and engaged POSCO about a JV on the topic. If Pilbara moved forward with a minimum 30% ownership of the POSCO JV, this would trigger an agreement to provide the processing facility up to 240,000 tpa of spodumene concentrate from Pilbara's Stage 2 expansion project. Furthermore, to secure this JV, POSCO would provide Pilbara a $79.6 million AUD unsecured convertible bond. Essentially, the JV would hold virtually no risk for Pilbara while ensuring POSCO with a guaranteed increased volume of spodumene for midstream conversion.[506]

The following year, Pilbara continued planning for Stage 2 expansion which they

[503] https://www.spglobal.com/marketintelligence/en/news-insights/trending/ztrwpa49_j463fa41bdlaq2

[504] Ibid.

[505] https://www.reuters.com/article/us-great-wall-motor-pilbara/chinas-great-wall-secures-lithium-supply-with-pilbara-deal-idUSKCN1C40JY

[506] https://www.annualreports.com/HostedData/AnnualReportArchive/ p/ASX_PLS_2018.pdf

anticipated would eventually contribute to a total of 840,000 tpa of spodumene concentrate. They also envisioned an even larger Stage 3 expansion if the market for lithium continued to grow. Stage 3 expansion was calculated to result in 1.2 million tpa of overall spodumene concentrate production. Simultaneously, Pilbara leadership continued to pursue the PSOCO JV where their lithium processing plant would have a capacity of 40,000 tpa of LCE. Importantly, in FY2019, Pilbara's mine became operational, shipping 174,952 tons of spodumene concentrate. They sold the concentrate at an average of $647.00 USD per ton for total sales of $113 USD million. This was only half of Pilbara's Stage 1 capacity. The price per ton that they could sell the SC6 for would increase dramatically in 2022.[507]

While Pilbara continued to ramp up their Stage 1 production, they stayed focused on their ambitious Stage 2 future expansion. GWMC had a conditional offtake agreement of 75,000 tpa while Ganfeng Lithium had a conditional offtake agreement of twice that at 150,000 tpa. And POSCO had a conditional offtake agreement of more than both of those combined at 315,000 tpa. These three agreements amounted to 540,000 tons per annum of additional production above and beyond the baseline Stage 1 production target of 330,000 tpa.[508]

At the end of FY 2019, Chinese battery giant CATL (Contemporary Amperage Technology Limited) bought an 8.5% stake in Pilbara at $55 million USD. Pilbara needed the money for its future expansion plans and CATL had the money and the technical capability to process the spodumene concentrate for midstream conversion. This investment provided more long-term upstream lithium security for CATL who had plans to expand aggressively in the global EV battery market. However, CATL sold their investment some four years later in March 2023 for $400 million USD, making more than a 700% profit.[509]

In FY2020, Pilbara cut back production to match customer demand, producing only 60,768 tons of spodumene concentrate while shipping 116,256 tons. With the global COVID pandemic hitting the world in March 2020, there was considerable associated supply disruption and demand destruction in the lithium industry.

[507] https://www.annualreports.com/HostedData/AnnualReportArchive/p/ASX_PLS_2019.pdf
[508] Ibid.
[509] Murdoch, Scott & Burton, Melanie. "China's CATL sells $405 mln stake in Australian lithium miner Pilbara", Reuters, March 2, 2023.

The Pilbara spodumene sales on the shipped tonnage were $84.15 million averaging $723.00 per ton, an increase of $76.00 per ton or 11.8% from FY2019. To put this in perspective, Pilbara's operating costs for the same period were $350.00 USD per ton including CIF (Cost, Insurance &, Freight) to China. Pilbara delivered the spodumene using eight ships, averaging 14,532 tons per vessel.[510]

This same year, Pilbara diversified its Stage 1 offtake regime by signing GWMC to a 20,000 tpa contract over a six-year period and Yibin Tianyi Lithium Industry Company for 75,000 tpa annum on a five-year contract. For background, Yibin Tianyi was formed in 2018 as a joint venture between seven different Chinese companies: CATL, Canmax (a machine company based in Shanghai), Changjiang Chendao Hubei New Energy Industry Investment Partnership, Yibin Tianyuan Group (a chemical manufacturer in Sichuan), Ningbo Hanyi Investment Partnership Enterprise, Ningbo Meishan Bonded Port Area Chaoxing Investment Partnership Enterprise (out of Zhejiang) and Suzhou TA&A Ultra Clean Technology (specializing in healthcare equipment). While Pilbara said they wanted to "diversify" their Stage 1 offtakes, one could argue they further enmeshed themselves in the broader Chinese market.[511]

The next year, the lithium industry had adapted to the pandemic and, accordingly, Pilbara increased production. In FY2021, they produced 281,098 tons of spodumene concentrate, which was 85% of their Stage 1 capacity. However, Pilbara shipped out slightly more, 281,440 tons for sales of $175.8 million, for $624.64 a ton. Operations costs averaged $389.00 USD per ton including CIF to China. Additionally, Pilbara began improving its Pilgan Plant to increase its Stage 1 capacity to 380,000 tpa. The money for these improvements would come from their strategic partner, Yibin Tianyi.[512]

To start, Yibin Tianyi provided Pilbara an upfront $15 million USD interest-free loan to be paid back in three years. In return, Yibin Tianyi secured another 40,000 tpa of spodumene concentrate for a three-year period. Combined with the previous 2020 offtake agreement, this secured Yibin Tianyi 115,000 tons of Stage 1 spodumene a

[510] https://www.annualreports.com/HostedData/AnnualReportArchive/p/ASX_PLS_2020.pdf
[511] Ibid.
[512] https://www.annualreports.com/HostedData/AnnualReports/PDF/ASX_PLS_2021.pdf

year through 2024. This meant that 30% of Pilbara's total Stage 1 spodumene capacity flowed directly to Yibin Tianyi.[513]

Importantly for Pilbara's production growth, they acquired the Altura Lithium Project in 2021 that was adjacent to their own ongoing operations. The Altura project was an existing hard rock mine with an onsite spodumene processing plant. Altura was operational in 2018 and produced 181,000 tons of spodumene in 2019. Pilbara renamed Altura's processing plant the Ngungajo Plant, with a capacity of up to 200,000 tpa. Also, since this acquisition was not forecasted, it's production was not tied to existing offtake agreements, meaning Pilbara had flexibility in how it sold this new capacity and to whom.[514]

Moving forward, Pilbara could achieve more offtake security if it diversified into the Japanese market as Pilbara is already heavily into China and have an existing relationship with POSCO, which is South Korean. Pilbara has several options in the Japanese market like Panasonic, that has large ongoing EV battery manufacturing contracts with Tesla and jointly runs the largest battery manufacturing facility in North America (Giga Nevada). Also, Murata Manufacturing is a Japanese company that comes to mind as they bought out Sony's battery business in 2017. Kyocera is another option, a Japanese company already established in the LIB market who is also targeting the growing EV battery industry.

Importantly, Pilbara needs to move downstream into the spodumene concentrate midstream conversion business ASAP as that is where they can capture the most value in the lithium chain. Let's look at their ongoing JV with POSCO, which has plans to produce 40,000 tpa of LCE or lithium hydroxide. In 2022, both LCE and hydroxide were selling at around $75,000.00 USD a ton in the China market. If the Pilbara/POSCO JV reaches maximum output and sells all their product, their revenue is $3 billion USD.

With a 6.3:1 spodumene concentrate feedstock conversion ratio, 252,000 tons of SC6 feedstock is required. At $650.00 a ton, that costs $163.8 million resulting in a $2.8 billion USD annual gain after conversion and sales. If Pilbara had its own solely owned 52,000 tpa conversion plant and sold its product at $75,000.00 USD per ton, that would result in revenue of $3.9 billion USD. This would require 322,000 tons of SC6 feedstock, priced at operating costs of $650.00 USD a ton, costing $209.3 million

[513] Ibid.

[514] Ibid.

USD. Total revenue after subtracting this cost would be $3.89 billion USD. To put that in perspective, if Pilbara reaches their Stage 3 goals of producing 1 million tons of spodumene concentrate annually and sells that product at $650.00 USD per ton, that is only $650 million USD in revenue.

The POSCO midstream conversion facility would make in a year what it would take Pilbara to sell at its theoretical maximum capacity for five years. With only 30% ownership, Pilbara would still make $900 million USD annually, far more than their theoretical maximum using their present business model. Currently, Pilbara is giving away most of the downstream lithium value chain to companies like General Lithium and Yibin Tianyi. Hence, why the POSCO JV should be Pilbara's main effort. After that processing facility is up and running, Pilbara should take the profits and knowledge from their JV and reinvest into their own 100% Pilbara owned LCE midstream conversion facility in Port Hedland. This would give them the offtake flexibility to sell across the Asia market while capturing much more of the lithium value chain.

Tianqi Lithium & Greenbushes Mine

As a refresher, Greenbushes Mine is managed by a JV – Talison Lithium. 49% of Talison is owned by Albemarle through Windfield Holdings. The other 51% of Talison is owned by the JV Tianqi Lithium Energy Australia (TLEA), which is itself owned 51% by Tianqi Lithium and 49% by Australian mining company IGO Limited. Thus, Tianqi owns the majority of TLEA, who owns the majority of Talison. However, due to the dilution of ownership within TLEA, Albemarle holds by far the single largest stake in Greenbushes. Greenbushes has three spodumene concentration processing plants capable of producing 1.2 million tpa.[515]

In FY2022 (meaning from July 1st, 2021 – June 30, 2022), Greenbushes was the worlds' largest hard rock lithium mining operation in the world, producing 1.14 million metric tons of spodumene concentrate.[516]

Tianqi has been the majority owner of Greenbushes mine since 2014, long before the lithium industry began to scale up. Tianqi is also the 100% owner of the Cuola lithium mine located in Yajiang County, Ganzi Prefecture, Sichuan Province. However, the

---

[515] file:///C:/Users/mreri/Downloads/2021%20Annual%20Report.pdf

[516] https://www.igo.com.au/site/pdf/c5d6ce55-e0f1-49ea-8e94-e3d95b1f3da2/Greenbushes-Site-Visit-Presentation.pdf

Cuola mine is not operational and does not produce anything. Thus, Tianqi now imported all its spodumene concentrate at cost from its own stake in the Greenbushes mine or through offtake agreements with other Australian mines.

Two years later, in 2016, TLEA began the on-again, off-again process of building a spodumene-to-lithium hydroxide midstream conversion plant on the coast in Kwinana, Western Australia. Kwinana is adjacent to and south of Perth. Kwinana is also where TLEA headquarters is located. The production of the plant took some six years based on Tianqi's own changing financial strength and the ups and downs of lithium pricing. Presently, the conversion plant is designed with two production trains, each with a capacity of 24,000 tpa for a combined capacity of 48,000 tpa. Train 1 was completed in 2021 with Train 2's anticipated completion in 2024. Kwinana already has long-term offtake agreements with LGES (South Korean), SK Innovation (South Korean), EcoPro (South Korean) and NorthVolt (Swedish).[517]

Obviously, the agreements with South Korea companies make sense as they are geographically the closest market. However, the supply chain to Sweden is a long one, prone to disruption and is 11,700 miles by ship. A ship loaded with lithium hydroxide will depart the Port of Kwinana, pass through the Gulf of Aden, putting the vessel at 5,700 miles. Then, it continues North through the Red Sea, passing through the Suez Canal, and west through the Mediterranean and passing through the Straights of Gibraltar – another 4,000 miles. The third leg of the voyage (another 2,000 miles) takes the lithium around the Iberian Peninsula, through the English Channel, around the northern tip of Denmark and onto the southern Swedish port of Gothenburg.

Once the ships offload their lithium at Gothenburg, NorthVolt's gigafactory is 573 miles to the northeast as the crow flies, east of Skelleftea. But the trip by truck is more than 700 miles as one heads north, works around giant Lake Vanern, and continues to Route E4 that connects the capital, Stockholm, with Skelleftea. E4 parallels the coast heading north and intersects Route 372 in Skelleftea. Route 372 heading east will take the lithium right to the gigafactory, three miles down the road. Or, the lithium can continue by sea, which is another 1,000 miles as it moves on past Copenhagen, across the Baltic Sea and the Gulf of Bothnia and then hitting the Port of Skellefteehamn, only four miles from the gigafactory.

---

[517] file:///C:/Users/mreri/Downloads/2021%20Annual%20Report.pdf

NorthVolt may be willing to endure this ridiculously long supply chain since Greenbushes operating expenses run about $250.00 USD per ton of spodumene concentrate, the lowest in the industry. (Author's note: I've seen different costs per ton for Greenbushes and it varies depending on the date of the reporting. Regardless, it's considered the lowest in the industry.) With Greenbushes producing a 1.2 million tons per year of spodumene, 600,000 tons goes each to Albemarle and TLEA. TLEA planned on sending approximately 300,000 tons of spodumene to their Kwinana conversion plant with the other 300,000 tons of their spodumene being exported by Tianqi Lithium to China for conversion there. TLEA calculates that 6.3 tons of their spodumene concentrate make a single ton of lithium hydroxide so 300,000 tons of spodumene = 47,600 tons of lithium hydroxide, or almost the max capacity of their first two production trains.[518]

The spodumene concentrate in excess of what Kwinana can use to fulfill offtake contracts with companies like NorthVolt, will be sold to Tianqi Lithium who will in turn ship it to their own midstream conversion facilities in China. However, this excess spodumene supply may have a limited run for Tianqi if Kwinana expands its lithium hydroxide production. There are already discussions of building trains 3 and 4 which would raise their capacity to 96,000 tpa.[519]

In May 2022, the Kwinana conversion plant was operational and produced its first converted lithium hydroxide. Of note, this was the first operational lithium hydroxide plant built on the continent of Australia. Even though Tianqi Lithium owned 51% of the operation, it broke the monopoly of China-based midstream conversion plants serving the Asia market. This allowed TLEA to skip the step in the established paradigm of Australian lithium being set to China for processing and then shipped out to the rest of the region as determined by established offtake agreements. Now, TLEA could ship lithium hydroxide directly to Chinese, South Korean and Japanese offtake customers. TLEA realized far more of the lithium value chain since their lithium hydroxide sold at many multiples above their spodumene concentrate and they had reduced seafaring CIF (Cost, Insurance, Freight) expenses by skipping the trip to China for conversion.

Two years after Tianqi began work on its Kwinana plant, in 2018, it began

---

[518] https://www.asx.com.au/asxpdf/20201209/pdf/44qs5gqdbb620t.pdf

[519] file:///C:/Users/mreri/Downloads/2021%20Annual%20Report.pdf

construction on its Anju midstream conversion plant located in Sichuan. Like the Kwinana conversion plant, the Anju plant was an on-again, off-again affair depending on the weakness of lithium pricing. Currently, the Anju plant is under construction and not yet operational. The Anju facility is designed as a battery grade lithium carbonate conversion plant with a 20,000 tpa capacity. The Anju plant is in Sichuan along with its earlier Shehong plant. From the southern port of Qinzhu to Anju is 625 miles as the crow flies, adding to the logistics supply chain distance. However, this does make geographic sense in that one of Tianqi's major customers is CATL, who has a battery manufacturing operation located in Sichuan as well.

To better understand why the Kwinana conversion plant took the better part of seven years to be completed and Anju is in its fifth year of development, we must look to Tianqi's investment in Chilean lithium powerhouse SQM. In 2018, the same year it began constructing the Anju plant, Tianqi bought a 24% share in SQM to the tune of $4 billion USD. This purchase placed Tianqi in considerable debt and directly impacted their decision to freeze development of their Kwinana and Anju conversion plants at various times. With continued lithium price weakness, Tianqi was confronted with possible bankruptcy. This precarious financial position led to Tianqi selling 49% of its Greenbushes and Kwinana operations to IGO.

In 2021, the overall Chinese conversion enterprise produced 298,000 tons of lithium carbonate and 190,000 tons of lithium hydroxide.[520] When Tianqi does complete the Kwinana and Anju conversion plants, it will have an overall installed capacity of 112,000 tpa. This means Tianqi can capture 23% of the 2021 Chinese conversion market. If we use a 6.3:1 spodumene conversion factor, it will take 705,000 tpa of spodumene concentrate feedstock to keep them operating at their maximum capacity. However, they are only getting 600,000 tpa from the Greenbushes mine of which IGO gets half. This means Tianqi must get offtake agreements from other Australian mining companies to reach their maximum capacity.

Albemarle's Hardrock Operations in Australia

As discussed, Albemarle assumed a 49% stake in the Greenbushes mine in 2015 when Albemarle bought Rockwood Holdings in a $5.7 billion USD deal. In doing so,

---

[520] China Non-Ferrous Metals Industry Association

Albemarle secured the single largest slice of spodumene concentrate offtake in the world. As we know, Tianqi's 51% share was cut almost in half in 2021 when IGO bought 49% of the Greenbushes operation for $1.4 billion USD. This left Albemarle with close to 600,000 tpa of spodumene offtake for its own direct use. Also, Greenbushes has the lowest hard rock operating costs in the industry at $250.00 USD per ton. This ongoing access to cheap spodumene feedstock at scale gives Albemarle a chance to maximize the lithium value chain to its advantage.

Not satisfied with just its holdings in Greenbushes, Albemarle bought a 60% interest in the Wodgina Mine located in Western Australia in 2019 for $1.3 billion USD. In doing so, Albemarle created a 60/40 JV with Mineral Resources Limited called "MARBL Lithium Joint Venture". This was later adjusted to a 50/50 ownership in early 2023. Wodgina has three spodumene concentration trains with an individual capacity of 250,000 tpa for a combined maximum capacity of 750,000 tpa. With a 50% stake, this gives Albemarle a 375,000 tpa cut of the total maximum offtake. Combined with Greenbushes production, this gives Albemarle a theoretical maximum feedstock capacity of 975,000 tpa. With a 6.3:1 midstream conversion factor, this can result in 154,000 tpa of battery grade lithium hydroxide sold.

However, soon after Albemarle bought into Wodgina, they put the mine into "care and maintenance" mode from 2019 through 2021 as weak lithium prices dominated. It wasn't until 2022 that the first spodumene train at Wodgina was put back into operation. This operational slowdown is okay in the bigger picture because Albemarle didn't have the midstream conversion capability in the region to handle the volume. The spodumene produced is shipped to Albemarle's two operational conversion plants in Chengdu/Meishan, Sichuan and Xinyu, Jiangxi for conversion to battery grade lithium hydroxide. Each one of these plants has an estimated 20,000 tpa capacity. (Author's note: Albemarle doesn't publish their conversion plant production numbers for these two locations. However, if we divide their reported 2021 lithium hydroxide production of 40,000 tpa by the number of active conversion plants, we can infer the annual capacity.)

When the spodumene production from Greenbushes surpasses what their two operational plants can handle, they run their excess feedstock through other conversion plants in China. These conversion plants owned by Chinese companies are called "tolling entities". With this process, Albemarle maintains ownership of the original feedstock and pays a fee per ton for the conversion. Upon conclusion of processing,

Albemarle still owns the final product like lithium hydroxide. Tolling is common in the lithium industry when a company has feedstock that exceeds conversion capacity. In 2021, Albemarle reported 10,000 tons in tolling volume and anticipated 20,000 tpa more in 2022. I have seen estimates for tolling fees at $2,00.00 USD per ton.

Albemarle understands it has a conversion capacity problem in the Asia market and has responded aggressively. In 2018, Albemarle began working on a lithium hydroxide conversion plant located in the Kemerton Strategic Industrial Area (KSIA). As background, KSIA is located just north of the Port of Bunbury which is about 95 miles south of Perth and 75 miles south of TLEA's Kwinana conversion plant. KSIA has been developed to attract strategic industries in Australia who process natural resources, like Albemarle. Kemerton's envisioned capacity is from 50,000-100,000 tpa depending on how many conversion trains Albemarle builds. Presently, the plant was still not in operation although $1.2 billion had been invested. Production value from the Kemerton JV will be split 85% Albemarle/15% Mineral Resources according to an updated agreement in 2023. Albemarle will operate the facility.[521]

In 2021, Albemarle purchased Tianyuan New Energy Materials Co., Ltd. for $200 million USD. Tianyuan, founded in 2017, is in Guangxi Province, which is southwest China, bordering Vietnam. In 2020, Tianyuan had a 10,000 tons per annum conversion facility in the well-positioned Port of Qinzhou.[522] By 2021, Tianyuan upgraded its capacity to 25,000 tons per annum for either LCE or Lithium Hydroxide.[523] As part of the 2023 deal reference the Kemerton facility, Mineral Resources received 50% ownership of this facility.

That same year, Albemarle continued to up their conversion capacity as they made an official agreement with the Pengshan Economic Development Park to develop a new 50,000 tpa battery grade lithium hydroxide conversion plant. The plant is in Meishan, an area just south of Chengdu in Sichuan province. This will be Albemarle's

[521] "Albemarle restructures joint venture with Australia's Mineral Resources". Reuters, Feb 22, 2023.

[522] https://news.metal.com/newscontent/101103015/guangxi-tianyuan-new-energy-material-to-see-first-batch-of-lithium-carbonate-output-in-late-may/

[523] https://www.prnewswire.com/news-releases/albemarle-to-expand-lithium-production-capabilities-with-acquisition-of-guangxi-tianyuan-new-energy-materials-co-ltd-301388704.html

second plant in the province. For geographic awareness, this conversion plant is located about 135 miles road distance (northwest) from CATL's battery pant in the Yibin Lingang Economic Development Zone. Just as with the Qinzhou facility, Mineral Resources also gained a 50% ownership in the Meishan facility in 2023.

Simultaneously, Albemarle announced similar plans to develop another 50,000 tpa battery grade lithium hydroxide conversion plant in Zhangjiagang Free Trade Zone in Jiangsu province. This is the same economic zone that Tianqi Lithium has one of their conversion plants. This is only 70 miles east of CATL's massive battery plant in Liyang, Jiangsu Province. Albemarle anticipates both plants being completed by 2024.

If we add this all up, when completed, Albemarle will have 195,000 tpa of midstream conversion capacity located in the Asia market by 2025. If we subtract 15% of Kemerton's 50,000 tpa capacity (minus 7,500 tpa, thus leaving 42,500 tpa) as it is run by the 85/15 AMRBL JV, that leave's Albemarle with 187,500 tpa of sole ownership conversion capacity. Let's do the same math as we did with Tianqi who we noted is on track to have 112,000 tpa of conversion capacity. This would give Albemarle 38% of the 2021 China midstream conversion market (488,000 tpa). With a 6.3:1 spodumene concentrate feedstock ratio, Albemarle will need 1.1 million tons of feedstock, or all of Greenbushes 2022 production.

However, Albemarle only gets half of this production (due to their 49/51 JV with Tianqi), or 600,000 tons. This means Wodgina would have to kick in the other 500,000 tons. Since Wodgina is run by the 50/50 JV MARBL, the mine would have to run at 1 million tpa for Albemarle to capture the additional 500,000 tons. If Tianqi can sell all its 112,00 tons at $75,000.00 USD per ton, that brings them revenues of $8.4 billion USD annually. If Albemarle can sell their 187,500 tons at the same rate, that brings them $14 billion USD a year in revenue.

Does China and Australia Have a Strategic Decoupling Problem?

For the past several years there has been increasing talk from both sides about a possible economic decoupling between China and Australia. Friction comes in part from China and Australia having diametrically opposed political systems with Beijing's dictatorship model having nothing in common with Canberra's democracy. Australia is critical of China's human rights record, to include their treatment of their Uyghur population, much as the U.S. is. Australia is also grappling conceptually with their loss of power and influence in the region as China has grown to become Asia's economic and political center of gravity.

If we are going to talk decoupling, then we need to talk economics. China is by far Australia's largest two-way trading partner. Both countries signed the *China-Australia Fee Trade Agreement in 2015* to enhance their economies. While the agreement eliminated import tariffs on copper and nickel, lithium wasn't mentioned.[524] In 2020-2021, Australia and China traded $267 billion AUD in goods, which was 32% of all Australia's trade.[525] Obviously, that's significant. Overall, almost 66% of Australian trade is in the Asia market with Japan and South Korea being the next largest trading partners.

Obviously, with one-third of Australia's trade coming from China, there won't be any immediate economic decoupling. If Australia was going to do so, they would have to set an aspirational date of, let's say, 2035. From now until then, Canberra would have to steadily find substitutes for its China trade elsewhere in the Asia market until it reconstructed an entirely new economic paradigm. If this were to happen, we will see the amount of trade between Australia and China decline incrementally from now until then. It will be obvious. If trade steadily dropped 2% per a year from now until 2035, it would bottom out at just 10%. We could then consider the two effectively decoupled.

One can argue that there is already a "soft" decoupling underway or at least a minor trade war. Problems started when Australia called for an inquiry into the origins of COVID-19 in 2020 which China took serious offense to. China responded by sanctioning a variety of Australian products like wine, timber, barley, beef, cotton, sugar, wheat, and copper. Iron ore was left alone so as not to harm China's own construction industry requiring mountains of steel. China was careful that any sector they sanctioned, they could get the goods somewhere else. (COVID is just one topic in a series of issues between the two).

However, some of the sanctioned sectors were global commodities, like copper,

524 https://www.dfat.gov.au/trade/agreements/in-force/chafta/fact-sheets/Pages/chafta-fact-sheet-resources-energy-and-manufacturing

525 https://www.dfat.gov.au/geo/china/china-country-brief

that Australia could easily sell elsewhere. And by doing a soft decoupling first, China helped prepare Australia for a larger decoupling if it were to come later. These sanctions conditioned the Australian economic body to find substitute markets to survive and thrive – it was an education at a national level. Importantly, the ability of Australia to adapt to minor trade warfare with China broke any psychological barriers they might have had in doing so. In other words, they weren't afraid and would not bend the knee to Beijing because of economic coercion.

Speaking of economic coercion, is Australia a partner of China's Belt and Road initiative? No, Australia is not, but the State of Victoria was, at least for several years. In 2018, Victoria signed a four-page Memorandum of Understanding with China that was an overly vague document meant to cement a partnership between the two. For example, a typical paragraph in the MOU outlined their undefined partnership as such: "The Parties will endeavor to carry out cooperation within their respective areas of responsibility and strengths as mutually agreed through bilateral communication". This wording meant nothing but could also mean anything. Regardless of its context, Canberra wasn't impressed and overrode Victoria, scrapping the agreement in 2021 because it ran counter to Australian national policy. Is this more evidence of decoupling?

Let's get to the good stuff and see what a decoupling of lithium looks like. For this discussion, let's assume a total permanent ban of all Australian lithium going to China with no exceptions. Since Tianqi Lithium owns 51% of the Greenbushes mine, they would be compelled to divest their holdings. Canberra could allow interested buyers on the open market to bid for the now available shares or the Australian government could just buy Tianqi out at fair market value and figure out the details later. Tianqi would also have to divest its interest in the Kwinana conversion facility in a similar manner.

Of course, Ganfeng would have to divest its 50% ownership of the Marion mine that it shares with Mineral Resources. All Chinese companies owning shares of Australian lithium companies, even though they aren't involved in running a mining operation, would also have to divest. CATL did exactly this when they sold their small position in Pilbara in 2023, possibly to hedge against the kind of risk we are exploring now. Importantly, all existing offtake agreements would be rendered null and void, allowing China to only receive what lithium was already in transit on the high seas. While all Australian mining companies would be prevented from trading with China, so would Albemarle. They could no longer ship their own lithium extracted in Australia to their own conversion facilities in China.

If we estimate that Australia's four major lithium mines (Greenbushes, Pilgangoora, Marion, Wodgina) produce 2.5 million tons of lithium concentrate a year, this equals 393,000 tpa of LCE or considerably more than half of all lithium extracted in 2022. If 65% of the world's midstream conversion capacity is in China, how is the remaining 35% capacity going to process the 57% of global lithium production coming from Australia? It isn't. Australia will have to put a hold on its mining operations while annual revenues from sales plummet. From China's side, even if they could secure the remaining 43% of all lithium production in the world, they still come up 22% short. They have a problem. Their battery and BEV industries will be devastated. So, where do we go from here?

For Australia to survive a lithium decoupling, they would need to develop their own domestic midstream conversion capacity of approximately 150,000 tpa capacity so that they are not held hostage by China's own robust capability. They would also have to identify and facilitate the construction of other midstream conversion facilities in the Asia market such as in Japan, South Korea, and Indonesia. If each of these countries had a 50,000 tpa LCE capacity, Australia would have another 150,000 tpa of regional capacity to feed its lithium concentrate to. This is probably a five-year process if Australia started now. And this still doesn't solve the problem that for this processed lithium to be useful, it must feed the global battery and BEV industry which means China. North America's and Europe's markets aren't developed enough to accept this much capacity.

China is equally held hostage by Australia's lithium imports and they know it. Consequently, they are already working on their own battery minerals decoupling plan by shifting to new sources of lithium. To start, China is pursuing new lithium mining opportunities domestically, in Africa, from the Lithium Triangle and any new sources that their BRI partnerships may bring them. This is also why China is exploring the extraction of lithium from deep sea nodules on the ocean floor. If these resources are within China's recognized territorial waters, they own them. Also, Beijing will continue its R&D efforts in attempts to find a substitute for LIBs, to cut their reliance on foreign sources. They, too, have a long journey to travel if they want to shift their entire existing supply chain paradigm.

Because the complete decoupling of lithium would result in devastating economic shockwaves across the global battery and BEV industries, I don't see this outcome happening as part of the ongoing trade war between Australia and China. If a decoupling of the battery minerals industry were to happen, it would have to be incremental and planned by both sides. Importantly, we will see this happening as the data will reveal it. It hasn't happened yet. We will explore the topic of economic decoupling and battery mineral disruption further in Chapter 20 when we look into Russia's invasion of Ukraine.

Looking Ahead

1. As we can see, to maximize capture of the lithium value chain, a company must be in the midstream conversion business. However, the barrier to entry is high as a 50,000 tpa battery grade lithium hydroxide plant can take several years to construct and costs upwards of $1 billion USD. However, the countries and companies that want a secure value chain will invest the capital to make it happen.

2. How much longer will we see China continuing to rely on Australia hard rock lithium concentrate to feed their battery and BEV industries? Just as the U.S. and Europe slowly woke up to the reality that they had no security in their battery minerals supply chains, Beijing is becoming aware of their own problems. The data will show a shift in Chinese policy when and if it happens.

3. Albemarle is in the planning stages of locating a future midstream conversion plant in Chester County, South Carolina with a capacity of 100,000 tpa to meet the needs of the growing U.S. EV battery industry. Is this a hedge against future potential disruption of their Australia-China operations? Where will their lithium feedstock come from, the Lithium Triangle or Australia?

4. When will see other countries in Asia develop their own midstream conversion facilities to take on Australia lithium feedstock? South Korea and POSCO have shown an awareness for the need to do so. Japan is an obvious country to do so as well due to Panasonic's ongoing battery efforts with Tesla and their growing tentative relationship with Toyota. Indonesia is another obvious choice due to their world leading reserves of nickel and the continuing interest by battery companies in doing business there.

5. Australia wouldn't be held hostage with the need to feed China's battery and BEV industries if they had their own domestic industries to feed. Where is Australia's own domestic battery enterprise? Where is the foreign investment in battery plants like in the U.S. and Europe? Where is the planned BEV plant in Australia? How have they missed most of the lithium value chain? Why are they content churning out millions of tons of lithium concentrate and then invest in nothing else downstream? Where is their national leadership in this space, where is their vision, where is their strategy, where is their economic strategy?

CHAPTER 14

Pricing Lithium

"You can't lose, it's a license to print money." – Elon Musk during a 2022 Tesla earnings call, referring to the prices that the lithium midstream conversion industry can charge

The Battery Minerals Supercycle

The world is experiencing a battery minerals supercycle where demand outstrips supply for an extended period. We have seen commodity supercycles before that coincided with the First, Second and Third Industrial Revolutions, global phenomena that changed almost every aspect of our modern societies. These events drove base metals commodity supercycles, at different times, that included iron, tin, and copper. However, we have never experienced a battery mineral super cycle before.

This battery minerals super cycle will be multi-decadal and continue through 2050. I say 2050, as that is the target that the Paris Agreements have set for global carbon neutrality. This is to keep manmade global warming, due to our industrial scale burning of fossil fuels, at an increase of "only" 1.5 degrees Celsius from previous global averages. Our warming Earth has already, and will increasingly, create catastrophic climate conditions for many societies and our collective humanity. Thus, national governments and the international institutions they support are driving the battery minerals supercycle.

On the path to 2050 carbon neutrality, the world's automobile industry is transitioning away from the ICE business model to a battery driven EV business model. In parallel, a fast growing solar and wind power generation industry continues to replace the existing antiquated fossil fuel-centric utilities model. These, too, depend largely on batteries for their energy storage. Additionally, the global charging infrastructure for vehicles (cars, trucks, motorcycles, bikes, boats, planes) and home distributed power systems will require batteries at a scale many cannot imagine. All these examples help to drive the present explosion of battery manufacturing and the associated battery mineral mining operations.

Experts have noted that this supercycle isn't cyclical as in "lithium prices always go up and down in concert with the usual dynamics of supply and demand". We have never seen this type of lithium supercycle before because the international state system has never pursued carbon neutrality before. By all accounts, the world's governments aren't going to get lithium fatigue and accept a much hotter Earth that devastates entire nations. This isn't a fad or an impromptu environmental campaign, it's long-term policy. To achieve carbon neutrality by 2050, Wood Mackenzie estimates the world will have to invest $50 trillion USD, with much of this going towards the lithium value chain.[526]

This persistent and growing demand for battery minerals by various industries in the value chain means that there is also a lithium supercycle. McKinsey estimates by 2030 world demand for lithium will reach 4 million tons of LCE.[527] This level of demand explains why we see an explosion of lithium mining start-ups trying to get into the game in Canada, the U.S., the Lithium Triangle and elsewhere. This is also why we see established lithium companies, like SQM, doubling production and previously unrelated industries, kike PSOCO, entering the lithium space. They are all working to provide the supply to fill the increasingly voracious global demand.

Lithium Prices

Historically, lithium prices have been low, selling at levels that didn't significantly interfere with downstream sales in the value chain like batteries and BEVs. Let's look back over the last five years or so at the lithium price trend. In 2017, lithium carbonate in the China market hit a high of roughly $23,900.00 USD a ton. Prices steadily declined from there, dropping 75%, until they hit a low of roughly $5,400.00 USD in December 2020.

[526] Mining.com, "Next mining supercycle will be different than any other – report", Jul 15, 2021.

[527] M. Azevedo, et al, "Lithium mining: How new production technologies could fuel the global EV revolution", McKinsey & Company, Apr 12, 2022.

From there, prices rose steadily until August 2021 when they absolutely exploded. By mid-November 2021, lithium carbonate in China hit historic highs at $83,650.00 USD a ton. Never had the world seen such incredibly high prices for lithium.[528]

It is important to note that when there is increased demand for a commodity, like lithium, there is lag time before prices catch up to the supply-demand mismatch. This lag time could be several months or even a year. It takes time for the existing supply chain, which is global and thus complex, to work through existing orders sold at previous prices. But rest assured, it does catch up. The same can be said for an oversupply of any commodity, it will take time for the prices to come down. Let's learn from my own ignorance.

Like many people, I read about the deal with SQM to provide LG Energy Solution with lithium over the course of an eight-year contract. This deal was announced in December 2020. I thought about it for a week and then bought a sizeable position in SQM in early January 2021. I just knew lithium prices would go up and then so would SQM stock value. I bought the stock at $55.00 USD a share. One year later, in January 2022, SQM stock had dropped to $51.00 USD a share, so I dumped it.

Obviously, there were better places to put my money since, SQM must have had some internal management problems. In November 2022, SQM was trading at $111.00 a share. What could I possibly have been thinking? It is evident that I didn't have the investing patience and I clearly didn't understand the dynamics of the global supply chain. Remember, price lags supply and demand. Don't be like me.

The price of lithium is important for many reasons as it drives the overall industry. When the price of lithium is high, the global industry goes into overdrive to capture its value. A high price gives companies incentive to explore unknown lithium hard rock and brine deposits, to begin new extraction operations and to get into the midstream conversion business. Consequently, high lithium prices, although limited in duration, serve to expand global lithium capacity at every level: upstream, midstream, and downstream.

But as companies race to extract maximum revenue from high lithium prices, they are increasing supply to meet demand that in turn drives the prices lower again. I have listened to many people in the lithium industry lament about the specter of decreasing lithium prices when they themselves are driving it by their own actions.

---

[528] https://tradingeconomics.com/commodity/lithium

Hence, a company has a defined window of time to maximize the value of the continuously changing lithium value chain before it cycles lower again.

This may seem obvious, but a company needs an existing mine or conversion facility to capture the value chain when lithium prices rise. Since it takes many years to get a mining operation online due to a whole host of disruptive factors (lawsuits, permitting, funding), a mining company can end up chasing a lithium mirage. For example, Nemaska Lithium moved out on their Whabouchi hard rock lithium mine and battery-grade lithium hydroxide conversion plant in Quebec starting in 2010. They went bankrupt in 2019. Now Livent and Investissement Quebec (IQ) own the mine 50/50 and anticipate a 2025 production schedule. We don't know what the lithium prices will be then, but they will most likely be lower than in 2023. Did they miss their window of opportunity?

An inescapable evil of high lithium prices, and this is really a comment on human nature, is that they mask operational inefficiencies and bad business models. As Elon Musk said, lithium companies have a license to print money when the prices are high. When prices come back to Earth, inefficient operations don't survive. A good comparison is the Quebec Lithium Mine that last ran with operation costs of $1,000.00 a ton and Albemarle's Greenbushes mine that perennially runs at $250.00 a ton. At $2,000.00 a ton, both companies are successful. At $750.00 a ton, only Albemarle is successful.

With an eye always to the future, mining companies must ruthlessly pursue operational efficiency. High demand with high profits lead to increased supply and lower future prices, meaning a company must always be looking to lower their operational costs per ton to survive in a soft lithium market. This seems obvious, but the trail that is littered with bankrupt lithium operations would say otherwise.

It is a common practice when lithium prices decline to the point that operational costs exceed profit, to put a mine in a "care and maintenance" mode. Basically, a company puts its mining operation in hibernation until lithium prices come up again to justify reopening. However, a company still must provide physical security for their operation, keep the electricity on and provide routine maintenance of their extensive equipment inventory. The harsher the climate where the operation is located, the more expensive the care and maintenance. For an idle hard rock mine in Canada, annual expenses run into the millions. A big company with multiple mines, like Albemarle, can eat these expenses. A small company with a single mine, like North American Lithium, probably won't survive (they didn't).

Besides the immediate maintenance costs, another issue with an idle mine is that the equipment continues to age. If a mine is idle for an extended period time due to suppressed lithium prices, their operational model and equipment can become dated and noncompetitive with newer systems. In one example, the Quebec Lithium Mine was idled from 1965 until 1990 when its new owners, Cambior, determined the entire operation was a total loss. 1965 technology wouldn't work in a 1990 world. Consequently, they leveled it.

A significant downside to high lithium prices is that it undermines other aspects of the downstream lithium value chain. As lithium prices go up, this causes downstream inflation in LIBs and the BEV's that use them. Consequently, the end-product BEV has skyrocketing prices, which less people can afford. The name of the game is reducing global carbon emissions by selling BEV's at scale and not gouging regular hardworking consumers.

In March of 2020, the average raw-material cost per BEV was only $3,381.00 USD. By 2022, average raw-material prices for BEVs more than doubled to $8,255.00 USD per vehicle due largely to battery minerals price inflation like nickel, cobalt, and lithium. This was a 144% increase, an unsustainable rate for consumers. BEV specific costs went up from $2,000.00 USD per vehicle to $4,500.00 USD.[529, 530]

In 2022, the average BEV cost $54,000.00 USD, which was a 22% increase from $44,200.00 USD the year before.[531] In 2020, the Tesla Model Y base price went from $54,000.00 USD and then jumped to $64,000.00 in 2022. A Mustang Mach-E was priced at $42,895.00 in 2021 and then increased to $46,895.00 in 2023. In another example, Rivian raised its R1T 2023 model prices from $67,500.00 to $79,500.00. This caused outrage from loyal Rivian customers who had submitted pre-orders and demanded that the original price to be honored. Rivian caved in and did just that. Angry customers didn't care about battery mineral inflation.

[529] https://www.alixpartners.com/media-center/press-releases/2022-alixpartners-global-automotive-outlook/

[530] CNBC, "Raw material costs for electric vehicles have doubled during the pandemic", by M. Wayland, Jun 22, 2022

[531] Autoblog, "EV prices rise to $54,000 average as material costs and demand soar", by C. Teague, Jun 28, 2022.

Pricing Intelligence

Since lithium is not tracked on the major indices and has no universally recognized price per pound like copper, finding out the price of lithium can be challenging. First, the different forms of lithium have different prices. Lithium spodumene concentrate (the percentage of lithia in the ore matters), lithium chloride, lithium carbonate and lithium hydroxide (the percentage of purity affects the pricing) are all priced differently. Also, the prices of these products are different depending on the region, although the prices for the China/Japan/Korea market dominate pricing comparisons as that is where most of the world's lithium is ultimately used.

Consequently, Price Reporting Agencies (PRA) have filled the void by providing pricing for those involved in the lithium enterprise. One of the leading PRA's in the lithium space is Fastmarkets, a London based firm who has been in the pricing intelligence business since 1999. In 2016, Euromoney Institutional Investor PLC, a financial information company, bought Fastmarkets and merged it with their own *Metal Bulletin*, with the result being Fastmarkets MB. *Metal Bulletin* was a journal specializing in pricing for the metals market since 1913, so they had considerable expertise in the field.

To start, Fastmarkets' goal is to produce accurate daily pricing of lithium. To do this, they developed a network of people in the lithium pricing industry (buyers, sellers, traders, market participants) who provide them with pricing data. In this capacity, they are a pricing intelligence organization that uses human intelligence (called a data contributor) and open-source intelligence to collect the information they need to provide a price. Fastmarkets uses a defined methodology where they seek diversity of data contributors across the lithium market and avoid overreliance on single source reporting that could skew accurate pricing.

Fastmarkets tracks a total of 22 battery grade lithium products, technical grade lithium products and spodumene. They break their pricing intelligence down between the two major global lithium markets: China/Japan/Korea and Europe/U.S. Their pricing distinguishes between spot prices (meaning what the market is selling at right now) and contract prices (think long-term and fixed). The prices for lithium carbonate and lithium hydroxide are broken down into these separate categories. Fastmarkets only provides spodumene pricing for China since they are by far the single largest consumer of hard rock spodumene coming from Australia. Presently, there are no other significant hard rock spodumene mining operations outside of the China-Australia nexus.

Let's look at some of Fastmarkets' pricing tags. For example, MB-LI-0029 tracks 99.5% pure lithium carbonate battery grade spot price for China/Japan/Korea in $USD/kilogram, including cost of CIF (cost, insurance, freight). MB-LI-0024 tracks 56.5% pure lithium hydroxide monohydrate battery grade contract price in Europe/ U.S., in $USD/kilogram and DDP (Delivery Duty Paid). DDP means the seller is responsible for the shipping and all the import requirements like VAT (Value Added Tax), customs charges and duty payment. In a third example, MB-LI-0012 tracks 6% minimum spodumene in China, including CIF, in $USD/ton. This is non-specific of spot or contract pricing.

As I mentioned, Fastmarkets is not the only PRA providing dedicated to lithium pricing intelligence. Benchmark Mineral Intelligence also provides this service. Benchmark follows a similar methodology as they capture pricing data from 90% of global lithium transactions and gather pricing intelligence from 200 industry sources. They track six lithium carbonate prices, four lithium hydroxide prices and one spodumene price in monthly assessments.[532] S&P Global Commodity Insights (formerly S&P Global Platts – it's confusing) provides weekly pricing of lithium carbonate and hydroxide in China and every other day pricing of Australian spodumene. I would have advised looking at the CME (Chicago Mercantile Exchange), but they also use Fastmarkets pricing intelligence now.

Also, one can follow the Shanghai Metals Market (SMM) at www.metal.com. SMM goes the extra mile to collect pricing intelligence by using their status to gain access to companies in the metals market. Specifically, SMM conducts continuing exclusive tours of relevant companies who provide them presentations on their company operations. Thus, the SMM team can have an extended question and answer session with company leadership. This enables SMM to better price the commodities it follows but also acts as a marketing tool for the company.

There can be disparities in pricing intelligence, so it is useful to compare differing assessments. For example, Fastmarkets tag MB-LI-0033 battery grade lithium hydroxide for China/Japan/Korea with CIF tracked a spot price of $76,500.00 USD/metric ton on September 1, 2022. In contrast, for the exact same date, S&P Global tracked battery grade lithium hydroxide with DPP at a spot price of $67,500.00 USD/metric ton. Different PRA's use different pricing methodologies and some are more thorough and

---

[532] https://www.benchmarkminerals.com/lithium-prices/

current than others. In fact, these differences become bulletized marketing points as PRA's compete with one another for customers.

London Metal Exchange

Most of the lithium in its various forms are not sold on metal exchanges, but through point-to-point offtake contracts. Metal exchanges overwhelmingly serve as a medium to trade commodities futures and serve a hedging function, although they will sell a physical product if a trade isn't settled beforehand – but this is extremely rare. Until 2020, metal exchanges didn't show much interest in lithium because it was a low quantity, low price, relatively niche commodity that didn't have much impact on the global market. This has changed. In 2022, about 689,000 tons of LCE were produced. If all this tonnage were theoretically sold at $80,000.00 USD a ton, that's a $55 billion USD value. That's real money. Now metal exchanges are interested.

The London Metal Exchange (LME) is the oldest metals clearing house in the world, formally standing up in 1877, the same year Thomas Edison announced his new invention, the phonograph. In the early 1800's, British traders moved out of the crowded Royal Exchange created in 1571 and congregated in the nearby Jerusalem Coffee House. Here, metal merchants could focus on their industry like tin and copper. Notably, the merchants would draw a circle on the sawdust floor, around which trading would take place. To this day, LME traders honor this tradition and sit in 'the ring', made up of semi-circular red sofas, to conduct business on the exchange floor.[533]

In 2021, LME stood up a Lithium Advisory Committee (LAC) comprised of fifteen representatives from across the lithium value chain. Members are from companies that include Albemarle, Tesla, Pilbara, and Chengdu Chemical Company. They are deliberately selected to represent different aspects of the industry to include diverse geographies. The committee's mission is to provide expert advice to the LME on lithium contracts. Other key tasks include promoting the use of lithium contracts, overseeing contract procedures, and recommending lithium related policy. Standing up this committee reflects the growing importance of lithium and how serious LME takes the industry. This gives lithium the same standing as other LME committees that already represent metals like steel, tin, cobalt, nickel, and copper.

---

[533] Mining Technology, "Times are changing: a history of the London Metal Exchange", by M. Lempriere, Aug 29, 2019.

For a company to sell their physical lithium product through LME, they must register their Brand to become an approved seller. The registration process includes meeting responsible sourcing requirements and OECD (Organization for Economic Cooperation and Development) published guidelines. If an approved Brand does not comply with LME policy, they are subject to suspension and/or delisting as well as canceling of existing warrants.

This Brand certification process ensures buyers get an ethically sourced product and protects them from their own future legal and reputational risk. A lithium mining company certainly doesn't want Greenpeace dropping a video about them to their 1.9 million Twitter followers exposing their use of a product derived from indigenous child labor with an extraction process that polluted local community drinking water and desecrated their ancient burial grounds. We would put that in the "bad" category. Because of the strict branding process, buying through LME is its own insurance policy.

Then there is the topic of storage and where the seller's physical product resides. For this part of the equation, LME has a Warehousing Committee that meets quarterly to ensure the LME warehousing process is executed effectively. In doing so, they oversee a global network of 500 warehouses in 32 separate locations to provide regional commodity storage solutions to their customers. Of note, there are no Chinese warehouses in LME's network, but there is history here.[534]

In 2012, the Hong Kong Stock Exchange (HKEx) bought LME for $2.2 billion USD. This move combined the exchange with the largest listing of Chinese companies in the world with the world's oldest metals house. Since much of the world's traded metals ended up in the Chinese market, the synergies were obvious. However, in 2008, the Chinese Securities and Regulatory Commission (CSRC) banned foreign exchanges from operating in mainland China. Because warehouses weren't specifically mentioned in the ban, HKEx thought they could get LME warehouses established in the newly created Shanghai Free Trade Zone. This never materialized because the CSRC continued to enforce the ban, expanding it to include LME warehouses. This was most likely done to prevent direct competition with the Shanghai Futures Exchange.[535]

Getting back to LME's storage network, LME does not own the warehouses nor

---

[534] www.lme.com

[535] Reuters, By F. Wong, P. Yam, "UPDATE 1-China's new free trade zone will not allow LME warehouses", Oct 23, 2013.

the physical product, but they ensure the warehouses meet LME regulations. These requirements include transportation capability, storage space, minimum daily load-out tonnage, and published storage fees. LME officers conduct physical on-premises inspections of these warehouses which can be delisted from LME's network for violating published LME Warehouse Requirements. Warehouses have incentive to participate in the LME network as it provides them business. Buyers trading through LME benefit from knowing that their newly acquired product is stored appropriately, in a logistically useful location and can be moved in a timely manner.

While deals through the LME can result in the actual transfer of physical goods between buyer and seller, this only occurs less than 1% of the time. The other 99% of the time, transactions are settled prior to actual physical exchange as they are overwhelming used as a hedging mechanism. However, these contracts are backed up by a physical product.

Beyond branding and storage, LME also expanded into the lithium pricing business when they hired Fastmarkets in 2019. One can assume LME, as newcomers to the lithium business, found it more economical to hire Fastmarkets' pricing services as opposed to hiring their own internal LME staff to do the same. However, there was drama with the decision as Benchmark Mineral Intelligence had competed for the same contract. Benchmark CEO Simon Moores responded to the hiring of Fastmarkets instead of Benchmark: "While the LME is new to lithium and we respect its decision, we wholly disagree. To provide truly reflective lithium pricing, you need a global team dedicated to analyzing and understanding the market. It is clear we have the only team in the world that meets this criteria."[536]

Just to show you how new I am to the business, as I mentioned elsewhere, I attended Fastmarkets' 2022 battery minerals conference in Phoenix. At the time, I had no idea who Fastmarkets was. I thought they were a contract event organizer. When I was there, I asked a Fastmarkets representative where the Benchmark booth was, because I couldn't find them anywhere. He kind of looked at me funny and politely replied that he didn't think they were at the event. Now that I know the background, it is obvious why Benchmark wasn't at an event organized by their chief pricing intelligence rival.

---

[536] https://www.benchmarkminerals.com/benchmark-minerals-reaction-to-london-metal-exchange-lme-lithium-decision/

Pilbara's Independent BMX Lithium Auction

Most of the lithium sold on the global market today is through long-term binding off-take agreements. These are legal contracts where a BEV or battery company agrees to buy a certain amount of a lithium product (spodumene, LCE, lithium hydroxide, etc.) from a supplier such as a lithium mining company. If a buyer can get a good price for many years on a bulk lithium product, it's to their advantage to lock it in. A long-term offtake agreement is a hedge against lithium inflation because once the deal has been inked, it doesn't matter if lithium prices go up.

For example, GM signed an offtake agreement with Livent in July 2022 for battery-grade lithium hydroxide starting in 2025.[537] This is a six-year contract where most of the lithium will come from Livent's Argentine brine operations. According to Fastmarkets, for July 2022, 56.5% pure battery-grade lithium hydroxide averaged $75,000.00 USD a metric ton in the Asia market. Four months later, in November of that year, the London Metal Exchange was selling 56.5% pure lithium hydroxide (futures) at $83,000.00 USD per metric ton.

As we can see, the exact date that a company signs an offtake agreement matters, as prices can and do change significantly. In this example, GM benefits from locking in a set price over six years that won't rise. However, Livent is locked into a deal where they are missing increased value over time. Livent is still getting a great deal as lithium prices are ridiculously high and they have guaranteed income for a set period. However, they would benefit from not committing all their lithium production in a market with rising prices, this way they can hedge against the high probability of continuing price increase.

This example also serves to illustrate how established companies like GM and Livent enforce information security and won't reveal details about their offtake agreements. They won't reveal the price paid for the lithium product nor the volume such as how many tons. GM doesn't want their competition to know how much their batteries will cost and Livent doesn't want other buyers to know if they are getting a bad deal. Sometimes a person can conduct business intelligence and gather data from a company's annual report, compare that to the previous year, and guestimate what a company paid for an offtake agreement. Other times, bankruptcy proceedings and

---

[537] https://ir.livent.com/news/news-details/2022/General-Motors-and-Livent-Enter-Long-Term-Lithium-Hydroxide-Supply-Agreement/default.aspx

related court documents will reveal pricing data. In contrast, small start-up mining companies are eager to reveal their offtake agreements, specifically the volume, to show that they are a viable business to attract investors and capital.

The above background serves to make the Pilbara case even more interesting. As we discussed in *Chapter 13: Lithium Hardrock Conversion*, Pilbara secured long-term offtake agreements with General Lithium Corporation, Ganfeng Lithium, Great Wall Motor Company, Yibin Tianyi and POSCO. But this means they are locked into binding contracts signed as long ago as 2016, which were probably priced at about $525.00 USD a ton. Since then, the average price of spodumene per ton has increased tenfold. However, if Pilbara committed all its capacity to binding long-term contracts, they missed out on the value increase of spodumene concentrate – a potential loss of hundreds of millions of dollars.

As we know, Pilbara was aware of these dynamics, and as they increased their overall production capacity with their Stage 2 expansion, they made sure not to tie up this additional tonnage in long-term offtake agreements. Instead, they made the decision to sell this tonnage on the open market, in an auction format, to maximize their value. Not only that, but Pilbara cut out any middlemen (like London Metal Exchange) and auctioned their tonnage in direct sales to customers just like Tesla selling cars directly to their customers, no dealerships required. Surprisingly, in an industry that overwhelmingly hides their sales data, Pilbara has a history of being very transparent with their offtake agreements to include volume and price per ton. Their auction was no different.

To sell their lithium concentrate, Pilbara established their Battery Material Exchange (BMX) where registered and verified buyers could bid on their lithium concentrate. To date, they held a series of digital auctions, holding them each time as more uncommitted tonnage becomes available through their expanded extraction operations. Remember, Pilbara's hard rock mining operations are in Australia and sell mostly to the China/Japan/Korea market. For all auctions, the concentrate sold is 5.5% lithia and the tonnage is shipped from Port Hedland. Shipping costs to China run about $80.00 USD a ton. Let's look at how these auctions did.

-   July 2021 (Auction #1): 10,000 tons, sold @ $1250.00 USD per ton, three-hour auction, with 17 bidders, 62 online bids placed, for a total of $12.5 million USD

- Sep 2021 (Auction #2): 8,000 tons, sold @ $2,240.00 USD per ton for a total of $17.9 million USD
- Oct 2021: (Auction #3): 10,000 tons 5.5% at $2350.00 a ton, 45-minutes, for $23.5 million USD
- April 2022 (Auction #4) 5,000 tons, sold @ $5,650.00 USD a ton for a total of $28.25 million USD
- May 2022 (Auction #5): 5,000 tons, pre-auction bid sold @ $5,955.00 USD per ton for a total of $29.77 million USD
- June 2022 (Auction #6): 5,000 tons, pre-auction bid sold @ $6,350.00 USD per ton for a total of $31.75 million USD
- July 2022 (Auction 7): 5,000 tons, received 41 bids, sold @ $6,188.00 USD per ton, 30-minute auction, for a total of $30.9 million USD
- Aug 2022 (Auction # 8): 5,000 tons, received 67 bids and sold @ $6,350.00 USD per ton, 30-minute auction, for $31.75 million USD
- Sep 2022 (Auction #9): 5,000 tons, received 22 bids, 30-minute auction, highest bid @ $6,988.00 USD per ton, for a total of $34.9 million USD
- October 2022 (Auction #10): 5,000 tons of spodumene bid @ $7,100.00 USD a ton, for a total of $35.5 million USD[538]
- November 2022, (Auction#11): 5,000 tons of spodumene bid @ $7,805.00 USD a ton, for a total sale of $39 million USD

Over the first few auctions, Pilbara was still figuring their system out, as well as conditioning their buyers to their BMX process. Their process evolved into selling 5,000 tons of spodumene concentrate every month through their online digital auction running for concise 30-minute periods. On occasion, they accepted pre-auction bids if the price was right, so they would forego the formal auction period. BMX worked out well for Pilbara and was an ongoing hedge against historic offtake agreements when the market price for lithium was still climbing. As long as demand for lithium remained high, combining fixed contracts with spot price auctions was a great way to achieve income stability and still capture rising profits.

Importantly, as we know, spodumene concentrate is the feedstock that kicks off the whole show and is later converted into lithium carbonate or lithium hydroxide.

---

[538] Pilbara publishes reports to the ASX reference its auctions

With this upstream feedstock inflation, all the midstream conversion products increase in price as well. The only way a company can counter this inflation is through vertical integration by owning not only the feedstock mining operation itself, but the midstream conversion facilities as well like Albemarle and Ganfeng. From a pricing intelligence perspective, one can bet that both Fastmarkets and Benchmark followed every one of these auctions closely and updated their China/Japan/Korea market price estimates for spodumene accordingly.

Strategic Stockpiling – Pricing Considerations

In 2022, the Biden Administration began conceptually working through the idea of stockpiling critical mineral resources to include battery minerals like nickel, cobalt, manganese, and lithium. The idea was to develop a buffer to global supply chain shocks to ensure the U.S.' low-carbon future could continue regardless of external impacts. An oft cited example of the need for stockpiling in the critical mineral space is when China stopped delivery of rare earth elements to Japan in 2010. This was due to a diplomatic row sparked by Japan's detention of a Chinese fishing trawler and its captain.

At that time, China already had a lock on the global REE industry, which has only increased since then. Japan, who must import everything, will always be vulnerable to supply chain disruption, meaning they should have a strong strategic stockpiling program in place. They didn't in 2010 and still don't. However, in the decade since that incident, Japan went from 100% dependence on China for REEs to 58%, meaning they are now only mostly dependent on their chief Asian rival.[539] This event was supposed to be a lesson to the world with similar supply chain dependencies. Yet here we are, 14 years later, and the U.S. is just starting to work through what a critical mineral stockpile program might look like.

There are many complexities to the topic, but for our purposes, let's look at potential impacts on the price of lithium. History often repeats itself and this case is no different. As we mentioned before in Chapter 7, the Atomic Energy Commission (AEC) had classified contracts with the three major American lithium companies from roughly 1955 through 1959. The AEC requested so much lithium for its hydrogen

---

[539] By M. Hui, "Japan's global rare earths quest holds lessons for the US and Europe", www.qz.com, Apr 23, 2021.

bomb program that its purchases were the chief driver of lithium production in North America and the world market. The amount of lithium supplied to the AEC and the prices they paid were and remain classified. Also, of interest to us, the U.S. Geological Survey stopped reporting on U.S. lithium production numbers after 1953. Intentional or not, this served to mask how much lithium was being stockpiled for the hydrogen bomb program.

What we do know, is that the AEC's purchases created an increased demand for lithium, raising prices and creating a bubble. This lithium bubble burst in 1960 when the AEC did not renew its contracts, flooding the market with uncommitted lithium. The Quebec Lithium Mine (QLM) lost 90% of its business after it had been supplying 17,000 units of lithium a month to Lithium Corporation of America (LCA) who then funneled it to the AEC. One unit of lithium is 20 pounds, so QLM provided upwards of 4 million pounds (2,000 tons) a year to LCA.

In turn, LCA lost 50% of its lithium business, even though the AEC warned them a year out that they would not be renewing their previous 5-year contract. Foote Mineral lost 33% of its business with revenues falling from $24 million a year to $16 million a year.[540] In the U.S., Lithium Hydroxide sold for $0.72 a pound or $1,440.00 USD a ton up until 1960. This dropped to $0.54 a pound or $1,080.00 a ton in 1961, a change of 25%. Prices remained depressed through 1970 when lithium prices rose to $0.59 a pound or $1,180.00 a ton. For today's prices, adjusted for inflation, multiple those numbers x 10. Imagine getting a ton of battery grade lithium today for just $10,000.00 USD.[541]

Six years after the end of World War II, the Cold War was in full swing. In 1951, the *Mutual Defense Assistance Control Act* was passed in an effort by the U.S. and its post-war allies to restrict goods of strategic value from Russia and its allies. *Under Title I – War Materials*, the embargo included arms, ammunition, petroleum and "atomic energy materials". Section 201 of the Act further stated that the U.S. would regulate the export of commodities to strengthen the U.S. and oppose the Soviet Union. However, in 1951, the U.S. and the AEC did not yet value lithium like they eventually would as their hydrogen bomb program was still immature.[542]

---

[540] Foote Mineral Company, 45th Annual Report, 1960.

[541] By O.W. Roskill, "Lithium: World Survey of Production and Consumption with special reference to future demand and prices" May 7, 1971.

[542] Mutual Defense Assistance Control Act of 1951.

By 1955, the AEC recognized the strategic importance of lithium to its own hydrogen bomb program. They recommended that lithium be added to Title I of the Act with the purpose of hampering the Soviet Union's own program. However, the Soviet Union was still able to acquire plenty of lithium for its own hydrogen bomb program, detonating test bombs in both 1953 and 1955. This meant Russia had already been successfully accumulating its own strategic lithium stockpile for several years.

We know this, because Russia began dumping its excess lithium on the open commodities markets in Europe in 1967, helping to keep lithium prices depressed. For example, West Germany imported 2,241 tons of lithium carbonate from Russia in the years 1967-1970 as compared to the 1,733 tons imported from the U.S. Not only did the U.S. and its Cold War alliance fail to prevent Russia from gaining access to lithium, but Russia also sold the excess lithium from its own hydrogen bomb program back to the U.S.' closest European allies.[543]

Regarding the U.S.' own strategic lithium stockpile, the AEC agreed to hold onto the lithium it bought from American lithium companies for a period of ten years. This was decided so that the AEC would not act as an unfair competitor to the existing U.S. lithium companies. Because the AEC was not a business and didn't function on the profit motive, it could sell its lithium at below market prices and suppress the entire lithium market. Every ton of lithium the AEC sold at below-market prices was a ton LCA or Foote Mineral couldn't sell at market prices.

In 1969, the GSA (General Services Administration) put up two lots of lithium hydroxide for bid, but the offers were low, and sales were small. Apparently, the market had enough lithium.[544] The next year, the Office of Stockpile Disposal received 13 million pounds of lithium hydroxide from the AEC and then sold it directly to LCA and Foote Mineral.[545] Presumably, since the lithium market was weak, the lithium was sold to both companies at below market prices. Curiously, Foote Mineral's annual reports for 1970 and 1971 don't mention receiving any lithium from the government. Foote's Chemical & Mineral Division's reporting was specific enough that they would have

---

[543] By O.W. Roskill, "Lithium: World Survey of Production and Consumption with special reference to future demand and prices" May 7, 1971

[544] Ibid.

[545] By J. Thomas, "Auditors allege mismanagement of defense stockpiles", July 22, 1979, Minneapolis Tribune.

nentioned the acquisition of 6-7 million pounds (3,000-3,500 tons) of lithium hydrox-
le at bargain basement rates, but they didn't.

Several years later, in 1974, GSA began negotiating the sale of an additional 80
illion pounds (40,000 tons) of lithium hydroxide through direct contracts with LCA
d Foote Mineral. Only then did we get a sense of how much lithium the AEC had
ckpiled during the 1950's. The previous 13 million pounds (6,500 tons) of lithium
droxide combined with the new amount equaled 46,500 tons of lithium hydroxide.
hat?!? That meant U.S. lithium companies had secretly funneled at least 9,300 tons
lithium a year to the AEC from 1955 to 1959. For comparison, estimated global
duction of lithium in 1958 was only about 5,000 tons. This means that the U.S.
rogen bomb lithium stockpile alone was almost double all known world lithium
duction for that five-year period.[546]

In 1974, global lithium production was still only about 7,000 tons that year. Thus,
held almost seven years-worth of global lithium production in their warehouses.
iously, GSA had a problem: they had more product than they could move, and
nding on how they moved it, they could crash the global lithium market. In the
ess, they could also potentially put out of business the very American companies
sold them the lithium in the first place. It was quite the dilemma. It looked like
was stuck with the single largest stockpile of lithium in the world.

s GSA was under pressure from the Nixon Administration to get rid of the ex-
ithium, they came up with the plan to sell this lithium back to LCA and Foote
al for one-third the going rate, which was $45 million below market rates.[547] This
help the GSA budget, free up warehouse space, and keep America's two major
n companies flush with lithium product. If a $45 million USD loss is two-thirds
market value, then GSA must have been negotiating a sale of the 40,000 tons
$22.5 million USD. Consequently, the going rate for 40,000 tons was $67.5 mil-
D, which equals $1,687.50 USD per ton. But at the 66% discount rate, LCA and
ould be getting it for only $562.5 USD a ton.

ile contract negotiations for GSA's mountain of lithium continued, GSA pro-
in 1977, auctioning 1.2 million more pounds (a mere 600 tons) of lithium

---

Kessler, "GSA Planned Sales of Surplus Below Market Price", Jun 22, 1978, The
ngton Post.

ERIC LYON

PHL9-76784132-LNLQZEJE-476

hydroxide using a sealed bidding process. As one could have predicted, Foote Minera
protested this competitive bidding process claiming it would disrupt their lithium op
erations. In other words, buyers would get the government owned lithium at muc
lower prices than Foote was selling it for. That was the "disruption". Accordingly, th
GSA stopped the bid.[548]

In the end, questions raised from an internal GSA audit and then investigatio
by the Department of Justice put the bulk lithium sale on hold. Also, another u
of lithium metal in alloys was discovered and GSA auditors recommended the b
lithium stockpile be saved for this use. Critics of the process described it as unethi
crony-capitalism that benefitted big business and the Administration's own dome
political allies. While DOJ did not find any wrongdoing reference the sale of lithiun
placed the entire process under severe public scrutiny. Of note, a wider ongoing
probe at the time into alleged GSA corruption did result in 117 criminal indictme
and 89 convictions.[549]

This previous experience in stockpiling, and specifically in lithium, should s
to inform the U.S. government as they move forward with their plans to rev
the strategic mineral stockpile. At present, the lithium market is tight and if the
Department of Defense starts buying up bulk quantities of battery minerals, p
will remain high or climb even further. These high prices undermine the overall
to transition to a low-carbon economy as zero-emission batteries and BEVs be
unaffordable to the larger population.

Also, the demand for battery minerals is so high, worldwide, there isn't er
being extracted to go around. In other words, a U.S. government stockpile pr
on a large scale, it would have to be massive to provide the necessary mine
curity it envisions, would undercut the transition to a green economy. The U
have to choose between securing a critical mineral stockpile in the near futu
years) or wait longer (7-8 years) until supply side forces catch up to runaway d
Otherwise, they'll undercut the very idea that is driving the current battery n
demand.

---

[548] By J. Thomas, "Auditors allege mismanagement of defense stockpiles", July
Minneapolis Tribune.
[549] By G. Goldenberg, "White House aid linked to 'bootleg investigations'", Sep 27, 197
Herald-Post.

When Will the Lithium Bubble Burst?

A report by Goldman Sachs (GS) in May 2022 predicting the impending rupture of the lithium bubble upset quite a few people in the lithium industry. What was so controversial about it? To begin, GS dared to proclaim that the green battery minerals bull market was over. Their fundamental thesis was that so much capital has been invested into the supply side of the equation (i.e., lithium mining) that a spot-market driven commodity was being traded as a forward-looking equity. They concluded that lithium, among other battery minerals like cobalt and nickel, had become fundamentally mispriced and a significant correction would come by 2024.[550]

GS further blasphemed the lithium market, predicting that the price per ton would drop from GS's own estimated price of $53,982.00 USD a ton in summer 2022 to a mere $16,373.00 USD a ton in 2023.[551] Since Fastmarkets' battery minerals conference was held only a month after GS's pricing prediction, I was expecting a lithium riot – company booths set on fire, buffets filled with pastries dumped on the nice carpet and anti-GS graffiti spray-painted on the bathroom walls. It wasn't quite that dramatic, but I did encounter some snide remarks and eye-rolling.

So, where did GS see this lithium oversupply coming from? They believed it would be from new mining operations coming online in China, Chile, and Australia. In China, they saw a growth in both hard rock and brine operations, adding 350 kilotons of LCE to the existing supply by 2025. From 2022-2025, GS predicted overall lithium supply would increase 33% annually, year over year (YoY) with demand only growing 27% YoY, creating a 6% gap that grew proportionally over that period. The GS report was well written by a competent team of experts in the field, but what did the professional price rating agencies think of their assessment?[552]

Benchmark responded to GS's report, disagreeing with some of its fundamental analysis. Specifically, Benchmark did not see a significant amount of lithium mining operations coming online until the end of 2023 or even early 2024. If this held true, then lithium prices would not drop to $16,000.00 USD a ton as forecasted by GS. Benchmark noted that Chinese mining operations suffered from delays and any new oversupply

---

[550] By N. Snowden, et. al.," Battery Metals Watch: The end of the beginning," May 29, 2022, Goldman Sachs Commodities Research.

[551] Ibid

[552] Ibid.

would not be coming from Beijing. In contrast to the GS report, Benchmark saw demand continuing to outstrip supply through 2025. Benchmark further predicted an increase in demand by another 1 million tons of LCE annually as we approached 2035.[553]

Whoever gets this right will have conducted the better analysis. From a demand side analysis, a team would need to understand the growth trends for every battery maker in the world. This battery growth would be tied directly to the BEV industry, so they need the production numbers of every auto company selling BEVs. Furthermore, the analytical team would need to cross over into overlapping supply side data to understand what level of output was physically possible. Thus, details about the entire lithium carbonate and lithium hydroxide conversion enterprise with output numbers from every facility in the world had to be known.

To understand the near-term supply-side inputs (1-2 years out), an analytical team would have to track every lithium mining project in the world. They would have to understand where every mine was in its overall trajectory, meaning they knew intimate details about each operation's permitting approvals, operational schedule, and financial health. Because of all the variables we discussed in *Chapter 6: The U.S. Mining Permitting Process*, I don't think one can accurately forecast a new mine's operational trajectory past 1-2 years. Anyone purporting to know the world's mining schedule three years out and more also has some beach front property to sell you in Arizona. If you don't believe me, I have three words for you: Rosemont Copper Mine.

Let's close out the chapter with a lithium pricing update. By the third week of March 2023, battery-grade lithium carbonate (LCE) prices had dropped in China to $46,875.00 USD a ton, down from historic highs in November 2022. This was a 45% drop in just four months from the previous ridiculously high prices. This was good news for battery manufacturers, BEV companies and the consumer buying the end product. This did mean that the owners of midstream conversion facilities like the big five (Ganfeng, Tianqi, Albemarle, Livent & SQM) would see their profits normalize for their 2023 annual reporting year.[554]

For one, Chinese BEV manufacturer Nio stated that every drop in lithium prices of $15,000.00 USD per ton of battery-grade LCE enabled them to realize an additional gross

553 "What is driving lithium prices in 2022 and beyond?" Aug 25, 2022, www.benchmarkminerals. com.

554 Zhang, Phate. "Lithium prices see biggest drop this year in China as decline accelerates, CnEVPost, March 20, 2023.

margin of 2%. Hence, Nio could expect to realize improved gross margins of almost 6% compared to previous historic highs. Nio also didn't think the drop in LCE prices were done as they anticipated a ton of battery-grade LCE would keep dropping until it hit $30,000.00 USD.[555]

Looking Ahead

1. Does the reader recognize that we are in a battery minerals super cycle, the likes of which are unknown to previous generations? Why or why not? Do you agree with the prediction that this super cycle will continue through 2050 or whenever humanity collectively achieves carbon neutrality?

2. What is your opinion on the supply and demand dilemma? Does the reader see supply catching up with demand like Goldman Sachs predicts or do you believe we will still experience a demand mismatch as Benchmark Mineral Intelligence predicts? Consider trying your own supply and demand formula and see how complex it gets. You can't do it unless if you have very specific data about many different operations which isn't easy to get.

3. What does the reader think about the differing price estimates from the competing agencies? Who do you trust more for accurate data? Shanghai Metals Market? Fastmarkets? Benchmark? S&P Global? Why do you follow one over the other, what is it about their pricing formula that you prefer over another?

4. What is the reader's opinion on a company hedging its bets through a combination of auctions, spot pricing and long-term offtake agreements? Do you like what Pilbara has been doing? Would you prefer to stick with established methods like what the LME offers? Both the seller and the buyer prefer different options depending on how it benefits them, now and in the future. How do we balance both needs?

5. Finally, is it even possible for a country to execute a realistic battery minerals stockpiling plan in the current super cycle environment? If there isn't enough lithium and cobalt to go around for the 80 million BEVs a year that will need them, how does a country think they are going to be able to stockpile these same resources? How does one balance a national stockpiling plan with achieving carbon neutrality? Which one is a bigger national security threat?

---

[555] Ibid.

Breaking Down the Cost of an
EV BATTERY CELL

The average cost of lithium-ion batteries has declined by 89% since 2010.

What makes up the cost of lithium-ion cells?

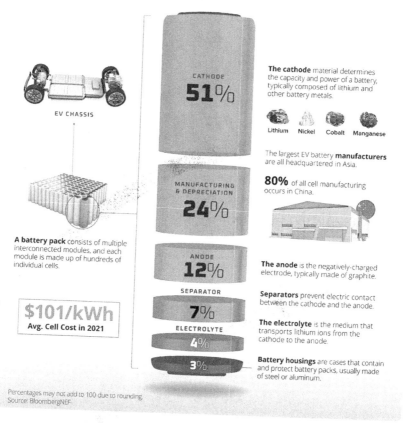

EV CHASSIS

A battery pack consists of multiple interconnected modules, and each module is made up of hundreds of individual cells.

$101/kWh
Avg. Cell Cost in 2021

CATHODE
51%

MANUFACTURING & DEPRECIATION
24%

ANODE
12%

SEPARATOR
7%

ELECTROLYTE
4%

3%

The cathode material determines the capacity and power of a battery, typically composed of lithium and other battery metals.

Lithium   Nickel   Cobalt   Manganese

The largest EV battery **manufacturers** are all headquartered in Asia.

80% of all cell manufacturing occurs in China.

The anode is the negatively-charged electrode, typically made of graphite.

Separators prevent electric contact between the cathode and the anode.

The electrolyte is the medium that transports lithium ions from the cathode to the anode.

Battery housings are cases that contain and protect battery packs, usually made of steel or aluminum.

Percentages may not add to 100 due to rounding.
Source: BloombergNEF

This is an interesting breakdown of the separate costs of the components within a lithium-ion battery. Notice that the cathode (positive terminal) is the most expensive component and involves the usual suspects: lithium, nickel, cobalt, and manganese. The anode (negative terminal) generally isn't discussed and is assumed to be graphite, either natural flake or synthetic. Professional PRAs have the challenge of estimating the cost and pricing for each one of these components in the different major markets. It takes a talented cross-functional team to get the most accurate estimates. (*by Getty Images*)

Lithium ore at the Greenbushes mine in Australia is transferred on a conveyor belt for further crushing and processing. Greenbushes is estimated to run costs at $250.00 USD per ton, the lowest in the industry. (by Getty Images).

The processed SC6 is dumped into piles for transfer to a midstream conversion facility, either Albemarle's Kemerton operation or onto China to feed their relentless lithium machine. (by Getty Images)

CHAPTER 15

Battery Electric Vehicles

"I think the biggest effect that Tesla will have will be to spur the other manufacturers to create compelling electric cars...to go electric sooner than they otherwise would." – Elon Musk

Global BEV Trends

The global ground transportation industry (cars, SUVs, trucks) is transitioning from traditional ICE (Internal Combustion Engine) vehicles to zero emission vehicles. The transition began in earnest in 2010 with the growth of Tesla. In many ways, Tesla spearheaded the global transition to BEVs (Battery Electric Vehicles). As Elon Musk intended, Tesla's success forced other traditional ICE OEMs (Original Equipment Manufacturers) like Ford and VW to pursue their own electrification programs or miss out on growing profits from the accelerating BEV trend or even face bankruptcy. Later, government mandates would spur on the transition to BEVs as low carbon transportation became law.

There has been an industry tendency to lump together both plug-in hybrid electric vehicles (PHEVs) and BEVs. PHEVs have both a small traditional ICE and a small rechargeable battery so that they can travel on either. Early reporting on the production of low carbon emitting vehicles did not distinguish between the two so it can be difficult to find good historical data on strictly BEV vehicles. For this chapter, we will focus on BEVs since the most efficient and profitable car company in the world pursues a 100% BEV business model. Additionally, PHEV's don't reduce carbon emissions nearly as much as BEVs and they will be phased out in favor of BEVs. Consequently, I assess PHEV manufacturing as a fundamentally flawed business model that will ultimately disappear.

In 2010, the global BEV market was microscopic. That year, Tesla sold its 1,500th Roadster and received 3,700 pre-orders for its Model S project which wasn't even in production yet.[556] Chinese carmaker BYD (Build Your Dreams) was selling their e6 BEV cross-over sedan with a 150-mile range to the Shanghai market in very low volumes – they sold just 33 that year.[557] That same year, Nissan introduced their 100-mile range Leaf sedan in Japan and the U.S., selling only 19 in the North American market.[558] Not a single German OEM made a BEV that year. It was easy to see, with only 0.01% of global vehicle sales, why the future of BEV transportation was in doubt.[559]

Fast forward five years to 2015 and things looked a little different when 540,000 PHEVs and BEVs were sold. This wasn't an overwhelming number, but it clearly showed the trend in rising BEV sales and declining ICE sales. The Chinese market grew from 58,000 BEVs sold in 2014 to 191,000 sold in 2015. The European market grew from 97,000 BEVs sold in 2014 to 193,000 sold in 2015. The U.S. market regressed from 120,000 BEVs sold in 2014 to 115,000 in 2015. Japan also regressed from an underwhelming 32,000 BEVs sold in 2014 to only 25,000 sold in 2015. In a growing trend, the China market accounted for 33% of global BEV sales.[560]

As would become customary, Tesla led the world in 2015 BEV sales with 50,580 vehicles.[561] However, there were new players in the field with GM selling their Chevy Volt in the U.S. In Germany, BMW was selling their i3 and i8 BEV series and VW their e-Golf. In South Korea, Hyundai started selling their Kia Soul EV. Toyota had already stopped production of their unpopular RAV4 EV that proved to be a low-performing

---

[556] https://ir.tesla.com/press-release/tesla-motors-reports-fourth-quarter-and-full-year-2010-results

[557] https://carsalesbase.com/china-byd-e6/

[558] InsideEVs, by M. Kane, "Nissan LEAF Sales Overview In U.S. From 2010-2019", May 02, 2019.

[559] https://www.iea.org/data-and-statistics/charts/global-sales-and-sales-market-share-of-electric-cars-2010-2021

[560] https://www.ev-volumes.com/news/global-plug-in-vehicle-sales/

[561] Elecktrek, by F. Lambert, "Tesla delivered 17,400 vehicles in Q4 for a total of 50,580 in 2015, Model X production at "238 units per week", Jan 03, 2016.

model with corresponding low volume sales. In China, BYD sold over 61,000 plug-in vehicles but only 7,000 were BEVs.[562]

In 2020, BEV sales grew considerably in the intervening five years with an estimated 2,187,500 sold globally. Tesla again led the field with 499,535 BEVs sold in all markets. China led the global BEV market with approximately 900,000 vehicles sold. The European market secured the next largest portion of global BEV sales with 740,000 units sold. There were increased sales by several European manufacturers like Renault, VW, Peugeot, BMW, Audi, Porsche, and Mercedes-Benz.

The North American market was by far the biggest laggards of the three. Only 252,000 BEVs were sold in the U.S. with Tesla dominating the field (200,000 vehicles sold) with contributions by the Chevy Bolt, Nissan Leaf, Audi E-Tron, Porsche Taycan, Hyundai Kona, and Kia Niro.[563] The Detroit OEMs consisting of Ford, GM, and Chrysler (Stellantis) remained far behind the competition with Tesla being the only credible American BEV manufacturer. Toyota, too, remained conspicuously absent from the U.S. BEV market.

In 2022, BEV sales continued to accelerate with an estimated 7.8 million sold worldwide out of 81 million manufactured.[564, 565] This was a 9.6% penetration rate meaning there were still tens of millions of ICE cars left to be displaced. For those and companies positioned to wreak the necessary ICE demand destruction, the future is bright. Tesla swung the biggest hammer, selling 1.3 million BEV units in 2022. As become the norm, China led the global BEV market with approximately 4.35 million BEVs sold.[566] In Europe, 1.58 million BEVs were sold, or about one-third of the China market.[567] In the U.S., less than 763,000 BEVs were sold which is less than half of Europe

562 CleanTechnica, by S. Hanley, "BYD Sold The Most Plug-In Cars In 2015", Jan 20, 2016.

563 InsideEVs, by M. Kane, "2020 U.S. Electric Car Sales: Tesla Captures 80% Of BEV Market", 15, 2021.

564 "Global car sales projected to rebound in 2023." https://evertiq.com, Feb 09, 2023.

565 Irle, Roland. "Global EV Sales for 2022." https://www.ev-volumes.com

566 Kane, Mark. "China: Nearly 6 million Plug-In Cars Were Sold in 2022". Inside, EVs, Feb 2022.

567 Kane, Mark. "Europe: Plug-In Car Sales Reached Spectacular Record in December 2 Inside EVs, Feb 07, 2023.

and one-sixth of China sales. Apparently, the U.S. enjoyed consistently missing out on most of the BEV and lithium value chain.[568]

China BEV Market Overview

With 26.9 million vehicles sold in 2022, China is the world's largest auto market – North America and Europe aren't even close seconds.[569] China's 1.4 billion population, which is as much as the populations of the other two markets combined, ensures that theirs will be the single largest market for the foreseeable future. In 2022, China's 4.35 million BEVs sold meant a 16% penetration rate, the second highest in the world after Germany. The primary reason why the Chinese BEV market is accelerating are the subsidies offered by the Chinese government. Because their market is so large and the incentives are meaningful, if a company wants to sell BEVs at scale, then they need to sell in China.

Until relatively recently, China was not a serious player in the automotive world. Chinese ICE brands weren't known or sold in the North American or European markets. The general template was that established foreign ICE manufacturers would set up joint ventures in China and then manufacture and sell their products to the Chinese market. For example, VW group is the single largest seller of cars in China, having established their first JV in Shanghai in 1984. In 2022, VW sold 3.18 million cars in China, but only 205,000 BEVs.[570] Historically, VW has earned half its annual profits from its China operations.

With BEV transportation really taking off around 2015, China saw an opportunity start a new industry from scratch. China was starting from ground zero like everyone else and could be as competitive as the established OEMs who had no more BEV expertise than they did. The Chinese government aggressively promoted the manufacturing of zero emission vehicles (ZEVs) by offering tax credits for new buyers. Also, from a strategic perspective, Beijing saw their fledgling BEV enterprise as a means to grow their national economy and become a major force in the global automobile industry much like Japan had in the 1970's.

Shahan, Zachary. "US Electric Car Sales Increased 65% in 2022". Clean Technica, Feb 25,2023.

"Global car sales projected to rebound in 2023."

Lincewill, Hillary. "Volkswagen Chairman: China is our most important partner". CarNews China.com, Feb 02, 2023.

In 2018, China sold over a million BEVs to domestic customers, the first country to do so in a single year. Moving forward from there, China increased their BEV sales by more than a million cars a year, every year. As of 2023, China had an estimated 450 automobile companies that manufactured some type of EV, either BEV or PHEV. Compare this to the U.S. who had only six. To be sure, all these 450 companies won't last, as the supply chain disruption and inflation of 2022-2023 will shake out the weak. However, these gaudy numbers show how much momentum the China BEV enterprise has.

The top selling BEV in China for 2022 was the Tesla Model Y with 315,000 units.[571] This is not surprising as Tesla recognized the potential for the China market early on and completed their Giga Shanghai plant there in 2020. The Shanghai government wanted very badly for Tesla to build a factory in their city, providing them $207 million in incentives.[572] Furthermore, a group of Chinese banks gave Tesla a $1.4 billion USD loan to build their factory. The five-year loan was financed at 90% of the one-year benchmark rate, something that is only done with Chinese banks' best clients.[573] Importantly, Tesla was the first company allowed to wholly own an auto manufacturing plant in China without forming a JV with a local Chinese company.

As of 2022, Tesla's Shanghai gigafactory was their production center of gravity, producing more than 710,000 BEVs for the year.[574] Importantly, over the course of the year, Tesla expanded and improved their production lines so that they had an annual installed capacity of 1.1 million BEVs. This made Giga Shanghai the single most productive BEV manufacturing plant in the world. There are multiple reports that Tesla intends to build a second manufacturing plant in China to produce a smaller, cheaper, $25,000.00 USD priced BEV – sometimes referred to as the Model 2.[575] This second plant

---

[571] Kane, Mark. "China: Nearly 6 million Plug-In Cars Were Sold in 2022". Inside, EVs, Feb 08, 2022.

[572] Opportimes, "Subsidies to Tesla: Shanghai government grants US $207 million", Sep 24, 2021.

[573] Reuters, by Y. Sun, et al, "Exclusive: Tesla to take new $1.4 billion loan from Chinese banks for Shanghai factory – sources", Dec 23, 2019

[574] O'Hare, Ben. "Over Half Of All Teslas Sold In 2022 Were Made In Giga Shanghai." InsideEVs, Jan 08, 2023.

[575] Reuters, by C. Randall, "Tesla confirms plans for second plant in Shanghai", May 4, 2022.

is predicted to be built near their first one to take advantage of the already established nearby domestic battery industry. Until this happens, it's just a rumor.

Let's discuss BYD, a homegrown Chinese auto manufacturer and Tesla's number one competitor. BYD has a distinct advantage over most of its peers because it first started out in the 1990's as a LIB manufacturer. This enabled BYD to build out their battery supply chain and develop deep relationships throughout the global battery enterprise. In 2022, BYD was the world's second largest producer of batteries for BEV's, one place behind fellow Chinese battery manufacturer CATL. BYD developed such a strong position in the battery space that they could sell their innovative Blade battery to their competitors, like Toyota, at a premium.

BYD got into the ICE automobile manufacturing game in 2002 when they bought Qinchuan Automobile Company. They eventually expanded from just producing ICE models by adding PHEVs in 2008 and then BEVs in 2009 – in low production numbers. Curiously, BYD was an early mover in low volume electrified segments like public and school buses, heavy trucks, and forklifts. For many years, BYD suffered from a dispersion of focus until 2022 when in stopped producing ICE vehicles altogether, building only PHEV and BEV models afterwards.

It was in 2022 when BYD hit its stride, finally taking off like many industry experts predicted they would. That year, BYD produced 1.85 million cars, including 911,000 BEVs and 946,000 PHEVs giving it the #2 rank in the world as a BEV manufacturer behind Tesla.[576] Personally, I would like to see BYD transition to a BEV-only company, but they have high volume PHEV sales because the Chinese government still offers subsidies for them. Chinese buyers won't transition away from PHEVs until their subsidies are gone and BEVs are the clear and only choice. However, I don't think BYD will ever be truly competitive with Tesla until they finish their transformation to a BEV-pure enterprise.

Japan BEV Market Overview

To date, Japan has been unable and unwilling to effectively pursue a BEV-centric enterprise. Japanese automakers have continued to mostly pursue an ICE business model to the exclusion of BEV models. The Japanese's main attempt at improved vehicle

---

[576] Kane, Mark. "BYD Closes Year 2022 With Record Plug-In Sales In December". Inside EVs, Jan 04, 2023.

efficiency has been the development of hybrid vehicles that does very little to reduce carbon emissions. This puts Japan in the position of importing the majority of the very few BEVs that the Japanese do buy despite having the largest auto manufacturing base in the world. For example, in 2022, Japanese automobile manufacturers sold 4.2 million cars in Japan.[577] Of these, domestic BEV sales remained microscopic at an estimated 59,000 units or just 1.4%.[578]

Japan does offer subsidies when purchasing a new BEV. New BEV owners get $5,200.00 USD while PHEV buyers get a smaller payout of $3,600.00 USD. Furthermore, Tokyo subsidized the installation of public charging stations throughout Japan about a decade ago to encourage BEV adoption. In 2021, there were about 29,000 BEV charging stations. However, this was down from 30,000 charging stations the year before. Japan installed more chargers than its tiny BEV population could use and many of them fell into disrepair from lack of regular use. Clearly, the Japanese government was out of step with its own auto manufacturers who had little interest in producing BEVs.[579]

Instead, it appears Japan would prefer to pursue a hydrogen approach as they offer subsidies of $18,500.00 USD when purchasing a new FCEV (Fuel-Cell Electric Vehicle), an unheard-of amount for a vehicle. According to the Next Generation Vehicle Promotion Center, Japan's goal is for 320 hydrogen filling stations constructed and 200,000 FCEVs on their roads by 2025.[580] They might reach the H2 station goal as they were halfway there in 2022. However, the FCEVs eligible for subsidies were the Honda Clarity (discontinued by 2022) and the Toyota Mirai (anemic sales). At the present rate of Japanese FCEV production, it might take them until the year 2300 to reach these FCEV goals.

Now, let's transition to details about Japanese BEV manufacturing. While Toyota was the world's largest automobile manufacturer at 10.5 million vehicles produced in 2022, their flagship bZ4X BEV only sold 3,844 units in China from its introduction in

---

[577] "Japan's 2022 New Car Sales Hit Lowest Level In 45 Years". Nippon.com, Jan 19, 2023.

[578] Take, Sayumi. "China's BYD starts EV sales in Japan as it chases Tesla". Nikkei Asia, Jan 31, 2023.

[579] InsideEVs, by M. Kane, "Japan: High Number Of EV Chargers Did Not Jump Start The Market", Aug 31, 2021.

[580] Next Generation Vehicle Promotion Center publication, 2018. Apparently, they stopped updating their English website in 2018.

October 2022 through January 2023.[581] The batteries for the bZ3 line, a JV between Toyota and FAW Group making BEVs in China, are provided by BYD as Toyota doesn't have independent battery technology. FWD versions will use batteries made by Panasonic. While Toyota is far behind in the BEV space, the other Japanese auto makers aren't doing any better.

As incredible as it sounds, Honda doesn't have a single BEV to sell and neither does Mitsubishi. Subaru did slightly better, selling 919 of its Solterra BEVs in the U.S in 2022.[582] However, the Solterra is actually manufactured by Toyota, so it is mostly a bZ4X clone using CATL batteries for its North American models. The Subaru Solterra easily wins the gold medal for "not being vertically integrated". Similarly, Mazda sold just 324 of its MX-30 BEVs in the U.S., which isn't surprising for an ugly compliance car with a mere 100-mile range.[583] It's under powered battery is made by Panasonic.

Nissan sells the most BEVs by volume of any Japanese auto maker. Nissan sold 12,000 of its Leaf BEVs in the U.S. in 2022 and just shy of 29,000 units in Europe.[584, 585] Nissan sold an estimated 12,000 Leafs in Japan as well. Nissan does not sell the Leaf in China, but they used to sell their Sylphy BEV there, which they recently discontinued due to continuing low sales volumes. In 2022, Nissan came out with the Ariya BEV and sold about 8,500 of them for the year in the Japan, China, European and U.S. markets combined.[586] The Ariya is a slight step up from the Leaf but will likely see low volume sales due to its mediocre range and overall antiquated design.

Nissan makes three BEVs for the China market in a JV with Dongfeng through their subsidiary called Venucia. The Venucia D60 BEV is a Sylphy clone and is their

581 Mihalascu, Dan. "Toyota bZX4 Price Cut By More Than $4,000 In China To Boost Sales". Inside EVs, Feb 17, 2023.

582 Flierl, Denis. "The 2023 Subaru Solterra EV Will Make Its Mark This Year But It's Not For Everyone". Torque News, Jan 07, 2023.

583 Kane, Mark. "US: Mazda MX-30 Sales Halted At Just 8 Units In Q3 2022". Inside EVs, Oct 12, 2022.

584 Kane, Mark. "Nissan Ariya Entered the US Market With 201 Sales in Q4 2022". Inside EVs, Jan 0, 2023.

585 "Nissan leaf Europe Sales Figures". CarSalesBase.com

586 Nissan Sales Data 2022. Nissan Motor Corporation Limited.

best-selling product with 43,528 sold in 2022.[587]. The Venucia T60 is a full-size SEV BEV on life support that sold just over 400 units for the year in China. Their Venucia e30 BEV was a Leaf clone that they stopped selling altogether in 2022 due to low sales.[588] I think the reader may see a trend here.

Nissan initially pursued some form of vertical integration for its battery production with the forming of AESC (Automotive Energy Supply Corporation) in 2008. AESC was a JV between Nissan, NEC Corporation and NEC Tokin focusing on the production of lithium manganese oxide batteries. In 2018, the Chinese Envision Group bought a majority share of the company, rebranding it Envision AESC with Nissan maintaining a 25% share in the company.[589] Envision AESC has existing battery manufacturing facilities in Japan, the UK, the U.S., and China with plans to build more in France, Spain, Japan, China, and the U.S. I take the sale of AESC to Envision as Nissan recognizing that they weren't a competent battery manufacturer and that they weren't serious about expanding into the LIB space. An absolutely baffling move considering the global trends.

Let's get back to the electrification of the largest car manufacturer in the word. In 2022, Toyota rolled out their "Beyond Zero" campaign which is tied to their "Achieving Zero" effort. Toyota seeks to achieve zero impact on our planet to preserve our environment for future generations. One can assume that Toyota is working towards achieving zero carbon emissions for its vehicle line-up. It's "BZ" line of BEVs is the physical manifestation of their Beyond Zero policy. To date, they have taken a three-track approach, developing primarily hybrid cars, then low production run FCEVs and finally BEVs. Since their hybrid car production lines contradict their Beyond Zero aspirations, it remains to be seen when they transition out these models.

Moving forward, Toyota must make a strategic decision about their business model: are they going to pursue a BEV line like their current bZ4X/bZ3 models or an FCEV line like their Mirai model? Their bZ4X line has already suffered from installing a non-competitive battery from Panasonic with below average range and charging speed.[590] It remains to be seen if their Chinese bZ3 JV with FAW Group takes off in

---

[587] https://chinamobil.ru/eng/dongfeng/venucia/d60ev/?view=sales

[588] Nissan Sales Data 2022.

[589] https://global.nissannews.com/en/releases/180803-01-e

[590] Edmunds, by J. Elfalan, "TESTED: 2023 Toyota bZ4X Falls Short of EPA Range Estimate", Jun 14, 2022.

the future considering the China market increasingly prefers local brands that are already technologically superior to anything Japan has to offer. It is interesting to see that Toyota looks to sell their products abroad and not in their own home country, although Japan's own stunted BEV market is part of Toyota's own doing.

On the topic of hydrogen FCEVs, the Toyota Mirai suffers from an underdeveloped hydrogen vehicle market with relatively few filling stations as compared to BEV public charging stations. Also, a person can charge a BEV in their garage, but they can't put an H2 filling station there. Perhaps Toyota will follow their sales and pursue the more successful line. Either way, as they haven't focused effectively on either approach, they suffer from a lack of unity of effort within their own business.

One would think the Japanese auto industry would have an advantage in transitioning to BEVs because of Panasonic. Panasonic is an established battery company who has been in the lithium battery space for 30 years. However, the Japanese BEV enterprise, although small, has not taken advantage of this resource. As we mentioned, the Nissan Leaf uses proprietary Nickle Manganese Oxide (NMO) batteries developed by Envision AESC, a Chinese company. Toyota's JV with FAW Group in China, the bZ3, uses BYD's proprietary Blade batteries. While Toyota's front wheel version of the bZ4X will use Panasonic batteries, the AWD version will use batteries by CATL. Clearly, the Japanese auto and battery industries are not working together to maximize the lithium value chain. They've ceded most of it to China.

Importantly, the foreign BEV invasion of Japan has already begun. Tesla has six stores in Japan through which they have been selling their Model 3 and then just started selling their Model Y BEVs in 2022. As of early 2023, Tesla had 62 separate supercharger locations dispersed throughout the country.[591] BYD started selling their Atto 3 BEV line in Japan in 2023 for less than the Tesla Model 3. BYD intends to rapidly expand their foothold in Japan as they establish 100 different dealer locations across the country by 2025.[592]

The Japan auto industry has resisted converting to BEVs in part because their ICE enterprise is so massive and it is easier, in the short run, to deny the need for change. It's a cultural groupthink problem. We have seen this with other ICE OEMs like GM

---

[591] https://www.tesla.com/findus/list/superchargers/Japan

[592] Take, Sayumi. "China's BYD starts EV sales in Japan as it chases Tesla". Nikkei Asia, Jan 31, 2023.

and Ford, even though both are further along than Toyota. In Japan, the auto industry consists of about 18.8% of all manufacturing and thus over 16% of its GDP.[593] In the long run, the negative repercussions to the Japanese economy will be devastating if they don't rapidly pick up the pace in their efforts to transition to BEVs.

South Korea BEV Market Overview

South Korean car manufacturers are doing slightly better than their much larger Japanese peers when it comes to BEV penetration. To begin, Hyundai Motors sold 3.94 million vehicles worldwide in 2022 and almost 689,000 units domestically.[594] Of these, they sold almost 195,000 BEVs consisting of their Hyundai and Genesis brands or just about 5% of their total sales. And just as Toyota does, they also pursue hydrogen fuel-cell vehicles (FCEVs), selling some 10,000+ units.[595] Hyundai sources its batteries from South Korean manufacturers LG Energy Solutions and SK Innovation as well as Chinese battery giant CATL.

The Kia Corporation sold 2.9 million cars worldwide in 2022 and 541,000 in South Korea.[596] Of this total, Kia sold an estimated 132,000 BEVS globally, most of them exported for sales.[597] This was just 4.5% of overall production as ICE models still dominate Kia's lineups. As with Hyundai, Kia has historically sourced its batteries from LG Energy Solution and SK Innovation. However, beginning in 2022, Kia sourced its batteries for is Niro BEV (48,000 sold) from CATL. Like Hyundai's decision, this indicates CATL has more competitive pricing, that Kia needs more overall battery capacity or Kia wants to diversify its sourcing – or possibly all three.

There were an estimated 25.5 million vehicles total on the roads in South Korea at the end of 2022. Of these, almost 390,000 were BEVs for an overall cumulative

---

[593] Route Zero Climate Group, "Japan and the global transition to zero emission vehicles", May 2022

[594] https://www.hyundai.com/worldwide/en/company/newsroom/hyundai-motor-reports-2022-global-sales-and-2023-goals-0000016948

[595] Kane, Mark. "Hyundai Motor Plug-In Car Sales Exceeded 24,000 in December 2022". Feb 04, 2023.

[596] https://www.best-selling-cars.com/brands/2022-full-year-global-kia-sales-worldwide-and-2023-forecast/

[597] Kane, Mark. "In 2022 Kia Sold Nearly 80,000 EV6". Inside EVs, Jan 17, 2023.

penetration rate of just 1.5%. Approximately 158,000 BEVs were sold in South Korea in 2022, revealing an accelerated pace of adoption.[598] South Korea enjoys the synergy of a robust domestic battery manufacturing base with several competent companies and Hyundai Motor Group (comprised of both Hyundai and Kia) that produces several competitive BEV lines. Not many countries can say that.

There are indications that the pace of BEV adoptions in South Korea is accelerating. For example, the Seoul City Government has offered $7,520.00 USD in subsidies per car for up to 27,000 buyers of BEV sedans in 2022. Seoul will offer upwards of $22,500.00 USD per electric truck depending on the class of vehicle.[599] This policy is similar to and surpasses the benefits offered by the U.S.' own *Inflation Reduction Act*. These subsidies work in conjunction with Seoul's ongoing efforts to create green transportation zones in the capital to reduce carbon emissions by encouraging BEV adoption and restricting ICE vehicles. Seoul intends to ban the registering of new ICE vehicles in 2035 and then ban them from the streets altogether in 2050.

A 2022 report by the International Energy Agency indicated that South Korea had the most robust charging network in the world relative to the size of its BEV fleet, with 2.6 charging points per BEV. In comparison, Europe had 15.5 BEVs per charging point while China had 7.2 BEVs per charging point. In 2021, South Korea had an estimated 105,000 charging points in total.[600] However, as Seoul wants 10% of its four million registered vehicles to be BEVs by 2026, they are installing 200,000 more charging points to help support this goal.[601] As BEV adoption is often perceived as being held back due to a lack of necessary charging infrastructure, that can't be said of South Korea.

South Korea's auto industry contributed an estimated 10% to their national GDP which hovers around $1.8 trillion USD annually with modest growth predicted. As the combined market caps of LG Energy Solution, Samsung SDI and SK Innovation are approximately $155 billion USD, the battery industry is a significant contributor to the

[598] "BEVs in South Korea rise by 68% in 2022, Hyundai-Kia surpass 1m globally". JustAuto.com, Jan 26, 2023.

[599] "South Korea increases subsidy funding pot for 2022". Electrive.com, Feb 15, 2022.

[600] The Korea Herald, by H. Yoo, "S. Korea has best EV infrastructure per unit in world: report ", May 31, 2022.

[601] Edelstein, Stephen. "Seoul plans more than 200,00 EV chargers by 2026". Green Car Reports, Sept 27, 2022.

national economy as well. Hyundai and Kia had combined market caps of just $57.7 billion USD in March 2023 compared to LGES' market cap alone of $104.5 billion USD. While South Korea is not as dependent on its auto industry as is Japan, a significant loss to its vehicle production during the global transition to BEVs would still devastate their economy.

North American Market Overview

Although the *Inflation Reduction Act* provides up to $7,500.00 in tax incentives for BEVs starting in 2023, the U.S. auto market remains dominated by ICE models. The U.S. has by far the largest auto market in North America with approximately 13.6 million vehicles sold there in 2022.[602] Compare this to Canada with 1.49 million vehicles sold[603] and to Mexico with just over 1 million.[604] Now we see why auto manufacturers in Canada and Mexico produce vehicles in their respective countries but ship most of them to the U.S. – because of the market size.

But the number of BEVs sold in the U.S. in 2022 was only a paltry 800,000 vehicles or about 5.8% of overall sales.[605] This is one-third of the national market penetration that China has, which is far ahead of the U.S. One car maker dominated U.S. BEV sales and that was Tesla, selling 536,000 vehicles in 2022 or 67% of all BEVs sold in the country.[606] Most Tesla vehicles sold in the U.S. were produced from their Fremont factory in California as their Austin factory was still ramping up. This proved to be very efficient as California bought more than 292,000 EVs in 2022, giving them the largest EV market penetration of any state in the U.S. at 16%.[607] This is line with California's recently passed legislation phasing out all pure ICE purchases in the state by 2035.

As we have seen with Japan and South Korea's auto industries, mainstream auto OEMs like Ford, GM, and Chrysler (Stellantis) historically resisted transitioning to

---

[602] https://www.goodcarbadcar.net/usa-auto-industry-total-sales-figures/

[603] "2022 auto sales worst since 2009, but December numbers offer hope". Automotive News Canada, Jan 04, 2023.

[604] "New car sales in Mexico in 2022 peaked in December". Mexico News Daily, Jan 04, 2023.

[605] Nedelea, Andrei. "US Car Market Shrunk In 2022 But EV Sales Went Up By Two Thirds". Inside EVs, Jan 18, 2023.

[606] https://www.goodcarbadcar.net/tesla-us-sales-figures/

[607] "New High: 16% EV Adoption in California in 2022". Clean Technica, Feb 16, 2023.

BEVs. This resistance to change directly led to Tesla seizing as much market share as it has and opened the door to other BEV start-ups. The old U.S. ICE OEMs have also suffered from deficient battery technology as compared to their chief competitor Tesla, but they have done much better than Japan's initial attempts. Of note, none of the U.S. OEMs turn a profit on their BEVs; they all sell them at a loss.

Ford and its sub-brand Lincoln sold 1.86 million vehicles in the U.S. in 2022. Of this total, they sold 61,575 BEVs that included 39,458 Mach-Es (made in Mexico), 15,617 F-150 Lightnings (made in Michigan) and 6,500 E-Transit vans (made in Kansas).[608] This is a 3.4% BEV penetration rate of the domestic Ford enterprise. Ford has historically sourced its NCM (Nickel-Cobalt-Manganese) batteries for its BEV lineup from South Korean manufacturers LGES and SK On but will increasingly use LFP (Lithium-Iron-Phosphate) batteries produced by CATL. Ford has hit three key areas (sedans, trucks, vans) with its line up and I suspect they can continue to grow these lines if they improve their BEV technology as well as their overall manufacturing process.

General Motors (GM) sold 2.74 million vehicles in the U.S. in 2022, substantially more than Ford did.[609] Of these, GM sold an anemic 39,096 BEVs including 38,120 Chevy Bolts, 854 GMC Hummers and 122 Cadillac Lyriqs. This is a microscopic 1.4% BEV adoption rate. Based on these numbers, we can only assume the Hummer and Lyrics are made by hand. GM is also making its BrightDrop electric van; they might have sold one hundred of them although GM does not release this data. GM historically sourced its batteries directly from LGES and now as part of their Ultium battery JV platform.

In my opinion, the BrightDrop van is their best line of effort due to the tremendous potential for disrupting the last-mile delivery van market segment. I think the rest are dogs but let me explain. The GMC Hummer 2022 edition costs $110,000.00 USD with a 212-kWh battery pack. It's overpriced and Tesla can make three Model Ys with the Hummer's one battery and make three times the profit. It will never sell in high volumes just like the old polluting ICE version it replaced. GM CEO Mary Barra admits they lose money on each one they make – so why did they make it?

The Cadillac Lyriq is a clean looking SUV with an MSRP of $62,000.00 USD in 2023. During test drives, the single-motor version with 102-kWh battery only went

---

[608] Ford Motor Company, December 2022 Sales Release.

[609] https://gmauthority.com/blog/gm/general-motors-sales-numbers/

270 miles, indicating that the overall powertrain and associated wiring is inefficient and poorly designed. In comparison, the Tesla Model X, who the Lyriq is designed to compete with, gets 350 miles of range. Also, for reasons known only to the Cadillac engineering team, they failed to design a front trunk (frunk) for the Lyriq, perhaps because their thinking is still stuck in the ICE age.

The original Chevy Volt was an ugly California compliance car. The "updated" Chevy Bolt is also an ugly California compliance car with antiquated technology and inefficient energy systems. Because of these inherent qualities, sales volumes have always been low and will continue to be so. The Chevy Volt/Bolt line surely wins the Darwin award for "failure to innovate". I believe the Hummer, Lyriq and Bolt reveal that GM has leadership, vision, creativity, and culture problems. The GM leadership team can't seem to make the right decisions to pull everything together to make a successful BEV enterprise.

Stellantis, who previously bought Chrysler, sold 1.5 million vehicles in the U.S. in 2022.[610] Stellantis sold just over 63,000 PHEVs through their Jeep and Pacifica hybrid lines (in other words, not BEVs). It took me a minute to digest Stellantis' word salad of a 2022 Sales Report to realize they didn't sell a single BEV in the U.S. Stellantis aims for 50% of all sales in 2030 to be BEV models which means 750,000 units in the U.S. Pro tip: this isn't going to happen. Overall, Stellantis shipped 5.78 million vehicles worldwide in 2022 with 288,000 of them being BEVs for a 5% penetration rate.[611] Stellantis has publicly stated their goal of manufacturing 5 million BEVs a year by 2030. This means transitioning 86% of their 2022 production numbers to electric units in just seven years. Pro tip: this isn't going to happen either.

The pure-play BEV start-ups in the U.S. all have low production numbers, inefficient production lines and can't sell their BEVs at a profit. They are in what Elon Musk called "production hell". First, electric truck and SUV manufacturer Rivian delivered just over 20,000 of its sleek BEVs in 2022.[612] Rivian uses batteries from Samsung SDI at its Illinois factory and may use SK On for BEVs made at its future Georgia manufacturing plant. Next, Lucid delivered 4,369 BEV sedans from its Arizona factory in 2022

[610] https://media.stellantisnorthamerica.com/newsrelease
[611] Stellantis, 2022 Sales Report.
[612] https://rivian.com/newsroom/article/rivian-produced-10020-vehicles-in-q4-2022

and only has enough money to last them to Q1 2024.[613] These good-looking cars are extremely energy efficient using batteries made by LGES and Samsung SDI, although Lucid recently signed a contract with Panasonic for future battery sourcing as well.

Truck maker Nikola delivered 83 electric semis in 2022 while simultaneously pursuing a hydrogen fuel-cell line of effort.[614] While Nikola sources its batteries from South Korean manufacturer LGES, it recently acquired Romero Power in an attempt reduce the costs of its battery packs. Nikola is still suffering a reputational hangover from its former CEO Trevor Milton recently being found guilty in federal court of fraud charges stemming from his time at the company.

From a volume production standpoint, all these companies are background noise. Let's discuss why Tesla is doing so much better than their competition by focusing on their manufacturing. Tesla has often said that their competitive advantage comes from "the machines that make the machines". What this means is that Tesla has built the most efficient manufacturing plant in North America based on simplification, parts reduction, and automation. In 2021, Tesla's Fremont factory produced an average of 8,550 cars a week. This was more productive than 70 other factories run by both domestic and foreign OEMs in North America.[615]

Tesla's Fremont factory is an old ICE plant originally built by GM in the 1960's. Tesla bought the New United Motor Manufacturing Inc. plant in 2010 for a pittance: $42 million USD. It doesn't have an inherently efficient BEV layout as it was made to build old school ICE vehicles in a rather inefficient manner. Tesla prefers massive, streamlined buildings with long assembly lines for fluid production with no interruptions. Another Tesla mantra is that the best part in a vehicle is the one that is never used. Importantly, BEVs have much fewer parts than complicated ICE models and Tesla takes extreme efforts to minimize the parts used in their BEVs. As an example of this, an electric motor has about 20 different parts while an internal combustion engine typically has over 2,000.

[613] https://ir.lucidmotors.com/news-releases/news-release-details/lucid-announces-fourth-quarter-and-full-year-2022-financial

[614] Doll, Scooter. "Nikola (NKLA) Q4 2022 results: Deliveries and revenues stumble, but plenty in the works for 2023". Elektrek, Feb 23, 2023.

[615] Bloomberg, by T. Randall, D. Pogkas,"Tesla Now Runs the Most Productive Auto Factory in America", Jan 24, 2022.

Tesla improved on antiquated OEM production models with the use of IDRA Gigapresses. IDRA is an Italian company that produces die-casting machines which Tesla uses to make its vehicles. Tesla started using Gigapresses to make the front and rear underbodies for its Model Ys in their Fremont factory in 2020. Now, several stampings have reduced upwards of 70 different parts, greatly simplifying their associated supply chains, and reducing manufacturing time per vehicle.[616] Other OEMs who cannot similarly reduce their vehicle parts used and lower their costs while increasing production are simply not competitive.

Another topic to discuss is the vertical integration of battery production. All ICE OEMs trying to break into the BEV market are behind the eight ball because they haven't developed their battery production supply chain and battery minerals sourcing. An early and critical move Tesla made was building its Nevada gigafactory in 2015 to make batteries for its U.S. fleet. The batteries for its BEVs are made in partnership with Panasonic who developed the cell level lithium-ion battery expertise from its previous two decades in the home electronics battery business. In 2022, Giga Nevada had an annual battery production capacity of 35 GWh that could outfit 350,000 BEVs.

While Giga Nevada was chosen largely for its extremely generous tax package from the state, Tesla has moved from a centralized to a decentralized battery production business model. Presently, Tesla has four factories producing BEVs in the world: Fremont, Austin, Berlin, and Shanghai. Tesla intentionally built battery plants onsite with their Austin and Berlin gigafactories to simplify their battery supply chain and better coordinate their integration. Tesla's Kato Road facility in Fremont produces its new 4680 batteries and their Shanghai factory sources batteries from CATL and LG Energy Solutions. Importantly, CATL has a battery manufacturing plant located just three kilometers from Giga Shanghai.[617]

As Tesla knows, and the ICE OEMs have just started to realize, the name of the game is battery mineral sourcing. If a company can't secure the necessary battery minerals for their BEV's far into the future, then they will suffer supply constraints and disruptions resulting in production delays and limitations. For instance, in 2018, Tesla

[616] ChargedEvs, by C. Morris, "Another Idra Giga Press delivered to Tesla Gigafactory Texas", Jan 17, 2022.

[617] InsideEVs, by M. Kane, "Report: CATL's New Battery Plant In Shanghai Already Supplies Tesla", Jan 09, 2022.

inked a deal with Ganfeng Lithium to supply 20% of its lithium hydroxide through 2020 with an option to renew supplies for an additional three years.[618] If Tesla secured fixed price contracts, then they not only secured a future supply of lithium, but they also insured themselves from future price inflation.

However, as mineral prices skyrocketed in 2021, more and more offtake agreements were variable meaning their prices went up according to the larger market and the insurance from inflation was lost. Also, lithium mining companies started aggressively renegotiating their existing offtake agreements to change them from fixed to variable. With limited amounts of battery minerals available in a tight market, the company who moved first to secure their supply chain ensured their own downstream BEV production capacity.

Although Tesla has much more experience sourcing battery minerals than its OEM competitors, it too could not insulate itself from the ongoing lithium inflation. With lithium running at $80,000.00 USD a ton in 2022, Tesla needed better insurance against lithium inflation and made moves to get into the lithium conversion business. Presently, Tesla is in discussion with Neuces County officials to buy land for their conversion facility in Robstown, TX near Corpus Christie. Tesla anticipates investing $365 million USD in the facility which would convert lithium feedstock into battery-grade product for its U.S. battery plants. [619]

Tesla understands the need to vertically integrate its battery supply chain to insulate itself against disruption, but I don't think they've gone upstream enough. Elon Musk has said before that he doesn't want Tesla to get into the lithium mining business, but I think they should. Until they control the battery mineral at the source, they are not vertically integrated and have not fully secured their supply chain in a growing market ravenous for lithium. Therefore, I think Tesla should buy a lithium mining company outright. Just think, for what Musk paid for twitter ($44 billion USD), he could have bought both Albemarle and SQM. As the BEV market becomes tighter and resources limited, true vertical integration will be the mark of the most competitive BEV manufacturers.

---

[618] The Motley Fool, by B. McKenna, "Who Are Tesla's Lithium Suppliers?", Apr 16, 2019.

[619] Elektrek, by F. Lambert, "Tesla lithium refinery project moves to private negotiations in Texas", Nov 17, 2022.

European BEV Market Overview

In 2022, 12.8 million vehicles were registered in Europe. Overall sales were suppressed partly due to Russia's invasion of Ukraine in February 2022. Because so many Western auto companies voluntarily pulled out of Russia, car sales in Russia plummeted from 1.5 million in 2021 to just 578,000 sold in 2022. Ukraine dropped from 105,000 cars sold in 2021 to just 37,000 in 2022.[620] When your national economy has collapsed and you need money just for survival, a new car is a luxury item – it can wait.

BEV registrations in Europe for 2022 hit 1.5 million or 12.1% of overall sales.[621] This puts Europe far ahead of the U.S but still behind China. The top selling BEVs in Europe for the year were: 1) the Tesla Model Y with over 138,000 sold, 2) the Tesla Model 3 with over 91,000 sold, 3) the VW iD.4 with over 68,000 sold, 4) the VW iD.3 with over 53,000 sold and 5) the Skoda Enyaq with over 52,000 sold.[622] After these five, there were many more with sales in the tens of thousands. Unlike the U.S. BEV market, the competition is much more diverse with many entrants with competent products.

Europe is a diverse region with each country pursuing its own BEV adoption measures of varying degrees based on their unique national dynamics. However, collectively, Europe is pursuing a path towards net zero emissions by 2050, thus driving their BEV transition. In 2022, the bloc of 27 countries composing the European Union voted to ban the sales of new fossil fuel burning cars beginning in 2035. This bans hybrid cars as well as PHEVs. Obviously, this has huge implications for the European car market. The companies poised to take advantage of this impending deadline are the pure BEV manufacturers and the OEMs that can transition in time with a competitive BEV product.

Norway is not part of the EU but is part of the European Economic Area that includes the EU countries. Regardless, Norway has the highest penetration rate of BEVs in Europe as they work to eliminate all ICE sales by 2025. In support of this, the Norwegian government offers an overlapping list of tax and fee incentives that make BEVs the most attractive choice when purchasing a new car. In 2022, Norwegians

[620] "Economic and Market Report State of the EU auto industry Full- year 2022", European Automobile Manufacturers Association, Jan 2023.

[621] https://www.acea.auto/fuel-pc/fuel-types-of-new-cars-battery-electric-12-1-hybrid-22-6-and-petrol-36-4-market-share-full-year-2022/

[622] Pontes, Jose. "Europe EV Sales Report – December 2022". Clean Technica, Feb 02, 2023.

bought over 174,000 new vehicles with 138,000 of them BEVs or 79% of all vehicles sold in the country.[623] Their expanding BEV market has attracted many new BEV manufacturing entrants to include Chinese companies like BYD and Nio. At the present rate of BEV market penetration, Norway may achieve its goal of selling 100% BEVs in 2025.

That means ICE dealerships in Norway will soon be out of business because they can't pay the rent on their dwindling sales. ICE used car sales will also collapse and owners will have to find buyers in neighboring countries if they can. ICE dominated manufacturers like Toyota will have one less market to sell their fossil fuel products in while BEV companies like Tesla and VW move in at scale. Associated ICE infrastructure like gas stations, oil change/muffler/brake shops will dwindle initially, consolidate, and then go extinct since BEVs don't require their services. Neighboring countries will accelerate their own BEV adoption as they realize Norway's national grid isn't crashing, has much less dependence on foreign oil and their cities no longer suffer from fossil fuel pollution.

England also isn't a member of the EU after Brexit but that didn't stop the Johnson administration from issuing a ban on ICE vehicles by 2030, a full five years ahead of the EU. In 2022, 1.6 million cars were registered in the UK with over 267,000 being BEVs or 16.6% of overall sales.[624] The BEV penetration rate is the same as California and China, but far behind Norway. Great Britain is ideal for the electrification of its ground transportation fleets due to heavy urbanization and low average daily miles traveled by drivers.

This means ICE manufacturers in the country have a real problem if they aren't pursuing a 100% BEV business model. For example, Toyota has two ICE manufacturing plants in Britain, one in Derbyshire and one in New Wales. As they did elsewhere, Toyota made the strategic error of pursuing hybrid production in Britain instead of BEVs. In response, Toyota says they will meet the 2030 zero emissions requirement (they will have to or they simply will be barred from doing business there) but as of 2023 they still don't have a viable BEV for sale. Toyota has invested almost $3.3 billion

[623] Kane, Mark. "Norway: Electric Car Sales Shoot Through The Roof In December 2022". Inside EVs, Jan 03, 2023.

[624] Carey, Nick. "UK car sales hit 30-year low in 2022, but could grow 15% this year – SMMT". Reuters, Jan 04, 2023.

USD in their two plants that will become stranded assets if and when they can't make the BEV transition in time.[625]

Across the Channel from England is France who registered 1.53 million light vehicles in 2022. Of these, almost 203,000 and close to 17,000 light commercial vehicles were BEVs.[626] This is a 14% penetration rate, less than England but still much better than the U.S. As France is a member of the EU, they are party to the impending 2035 ban on ICE vehicles and must transform their domestic auto industry accordingly. However, Paris, like the UK, has moved up their city ban on ICE vehicles to 2030. Also, starting in 2024, the oldest part of the center of Paris will have a complete ban on automobiles to reduce congestion, lower fossil fuel pollution and encourage a pedestrian friendly environment.

Renault Group is the largest auto manufacturer in France, selling 2 million cars worldwide in 2022, to include 470,000 in France which is its biggest market.[627] There is talk that Renault may spin off its BEV division to become its own company as they recognize their ICE culture will hold back their electrification goals. Almost 1.53 million passenger cars were sold in France in 2022 as well as 348,000 light commercial vehicles. 203,000 passenger car BEVs were sold for a 13% penetration rate.[628] Renault Groups best-selling car in France was the Dacia Spring with more than 18,000 delivered in 2022.[629] This small compact car has a short range of 120 miles and is not offered in North America as it wouldn't sell there. It's a European urban-centric vehicle.

As a large, diverse company, Renault has growing battery needs. Renault has an established relationship with LGES for NMC batteries made at their Wroclaw, Poland plant with plans to develop a JV in France itself. Renault is also working with Envision AESC to build a battery plant in Douai, France. (Remember, a Chinese company bought the majority of AESC from Nissan while Nissan still holds a minority share.) Additionally, Renault is working with French start-up Verkor to develop a battery

[625] https://www.toyotauk.com/

[626] Kane, Mark. "France: Plug-In Car Sales Increased Slightly in 2022". Inside EVs, Jan 15, 2023.

[627] https://media.renaultgroup.com/renault-group-2022-sales-results-continued-growth-in-value-creating-segments/?lang=eng

[628] https://www.best-selling-cars.com/france/2022-full-year-france-new-car-market-overview-and-analysis/

[629] Kane, Mark. "France: Plug-In Car Sales Increased Slightly in 2022". Inside EVs, Jan 15, 2023.

operation. Although Verkor, created in 2020, is still in the funding stage and is many years away from starting production. Renault has even inked a deal with Australian start-up Vulcan Energy in anticipation of its German geothermal brine extraction operations getting off the ground.

More important than France for overall BEV trends is Germany. Although Germany is a member of the EU, they have initially opposed the proposal to ban all ICE vehicles by 2035. Germany contends that there will still be small use cases for ICE vehicles and the use of carbon neutral fuels (i.e., synthetic fuels). However, the European Commission passed the ICE ban based on a majority vote. In contrast to Berlin's opposition, Mercedes publicly stated they were prepared to sell only BEVs by 2030. VW also voiced their support for a 2035 ICE ban, indicating they thought they would have the battery capacity to do so by then. At 5% of Germany's GDP, it is important that their auto industry get the transition to BEVs right.

Germans bought 2.65 million passenger vehicles in 2022 with VW, Mercedes, Audi, BMW, and Opel being the top five sellers in that order.[630] Of these, more than 470,000 were BEVs for a 17.7% penetration rate, the highest for a country of that size. The five top selling BEVs were in this order: Tesla, VW, Hyundai, Opel, and Fiat. The single largest auto manufacturer in Europe is the VW Group who sold 8.26 million vehicles worldwide in 2022 and more than 572,000 BEVs for a 7% penetration of overall sales.[631]

VW currently sources its batteries for its European BEVs from LGES and Samsung SDI and its Chinese BEVs from CATL. However, VW wants to vertically integrate its battery supply chain and is determined to manufacture its own batteries through its newly formed subsidiary PowerCo. PowerCo has plans to invest $20 billion USD to develop six battery gigafactories in Europe and one in North America. But if VW is going to enter the battery business, they also need to secure their own battery mineral supply.

Correspondingly, VW is developing a JV with Chinese firms Huayou Cobalt and Tsingshan Group for nickel and cobalt extraction operations in Indonesia. The

[630] https://www.best-selling-cars.com/germany/2022-full-year-germany-best-selling-car-brands/

[631] Kane, Mark. "Volkswagen Group Global BEV Sales In 2022 Reached 572,100". Inside EVs, Jan 18, 2023.

JV anticipates extracting 120,000 tons of nickel and 15,000 tons of cobalt annually for VW's growing battery enterprise. VW is also forming a separate JV with Huayou Cobalt in China for additional nickel and cobalt refining activity to include precursors and cathode production.[632] As VW says they have strict ethical guidelines in reference to their cobalt acquisitions, how do they square this partnership knowing Huayou sources their cobalt from the Congo?

Looking Ahead

1. What does the reader think future global BEV adoption rates will be next year? In 2025? 2030? Will we see continued incremental penetration of the existing ICE enterprise or will we hit a tipping point where mass adoption ensues? To hit a tipping point, the battery minerals supply chain, battery factories, BEV manufacturers and charging infrastructure all must be lined up and ready to go at scale. There can be no space between the separate but mutually supporting industries.

2. Will the Chinese BEV market continue to dominate adoption trends? When might European or North American markets have all the necessary pieces in place (technological, political, financial, social) to make higher adoption rates possible? Will Tesla and BYD continue to dominate the China market? Will other BEV manufacturers sprint pass them (like Nio, LEAP Motor, VW) or will the top two double down on their existing efforts to increase their market cap?

3. How is the Japanese auto manufacturing enterprise going to evolve moving forward considering that they have the most to lose if they fail to transition effectively to BEVs. I believe their continued high ICE sales only enforces their existing groupthink and masks their long-term vulnerability. What impact will a failed transition have on the Japanese national economy? We already see Tesla and BYD moving in on Japanese turf, will there be others like VW, Hyundai, and Nio?

4. North America is a BEV laggard, allowing China and Europe to realize far more of the lithium value chain to date. Does the *Inflation Reduction Act* offer

---

[632] "Volkswagen forms Chinese ties to secure EV battery materials". Nikkei Asia, March 21, 2022.

enough incentives to get the U.S. ICE OEMs off the stick and moving out? Will the U.S. help energize Canada and Mexico to work together to develop a true North American battery mineral supply chain to feed the growing battery and BEV industries? Will the U.S. rely on foreign auto makers to come in and make BEVs because the Detroit Dinosaurs can't figure it out? In that same vein, how much market cap will Tesla steal from the ICE enterprise moving forward?

5. In March 2023, the EU passed their *Critical Raw Materials Act* to secure their critical mineral supply chain in support of their net zero low carbon initiatives. Identified critical raw materials include lithium, nickel, platinum group metals and rare earth elements. By 2030, 10% of these critical raw materials consumed annually will be extracted in the EU; 40% of critical raw materials processing will occur in the EU; 15% of critical raw materials will be recycled in the EU; not more than 65% of a critical raw material will be sourced from a third country. How does this impact future battery manufacturing plant develop in Europe? How does this impact future BEV production in Europe? Will we see BEV manufacturers moving upstream into mineral extraction and battery manufacturing to vertically integrate their value chain? Will this law accelerate the European BEV enterprise like the *Inflation Reduction Act* is doing in North America?

CHAPTER 16

The Lithium-Ion Battery Industry

"We can't be blindsided by new technology. Look at what happened to IBM where the business model was turned around by the arrival of Windows and Microsoft's operating system. It's sensible to be cautious." – Robin Zeng, CEO CATL, 2014 interview

Global Lithium Battery Overview

In 2022, an estimated 518 GWh of batteries were manufactured and deployed as the overall global battery industry attempted to keep up with the accelerating demand for BEVs. Upwards of 750 GWh of batteries will be produced in 2023, depending on a whole host of factors that we have already discussed. However, demand is not a factor currently impacting battery production as there is clearly an overdemand. At present, there are two primary constraints on battery production: 1) the capacity of existing battery manufacturing plants and 2) the capacity of existing battery minerals extraction and manufacturing (i.e., synthetic graphite is made, not mined). In other words, the battery industry can't make them fast enough. [633]

The upward trend for EV/BESS battery demand and manufacturing has been as dramatic as it has been consistent. 100 GWh of battery capacity was deployed in 2018, 118 GWh in 2019, 147 GWh in 2020 and then a big jump forward to 301 GWh in 2021. The jump to 518 GWh in 2022 confirmed the accelerating demand for more LIBs of all

---

[633] SNE Research, 2022 EV Battery Report, Feb 08, 2023.

types. By all indications from available data by various market intelligence companies, this acceleration will continue into the foreseeable future.[634]

The global battery industry is dominated by the Asia market with three key players (in this order): China, South Korea, and Japan. All three countries got into the small LIB space in the 1990's to support the home electronics industry (cell phones, laptops, watches, and small electronics of all types). When the world started transitioning to BEVs, they already had extensive industry connections and infrastructure enabling them to shift focus to the BEV space. Incredibly, the entire European and North American markets missed this opportunity. Consequently, there is not a single country today that produces BEV batteries at scale outside of Asia or by Asian companies.

In 2022, six out of the ten top EV battery manufactures in the world were Chinese. These included: CATL (Contemporary Amperage Technology Limited) with 191.6 GWh of capacity manufactured, BYD (Build Your Dreams) with 70.4 GWh, CALB (China Aviation Lithium battery) with 20 GWh, Guoxuan High-Tech (or Gotion) with 14.1 GWh, Sunwoda Electric Vehicle Battery Company with 9.2 GWh and Farasis Energy with 7.4 GWh. Combined, these six companies produced 312.7 GWh for the year or 60% of the global market.[635]

There were three South Korean companies in the top ten to include: LG Energy Solutions (spun off from LG Chem) with 70.4 GWh, SK On (spun off from SK Innovation) with 27.8 GWh and Samsung SDI with 24.3 GWh. These three companies manufactured a total of 122.5 GWh in 2022 or 23.6% of global lithium-ion battery production. The only Japanese company in the top ten was Panasonic with 38 GWh of production or 7% of global production capacity. In total, these top ten companies produced more than 90% of the world's BEV batteries.[636]

We can expect Asia's dominance in the LIB space to continue for the foreseeable future. Although the rest of the world is finally waking up and getting more into the LIB space, as we will discuss more in this chapter, they have 25 years of lost time to try and make up. China fully understands its dominant position in the battery space and they have no plans to relinquish this status – none. The Chinese plan is to double down on their current trajectory and not let up on the gas (so to speak). Importantly,

---

[634] Ibid.

[635] Ibid.

[636] Ibid.

China is maneuvering to remain the world's leading battery provider as opposed to just servicing their own domestic market.

One thing to focus on as we dig deeper into these battery companies is their vertical integration and ability to capture more of the value chain, both upstream and downstream from their immediate industry. A successful battery company has secure, redundant supply chains and has planned for disruptions. We would also expect them to "see" the industry and know where to go to expand their business; in fact, it should be obvious. Additionally, the name of the game is scaling up. If a battery company has good chemistry and a quality overall product, they can sell each one they make. It is then a race as to how many batteries hey can manufacture and how effectively they can secure their own battery mineral supply chain.

China's Battery Industry

As China's BEV industry began to expand, Beijing ensured that domestic manufactures would be the ones providing the batteries, not the more established industries from South Korea or Japan. As there were no other BEV battery manufacturers outside of Asia, these were the only competitors in the business. China locked them out through the effective application of bureaucratic warfare doled out by the Ministry of Industry and Information Technology (MIIT). MIIT has many functions, one of which is establishing battery industrial policy.

Beginning in 2015, MIIT published lists of BEV batteries that met industry "technical standards". This became known as the "white list". The batteries on the white list were approved for use in Chinese BEVs. If a battery wasn't on the white list, that meant they didn't meet MIIT published "technical standards" and couldn't be used. While this was just good old-fashioned protectionism, "technical standards" provided the guise that it was a production safety issue. Importantly, Chinese BEV manufactures who used approved white list batteries were the ones that received government subsidies for their products. [637]

Judging from subsequent results, MIIT's protectionist measures had the desired impact. In 2016, the last time the white list was updated, there were 57 companies recognized by MIIT – all of them were Chinese. Therefore, it was no surprise in 2018 when

---

[637] Quartz, E. Huang, "China's breaking up the EV battery monopoly it carefully created", June 25, 2019.

the China Battery Industry Association posted its list of top ten battery manufacturers and all of them were domestic Chinese firms. The system was rigged and all the regional battery industry players knew it. But this closed system couldn't last forever as insulating their battery industry had long-term consequences.

To start, China is a member of the G20 (Group of 20), an intergovernmental forum where 19 of the world's richest economies and the EU discuss and coordinate global economic activity. As such, the G20 represents some 80% of global wealth. China couldn't continue its protectionist policies in perpetuity and still abide by the spirit of cooperation in the G20. Afterall, South Korea and Japan were G20 members and regional neighbors. They could enact their own protectionists policies and hold back support to Chinese G20 financial initiatives if they wanted to.

Additionally, as the global battery industry grew, including China's, protectionism could be detrimental in that it would confine growth to their own domestic market. What would happen in the future when China wanted to sell its batteries in North America and was confronted with a wall of retaliatory polices from Canada, Mexico, and the U.S.? It was better in the long run for China, from an economic growth perspective, to establish a strong battery industrial base, drop its own protectionist policies and then expand their lithium-ion business globally. And that's what they did.

It was in 2019 that MIIT ended its protectionist policies and abolished its white list. China opened up its BEV market that same year as well. Previously, foreign car manufacturers operating in China, like VW and GM, had to partner with an established Chinese auto company in the form of a JV. Tesla was the first foreign car manufacturer to build an independent manufacturing plant without being encumbered with a JV. China intentionally opened its battery and EV industries to encourage competition, to shake out its own domestic companies with poor fundamentals and to accelerate overall battery and EV adoption in the country.

Contemporary Amperage Technology Limited (CATL)

The CEO of CATL, Robin Zeng (aka Zeng Yuqun), who was born in 1968, began his career in academics. He earned a Doctorate in Condensed Matter Physics from the prestigious Institute of Physics, Chinese Academy of Sciences. After graduating, he found work at SAE Magnetic, a Hong Kong company specializing in magnetic heads for computer hard drives. After ten years at SAE, Zeng moved on and founded the Hong Kong based company ATL (Amperage Technology Limited) in 1999. Under

Zeng's leadership as CEO, ATL grew to 3,000 people, specializing in lithium polymer battery manufacturing for small consumer products like laptops and cell phones. In 2005, Japanese company TDK Corporation, who focused on electronic components manufacturing, bought ATL outright for $100 million USD. [638]

Not satisfied with the limited scope of work at ATL, Zeng started new business CATL in 2011 to focus on the development and manufacturing of LIBs for the growing EV and BESS markets. He positioned his new business in his hometown – the port city of Ningde, Fujian Province. Zeng, himself, is brilliant, practical and an absolute workhorse. He sees where the market is going, he understands the value of speed and he knows how to operate at scale. One would be hard pressed to find a CEO who has imprinted their personality more on a company than Zeng has with CATL. Consequently, one would be equally hard pressed to find a business leader who has moved their business forward in such a way to meet their strategic vision in such a compressed timespan.

As we can see with Zeng's quote at the beginning of this chapter, he values innovation above all else. For example, in 2014, CATL employed just 500 people in their R&D department.[639] By 2022, CATL increased their R&D efforts twenty-fold and now employs an army of over 12,000 people in R&D.[640] To put this in context, the American lithium services company Albemarle only has 5,600 employees total.[641] Let that sink in. In 2021, CATL spent $1.2 billion USD on their R&D and was on pace to spend $1.7 billion USD in 2022.[642] CATL intends to protect their battery technology lead through an impenetrable wall of patents: they have over 5,400 already approved and another 7,400 pending.[643] I don't know of another company in the lithium value chain that puts so many resources into their R&D.

As with other companies who develop proprietary technology that is key to the success of their business model, CATL protects their intellectual property (IP).

---

[638] Batteries International, by M. Halls, "Next generation lithium: from electronic components to the smart grids of the future", Issue 92, Summer 2014.

[639] Ibid.

[640] CATL, H12022 Report.

[641] https://www.albemarle.com/

[642] CATL, H12022 Report.

[643] Ibid.

As we noted with the deluge of patents above, part of protecting a company's IP is filing patents which provide a certain level of official and recognized IP security. But it's not enough. Journalists who conduct tours of CATL facilities are given general access to non-essential structures but don't get to see sensitive battery production lines. Another problem in the battery industry (and any industry) is the movement of trained personal from one company to another – this is the physical embodiment of IP transfer.

Companies typically try to prevent departing employees from disclosing the IP kept in their brains to the new company that hired them by the signing of NDAs (Non-Disclosure Agreements) or Non-Compete Clauses (NCC). In 2022, CATL sued much smaller Chinese EV battery manufacturer Svolt Energy after nine CATL employees left to join Svolt affiliated companies. CATL accused these employees of providing Svolt with proprietary information which Svolt denied. Ultimately, the Ningde Intermediate People's Court made a judgement in favor of CATL with Svolt awarding CATL a paltry $740,000.00 USD. This small award meant that CATL didn't have much of a case or at least couldn't prove it in court. While this was nothing but budget dust for CATL, it did set a precedence for legal action. [644]

CATL also went after their junior battery competitor CALB for patent infringement. CALB denied the claims arguing that the initial case brought against them involved outdated technology and that all their present technology was far more advanced and thus did not meet CATL's patent protection. The Fuzhou Intermediate Court partially ruled in CATL's favor with CALB paying only $444,000.00 USD and mandating that CALB stop producing any battery specifically using one CATL's patents (patent # ZL201810039458.6). CALB wasn't satisfied with this judgement. [645]

Subsequently, CALB followed up with the China National Intellectual Property Administration (CNIPA), disagreeing with their determination that some of CATL's patents in dispute were deemed valid. CNIPA had previously determined that parts of CATL's patents were deemed invalid. CALB was seeking a judgement that they all be deemed invalid. CALB also submitted litigation over the validity of CATL's patents through the Beijing Intellectual Property Court (BIPC), seeking a return of a favorable

---

[644] CnEVPost, by P. Zhang, "CATL settles lawsuit against Svolt Energy, wins about $740,000 in compensation", July 9, 2022.

[645] CALB Press Release, "Announcement on Progress of Litigation", Nov 30, 2022.

judgement. If either CATL or CALB disagrees with BIPC's decision, the issue can then be raised to the Supreme People's Court. CALB emphasized that neither the present judgement nor ongoing litigation would negatively impact their battery production. [646]

We will let CALB's lawsuits simmer while we move on to defining CATL's business architecture. To start, they have five R&D centers with two in Fujian Province (one in Ningde and one in Xiamen), one in Liyang, two in Jiangsu Province (one is in Shanghai) and one in Munich, Germany. The business logic for placement of the two centers in Fujian province are obvious as that is where CATL's headquarters and two battery manufacturing plants are. Jiangsu is another obvious location as Shanghai, which is in Jiangsu, is the center of BEV manufacturing in China and thus the center of world BEV production. Importantly, CATL has been in Munich since 2014 as they see Germany as strategic point of insertion for expanding battery operations on the European continent.

In 2017, CATL spread their battery tentacles into key global markets, setting up wholly owned subsidiaries in the U.S., Japan, Canada, and France. Each one of those are key market players in the BEV world, even if some of that potential is a ways down road. These locations are strategic in nature. CATL USA was placed outside of Detroit in Auburn Hills to establish business ties with the major car manufacturers there: Ford, GM and Stellantis. CATL's office in Japan is in Yokohama City, just outside of Tokyo with the mission of building inroads with the world's largest car manufacturer, Toyota. France is home to several major car manufacturers (Renault) and Canada feeds the U.S. market with parts, cars and has a robust mining industry.

CATL has twelve battery manufacturing plants with more scheduled. To date, they have concentrated their efforts in China but are beginning to expand into the European and North American markets. CATL has ten battery plants in China, with most of them in south-central China near the coast. The first five are located in: Ningde, Fujian Province (collocated with the company HQs and is a JV with car manufacturer FAW); Xiamen, Fujian Province (just south of CATL HQs); Xining, Qinghai Province (about 350 miles east of China's largest lithium brine operations); Jining, Shandong Province (this will come on line in 2024); and Shanghai (actually these are two plants with one operational in 2022 and the other coming online in 2023).

Another five are in Liyang, Changzhou Province (this is a JV between CATL and car

---

[646] Ibid.

manufacturer SAIC, called United Auto Battery Company); Yibin, Sichuan Province (this is a JV with car manufacturer Geely and came on line in 2022); Guiyang, Guizhou Province (CATL has also signed a deal with the provincial government to establish a battery swap network); Yichun, Jiangxi Province (CATL is also developing a hard rock lithium mine near the plant) and Zhaoqing, Guangdong Province (this $1 billion USD plant began production in 2022).

CATL has one active battery plant in Europe, located in Erfurt, Thuringia, Germany. CATL began building the plant in 2019 and brought it online at the end of 2022 when it could make its own cells on site. The $1.8 billion USD plant has a 14 GWh capacity that can outfit about 350,000 BEVs depending on their battery size. CATL has plans to expand the plant's battery capacity to 24 GWh sometime in 2023. I suspect CATL has plans to expand this factory as big as they can get it as they can and will sell every single battery they make. It is interesting to note that Germany, with a highly educated work force, a technologically sophisticated society and a massive car industry completely missed the boat on the battery revolution and must import battery expertise from abroad because they have none themselves.[647]

CATL is developing a second European battery plant in Debrecen, Hungary with a planned investment of $7.5 billion USD to build out 100 GWh of capacity. CATL CEO Robin Zeng recognized this second plant as critical in their strategy to expand outside of China and into the continent to service the growing BEV market in both Germany and all of Europe. The Hungarian Minister of Foreign Affairs and Trade welcomed the investment to counterbalance the European recession as it would add 9,000 new jobs. The Minister further described CATL's plant as the biggest greenfield investment in the history of Hungary.[648]

As we well know, these factories produce batteries but they don't all produce the same kind of batteries. CATL makes several different kinds of batteries but mainly NMC batteries (Nickel-Manganese-Cobalt), technology developed by Professor Jeff Dahn out of Dalhousie University in Canada. NCM batteries are called ternary batteries and are what BEV manufacturers have traditionally used for their LIBs because

---

[647] Reuters, "CATL's German plant targets six battery cell production lines by the end of 2023", Jan 26, 2023.

[648] Inside EVs, by M. Kane, "CATL Will Build Massive 100 GWh Battery Plant In Hungary", Aug 12, 2022.

they have high energy density characteristics. However, they degrade over time, lose their charge in cold weather and cannot be charged to 100% very often or it damages the battery.

CATL more recently began producing LFP (Lithium-Iron-Phosphate) batteries and sells many of these to Tesla who installs them in their vehicles made in Shanghai. LFP batteries have several advantages over NCM in that they are less expensive, can be charged regularly to 100% capacity, perform better in cold weather and have a longer life cycle. However, they do suffer from lower energy density meaning a company must make a larger, heavier battery to get the same range as a ternary battery. On the positive side, iron and phosphate are relatively plentiful and a company doesn't have to worry about the human rights problems that are associated with cobalt mining. Because size and weight aren't a concern, LFP batteries are ideal for BESS.

While NMC and LFP both have their own advantages and disadvantages, CATL is creating a new M3P battery to split the difference. Reporting indicates that the battery went into production in 2022 but won't be delivered until 2023. CATL has been tight-lipped about what the exact chemistry is, but many observers think it must be similar to an LMFP (Lithium-Manganese-Iron-Phosphate) battery. Other reporting indicated zinc, magnesium and aluminum were being added to an LFP chemistry. Allegedly, the M3P battery will have 15-20% more energy than an LFP battery but cost the same. If the M3P comes into production at scale and retains the positive qualities, this will instantly make all previous LFP batteries non-competitive. [649]

The more variety a company has in their battery production architecture, the more diverse mineral supply chain they must develop and secure. Although CATL is increasingly producing nickel-fee batteries, they are still in their inventory and most likely will be for many years. Hence, they still must secure a nickel supply chain. Since they know this, CATL bought the single largest share of Lygend Resources, who IPO'ed on the Hong Kong Stock Exchange in December 2022. In 2021, Lygend was recognized as the single largest nickel producer and trader in the world. As if that weren't enough, Lygend is currently expanding their portfolio into Indonesia, who has some of the

---

[649] CnEVPost, by P. Zhang, "CATL's M3P battery to be put into use next year, says chief scientist", July 22, 2022.

largest nickel deposits on the planet. It is safe to assess CATL's nickel supply chain as being secured. [650]

There is nickel in Indonesia but a company generally must go to Africa to secure cobalt. While CATL is producing several cobalt-free battery models, they still need cobalt for their ternary batteries. Accordingly, in 2021, CATL bought a 25% stake in China Molybdenum Company's Kisanfu mine in the DRC (Congo) for $135 million USD.[651] This means CATL will receive 25% of the cobalt and copper from the mine moving forward. The following year, China Molybdenum changed its name to CMOC Group. Not satisfied with their initial purchase into the Kisanfu mine, CATL bought a 25% share of the entire CMOC Group in 2022 for approximately $4 billion USD.[652] This ensured CATL would receive a continuing supply of cobalt, copper, and phosphate for its battery enterprise.

And, of course, CATL must secure its lithium supply chain as there is no substitute for it now or on the horizon. As we would expect, CATL has already bought into several lithium mining operations in China (Sichuan & Jiangxi Provinces), but let's focus on the big fish. In January 2023, CATL won a competitive bidding process to develop lithium operations in Bolivia. Specifically, the CBC Consortium, where CATL is the majority owner, will spend an estimated $1 billion USD to develop lithium brine extraction operations using DLE (Direct Lithium Extraction) technology.[653]

As a reminder, Bolivia is believed to hold the largest reserves of lithium in the world. And as the reader may have guessed, Bolivia is a member of China's Belt and Road Initiative. When this brine operation becomes operational, CATL will have secured its lithium supplies for the foreseeable future. It is interesting to note that neither a European nor a North American company won the contract. Importantly, CATL may be able to use its LCE extracted from the Lithium Triangle to supply its future battery plants in the U.S.

So, who is buying all these EV batteries from CATL? Is it mainly local Chinese BEV

[650] China Business Law Journal, "Nickel trader Lygend raises HKD3.67bn in IPO to fund projects", Dec 5, 2022.

[651] Reuters, "CATL takes stake in China Moly cobalt mine for $137.5 million", April 11, 2021.

[652] CMOC Group Limited, Press Release, Oct 31, 2022.

[653] Reuters, by D. Ramos, "Bolivia taps Chinese battery giant CATL to help develop lithium riches", Jn 20, 2023.

manufacturers and regional buyers? Or do they have a global customer base? Well, the answer is "yes". To start, CATL sells their batteries to the major Chinese BEV manufacturers like Nio, Li Auto, Zeekr and telecom giant Huawei (who is entering the BEV business). CATL also landed Tesla as a customer in 2021, when Tesla announced in Q3 that they would begin outfitting all their standard range models with LFP batteries globally.[654] Regionally, CATL has inked contracts with Toyota, Nissan, Honda, and Kia. How about Europe? They already have a foothold there with deals that include VW, BMW, Mercedes, and Renault. Did I miss anybody?

South Korea & LG Energy Solutions

As we noted in the beginning of this chapter, South Korean battery manufacturers are major players in the global EV battery market. This isn't particularly easy for them seeing as how they have no natural battery mineral resources to exploit on their peninsula. Hence, they must import everything for their onshore battery plants or they must offshore their battery operations. This puts them in a precarious position from a strategic critical minerals security perspective as they are prone to disruption. Also, South Korean car manufacturers have been slow to adopt BEVs at scale, even though they are doing better than their neighbor, Japan.

While there are three major South Korean battery manufacturers, for the purposes of our discussion, let's focus on the biggest one, LG Energy Solutions (LGES). LGES is a relatively new company in its present form as it spun off from its parent company, LG Chem, only in 2020. I wholly agree with this strategic decision as it enables LGES to focus on its core business without distractions from their parent company. It also allows them to develop their own culture which must be based on speed, innovation, and scale. Remember, CATL is literally next door to them and is moving out at a fierce pace. While this was a necessary move, LG Chem shareholders were angry that the biggest workhorse in the company with the most growth potential was departing their portfolios.[655]

LGES' business strategy rests on four key pillars: product competitiveness, smart

---

[654] Tesla, Q32021 Update

[655] The Korea Times, by B. Byeung-yeul, "LG Chem fails to address investors' concerns", Oct 12, 2020.

factories, supply chain management and future readiness.[656] Let's start with the first pillar: product competitiveness. By this, LGES means that they must provide specific markets the products that they need that are of high quality. For example, Hyundai wants NCMA (nickel-cobalt-manganese-aluminum) batteries in its BEVs and LGES needs to accommodate that. And seeing as how CATL is providing Tesla the majority of its LFP batteries, how does LGES break into that segment and compete effectively? They can't afford to be beaten to the punch and allow competitors to come out with a better product. The company with a better product has a much better chance of securing long-term binding relationships with thrifty buyers.

It is interesting to see LGES identify the development of highly efficient smart factories as key to their strategy. I couldn't agree more. Tesla has famously built the most efficient BEV factory in the world in Shanghai. Similarly, one of Robin Zeng's earliest initiatives at CATL was developing their "301 program" where they cut manufacturing processes and equipment by 30%.[657] What LGES must avoid is the debacle where GM recalled every single Chevy Bolt using LG batteries due to risk of fire. Chevy recalled 140,000 of its BEVs in 2021 resulting in LG Chem paying out $1.9 billion USD to GM to fix the problem.[658] What was the source of the problem? A failure in the manufacturing process where a battery anode gets torn and a separator is folded resulting in a potential fire hazard.[659]

Thirdly, LGES correctly recognizes supply chain management as critical with the need to localize battery mineral sourcing with their offshored battery factories. This is especially true when we look at the U.S.' *Inflation Reduction Act* which only rewards regionally sourced batteries. As we know, the EU just passed their *Critical Raw Materials Act* that mandates increased onshoring of battery minerals. Overall, the BEV industry is moving towards collocated battery/EV manufacturing plants as opposed to shipping their components all around the globe. LGES also recognizes the need for more

---

[656] LGES, Q4 2022 Earnings Conference Call

[657] Batteries International, by M. Halls, "Next generation lithium: from electronic components to the smart grids of the future", Issue 92, Summer 2014.

[658] Reuters, by H. Yang, "GM settles $2 bln Bolt EV recall cost deal with S.Korea's LG", Oct 12, 2021.

[659] Design News, by D. Carney, "GM suspended Chevrolet Bolt EV production in August due to battery fires.", Sep 29, 2021.

upstream sourcing. They need to get into the battery metals mining business or at least buy large enough shares into existing companies to secure their offtake. LGES is doing this as we will see in a moment.

Finally, future readiness is the final crucial pillar in their strategy which we can take to mean operational innovation and R&D. Specifically, LGES is pursuing next generation battery chemistries like lithium sulfur and solid-state batteries. They are also investigating Baas (Battery as a Service) like Nio and CATL are already doing and EaaS (Energy as a Service) although their BESS (Battery Energy Storage Solutions) growth has been flat from 2021-2023. Clearly, LGES has prioritized their BEV battery manufacturing over their BESS efforts, like other major market players like Tesla, CATL and BYD.

Let's look at LGES R&D efforts. LGES has over 27,000 employees worldwide with more than 2,500 working in R&D. They have steadily increased their R&D budget, investing $3.2 billion USD in 2020. This is a common trend in the EV battery space as companies compete to develop better products with more range at lower prices. Additionally, LGES has 24,731 patents to protect their Intellectual Property (IP). They have numerous Advanced Automotive Battery technology research centers as well as dedicated teams studying the advancement of battery cells and battery packs.[660]

LGES has a dispersed manufacturing architecture with battery plants located in South Korea (Ochang), China (Nanjing), Europe (Poland) and the U.S.(Michigan). LGES has two battery plants in South Korea: Ochang 1 which was built in 2004 and Ochang 2 that was built in 2012. LGES began building a new battery line in 2022 at the Ochang campus to produce 9 GWh per year of 4680 cylindrical cells that are most likely for Tesla. LGES is also expanding its 2170 cylindrical cell capacity by 4 GWh, also most likely for Tesla. This expansion will cost $567 million USD and bring Ochang production up from 22 GWh to 35 GWh annually by the end of 2023.[661]

As early as 2009, LG Chem and GM collaborated on the Chevy Volt with LG providing the battery cells and battery packs for the vehicle.[662] LG Chem then expanded

---

[660] https://www.lgensol.com/en/index

[661] The Korea Herald, by S. Ji-hyoung, "LG Energy Solution unveils W730b EV battery plan", June 13, 2022.

[662] EE Power, by J. Shepard, "Chevrolet Volt Battery Packs Will Be Manufactured By General Motors In US", Jan 20, 2009.

into the U.S. in 2010, establishing a small battery manufacturing plant in Holland, Michigan, about two and a half hours west of Detroit on Lake Michigan. After LG Chem manufactured the battery cells at the Holland plant, they shipped them to the GM Battery Assembly Plant in Brownstown located just outside of Detroit. Today, this is where the batteries are assembled for GM's Hummer and Cadillac Lyriq vehicle lines. In 2022, LGES announced plans to invest $1.7 billion USD to expand and upgrade its very small Holland operation from only 5 GWh to 25 GWh of annual capacity.[663]

It was in Nanjing that LG Chem began building their first EV battery plant in 2014 to serve the growing China battery market. Nanjing is only 165 miles from Shanghai, the BEV manufacturing center of the world, so I'd say this is a strategically placed location. They intended to be operational by 2015, the same year that the Chinese regulatory body MIIT began publishing battery "technical standards" that effectively shut out foreign competition until 2019. In 2018, LG Chem invested another $1.9 billion USD to start construction of a second EV battery plant in Nanjing which would be built in stages and completely finished in 2023.[664]

When the foreign EV battery ban was lifted, LGES was ready to provide batteries for Tesla's new Model 3 built out of Shanghai, which began production at the end of 2019. At the end of 2020, LGES planned to invest $500 million USD more into one of its Nanjing plants to go from just eight to seventeen production lines making 2170 cylindrical battery cells. This would increase plant production by 8 GWh a year. The Nanjing plant also planned to ship their batteries to Germany and the U.S. to supply Tesla BEV production at those locations. One would be hard pressed to find a more inefficient supply chain prone to disruption than that. But it also makes a strong case for the need for locally sourced battery plants. [665]

After securing two manufacturing bases in Asia, LG Chem established a European foothold in Wroclaw, Poland in 2016. This was the first EV battery plant on the European continent and it was large with a 30 GWh annual capacity. This was a

---

[663] Holland Sentinel, by C. Muyskens, "MEDC chief: LG's $1.7B expansion in Holland comes at critical time", Mar 22, 2022.

[664] Pulse News, by L. Jae-Chul & C. Mira, "LG Chem breaks ground for 2nd EV battery plant in Nanjing, China", Oct 23, 2018.

[665] Reuters, Exclusive: LG Chem to double China battery capacity to meet Tesla demand – sources", Nov 30, 2020.

brilliant strategic decision by the LG Chem leadership. In 2020, LG Chem wanted to expand and modernize their existing facilities at a cost of $1.65 billion USD. In order to make this expansion possible, the European Investment Bank (EIB) provided LG Chem with a loan of $536 million USD or one-third of the total project cost. This investment would more than double the Wroclaw plant capacity to 65 GWh annually. This was good news for Poland as the project would add 1,800 more jobs for a total of 6,000 people employed at the plant.[666]

LGES is also working to expand its current footprint beyond what we have just discussed, with the intent to scale up and diversify geographically to reach new markets. To begin, they have three plants in the U.S. (OH, MI, TN) in the works through a JV with GM called Ultium Cells which is GM's priority effort. Honda and LGES are forming a JV in Ohio to build batteries to supply their BEVs in the U.S. They are also looking into a wholly owned operation near Phoenix, AZ to potentially supply Tesla with batteries. In Canada, LGES is working a JV with Stellantis to build batteries out of Ontario for the North American market. Also, Hyundai and LGES are presently working through the details of building out battery plants in Indonesia and the state of Georgia, US. Finally, Ford and LGES have agreed to build a JV battery plant near Ankara, Turkey.

When looking at these nine battery operations, we see LGES scaling up at a pace that will easily triple their current annual production capacity. It is also apparent that LGES is regionally aligning its operations, as are their JV partners, in response to laws instituted by the U.S. and EU to incentivize onshore battery manufacturing to secure their respective critical supply chains. Seven out of nine of the plants are in North America, indicating that they accurately see the huge opportunity to expand in the U.S.' severely underdeveloped market. This is an aggressive plan that hits the three major regional car markets and locks them into secure long-term contracts with willing BEV manufacturing partners.

Where is LGES securing all the lithium tonnage to meet the requirement for hundreds of GWhs a year? To start, they already have an eight-year binding offtake agreement with Chilean company SQM for battery-grade LCE and lithium hydroxide.[667]

---

[666] Inside EVs, by M. Kane, "LG Chem Gets €480 Million Loan From EIB For Battery Plant In Poland", March 26, 2020.

[667] Mining Journal, "SQM inks long-term lithium supply accord with LG", Dec 22, 2020.

They have also signed a ten-year deal with Snow Lake Lithium in Canada to produce lithium hydroxide with production estimated to begin in 2025.[668] In the U.S., LGES signed a binding six-year agreement with Utah-based Compass Minerals for an initial 4,400 tpa of LCE from their brine evaporation operations.[669] For the Asia market, LGES signed a binding five-year offtake agreement with Australian miner Liontown Resources for 700,000 tpa of lithium contrate from 2024-2028.[670]

From a circular economy perspective, LGES understands recycling is the new mining and has pursued several regionally aligned effort in this space. For the North American market, LGES has signed a binding ten-year agreement with U.S. company Li-Cycle, providing them with expended LIBs and in return receiving approximately 10,000 tpa of recycled nickel sulphate.[671] For the China market, LGES is working with Zhejang Huayou Cobalt to develop two battery recycling centers to recover nickel, cobalt and lithium from expended batteries.[672] In another effort, LGES is partnering with Korean steelmaker POSCO to recycle its batteries in both Poland and South Korea to recover nickel, cobalt, manganese and lithium.[673]

In my assessment, LGES is doing everything it should be to grow its business. Importantly, it's hitting every line of effort it must in each of the three strategic markets (China, Europe, U.S.). LGES has had some tough breaks in its history: partnering with GM on the Chevy Bolt which has never sold well, China shutting them out of BEVs from 2015-2019 and the battery recall incident which reflected a manufacturing failure. But that's all lithium brine under the bridge. The degree of LGES' future success will be determined by the competence of their own leadership, the ability to execute their plans effectively and their desire to scale up battery capacity.

[668] Snow Lake Lithium, "Snow Lake Lithium and LG Energy Solution Collaborate To Establish Lithium Supply Chain in North America", Sep 22, 2022.

[669] Compass Minerals, "Compass Minerals Signs Binding Multiyear Agreement to Supply LG Energy Solution with Battery-Grade Lithium Carbonate", Nov 10, 2022.

[670] Pulse News, by L. Eun-joo, "LGES secures 700,000 0lithium concentrate from Australian miner Liontown", May 02, 2022.

[671] Li-Cycle, "Li-Cycle Completes Commercial Agreements with LG Chem and LG Energy Solution", April 21,2022.

[672] Just Auto, "LGES, Huayou to establish EV battery recycling JV", July 26, 2022.

[673] The Korea Herald, by K. Byung-wook, "Posco to launch new entity to recycle LGES batteries", April 30, 2021.

Japan – Panasonic

Panasonic is the LGES of Japan – well, sort of. While it is the largest producer of EV batteries in Japan, it also the most underperforming of the top ten companies. Panasonic has been producing LIBs for thirty years, but you wouldn't know it by their mere 35 GWh of production in 2022. For example, in 2009, Panasonic was already making EV batteries while CATL didn't even exist. But only fourteen years later, CATL had sprinted past Panasonic with a commanding 600% relative lead in annual battery production capacity.

To be sure, the biggest drag on Panasonic has been the lack of a domestic BEV industry in their own country. Toyota is the largest car manufacturer in the world with Japanese companies collectively outproducing every other single country in the car business. However, Toyota has made the strategic error of resisting the transition to 100% BEV manufacturing which undercuts their future market position. A Toyota-Panasonic BEV-battery marriage could be the most powerful partnership in the world as opposed to the disappointing flop that it presently is.

The story of Panasonic is really the story of their relationship with Tesla. However, AC Propulsion out of California initially provided electric powertrains for Tesla's original Roadster. The Roadster was always a low-volume production model and from 2008-2012 Tesla only made 2,500 models. As the vehicles were handmade, it was easy to keep up with an equally unsophisticated and unautomated battery supply process. As such, the battery packs provided by AC Propulsion were part of a learning process where Tesla evolved its understanding of their product and what they needed.[674]

The packs were made of commercially available rechargeable 18650 cylindrical cells with a lithium-ion chemistry. The Roadster battery pack had 6,800 of these cells and weighed in at a hefty 990 pounds.[675] In 2009, Tesla stopped using ACP's battery packs because they wanted different design features and began using a heavily modified version that they made in-house.[676] Tesla quickly realized that they needed a pro-

---

[674] EV Annex, by M. Pressman, "From tzero to Model S; How AC Propulsion was a catalyst for Tesla Motors", Feb 06, 2016.

[675] Tesla Paper, by G. Berdichevsky, et al., "The Tesla Roadster Battery System", August 16, 2006.

[676] Road and Track, by B. Sorokanich, "Elon Musk Admits to Shareholders That the Tesla Roadster Was a Disaster", June 1, 2016.

fessional battery manufacturer who operated at scale if they were going to grow their business. Making the battery packs by hand wasn't cutting it.

After conducting a search for such a manufacturer, they agreed to a deal with Panasonic, who had been in the battery business since 1923 and developed their first lithium-ion battery in 1994.[677] As outlined in the original supply agreement signed in 2009 between Panasonic and Tesla, Panasonic would make its battery cells in Japan and then ship them to Tesla's Fremont plant in California. Tesla was responsible for recycling the batteries if they chose to, although they weren't interested in doing so at the time. The agreement allowed Tesla to source its batteries from other companies and Panasonic could sell to other BEV manufacturers as well. The original contract was for six months but would automatically extend year by year after that.[678]

In order to support the new battery requirements for Tesla's low-production run Roadster, Panasonic opened their new factory in Suminoe, Japan in 2010. Here, Panasonic made their NCR (Nickel-Cobalt-Rechargeable) 18650A cylindrical cells with a 3.1 Ah (ampere hours) capacity which was an improvement over their previous 18650 cell with 2.9 Ah.[679] These batteries are widely known as NCA (Nickel-Cobalt-Aluminum) cells. As a side note, Panasonic has since worked to wean itself off cobalt and today they use less than 5% of it in their batteries.[680] From a capacity perspective, the Suminoe factory was set up to manufacture 300 million cells a year.[681] This was enough to fill battery packs for 44,000 BEVs annually using the previous battery pack configuration. Clearly this volume was not intended for Roadster production, but in preparation for Tesla's impending release of a new model.

As Tesla closed out production of its Roadster in January 2012, it released its next model, the Model S. The Model S would also receive battery packs made from 18650 cylindrical cells. In 2012, Tesla delivered 2,650 of its Model S BEVs, in 2013 they sold 22,350 and in 2014 they sold another 32,000.[682] Based on the production capacity of

[677] https://www.panasonic.com/global/energy/products/battery/profile/ history.html

[678] Panasonic Corporation, Supply Agreement, July 21, 2009.

[679] Panasonic Group Press Release, "Panasonic Starts Mass-Production of High-Capacity 3.1 Ah Lithium-ion Battery", Dec 18, 2009.

[680] Panasonic Group, Annual Report 2022.

[681] https://www.tesla.com/blog/panasonic-presents-first-electric-vehicle-battery-tesla

[682] Tesla Annual Reports 2012,2013,2014.

Panasonic's Suminoe factory, they were able to keep up with these readily modest numbers. However, Tesla began preparations to scale up production, signing an agreement with Panasonic to produce 1.8 billion cells from 2014-2017.[683] Based on the original 18650 battery pack configuration, this equaled 264,000 BEVs or 66,000 a year. In 2014, Tesla and Panasonic also agreed to build a battery Giga factory in Nevada in anticipation of further growth.

In 2015, Tesla sold 50,000 Model S units and just 214 of its new Model X full-size SUVs.[684] This meant Panasonic had expanded its battery production which would have to keep up with Model S/X sales moving forward. Tesla manufactured almost 84,000 Model S/X BEVs in 2016 and then 103,000 Model S/X/3 models the next year in 2017.[685, 686] Although Model 3 sales were limited in 2017, future growth would be explosive as Tesla ramped up sales of its family sedan. Could Panasonic keep the pace?

Giga Nevada became operational in 2017, producing the new 2170 cylindrical battery cell that would be used in Tesla Powerwalls, Powerpacks and Model 3's.[687] Panasonic owned the battery making equipment in the gigafactory with Tesla buying the finished battery cells. The 18650 cells were 18 mm in diameter and 65 mm tall while the 2170s were 21 mm in diameter and 70 mm tall. The larger 2170s were slightly more efficient due to more battery mass with the battery pack benefiting from less battery packaging meaning it had increased energy density. The Model S/X continued to be powered by the legacy NCA 18650 cells.

The following year, in 2018, Tesla manufactured 245,000 Model S/X/3 units, a big jump from 2017 because of the success of the Model 3.[688] That same year, Panasonic began production of NCM (Nickel-Cobalt-Manganese) prismatic EV battery cells at its manufacturing plant in Dalian, China in order to serve the North American and

---

[683] Tesla Annual Report 2014.

[684] Inside EVs, by M. Kane, "Tesla Motors – Model S/X Road To 50,000+ Sales In 2015 & Cumulative Total Of Nearly 110,000", Jan 5, 2016.

[685] https://ir.tesla.com/press-release/tesla-q4-2016-production-and-deliveries

[686] https://ir.tesla.com/press-release/tesla-q4-2017-vehicle-production-and-deliveries

[687] https://www.tesla.com/blog/battery-cell-production-begins-gigafactory

[688] https://ir.tesla.com/press-release/tesla-q4-2018-vehicle-production-deliveries-also-announcing-2000

Chinese markets.[689] However, China was still limiting EV battery production until 2019 and Tesla didn't use prismatic cells. Also, curiously these batteries were intended to target the Plug-in Hybrid EV (PHEV) segment. In 2019, Panasonic would go on to form a prismatic battery manufacturing JV with Toyota which would also be in Dalian.[690] Clearly, Panasonic was trying to diversify its portfolio.

While Panasonic moved into the prismatic battery business, Tesla was ramping up production with 367,000 Model S/X/3 models sold in 2019.[691] More importantly, in December, Tesla opened their Giga Shanghai plant for production with Model 3's quickly rolling out its doors. Soon after, this would become the most efficient, profitable auto manufacturing plant in the world. Whatever company landed the contract to supply Giga Shanghai would potentially set themselves up for the single most lucrative battery deal in the world. And it wouldn't be Panasonic. Instead, Tesla partnered with LG Chem whose Nanjing battery plant would produce 2170 cylindrical cells for the Model 3 in China.

2020 was a big year for Tesla as they started manufacturing their very popular Model Y crossover utility vehicle at both their Fremont and Shanghai factories. That year, Tesla produced 509,000 Model S/X/3/Y units.[692] The Shanghai factory alone had a 250,000 unit run rate for its Model 3/Y product lines. Also in 2020, Tesla diversified its battery supply chain when it inked a deal with CATL to supply LFP (Lithium-Iron-Phosphate) prismatic batteries for its standard range Model 3's.[693] This was the first time Tesla departed from the cylindrical cell form factor for its BEVs. This was also the first deal between CATL and Tesla, but it would not be the last. At that time, neither LG Chem nor Panasonic manufactured LFP batteries.

For LG Chem, their Nanjing plant ramped up production of NCMA (Nickel 90%-Cobalt 5%-Manganese-Aluminum) 2170 cylindrical cells for the new Model Y.[694] Not only did Panasonic not get the Model 3 contract, but they also missed the Model

[689] https://news.panasonic.com/global/press/en180313-3

[690] Panasonic Corporation, Press Release, January 22, 2019.

[691] https://ir.tesla.com/press-release/tesla-q4-2019-vehicle-production-deliveries

[692] https://ir.tesla.com/press-release/tesla-q4-2020-vehicle-production-deliveries

[693] Electrive, "CATL to kick-off LFP cell supply for Tesla China Model 3", July 20, 2020.

[694] The Korea Times, by K. Bo-eun, "LG to supply NCMA battery for Tesla next year", Dec 17, 2020.

Y contract as well. Both CATL and LG Chem were simply more competitive with battery plants near Giga Shanghai with locally sourced supply chains. Panasonic didn't even have a battery plant in China that could make the needed 2170 or LFP battery cells; they were inexplicably focused on the much smaller PHEV market.

Tesla continued to pick up the pace in 2021, producing 930,000 total BEVs with most of them made at Giga Shanghai.[695] The Shanghai factory delivered 484,000 Model 3/Y units, surpassing Fremont for the first time.[696] This meant Panasonic was making batteries for just 48% of Tesla's vehicles while LG Chem and CATL provided the other 52%. The battery gap only widened for Panasonic in 2022 with Tesla producing 1.3 million vehicles and over 710,000 being made in their Shanghai plant.[697] This again confirmed Shanghai and China as the BEV center of the world and competitive battery manufacturers recognized that. That same year, there were persistent rumors that Tesla would soon begin using CATL's M3P batteries in their Model 3's as the M3P had a superior range to existing LFP technology.[698]

The reality and rumor of Tesla diversifying its battery supply chain with manufacturers other than Panasonic went hand in hand with long-standing speculation that the two had an increasingly strained relationship. Specifically, the issue was over Panasonic's unwillingness to produce batteries in China for Tesla's Shanghai plant.[699] Also, in 2021, Panasonic sold all its shares in Tesla for $3.6 billion USD, making itself a hefty profit on its original investment of only $30 million USD in 2010.[700] Did this show a lack of faith in Tesla's continuing growth or did Panasonic merely need the money to

[695] https://ir.tesla.com/press-release/tesla-q4-2021-vehicle-production-deliveries

[696] CnEVPost, by P. Zhang, "Tesla Giga Shanghai reaches 1 millionth production vehicle milestone", Aug 15, 2022.

[697] Inside EVs, by B. O'Hare, "Over Half Of All Teslas Sold In 2022 Were Made In Giga Shanghai", Jan 08, 2023.

[698] Inside EVs, by M. Kane, "Rumor: China-Made Tesla Model 3 To Get CATL's M3P Batteries", Aug 19, 2022.

[699] Zacks Equity Research, "Tesla-Panasonic Relation Strains Over Gigafactory 3 Production", Nov 26, 2019.

[700] Financial Times, K. Inagaki, "Panasonic offloads Tesla stake for $3.6bn", June 25, 2021.

bankroll its $8.5 billion USD acquisition of autonomous supply chain company Blue Yonder?[701]

While Panasonic is not all in on their relationship with Tesla, they are and will remain an important partner for the foreseeable future. Panasonic is particularly key in developing Tesla's new 4680 batteries which Tesla envisions outfitting its future vehicles with. Panasonic first started building 4680's on a pilot line in Japan and later moved to production at Tesla's Giga Nevada factory. Furthermore, Panasonic has plans to update its Wakayama plant to introduce 4680 production there and they also intend to build a new 4680 battery plant in Kansas with a start date of 2025.[702]

So, why isn't Panasonic all in on Tesla? Why aren't they capitalizing on the most significant transition of the global transportation industry in 120 years? Afterall, they have been in the battery industry for a century and have 15 years of experience in producing EV batteries at scale. We know for a fact that the battery space is one of the great financial opportunities of our time. Just look at CATL with a $144 billion USD market cap and LGES with $104 billion USD (parent company LG Chem's market cap is $36 billion USD). Now compare that to Panasonic with only a $20 billion USD market cap. What are we missing here?

To start, Panasonic's battery business suffers from operational dilution as they are just one of five corporate lines, the other four being Lifestyle, Automotive, Connect and Industry. As an example of Panasonic's distraction, they have identified their most important technological pillar for future growth as creating a new hydrogen energy division. What? Why aren't they doubling down on EV batteries which is their cash cow? However, this is in line with Tokyo's and Toyota's continuing interest in hydrogen fuel-cell transportation even though it has clearly lost out conceptually and practically to BEVs. I believe Panasonic has made a strategic error in prioritizing its hydrogen line of effort when it already has a well- developed battery business in an industry exploding with no end in sight.

One only has to read Panasonic's 70-page 2022 annual report to quickly realize the energy division and the battery production efforts within it are simply not

[701] https://media.blueyonder.com/panasonic-completes-acquisition-of-blue-yonder/

[702] Teslarati, by J. Klender, "Tesla battery partner Panasonic to lean on 2170 and 4680 batteries for profitability", Feb 02, 2023.

a priority. Because of their corporate structure, Panasonic's battery production will never reach its full potential under its current business model. As we already saw, LG Chem realized that it had to spin off its battery division into LGES for it to become focused and productive. Panasonic's Energy division accounted for 11% of revenue in 2022 or $6 billion USD out of $54.6 billion USD net sales for the larger Panasonic Group. Ironically, while Panasonic only ran a 3.5% net profit in 2022, its energy division was by far the most successful of the five divisions, running an 8% profit.[703]

These numbers indicate that their battery division would do much better on its own. To me, this is clearly a reflection of the Panasonic leadership who can't see the market and are unwilling to scale up and expand their established battery business model. In 2010, CATL didn't even exist, yet today they are worth many multiples more than Panasonic. CATL identified the enormous future potential of the global LIB market quickly and has reaped the benefits while plodding Panasonic still hasn't. I expect to see the battery companies who are willing to scale up and develop new technology to expand their market share at the expense of those who can't and won't do the same.

Looking Ahead

1. How is the top ten category going to look next year and then every year moving forward? Who will be the new winners and losers? There is no indication that the Chinese companies will lose market share, quite the opposite. They are aggressive, well-funded and continue to pursue new technological breakthroughs.

2. Who will be the first battery company to reach 1 TWh of annual battery capacity? The obvious front runner is CATL as they have built the foundation for continued growth and are scaling up more aggressively than their peers. What kind of strategic influence will CATL have when/if they provide most of production for the global transportation fleet? Can their competitors match their continually evolving battery technology? Unsurprisingly, in 2022, Time Magazine named CATL's new Qilin battery one of the best inventions of the

---

[703] Panasonic Group, 2022 Annual Report.

year. In an industry based on technological sophistication, CATL's 12,000-person R&D division provides a decisive advantage in the global battery space.

3. Will Panasonic eventually spin off its battery division so it can expand and reach its full potential? Will Panasonic form a long-term relationship at scale with Toyota? This dynamic duo should make their competitors tremble in fear as they gobble up huge chunks of the total addressable battery and BEV markets. Or will Panasonic continue to dilute its efforts by supporting the hybrid vehicle industry even though this path leads to a dead end?

4. When (if ever) will North America develop the technical expertise to develop their own domestic battery industry built by Canadian, Mexican, and American companies? How much of a battery foothold will China secure in North America? What are the associated implications of this market penetration relating to the idea of securing a critical mineral supply chain? Now, ask the same questions of Europe.

The TZero made by AC Propulsion is the original BEV design that would inspire the founders of Tesla to move forward with their own production plans. The battery pack for the vehicle is not on the floor of the car, rather filling the insides of both car doors. *(by P. Gruber)*

Tesla's gigfactory in Shanghai is the most efficient automobile manufacturing plant in the world, either BEV or ICE. With a 1.1 million unit annual run rate, this one factory produces more BEVs than any other competitor. Of note, the Shanghai plant was the first foreign operation allowed to function independently in China. *(by Tesla).*

In this picture we see a comparison of Tesla's cylindrical cells and their relative size. A Tesla Model S battery pack has 7,000 thousand of these 18650 battery cells in it lined up next to one another. Essentially, many BEVs are powered by rows upon rows of Double A-sized batteries. *(by Author)*

The cathode material of a LIB moves through the manufacturing process. Cathodes and anodes are made into long sheets of material that are divided by separators. For cylindrical batteries, these sheets are rolled tightly together before being fitted into their outer shell. *(by Getty Images)*

CHAPTER 17

Urban Mining: Recycle Everything

"The Congress finds with respect to materials, that the recovery and conservation of such materials can reduce the dependence of the United States on foreign resources and reduce the deficit in its balance of payments." – Resource Conservation and Recovery Act of 1976

Urban Mining

No, urban mining is not digging a giant open pit mine in the middle of Manhattan across from Grand Central Station to extract cobalt beneath underground subways through ethical means (although I am sure some may like to see that). Urban mining is recycling previously used batteries from BEVs, BESS, computers, phones, and anything/everything else that uses a lithium-ion battery (LIB). Why do we want to pursue urban mining when the world already has a steady and accelerating flow of battery minerals to feed the global BEV transition? The reasons are many.

There is little if any politics involved in urban mining as compared to hard rock mining and brine extraction. There is no concern with land ownership, fights over extraction royalties or debates about being pro-business or pro-environment. Since a recycling facility can literally be built anywhere, urban mining operations can avoid any cultural disputes reference land and location like we have seen many times with Thacker Pass, the Grand Canyon and more. Because of this, urban mining keeps a company out of the courtroom where lawsuits can drag out a traditional mining operation for many years. The real politics of urban mining revolve around what incentives local and state government will provide to a recycling company to bring in their business. Urban mining brings with it jobs, economic development, and tax revenue.

Because a recycling facility has a very small physical footprint compared to the hundreds of square miles of a hard rock mine or brine extraction operation, the permitting process is simplified. Imagine if an urban mining operation buys or leases an existing structure in an area already zoned for local industry – what are the permitting concerns? An urban mining business will have to navigate the usual approvals for any industrial process, including permits for air quality, aquifer protection from wastewater, solid & biohazardous waste, and an approved waste facility plan. Also, they may require a special waste ID number and a hazardous waste treatment, storage, or disposal facility (TSDF) permit.

From an Environmental, Social, Governance (ESG) perspective, it is much easier for an urban mining operation to fulfill these principles. For example, one can't produce batteries for a BEV company to reduce carbon emissions that cause global warming and then dump the expended batteries in a landfill and claim they are concerned with our environment. In order to fulfill ESG principles, it is imperative that every single EV battery is recycled. The brand damage and reputational fallout from a BEV or battery company that does not ensure 100% recycling of its products would be significant.

The most important aspect of urban mining is that the associated supply chain becomes incredibly shortened and simplified. For instance, if an urban mining operation sources all its required battery metals from expended batteries from BEVs registered in New Your City, then their supply chain is the length and width of NYC. There is no need for shipping in lithium from Argentina. There is no need for shipping in manganese from South Africa. There is no need for shipping in nickel from Russia. There is no need for shipping in cobalt from Africa. The supply chain becomes whatever the nearest population of BEVs is that has the volume to sustain the collocated recycling business. Correspondingly, the chances of disrupting this urban mining supply chain becomes nil.

With a localized supply chain, there is no longer a far-flung global enterprise consisting of ships filled with various battery metals making their way through the Suez Canal to ports thousands of miles away from their original destination. This means the associated carbon footprint that comes with the existing global network of fossil fueled shipping, trains, air transport and long-haul trucking is eliminated. A localized urban mining business can transport locally expended LIBs with BEV class-8 trucks (i.e., Tesla Semis) to reduce its carbon footprint. Also, the same company can ensure it only uses renewable energy to power its recycling process.

Ultimately, for urban mining to be successful as an enterprise, it must be more cost-effective to recycle expended batteries than to continue with the existing model of mining and brine extraction. In this regard, recycling has many advantages from a perspective of operations expenses. As mentioned previously, the cost of shipping from a global supply chain thousands of miles long is eliminated. When a company recycles a battery, they get all the needed metals on the spot: nickel, manganese, lithium and so on. Additionally, the entire open pit mining architecture is eliminated with no need for dump trucks, excavators, explosives, rock crushers and all the employees to run them. Also, there is no need for the many square miles of evaporation ponds positioned in very remote locations.

Shipping Lithium-Ion Batteries as HAZMAT

The urban mining of depleted LIBs does come with additional concerns in that it is considered a hazardous material or HAZMAT. The procedures that must be followed to transport batteries can cause additional expenses. In the U.S., the transportation of LIBs is regulated by the Pipeline and Hazardous Material Safety Administration which falls under DOT (Department of Transportation). Published Hazardous Material Regulations (HMR) provide details of how LIBs are packaged and shipped. A failure to follow the HMR can result in fines or based on the seriousness of the violation, criminal prosecution.

To start, LIBs are classified as HAZMAT due to their chemical qualities making them prone to fires, thermal runaway, corrosion, and electrical hazards. With thermal runaway, lithium-ion cells are likely to ignite adjacent cells and entire batteries are likely to ignite adjacent batteries. Because LIBs have such high energy density, fires tend to be powerful and hard to put out. Battery fires tend to spread to surrounding material and the mode of transportation itself. Obviously, with aerial modes of transportation, this can be catastrophic.

All shipments to, from or within the U.S. are subject to the HMR. However, when conducting international transportation of LIBs, additional recognized regulations are followed. For international air shipments, International Civil Aviation Organization's Technical Instructions for the Safe Transport of Dangerous Goods by Air (ICAO

Technical Instructions) are enforced. Similarly, for shipments by sea, the International Maritime Dangerous Goods Code (IMDG Code) is in effect. Also, states may have additional shipping regulations as might the shipping company itself.

Another consideration is that LIB shippers must ensure that their batteries have passed the design tests under the *United Nations (UN) Manual of Tests and Criteria, Section 38.3.* There are a variety of tests that include forced discharges, crush/impact scenarios and the effect of vibrations. As of January 01, 2022, the manufacturers of lithium cells/batteries and their subsequent distributors must make the testing summaries available to the supply chain. This requirement applies to all batteries made after January 01, 2008, which is, essentially, more than 99% of the current battery supply in circulation. [704]

A BEV (with its battery still attached) being shipped to a recycling facility is governed by *UN3171 Battery-powered vehicle.* Just the LIB being shipped by itself is governed by *UN3090 Lithium metal batteries including lithium alloy batteries.* The size of the lithium-ion cell or battery measured in Watt-hours (Wh) also affects shipping standards. If a cell or battery meets the definition of "small" then they receive less stringent shipping standards. For shipping by highway or rail, a cell that is 60Wh or less and a battery that is 300Wh or less are considered "small". Those measurements are so small that they don't apply to modern BEV batteries.[705]

However, expended batteries being shipped by a motor vehicle for recycling purposes are granted two exemptions under the HMR. First, they are exempted from the above-mentioned UN Section 38.3 so that the shipper does not have to prove the batteries' testing regimen. Second, they do not have to meet UN packaging specifications and requirements. Most likely, the packaging used to transport LIBs for recycling must meet DOT-SP (Special Permit) requirements. These requirements are meant to ensure that the HAZMAT is shipped in a safe a manner.

For example, palletized lithium batteries shipped via truck must be packaged in manner so that negative and positive terminals are not exposed and can cause a spark. Terminals need to be covered and the batteries inner wrapping must be a non-electrically conductive material. The outer packaging must be a strong, durable form like metal or plastic boxes or even drums. Damaged, defective, or recalled batteries

---

[704] DOT, "Lithium Battery Guide For Shippers", September 2021

[705] Ibid.

(like the LG Chem batteries in GM's Bolt BEVs that were recalled in 2021 due to fire hazards) receive special packaging considerations as these are considered especially hazardous.

These categories of HAZMAT batteries can only be shipped by road, rail, or vessel – not by air due to the risks. Each battery in this category must be individually wrapped according to published regulations described above. They must also receive additional packaging that provides cushioning and stability and then placed in a durable outer packaging. Then, the outer packaging must be appropriately marked such as "Damaged/defective lithium-ion battery" with minimum half-inch tall letters. Additionally, a standard Class 9 Lithium Battery Label must be attached to the package.[706]

Furthermore, emergency contact telephone number must be provided on the outside of the packaging. Personnel must be assigned to monitor the emergency contact line and be on stand-by for a response if needed. They must be knowledgeable of the HAZMAT being shipped and be able to provide emergency response coordination for first responders if necessary. Also, prior to shipping, personnel preparing the batteries must receive HAZMAT training. Training records will be maintained for three years for company personnel and then retained for at least 90 days when they terminate employment. [707]

The above information in this section is not meant to make it look like these safety procedures inhibit the successful shipping and recycling of LIBs at scale. These details do illustrate that there are federally mandated and enforced requirements that must be followed during the overall battery metals recycling process. Consequently, the regulations and their second-order effects must be calculated into the urban mining operations model. Just so you know, Elon Musk isn't going to throw a bunch of expended Model S batteries in the back of his new bulletproof Cybertruck and then dump them off at his buddy's (J.B. Straubel) recycling plant on his way home from Fremont. No, I will not make a bet on that last statement.

---

[706] DOT, "Safety Advisory Notice for the Disposal and Recycling of Lithium Batteries in Commercial Transportation", May 17, 2022.

[707] Ibid.

EPA Regulations for Recycling Lithium-Ion Batteries

Urban mining is far simpler from a permitting perspective than hard rock mining because there are fewer regulatory hoops to jump through. Legally, it is much less complicated in every way. But there are still regulations to follow. The Environmental Protection Agency is not going to give a recycling company a free pass just because they lowered their carbon footprint. The EPA is going to ensure any recycling facility meets all air, soil and water permitting requirements or they will shut them down and hit them with fines so big that their eyes will water (up to $25,000.00 USD a day and 1-year in prison). It's nothing personal.

To begin, the *Resource Conservation and Recovery Act* (RCRA) is 47-pages long and provides regulatory guidance in areas such as hazardous waste disposal and recycling operations. RCRA was enacted in 1976 and superseded the *Solid Waste Disposal Act* of 1965. The EPA manages the overall RCRA program in conjunction with the states who may also have their own solid waste legislation. Associated EPA standards regarding the RCRA are published under *Title 40 of the Code of Federal Regulations.*

Under Title 40, LIBs are classified as solid waste which means they can be determined to be hazardous waste as well if they meet certain criteria. A solid waste is considered a hazardous waste if it has any of the four characteristics of ignitability, corrosivity, reactivity and toxicity (*CFR 40, Chapter I, Subchapter I, Part 261, Subpart C, Paragraph 261.20*) LIBs meet the first three criteria but do not meet the solid waste/hazardous waste exclusion criteria under Part 261. Hazardous waste that can be recycled is termed "recyclable materials".

While the RCRA of 1976 showed an understanding of the "reduce, recycle, reuse" concept that is critical for a circular economy, the writers of the document in no way anticipated the eventual mass recycling of batteries at scale from tens of millions BEVs. But that's okay. For laws to be effective, such as those in the Code of Federal Regulations, they need to evolve over time. To their credit, the EPA recognized that their regulations designed decades ago for home waste products like batteries for calculators needed to be updated. In 2021, they held a *Lithium-Ion Battery Disposal and Recycling Stakeholder Workshop* to brainstorm the way ahead.

Overall, the workshop failed to recognize the macroeconomic significance of recycling LIBs from BEVs at scale. Instead, the group focused mainly on the habits of residential consumers of home batteries. The workshop also missed the implications of the future shift away from traditional mineral extraction and how this would impact national critical mineral supply chain policy. How could this be possible? Eighty-six separate stakeholders attended the workshop from across the recycling spectrum to include private industry, recycling companies, state, and federal representatives. Also attending were representatives from Toyota, Stellantis, Honda and Volkswagen. Tesla was noticeably absent.[708]

Let's sift through the summary of the workshop and see what ideas were presented that might impact the recycling of LIBs from BEVs at scale. One thought was to consider classifying large LIBs as solid waste (not hazardous waste) if the state of charge of the battery was below a certain level. If an expended BEV LIB was reclassified, from a regulatory and actual shipping perspective, this would simplify and speed up the overall collection process. In a similar vein, it was suggested that LIBs be treated under the category of Universal Federal Waste which benefit from streamlined hazardous waste standards.

Workshop discussions on large LIBs were more productive but still did not grasp the scale of future BEV LIB recycling nor did they conceptually integrate BEV LIB recycling with a national critical minerals strategy. Thoughts on the topic included:

- Transporting large LIBs are challenging due to size/weight; skilled workers are needed to package/handle LIBs
- Reusing old BEV LIBs for BESS is not competitive with new purpose-built BESS solutions with better chemistry
- Variety of LIBs from different manufacturers with different designs makes recycling more challenging
- Because BEVs are relatively new and there isn't a large volume of expended LIBs available for recycling, no one has developed a comprehensive BEV-specific LIB recycling framework; U.S. lacks a domestic refining capability for battery minerals
- Where will a recycling facility get their BEV LIBs from? A salvage yard? How do you get a massive BESS for recycling? What is the process?

---

[708] "EPA Lithium-Ion Battery Disposal and Recycling Stakeholder Workshop". Prepared by ERG, Inc & JSE Associates, Jan 28, 2022.

Another discussion was held addressing how to provide necessary incentives to encourage BEV LIB recycling. Their thoughts included:

- Tax incentives for recycling companies; Rebates for companies using recycled battery minerals; A core charge (refundable deposit) for returned LIBs – this would have to be rethought to work for BEV and LIB manufacturers at scale
- Pursue a battery leasing model that makes it easy for EOL (End of Life) turn-in like Nio and CATL's BaaS (Battery as a Service) programs
- Mandate recycled battery mineral content in new BEV LIBs

A third brainstorming event asked what the EPA could do differently to facilitate an expanding recycling enterprise.

- Incentivize regional recycling capabilities as there is presently a lack of capacity (this is because there aren't enough BEV LIBs in circulation)
- Exempt LIBs from hazardous waste regulation at certain parts in the recycling/transportation cycle to streamline the process – safely
- Effectively regulate polluting emissions during the LIB recycling process; No exemptions from safeguarding our environment
- Establish overarching LIB recycling management best practices for the U.S. market to guide the larger enterprise

This EPA sponsored workshop illustrated how early the U.S. is in its recycling enterprise journey. Clearly, based on the inputs from across the American LIB recycling enterprise, the U.S. is not prepared for large scale BEV/BESS LIB recycling. However, they have time to work out the details because mass BEV/BESS LIB recycling is still many years away, perhaps in 2030 there will be enough LIB EOL throughput to support the industry. The recycling industries in China and Europe will mature faster as they have a higher mass BEV adoption rate earlier than the U.S. The U.S. should be observing those industries closely for useful lessons.

What is the Battery Act?

Learning about the DOT's and EPA's roles in the LIB recycling enterprise shows that there isn't any single entity responsible for coordinating this effort. This fact raises interesting questions to consider. Should there be an Office of Recycling created at the federal/national level? Should the recycling effort be left to the States to manage? Should private industry be left to pursue their own ideas on the topic and let the invisible hand of the battery economy figure it out? Or, maybe, the U.S. needs to update and modernize the *Battery Act* to reflect the biggest revolution in the battery industry in over a century.

The *Mercury-Containing and Rechargeable Battery Management Act* (MCRBMA), commonly referred to as *The Battery Act,* was a 9-page document signed into law in 1996. The EPA was mandated to enforce the Act and its enclosed regulations. The purpose of the Act was to phase out the use of mercury in commercial batteries as it was in the public interest to do so. Additionally, the Act was aimed at efficiently recycling specific categories of batteries to include nickel cadmium and lead-acid batteries. Other goals included educating the public on the need and procedures for recycling these batteries as well as establishing universal battery labeling standards. The Act was directed towards the individual public consumer.

Enforcement of the Act was an essential part of making it work. Violations could result in up to $10,000.00 USD in penalties. If the initial violation was not corrected in the allowed specified period, a subsequent $10,000.00 USD penalty would be applied. Regulated battery manufacturers, makers of rechargeable battery products and importers of the described batteries were not only subject to the laws of the Act, but they must also maintain and provide records of their activity when requested by the EPA.

Title I of the Act specifically addressed the details of enforcement. As mentioned previously, this portion of the Act specifically addresses nickel-cadmium and lead-acid batteries. One aspect of Title I was mandating labeling procedures with nickel-cadmium (Ni-Cd) labeling being, "BATTERY MUST BE RECYCLED OR DISPOSED OF PROPERLY" and lead-acid batteries (Pb) would clearly state "CONTAINS SEALED LEAD BATTERY. BATTERY MUST BE RECYCLED." This mandatory labeling was a form of public education and notification of the requirements regarding processing of these batteries.

Title II of the Act specifically addressed the provisions to phase out the use of mercury-containing batteries. Several types of mercury-containing batteries were designated as illegal as of the date of the signing of the Act meaning this was a total ban. Other types of mercury-oxide containing batteries could still be imported and sold in the U.S. if they met several conditions. The thrust of the conditions was that the seller must advise the buyer of mercury-oxide batteries of the EOL collection procedures that must be followed after purchase. While the *Battery Act* does not address LIBs, it is instructive in that it is another example of the U.S. federal government regulating the battery industry in the interests of the nation. Specifically, the recycling of certain types of batteries became mandatory and certain types of batteries were deemed to be illegal and no longer eligible for sale in the U.S. Importantly, the Act provided a national framework for managing aspects of the larger battery enterprise instead of relying on a patchwork of state, local laws, and initiatives.

In my opinion, the U.S. needs to be forward looking and should pass legislation addressing the need for mass BEV LIB recycling. Let's call this document the *Lithium-Ion Battery and Critical Minerals Conservation Act of 2023*. Personally, I like the directive nature of the Battery Act and the LIBCMC would use similarly mandatory language as well as providing a national framework for execution. If the U.S. does not create a national BEV LIB recycling framework, then it is incapable of executing an effective critical minerals strategy. The two go hand in hand. In the future, a national recycling framework for critical minerals present in EV batteries is crucial for achieving battery minerals independence and securing its associated supply chain.

To start, the LIBCMC would direct that all EV batteries in the U.S. be recycled either by the selling BEV manufacturer or an established urban mining facility. The selling BEV manufacturer will have a responsibility to ensure that their EOL LIB product is recycled at a recognized and certified facility. This will take coordination between the owner and the manufacturer to ensure that the battery is recovered and recycled. The LIBCMC will also make it illegal for an EOL EV battery to be disposed of in any way other than turning into a certified facility with no exceptions.

Additionally, EV batteries in the U.S. need to stay in the U.S. when they reach EOL. This means, recycled EV batteries and the battery metals recovered from them need to be reused in future domestic LIB production. From a critical mineral strategy, a country can't have their battery metals recovered from EV batteries subsequently sold overseas – this defeats the entire purpose of recycling. To ensure domestic reuse of battery metals, this can simply be mandated as law. Also, domestic reuse can be encouraged through high battery metals export tariffs making it prohibitively expensive to do so. Also, an established percentage of recycled battery metals can be mandated for domestic battery production. For example, in 2025, domestically produced EV batteries must contain 10% recycled battery metals, in 2026 it's 15%, in 2027 it's 20% etc....

Global Battery Alliance Passport

The Global Battery Alliance (GBA) is a battery recycling advocacy group founded in 2017, sponsored by the World Economic Forum. Members agree to promote the core principles of the GBA which include establishing a circular battery economy in support of the Paris Agreement, contributing to a low carbon economy, and supporting ESG principles in line with UN Sustainable Development Goals. There are 135 members which include some big players like CATL, LG Energy Solutions, Tesla, SQM and the London Metal Exchange. However, other big names are noticeably absent like Albemarle, BYD, Samsung SDI and Panasonic.

GBA sponsors a very progressive Battery Passport (BP) program which is an effort to provide information about and transparency to the battery value chain. The BP program creates a digital twin for a physical battery that contains information about the battery's life. The information is stored on a cloud server that GBA members can access. Data about the battery includes where the minerals from the battery was mined and refined, where the battery cells were made and where the battery pack is assembled. The battery gets an ID number, a barcode and a QR code. The digital twin also stores information about the battery EOL and when, where, and how it is recycled. The battery can earn a Quality seal if it meets Battery Passport standards for being responsibly manufactured in a way that considers the climate, the environment, and local communities.

What I find most useful about the initiative is the ability to access data about upstream mineral acquisition. Categories include the type and amount of recycled material used in the battery. This is important to verify that a company is using recycled battery metals and to what extent. Otherwise, how does one verify that companies are adhering to regulation? Tied to recycling data is material traceability where we have information about the minerals in the battery, where they are from and how they move through the larger value chain.

Ultimately, there must be a battery tracking system established to enforce recycling mandates and collect data to understand the larger process. Only with this overarching perspective can the industry change paths and implement better decisions when necessary. Also, only through regulation will battery and BEV manufacturers introduce such a system. Presently, they don't have the incentives to voluntarily provide this information or they would already be doing it. For example, countries that source cobalt from the DRC that employs child labor will not self-report these practices.

From the perspective of drafting my extremely well thought out *Lithium-Ion Battery and Critical Minerals Conservation Act* of 2023, I would add a paragraph that mandates a battery data program. In the language I would tag the DOE with creating such a program as part of an ongoing focus on energy resilience and independence. This would be fully in line with the existing *Inflation Reduction Act* that mandates a growing North American supply chain for BEVs and associated batteries. Unfortunately, writers of the IRA didn't understand the overall lithium value chain enough to encapsulate urban mining, so separate legislation will be needed.

Battery Recycling Perspectives: China, U.S., Europe

From a strategic perspective, China understands that they must develop a comprehensive EV battery recycling regime to ensure their own critical mineral security. China is in a vulnerable position because they import most of their lithium and other battery minerals, mining very little of it in mainland China. For instance, if Australia were to shut off its supply of hard rock lithium concentrate that it regularly sends to China, the Chinese EV and battery sectors would collapse. This in turn would send shockwaves through the global EV and battery spaces. Consequently, from a national perspective, China wants EV battery minerals to stay in China once they reach their EOL.

Just as with BEV and battery manufacturing, China is far ahead of its North American and European peers in EV battery recycling. They are ahead largely because of necessity since they adopted BEV manufacturing to scale much earlier than the U.S. or Europe. Consequently, China is already confronted with the reality of millions of pounds of EOL batteries from the transportation sector – cars, buses, motorcycles, bicycles, mopeds, and heavy equipment. In 2020, China produced an estimated 240,000 tons of EV battery waste, an amount that was predicted to double in 2022.[709] China has had several years to evolve its recycling policies and learn from its challenges and mistakes.

---

[709] https://ellenmacarthurfoundation.org/circular-examples/gem-china

China's Ministry of Industry and Information Technology (MIIT) has over-all responsibility for coordinating and developing their national recycling program. According to the Vice Chairman of MIIT, Zhang Yumming, China had already es-tablished at least 10,000 battery recycling centers by the summer of 2022. Yumming recognized that there was still much work to be done coordinating recycling efforts between all these recycling sites and central/local governments. Ongoing challenges included the ability to effectively manage such a large enterprise, standardizing recy-cling procedures and improving recycling technology.[710]

Two of the largest officially recognized recycling businesses in China are GEM and Brunp who, when combined, own approximately 50% of all recycling business in the country. GEM (Green Eco-Manufacture), founded in 2001, is a publicly traded company with its headquarters in Shenzhen. In 2020, GEM recycled about 25,000 EV batteries (12,000 for the first half of 2020), which isn't very much considering how big the Chinese EV industry was in 2020. GEM has established recycling centers in 16 major industrial hubs and has also established recycling agreements with 280 separate auto and battery manufacturing companies. As of 2020, GEM was recycling 10,000 tons of nickel and 5,000 tons of cobalt annually from EOL battery waste in China.[711]

Brunp Recycling Technology Company Limited is headquartered in Guangdong Province and is a subsidiary of the world's leading EV battery producer CATL. This makes sense, and is strategic move by CATL, as recycling at scale is a chance for CATL to control its own battery mineral supply chain through urban mining. CATL chairman, Robin Zheng, understands this clearly and estimates that the recovery rate of nickel and cobalt from EV batteries is at 99% and the recovery rate of lithium is at 90%. Furthermore, Zheng believes that by 2035, the recovery of battery min-erals from EOL EV batteries through urban mining will meet most of the market demand.[712]

Brunp/CATL is already putting their urban mining operations into high gear so that recovered battery minerals can be used in the next generation of CATL batteries. In 2021, Brunp started construction of their $4.9 billion USD battery material complex

---

[710] Pandaily, "China Establishes Initial Power Battery Recycling System", July 21, 2022.

[711] https://ellenmacarthurfoundation.org/circular-examples/gem-china

[712] Pandaily, "China Establishes Initial Power Battery Recycling System", July 21, 2022.

in Yichang with plans to be operational by 2023. This massive complex will have the capacity to produce 360,000 tons of iron phosphate annually, 220,000 tons of lithium iron phosphate (LFP), 180,000 tons of lithium nickel-cobalt-manganese (NCM) precursor, 40,000 tons of lithium cobalt oxide (LCO) and 40,000 tons of graphite. Additionally, the complex will be able to receive and recycle some 300,000 tons of EV batteries a year.[713]

While Brunp was building out its recycling empire, the U.S. was just starting to get organized. Under the Biden Administration, the federal government recognized that battery recycling at scale was an integral part of its North American battery supply chain and critical minerals strategy. As mentioned previously, the *Infrastructure Investment and Jobs Act* (also known as the *Bipartisan Infrastructure Law*) provided DOE $62 billion USD to pursue different clean energy initiatives. Of this amount, $7 billion USD was provided to support the U.S. battery supply chain to include EOL recycling. Guidance for awarding grants included addressing the commercial scale recycling of EV batteries and BESS.

DOE's Office of Energy Efficiency and Renewable Energy (EERE) manages the awards such as the Battery Manufacturing and Recycling Grants Program. This program has $3 billion USD available until expended. The Office of Manufacturing and Energy Supply Chains disburses the grants to eligible entities such as universities, national laboratories, private companies, and local/state governments. Similarly, the same office manages the Battery and Critical Mineral Recycling program, disbursing up to $125 million USD in federal funds. Any educational, governmental or company that touches the battery recycling value chain is eligible.

More specifically, an award of not less that $100 million USD can be provided for a new commercial battery recycling facility. Not less than $50 million USD can be awarded to efforts to retool or retrofit and existing facility for recycling operations. Additionally, not less than $50 million USD can be awarded for a battery recycling demonstration project. These three categories provide some flexibility in approaching the topic depending on what stage an awardee is at in their trajectory. A university may move forward with a demonstration plant, a start-up may retool an existing plant to save on costs and an established company with access to more funding may build a completely new facility.

---

[713] Argus Media, "China's Brunp builds Yichang battery material complex", Dec 6, 2021.

The European Union, with its 27 member states, also recognizes the role battery recycling plays in constructing an overarching framework for a regional-centric battery strategy. The European Parliament studied the problem and has proposed legislation like the U.S. did to promote a circular economy and reduce their dependence on battery metal imports. The EU recognizes the present disruption to both utilities and transportation by industrial batteries (what they classify BESS as) and EV batteries. Since the EU suffers from a lack of regionally sourced battery minerals to include cobalt, nickel, lithium, and lead, it is critical that they recycle and recover all the battery minerals that are present in industrial and EV batteries. Once these battery minerals are physically in the EU, they want them to stay in the EU. Starting in 2030, regulations will require EV batteries to contain 12% recycled cobalt, 4% recycled nickel and 4% recycled lithium.[714] While those numbers aren't very ambitious, it is a start and the requirements can change as the industry evolves.

The way ahead for EU member countries include labeling batteries to convey basic information about them, to include a QR code. Starting in 2026, every EV battery and BESS sold will have an electronic record further described as a "battery passport". In 2027, every battery manufacturing plant will have to provide "technical documentation" for each battery showing how much and what kind of recycled battery minerals are in it. Also, the EU is very concerned with the nexus of human rights and minerals derived from conflict zones involving the extraction of tin, tantalum, tungsten, and gold. A comprehensive blockchain systems for batteries could help them effectively regulate these "conflict minerals".

The EU emphasizes the need for accountability between who manufactures the batteries are how they are ultimately recycled. Meaning, battery producers have an EOL commitment to the batteries they manufacture – it isn't someone else's problem to deal with, it's their problem. Furthermore, battery manufactures have a financial obligation to the batteries recycling process. This implies a battery manufacturer should manufacture batteries in a way that can be efficiently recycled in a cost-effective way. A good example of how to achieve this is illustrated by Chinese BEV manufacturer Nio whose batteries are designed to be swapped out from the actual BEV from inception.

---

[714] European Commission, "REGULATION OF THE EUROPEAN PARLIAMENT AND OF THE COUNCIL, concerning batteries and waste batteries", Dec 10, 2020.

Now, here is where it gets interesting. In the future, all batteries entering the EU market must comply with this regulation, regardless of country origin meaning China, Japan, South Korea, etc.... We have already seen with the U.S.' *Inflation Reduction Act* how affected trading states will react. Some will try to get exemptions for the policy, others will ask for several years to get in compliance and others will retaliate with similar protectionist policies in their home markets. However, if the EU doesn't stay the course, then they won't get a regionally sourced battery minerals supply chain that is secure from disruption.

The EU mandate on recycling will effectively force all European countries to adhere to their agreed upon regime regardless of if they are a member of the EU or not. Countries not in the EU include England, Norway, and Switzerland. However, English BEV manufacturers will have to follow EU battery passport requirements or they won't sell their product on mainland Europe. The same goes for Norwegian battery company Freyr – they too will adhere to EU recycling regulations or they are effectively out of business. Switzerland produces neither BEVs nor batteries so this is irrelevant to them until they do.

It will take a while to produce a detailed and enforceable battery recycling regime in Europe because of all the stakeholders. The major players need to be on board like Germany who is home to the big dogs like Volkswagen, Mercedes, Audi, BMW, and Porsche. France must be on board as well with Peugeot, Renault, and Citroen. Also, let's remember Stellantis, which resulted from the merger of Fiat Chrysler and PSA Group, has its headquarters in the Netherlands. However, it is in every European country and BEV manufacturers' interests to support a European battery recycling regime that keeps battery minerals in their respective countries.

Redwood Materials

Let's look at the rapidly growing American battery recycling company, Redwood Materials. Redwood, whose headquarters is in Carson City, NV, was founded in 2017 by its current CEO J.B. Straubel. Straubel was one of Tesla's first employees and worked there as its CTO (Chief Technology Officer) from 2004-2019. It is safe to say Straubel understands Tesla, the larger BEV industry, LIB technology, and how recycling ties into the overall circular economy.

They chose to put their first recycling facility in Carson City, which is about half an hour south of Reno. The facility is in the northeast part of town positioned in an industrial district near the Carson City airport. The original facility is good-sized at 150,000 square feet, although they have plans to expand it to a massive 400,000 square feet.[715] Because of their location, they can only expand to the east and south of their present structure and then they are out of room due to the size of their existing lot.

Carson City was chosen due to its proximity to the Tesla Giga Factory located in Sparks, NV which is 20 miles east of Reno proper. Giga Nevada, built in 2015, began as Tesla's primary EV battery manufacturing facility but also produces drivetrains and BESS products like their Powerwall and Megapack. While Giga Nevada builds finished battery products, Tesla's battery partner, Panasonic, actually makes the battery cells that are then assembled into a finished product. In 2021, Redwood expanded their Nevada footprint and began constructing a battery material facility just a few miles down the road from Tesla's Giga factory.

Accordingly, Redwood has a contract to provide Panasonic with recycled battery minerals that are then used to make new EV battery and BESS products. Redwood also has contracts with other major companies that have the potential to take off in the future such as with shipping giant Amazon. Amazon believes enough in Straubel's business model that they invested in Redwood through their Climate Pledge Fund that is valued at $2 billion USD. In this relationship, Redwood will recycle small LIBs and EOL EV batteries for Amazon.

So, what does this look like? Amazon facilities all over the country will send their various expended small LIBs to Carson City where Redwood recycles them and extracts their battery minerals like lithium, nickel, and cobalt. Then, Redwood sells these minerals up the road to Panasonic. The same goes with Amazon's future BEV fleet which they anticipate will consist of 100,000 electric delivery vans. These vans will most likely be developed by electric pick-up manufacturer Rivian. By the end of 2022, Amazon already had at least 1,000 electric delivery vans in operation that were built by Rivian. In 7-8 years, depending on the vans' battery EOL trends, Redwood will begin to cycle through increasingly large amounts of LIBs from Amazon's delivery fleet. [716]

---

[715] TechCrunch, by K. Korosec, "Redwood Materials raises $700 mil to expand its battery recycling operation", Jul 28, 2021.

[716] Business Insider, by M. Meisenzahl, "Amazon says it has more than a thousand electric Rivian vans making deliveries across the US — see how they were designed", Nov 7, 2022.

Another interesting relationship Redwood has is the contract they inked with mobility company Lyft in Q42022. With this deal, Lyft ships its EOL batteries from its e-bike/e-scooter program to Redwood's Carson City facility. Lyft estimates that the batteries on these platforms have a five-year lifespan before they need to be taken out of service and recycled. According to Redwood, 130 e-bike/e-scooter batteries provide enough recycled minerals to make one new EV battery. While this is a relatively small volume of LIBs to recycle, this establishes a potentially significant relationship with Lyft with larger future implications. [717]

Lyft is moving towards only employing drivers of BEVs by 2030 and in order to reach their target they provide a variety of incentives. It is hard to tell how many drivers a ride-hailing company like Lyft or Uber employees as it is constantly changing and depends on a lot of circumstances like the impact of COVID, the overall economy, jobs outlook, etc... However, Lyft employed an estimated one million drivers in 2020 in the U.S., a number that was similar to their competitor Uber (many drivers work for both companies). If Redwood can help Lyft figure out a way to get their 1 million drivers' future EOL EV batteries into their established recycling pathways, that would be a considerable win for them. [718]

Redwood has aggressively expanded its EV battery recycling program in other ways, instituting a partnership with both Ford and Volvo in the state of California. California is a natural starting point for a comprehensive recovery program because they have by far the highest EV adoption rate in the country. While Ford and Volvo do not presently manufacture high-volume BEVs, this is a critical starting point for Redwood to establish and evolve their program which can then be replicated elsewhere. From a logistics perspective, Redwood is strategically located as Nevada and California are bordering states and Carson City is positioned across the border from Sacramento (100 miles direct line distance), connected by Routes 80 and 50.

With the California program, Redwood accepts lithium-ion as well as nickel-metal-hydride (NiMH) batteries that are commonly used in cars like Toyota's Camry and Corolla hybrid models. Specifically, Redwood will work directly with any business

[717] Tech Crunch, by R. Bellan, "Lyft, Redwood Materials partner to recycle shared e-bike and e-scooter batteries", Nov 23, 2022.

[718] Ride Share Guy, by M. Berry, "How Many Uber & Lyft Drivers Are There?", Nov 1, 2022.

that deals in the dismantling of BEV and hybrid batteries. Importantly, as we discussed earlier in this chapter, Redwood provides them expertise in navigating existing HAZMAT shipping regulations to get them to Carson City. While Volvo and Ford initially supported this program in 2021, Redwood has since developed further recycling partnerships with Toyota, Volkswagen, Audi, and the American electric bus start-up Proterra.[719] I expect Redwood will continue to grow their partnership program as they moved forward.

After the first year of its program ending in 2023, Redwood collected 1,268 separate EOL battery packs weighing 500,000 pounds from a dozen different car companies it had established relations with. Most of the batteries recovered were LIBs (82%) while the remaining 18% were NiMH chemistry batteries from hybrid cars. Redwood was able to recover 95% of the battery minerals from the EOL units it received. Of note, the largest expense for Redwood was the shipping of the batteries to their facility in Nevada. This underlines the added expenses of HAZMAT shipping and the need to collocate a recycling facility as close to its EOL battery population as possible. Redwood anticipated overall shipping costs would come down as the scale of their efforts increased.[720]

As indicated by Brunp and CATL's movement into the EV battery recycling business at a massive scale, a company like Redwood must expand along with the exploding BEV market to capture its associated TAM. Small, incremental movements won't get Redwood where they want to be as an industry leader in a domestic car market with annual sales of 15 million vehicles. While their Carson City recycling facility is strategically placed in relation to the California battery recycling market and their Panasonic partners in Nevada, this single hub won't cut it at the national level. They need to expand and develop regional hubs to improve operational efficiencies and lower continuing costs like HAZMAT shipping.

Redwood announced their plans to do just this in December 2022 by constructing a Battery Materials Campus near Charleston, SC. The campus will be served by a nearby rail access and the Port of Charleston gives them ready access to the global shipping network. Geographically, this shortens their recycling supply lines as one

[719] https://www.redwoodmaterials.com/partner-with-us/
[720] Merano, Maria. "Redwood Materials recovers 95% of metals from EOL battery packs". Teslarati, March 02, 2023.

can use the Mississippi River as a conceptual dividing line between West Coast operations (Carston City) and East Coast operations (Charleston). Redwood anticipates investing $3.5 billion USD in their new campus with recycling operations beginning in Q4 2023. [721]

Redwood also continues to strengthen and grow its ongoing relationship with Panasonic. Panasonic began building a new battery manufacturing plant in De Soto, KS in Q3 2022 with plans to begin production in Q1 2025. The plant is forecasted to produce 30 GWh annually of lithium-ion batteries for the American EV industry. Redwood has secured the contract to provide Panasonic with their cathode material for the Kansas operation. Overall, Redwood anticipates producing 100 GWh of anode and cathode material by 2025, enough for one million BEVs. By 2030, Redwood wants a five-fold increase to 500 GWh, enough for five million BEVs.[722]

The reader must have noticed that during our brief overview of Redwood, there has not been a single mention about Straubel recycling Tesla batteries for his old friend Elon Musk. Why is this? How come Straubel couldn't and didn't leverage his ongoing relationship with Musk to ink a deal? It may seem odd that they didn't, seeing as Straubel was a Tesla co-founder and CTO for many years to boot. I think the relationship doesn't exist merely because Tesla strives for vertical integration of its operational model, especially for key aspects of the business.

Hence, as of 2023, Tesla has already developed a robust in-house battery recycling program where it claims to retrieve and recycle 100% of Tesla EOL batteries.[723] As we mentioned, Tesla is working towards developing its own proprietary EV batteries and battery cell expertise and is working towards controlling all aspects of this process. Consequently, Tesla recognizes the need to retain and reuse the critical minerals in its own batteries to secure its own associated supply chain and, in doing so, control its battery mineral costs. Elon Musk has stated publicly that he doesn't want Tesla to get directly involved in the traditional mining industry, but he clearly sees the imperative to get into the urban mining business.

The Department of Energy (DOE) believed enough in the importance of recycling to achieve critical mineral independence as well as the viability of Redwood's

[721] https://www.redwoodmaterials.com/news/announcing-redwood-south-carolina/

[722] https://www.redwoodmaterials.com/news/redwood-high-nickel-cathode-panasonic/

[723] https://www.tesla.com/support/sustainability-recycling

business model that they provided them a $2 billion USD conditional loan in February 2023. The money is intended to support expansion of Redwood's recycling efforts in Nevada. DOE anticipates their investment resulting in Redwood recycling and producing enough anode copper foil and active cathode material to support the production of one million BEVs annually.[724]

Redwood is and isn't a profitable recycling company. Let me explain. By 2022, Redwood was recycling 6 GWh of LIBs annually, or the equivalent of about 60,000 EV batteries.[725] Straubel has publicly stated that this scale of battery recycling is profitable already. But that is for the specific operations pertaining to battery recycling itself. Overall, Redwood isn't profitable because they incur a lot of other operational costs as they scale up for mass recycling. We see this same phenomenon with the BEV charging infrastructure business – the specific charging operations are profitable but not enough to put the overall company in the black. Redwood may reach profitability around 2028 as they expand their anode and cathode sales in large volumes. If they can execute their current business plan, which is ambitious, I think their success is inevitable.

Redwood is not the only company in the U.S. recycling game, there are many others trying to grow in the space. For example, Canadian recycling company Li-Cycle (NYSE:LICY) is on the move, although they are a relatively young company, founded only in 2021. Li-Cycle is already building out battery recycling hubs in Rochester, NY, a second one in Gilbert, AZ (a suburb of Phoenix), a third in Tuscaloosa, AL and a fourth in Ontario. Li-Cycle has established several relationships with significant lithium value chain players like Ultium Cells (a GM & LGES battery JV), mining giant Glencore and Vines Energy Solutions (part of Vietnamese conglomerate Vingroup). Li-Cycle closed out 2022 with $12 million USD in battery material sales and a net overall loss of $100 million USD.[726]

However, Li-Cycle also received a conditional loan from DOE in February 2023

---

[724] https://www.energy.gov/lpo/articles/lpo-offers-conditional-commitment-redwood-materials-produce-critical-electric-vehicle

[725] https://www.redwoodmaterials.com/news/electric-vehicle-and-hybrid-battery-recycling-california/

[726] https://li-cycle.com/press-releases/li-cycle-reports-fourth-quarter-and-year-2022-financial-and-operational-results/

to the tune of $375 million USD which would ensure them the needed cash flow to maintain operations for at least another four years. The loan will support Li-Cycle's Rochester recycling facility and is intended to result in the recovering the battery materials required for 203,000 BEVs annually.[727] These 100% guaranteed DOE loans are issued by the Federal Financing Bank at the going U.S. Treasury rate that was at 4.07% when DOE made its announcement. Additional rate adjustments include a 37.5 basis points (bps) liquidity spread and then an additional 37.5 to 200 bps based on the credit rating of the project.[728]

The Future of Urban Mining is Bright

Urban mining offers the possibility of critical mineral independence and security. Once a country gets large amounts of battery minerals in their country in the form of BESS and EV batteries, they need to ensure they capture and reuse 100% of it. For this circular battery economy to develop, governments must give it life by passing effective recycling laws, offering meaningful incentives, and creating an overall environment conducive to growing the industry. A disciplined national recycling enterprise will take many years to develop, so those who start on this path soonest will reap the rewards.

The global recycling industry has much to learn from China's efforts as they have begun dealing with these challenges at scale, earlier than Europe and the U.S. have. China, too, can learn from other developing regional recycling efforts as we can see by the growing idea of a "battery passport" in Europe. Integrating blockchain technology facilitates recycling at scale in many ways not possible by current "dumb" processes. In these early stages of recycling, there is tremendous opportunity for the exchange of ideas and best practices across nations, regions, and continents. For example, we see this international comingling of business models as Redwood (an American company) recycles Volkswagen batteries (a German company) to be reused by Panasonic (a Japanese company) all using lithium originally extracted by SQM (a Chilean company).

It will be many years and several decades before urban mining reaches its full potential and can provide most required battery materials for the expanding BEV

---

[727] https://www.energy.gov/lpo/articles/lpo-announces-conditional-commitment-loan-li-cycles-us-battery-resource-recovery

[728] DOE, Credit-Based Interest Rate Spread for Title XVII

industry. However, the trend is clear that urban mining will continue to accelerate at scale with the potential to disrupt the traditional mining business. Until this happens and for the foreseeable future, both urban and traditional mining will grow in parallel as they work to meet accelerating demand. There is enough business across the globe that they are not presently in competition with one another.

It will be interesting to see as the recycling industry reaches maturity and efficiency when it does in fact produce anode and cathode material to scale at costs much less than traditional mining. When this happens, battery manufacturers will naturally choose the lower cost option. Importantly, urban mining benefits from a supply chain that can truly be local in comparison to traditional battery material that travels on average 50,000 miles to get to its final destination.[729] The new urban mining business model destroys this preposterous reality. Long before this happens, it will be in the interest of established mining companies to hedge their bets like Glencore did with their investment in Li-Cycle.

Looking Ahead

1. How much room is there in the recycling space for different companies before it becomes saturated? Will BEV manufacturing and traditional mining companies move into the recycling industry or will they contract it out to dedicated private recycling companies? When will urban mining become a superior business model in comparison to traditional extraction methods? Could we see urban mining become so successful that they move upstream in the value chain?

2. When will the cost of recycled lithium from batteries be incorporated into the existing lithium pricing regimes? Will pricing agencies eventually create recycled battery mineral tag lines? The same can be said for the other associated battery minerals as well like nickel and cobalt. Of note, S&P Global began daily coverage of recycled black mass spot prices in mid-April 2023 for both the China and Europe markets. Similar to lithium, graphite has been given short thrift as a commodity since it hasn't been a global money-maker compared to other big sellers like copper and iron. As the battery industry

---

[729] https://www.redwoodmaterials.com/news/announcing-redwood-south-carolina/

continues to grow at an accelerated pace, when might we see graphite attain the status of other valued commodities?

3. Although we only briefly discussed the DOE loan programs, how does the readers assess their impact on the battery recycling space? Is the amount of money provided by DOE a game-changer? Is it enough to launch these companies into future profitable ventures? Will we look back in several years, as we do with DOE's loan to Tesla, and say that these loans changed the course of the entire industry?

4. What is the reader's opinion on the necessity of recycling as it relates to a critical minerals strategy and how should governments approach the topic? Should governments establish laws mandating the recycling of battery minerals or offer incentives instead so that the invisible hand of the market takes over? One can go online and buy entire EV batteries or even battery modules; many are from car wrecks. At present, there are so many loopholes in the U.S. battery recycling system, it is not effective.

5. Apple developed a robot in 2018, named Daisy, to disassemble its iPhones. Part of the disassembly process at their Materials Recovery Lab includes removing and recycling their lithium-ion batteries. The four-module Daisy machine can disassemble 1.2 million iPhones a year. When is the LIB industry going to achieve this same level of automated battery disassembly and recycling? Until the recycling process reaches maximum automation, the process will remain inefficient and black mass battery mineral pricing won't be as competitive as it can be.

CHAPTER 18

BEV Charging Networks

"But in totality, the network will be built at the same pace as cars, generally. And it has been for 15 years. You might have a year where something bursts ahead a little bit, but if you average over just a few years, the network will pretty much grow with cars. And it doesn't need to go any faster." – Pasquale Romano, CEO ChargePoint[730]

My Personal BEV Charging Experience

Obviously, BEVs require a charging network to recharge their batteries, but the topic is complicated. The debate includes: should we build the charging network first before we roll out BEVs at scale or is it the opposite? Can everyone charge at their home or do they need public charging stations, and if so, how many, and where? Also, who is supposed to pay for these networks – the government? BEV manufacturers? Private companies? BEV owners? To date, the approach has included everything combined. Overall, most observers would agree that there are not enough established charging systems presently installed to support the growing sales of BEVs.

However, nobody knows how many chargers are required for a global BEV fleet and every statistic is merely an educated guess. It is safe to say that the number is large. In early 2023, S&P Global Mobility estimated that with a 40% BEV adoption rate in the U.S. by 2030, there would be 28.3 million BEVs on U.S. roads. They guessed that 2.13 million level 2 destination chargers and 170,000 DC fastchargers would be needed in

---

[730] Jenkins, Lisa. "What the future of EV charging holds, according to the CEO building it". Protocol, May 10, 2022.

the U.S. alone. This does not include all the level 2 home chargers installed in homes across the country – a number that would most likely be in the tens of millions.[731]

Now, multiply those numbers by three to account for similar adoption rates in Europe and China. That gives us an estimated need for 6.39 million level 2 destination chargers and 510,000 fastchargers. There are a lot of unknowns with these estimates such as: do the number of chargers required increase proportionately with the increasing number of BEVs or do the numbers level off? I think the first accurate numbers will come out of Norway in the next several years as they will be the first nation to achieve a near 100% BEV adoption rate in 2025.

If we can get accurate data on the number of level 2 home chargers, level 2 destination chargers and level 3 fastchargers deployed in Norway and then match that with the number of BEVs on the road, we should be able to get a reasonably accurate ratio required. As we have seen with gas stations, the number of chargers deployed should self-regulate over time. If Norway over-deploys chargers, they will become inoperable over time due to lack of use or they will fail to generate revenue and will be removed. We have already seen these dynamics in Japan where the charging network has actually shrunk due to a lack of use.

As a frame of reference, in early 2022, Norway had around 480,000 BEVs registered in the country. They had approximately 14,000 level 2 destination chargers and 3,000 fastchargers. By direction of the government, fastchargers were place on all major roads, no more than 30 miles apart. The Norwegian government provided initial funding to build out the national charging network, including a concerted effort to provide chargers for housing associations. Since 99% of Norway's national electric grid is provided by renewable energy, electricity is inexpensive compared to much of Europe. Also, this high level of green electricity ensures that running a national BEV fleet is exceptionally clean as opposed to powering it by polluting fossil fuels.[732]

Let's discuss my own personal experience with charging. We own a Tesla Model Y BEV and primarily use home charging. When we bought our Model Y in April 2022, we lived in our old house and weren't going to install a permanent charging outlet as we were putting the house up for sale. So how do we charge our BEV? Well, our washer/

---

[731] Elektrek, by M. Lewis, "Here's how many EV chargers the U.S. has – and how many it needs", Jan 09, 2023.

[732] Mer, "EV Charging Infrastructure Best Practice: Learnings From Norway", March 17, 2022.

dryer room was in a small room adjacent to our garage, so we could use the dryer outlet to charge our BEV. Our car came with a 240-volt adapter for the level 2 charging cord which plugged directly into the dryer outlet to charge our BEV.

However, this was a royal pain in the ass because each time I had to pull the dryer out a few inches from the wall and unplug the dryer. Then I had to plug in the BEV charger and push the dryer back in against the wall. Pulling and pushing the plug in and out of the dryer took some effort. My wife pretended not to know how to do the process because it was such a hassle, so I had to do it every time.

After a month of that nonsense, I said I'm done with this. I started surfing the web, looking for a solution. I found that there was already an established industry to deal with my dryer problem which dealt in splitter boxes. I ended up buying a Splitvolt box for $350.00 USD that plugged directly into the 240-volt wall outlet. The box then sat on top of the dryer where I plugged in both the dryer plug and the car charging plug. I could either use the dryer or charge the car, but not at the same time. However, that was easy, as I would just plug our car in at night before we went to bed – problem solved.

When we moved to the other side of town to our new house, we installed a 240-volt outlet in our garage after running about 18 feet of wire from our closest circuit breaker box. We paid to have it installed in June 2022 and it cost $2500.00 USD, which I thought was a lot. However, COVID had contributed to a global supply chain disruption and there was a copper squeeze, so wiring prices had increased. Either we paid the installation cost, or we would have to back our Model Y into the garage so we could get the charging cord close enough to the dryer outlet to use the splitter box again. No thanks. I craved convenient charging. I admit it.

Our electricity provider is Tucson Electric Power or simply TEP. To promote BEV adoption, they offer up to a $500.00 USD rebate when installing a level 2 EV charger. The rebate takes the form of being credited to the TEP user account. To apply and qualify, the homeowner submits an *Electric Vehicle Charger Program Application Form. Also, the homeowner must opt into a Time of Use rate plan for two years if they are participating in net metering. With this rate plan, the homeowner is incentivized to charge their vehicle in off-peak hours from 10 pm to 5 am to receive reduced electricity rates.* I have calculated, based on what I am charged from TEP, that it costs me $8.00 to charge my Model Y from 0 to 300 miles range.

Let's talk about my Tesla's battery. Our Model Y has a battery pack made from 2170 batteries meaning that we keep our BEV charged between 20% and 80% of capacity. The thought is that if you consistently charge to 100%, you are shortening the life of the battery.

It takes several hours on the typical day to charge our car to give it a 100-mile charge back to 80% capacity. Because it takes several hours to charge it, if I forget to plug it in at night, I'm screwed the next morning. And, yes, I have done that more than once. If I forget, then I would need to drive to the closest supercharger and charge up if I am going on a trip. Our nearest Tesla supercharger is only two miles away from our house. If you don't have a supercharger nearby, you will be inconvenienced as you delay your trip to charge up. Obviously, nobody likes that and they will complain that an ICE car is more convenient.

Now, let's talk road trips. I've done several trips from Tucson to San Diego for the weekend and back. After departing Tucson and on the way to San Diego, we stop at the Tesla supercharger in Yuma, AZ on the border with California. The distance is about 235 miles, so we charge back up to max capacity. Since it takes about an hour to charge, we walk to the nearby hotel and get lunch. From there, we are onto San Diego which is another 175 miles but it uses a lot of energy because we must go up and over the mountains before descending to the coast. So, if we have a full charge in the morning when we depart, we stop once to charge and then are good to make our destination. We've done the trip so many times now, it's easy and we don't even think about it.

Charging Networks

Let's get back to the topic of where you charge your BEV. While an estimated two-thirds of Americans have a garage or carport that could potentially be used to charge a BEV, what if you live in an apartment complex or condo that doesn't?[733] Then what? Well, the building owner is going to have to spend money to invest in charging infrastructure for either the parking garage or parking lot. That can be a lot of money. And you know the only way to raise this money is to increase HOA fees which means you, the renter/owner, is paying for it.

While it depends on what kind of charger an apartment gets, I am going to guess that they start at around $2,500.00 USD for installation and the charger. One hundred

---

[733] Insideevs., by M. Kane, "U.S.: New Report Reveals Share Of Housing Units With A Garage Or Carport", Dec 20, 2022.

renters each requiring a charger comes out to a hefty $250k bill. Certain towns or counties offer rebates to encourage electrification, but it all depends. I've also seen people run electrical cords out of their apartment windows to their cars because apartments wouldn't install chargers. But that kind of level 1 charging isn't acceptable and it takes about 48 hours straight to charge your battery.

So, if you can't charge where you live, then you must charge somewhere else. Also, when you are traveling, it doesn't matter if you charge at home or not because you need to recharge periodically. This brings us to charging networks which most people agree, including me, are insufficient in most areas of the U.S. and the world. I am of the mind that a robust charging network needs to be built to encourage BEV adoption but that takes money and civic leadership that are sometimes lacking. Let's look at several examples of charging networks to assess their effectiveness and shortcomings.

Tesla's Charging Network

Tesla was not just an early mover in the BEV space, they are also industry leaders in the charging network business. They understood early on that a publicly accessible BEV charging network at scale was critical to move BEVs forward. They began installing the first superchargers in 2012 of what would become the most robust private global charging network by the time you are reading this. For sure, Tesla has a very large task in front of it as it tries to build out its own BEV charging network in the U.S., Europe, and China. However, an extensive proprietary charging network can provide a competitive edge to a BEV company and can also be a source of extensive revenue. With BEVs, electricity is the new oil.

By the end of 2022, Tesla had 4,653 separate supercharger locations and more than 42,142 individual supercharger stalls worldwide. In the United States, Tesla had 1,626 separate supercharger locations. Although they had charging locations in all 50 states, fully 20% of them were in California. This makes sense since Tesla first manufacturing plant is in Fremont and the largest number of buyers of Teslas reside in California. The charging locations tend to be in urban areas or established towns so, as you travel longer distances, you are essentially island hopping from station to station. Smaller towns away from major highways generally won't have superchargers installed.[734]

---

[734] https://supercharge.info/charts

I'll use my personal experience as an example. The superchargers I use in Tucson are 15 minutes east of Route 10, a major route connecting Phoenix and El Paso. The supercharger location is near a mall called La Encantada. They have ten 150 kW chargers in the back parking lot. I've never seen more than 3-4 cars charging there at any one time. La Encantada is a very nice mall with shops, cafes, and restaurants. You can easily spend 30-45 minutes having lunch, getting coffee, or eating ice cream as your BEV charges. There is another location with ten superchargers about 45 minutes away in Rita Ranch which is the southeast part of Tucson. Those chargers are at a gas station right off Route 10. The gas station has a Subway sandwich shop there. If you are ever passing through Tucson, I recommend you hit La Encantada.

When I travel to San Diego to visit family, I charge my Model Y in town. The location I go to is situated in the parking lot of a good-sized mall. They have 20 supercharges at that location and the first time I showed up, 19 cars were already parked and charging. I was lucky to get the last space. They could increase the number of superchargers there to 30 easy and have them all filled on a weekend evening. This is where all the apartment dwellers charge because they have no options where they live. But there are plenty of things to do for 45 minutes like shopping or eating at several adjacent restaurants. This is a good location that makes sense.

While Tesla's exclusive charging network is a great incentive for Tesla owners, it uses its own proprietary charging cable and port. If we look at ICE cars, gas pumps and their nozzles are universal and work across all car models no matter where they were made. This is what, in part, enabled the mass use of ICE vehicles – the universality of powering whatever model you had. American, German, French and Japanese all had commonly designed gas ports which worked with a standardized nozzle size. I suspect we have all grown to take this universality for granted.

In North America, the most used charging plug is the SAE (Society of Automotive Engineers) J1772. In fact, every BEV sold in the United States uses the J1772 for level 1 (120 volt) and level 2 (240 volt) charging – except Tesla. Tesla uses their own proprietary product. However, this isn't that big a deal because Tesla sells an adapter which allows all Tesla vehicles use the J1772 plug. When it comes to level 3 (480 volt) DC (Direct Current) fast charging, the most common format is the J1772 Combined Charging Systems (CCS) which has an additional two connectors below the original plug.

Tesla's proprietary plug is more efficient in that both level 2 and level 3 charging use the same plug, unlike the J1772 that uses the different CCS version for DC fast charging. Tesla's product is smaller, has a simpler design and can handle charging up to 1MW during DC charging. In 2022, Tesla renamed its plug the "North American Charging Standard" or NACS in an attempt to get the rest of the industry to adopt its proprietary plug. To push their NACS plug, Tesla even provided free access as how to design their charging port to encourage other companies to adopt it. However, they tried to push this idea much too late in the game. It might have been adopted if they did this in 2012 not 2022.

Tesla is part of the Charging Interface Initiative e. V. (CharIN) which is a global association with over 300 members whose purpose is to advance global interoperability of the previously discussed CCS. Obviously, Tesla didn't coordinate their NACS offensive with CharIN as their response stated the move would "lead to further consumer confusion and delay EV adoption." CharIN was further concerned that Tesla's effort would disrupt the association's ongoing effort to develop CCS standardization through the diversion of limited resources.[735] We already know what Tesla's decision is on the topic. They will continue to build their proprietary charging port and interface while also selling a CCS adapter for Tesla owners. Thus, two parallel charging models will continue to develop side by side in North America.

In late 2021, Tesla discussed their plans to triple their 27,600 charging stalls to 90,000 by the start of 2024.[736] From the time of that statement in October 2021 through December 2022, they added another 14,000 stalls, so they are coming up short – but the intent is there.[737] It remains to be seen if Tesla's 1.5 megawatt Megachargers for its Tesla Semi Trucks are eventually developed in line with CharIN's Megawatt Charging Standard (MCS). As of today, they have not.

While Tesla has only been manufacturing their BEVs in Shanghai since 2020, their China/Asia charging network already surpasses their North America efforts with 1,897 different supercharger locations established.[738] Of these, more than 1,500 were

[735] https://www.charin.global/news/charin-response-to-tesla-announcement-to-open-the-north-america-charging-standard/

[736] Cleantechnica.com, by S. Hanley, "Tesla To Triple Size Of Supercharger Network Within 2 Years". Oct 21, 2022.

[737] https://supercharge.info/charts

[738] https://supercharge.info/charts

in China. By the start of 2023, Tesla had over 10,000 individual charging stalls across China. Tesla positioned these tactically with a focus on major international hotels, airports, shopping malls, vacation resorts and major business centers. In the summer of 2022, Tesla opened its first store in Inner Mongolia. At the time, Inner Mongolia had seven supercharging stations with 47 charging stalls and 13 destination chargers with 23 separate charging pilings.[739] If you want to compare BEV companies to assess their competitiveness with Tesla, see what kind of footprint they have in Inner Mongolia. If they are not there, they are not competitive.

China BEVs have used the GB/T charging standard since 2013 which is different from the North American and European standards. The GB/T = Guojia Biaozhun/ Tuijian = National Standard/Recommended. Thus, Tesla models made in China (MIC) use the GBT connector as does their supercharger network. This has manufacturing considerations in that the models Tesla makes in China but ships to Europe are made with the European CCS standard. However, if Tesla ships a model with a GBT standard to, say, South Korea, which uses the European CCS standard, then the owner can simply buy a connector adapter for charging.

To make things even more interesting, Japan developed their limited production BEVs, like the Nissan Leaf, with the CHAdeMO (CHArge de MOve) connector standard. The CHAdeMO association developed their protocol in 2010 with support from the Toyota Electric Power Company (TEPCO) and the major Japanese car manufacturers. CHAdeMO has limitations in that it is designed for DC charging only and Japanese BEVs must have a different connector port installed to accept AC connections. CHAdeMO does support V2G (Vehicle to Grid) bidirectional charging meaning that it can connect BEVs to a smart grid. In 2021, Japan had 7,700 CHAdeMO chargers in-country.[740] Compare that to Tesla who only has 57 superchargers in the country, reflecting their relatively low penetration rate.[741]

In Europe, by the end of 2022, Tesla achieved more than 10,000 individual superchargers distributed in 930 different locations in 30 countries. Supercharger stations

[739] Tesmanian, By E. Fox, "Tesla Opens its First Store in Inner Mongolia, Expanding into Northern China", June 8, 2022.

[740] Insideevs, by M. Kane, "Japan: High Number Of EV Chargers Did Not Jump Start The Market", August 31, 2021.

[741] https://supercharge.info/charts

were deployed in clusters about 200 kilometers apart to provide maximum travel range. About half of the charging locations were in just four countries: Germany, France, the UK, and Norway. This makes sense as the first three are large countries that have aggressively pursued electrification while Norway is forecasted to achieve 100% annual BEV sales by 2025.

In Europe, there is still no universal charging standard, but they mostly use the Mennekes connector for level 2 AC charging and the Combined Charging System (CCS) Combo 2 connector for level 3 DC charging. In 2018, Tesla announced that they would start building their Model 3's designated for the European market with the CCS Combo 2 charge port and their Model X and Model S would get CCS Combo 2 adapters.[742] Soon after, Tesla began retrofitting their supercharger network that was installed with Mennekes connectors with an additional CCS Combo 2 charging cable. This retrofitting was largely completed by 2019.

Overall, Tesla is the only BEV manufacturer with such a robust global charging network that they own and operate themselves. Unlike other BEV companies, they don't need to rely on anyone else to charge their own products. Personally, where I live in Arizona, the Tesla Supercharger network is robust enough that I have not seriously considered using anything else. Importantly, Tesla makes it very easy to use their network. All I have to do is plug in anywhere in the U.S. and my credit card is automatically charged through my Tesla phone app. It's simple.

So, if electricity is the new oil for BEVs, there is money to be made owning and operating a charging network. The more charging stations Tesla has and the more BEVs there are on the road each year using them, the more they make. Elon Musk stated in 2022 that Tesla makes a 10% profit on their charging operations, much less than some analysts had predicted.[743] Goldman Sachs estimated that with 500,000 Superchargers in place, with each one charging 15 BEVs daily, Tesla could make $28 billion USD a year.[744] As Tesla presently only has about 8% of that number, they might be making

---

[742] Elektrek, by F. Lambert, "Tesla confirms Model 3 is getting a CCS plug in Europe, adapter coming for Model S and Model X", Nov 14, 2018.

[743] Torque News, by T. Aregay, "Elon Musk Reveals Tesla's Supercharger Profit As The EV Maker Prepares To Open The Network", April 4, 2022.

[744] Goldman Sachs Global Investment Research, Tesla Charging Network Assessment, 2021.

$2 billion USD a year off their charging infrastructure. I don't see Tesla ever reaching 500,000 separate stalls, but 100,00 is possible as they are half-way there.

Electrify America

Electrify America is an interesting story. From 2009 through 2016, Volkswagen Automotive Group and several of its sub-brands (Audi, Porsche) conspired to defraud the U.S. government by illegally bypassing American emissions standards. During this time, VW sold 590,000 diesel engine models that employed software designed to cheat the U.S. emissions testing process. The cheat software was effective since emissions equipment determined that these vehicles met U.S. emissions standards when in fact they did not.[745]

Ultimately, this reflected a corrupt VW business culture where they made the strategic decision to cheat U.S. emissions standards rather manufacture low-emission BEVs. This was also an explicit admission by VW leadership that their ICE business model was invalid and could not compete with modern pure BEV companies like Tesla. To be fair, all the major ICE OEMs exhibited some level of denial when confronted by the current BEV revolution (GM, Ford, Toyota). It is a tough thing to admit that most of the company's decades old enterprise is rapidly evolving into stranded assets.

Over the course of several legal judgements in the U.S. and Europe, VW was hit for $30 billion USD in penalties. However, it took this very public scandal and massive reputational hit to VW's brand to force them on a different path that moved them towards a BEV-centric business model. For example, VW established a permanent Sustainability Council whose mission was to ensure company strategy was grounded in ESG (Environmental, Social, Governance) principles moving forward. Also, VW has voiced its support for the EU's mandate to ban new ICE vehicles in Europe beginning in 2035.[746]

As part of VW's settlement with the EPA and the State of California in 2016, they agreed to spend $2 billion USD by 2026 to develop EV charging infrastructure in the

---

[745] https://www.epa.gov/vw/learn-about-volkswagen-violations

[746] Forbes, by G. Kell, "From Emissions Cheater To Climate Leader: VW's Journey From Dieselgate To Embracing E-Mobility.

U.S.[747] To build out this level 2 and level 3 charging network, VW formed Electrify America LLC to manage the enterprise, with its HQs in Reston, VA just outside of Washington, DC. In 2022, Electrify America raised $450 million USD in equity investments giving the company a $2.45 billion USD valuation. One of the major investors was Siemens Financial Services.[748] With this round of investments, Electrify America acknowledged that they were investing beyond just the minimum originally mandated $2 billion USD.

By the summer of 2022, Electrify America had 800 charging stations with 3,500 individual charging stalls from coast to coast in the U.S. and select locations in Canada.[749] To put this in perspective, Tesla had over 5,000 individual stalls at the start of 2017.[750] However, Electrify America is on the move and plans to have 1,800 separate superchargers sites by 2026 with 10,000 individual stalls in both the U.S. and Canada.[751] To build out the charging network in Canada, VW stood up Electrify Canada. Electrify Canada efforts are much smaller than in the U.S. and reflects the lower actual and expected BEV penetration rate there. For example, as of January 2023, there were no charging sites in the City of Montreal and only two with a total of eight stalls in adjacent suburbs. By 2026, Electrify Canada intends to have 100 sites with 500 fast charging stalls.[752]

In 2021, Electrify America dispensed 41.4 GWh of electricity through 1.45 million individual charging sessions. By comparison, in 2020, they only recorded 268,000 charging sessions. Electrify America believes that the 41.4 GWh was enough energy for BEVs to drive some 145 million miles. This equaled 5.7 million gallons of gasoline not burned by ICE vehicles. From a user perspective, not all charging sessions were equal timewise as Electrify America had chargers ranging from 150 kW to 350 kW

[747] CNBC, by P. Eisenstein, "VW's $2 billion penalty for diesel scam, Electrify America, builds electric charging network across US to boost EV market", May 10, 2019.

[748] https://media.electrifyamerica.com/en-us/releases/190

[749] Elektrek, by S. Doll, "Electrify America reports a fivefold increase of charging sessions in 2021 compared to 2020", May 2, 2022

[750] https://supercharge.info/charts

[751] https://media.electrifyamerica.com/en-us/releases/190

[752] www.electrify-canada.ca/getting-started/

capabilities. However, from a pricing perspective, users were charged per kWh based on either a guest or member rate.[753]

Because VW was also sued by the State of California, they must make regular quarterly reports to their friends at the California Air Resources Board (CARB). By the end of Q3 2022, Electrify had built a total of 244 ultra-fast charging stations in the state. For Q3, they provided 687,000 separate charging sessions for BEV owners. In total to date, Electrify provided 22 gigawatt hours of charging in California which enabled 79 million miles of electric driving by BEVs. Electrify identified that the average design, permitting and construction costs for charging stations in California were 48% higher than the national average. Also, the average utility interconnection process took 38 weeks or 63% longer than the national average.[754]

As we discussed briefly with Tesla's charging network, it is interesting to estimate what kind of revenues Electrify America might be making with their own network. It is hard to think investors put almost half a billion dollars into Electrify America if they didn't think that electricity was the new oil for BEVs. Inside EVs did the math and calculated that in 2021, 28.6 kWh of energy per session was dispensed. Based on monthly user fees and at the charger fees (an educated guess, only company insiders managing the books know the specific details), Electrify America brought in estimated revenues of $18 million USD.[755]

If we want to be generous and round up this revenue to $20 million USD, it will take some 100 years to make up the original $2 billion USD investment. If Electrify America can get to 10,000 stalls while maintaining their current energy sales rate, they could cut this payback period to perhaps 35 years. This example highlights the reality that a charging network must operate at scale and dispense large amounts of energy in order bring in the revenue to justify the investment. Also, it takes more time to establish new charging sites due to permitting delays than companies want to admit. Tesla clearly isn't on track to have 90,000 charging stalls by 2024 and Electrify America won't have 10,000 stalls by 2026.

[753] https://insideevs.com/news/583693/electrify-america-145million-charging-sessions-2021/

[754] Electrify America, Q32022 Report to CARB.

[755] https://media.electrifyamerica.com/en-us/releases/181

GM's Charging Efforts

GM's is late in the game when it comes to charging operations as are many ICE OEMs. Because the OEMs were late transitioning to BEVs, they had no reason to invest in battery supply chains nor charging infrastructure either. Hence, GM doesn't manufacture their own proprietary charging equipment like Tesla or VW, so they won't benefit from the revenue of a wholly owned charging network. However, they have plenty of options to advance their BEV enterprise by partnering with existing private charging companies.

GM's current strategy is to create a platform to coordinate multiple charging companies to advance their electrification program. Their platform is called Ultium Charge 360, named in reference to their Ultium battery platform that their BEV program is based on. GM's different brands will have different apps that will be used to coordinate with their charging partners, whomever the driver chooses to use. GM is partnering with several private charging companies to include EVgo, Blink Charging, EV Connect, ChargePoint, FLO, Greenlots (owned by Shell) and SemaConnect (owned by Blink). GM estimates that these companies have a combined network of 80,000 charging locations (level 2 and level 3) which a user will be able access through their GM mobile charging app. Additionally, by 2025, they anticipate their partner, EVgo, to have 2,700 fast charging stations online.[756]

In 2022, GM launched their Dealer Community Charging Program. This program provides ten level 2 chargers (in partnership with FLO) to each member of GM's dealer network. The dealership then positions these chargers at key locations in their community that encourages maximum charging opportunity. By the start of 2023, 1,000 of GM's dealers had signed up for the program while GM intended to get the rest on board. If all 4,000 dealers participate, GM can install a 40,000-charger network to advance their BEV program. GM emphasizes that 90% of the American population lives within 10 miles of a GM dealership.[757]

To address the home charging segment, GM has partnered with Qmerit, a full-spectrum electrification provider who also sells level 2 charging solutions. The idea is that a GM BEV owner will use an app to get three competitive quotes from pre-approved home charger providers. The owner will then select one of these vetted electricians to install their 240-volt charger, including handling the permitting process. GM

[756] https://www.gm.com/stories/evgo

[757] https://investor.gm.com/news-releases/news-release-details/gm-advances-dealer-community-charging-program

also offers to pay for the installation outright as part of their effort to promote buying or leasing one of their 2022/2023 model Chevy Bolt BEVs.[758]

Nio's Novel Approach

Since we have seen how several U.S.-centric companies approach charging networks, let's examine Nio's operations. Nio is a Chinese BEV manufacturer founded in 2014 by William Li. Nio, based in Shanghai. Nio offers a line of three SUVs and two passenger sedans. Nio has specifically targeted BBA (Mercedes Benz, BMW, Audi) as their direct competition in the premium auto market and does not consider Tesla their competition. Li recently commented, "People who originally drove BMWs won't go back to buying BMWs after buying NIO vehicles. That is the trend."[759] In 2022, Nio sold 122,000 BEVs, most of them in the China market, although they have already laid the groundwork to expand sales into Europe.

Following in the steps of Tesla, Nio too sees the benefits of operating its own charging network for its BEV fleet. In 2018, Nio began installing charging stations, both destination chargers and superchargers. By November 2022, Nio had installed over 1,200 fast-charging stations with more than 5,700 individual fast-chargers (level 3 chargers). They also had installed 948 destination charging stations (level 2 chargers) with over 6,000 individual destination chargers. In January 2023, Nio produced it's 300,000[th] car meaning they had roughly one charging pile for every 25 BEVs they have manufactured – a very high ratio. Furthermore, Nio had standing agreements with various third-party charging companies that gave them access to another 590,000 chargers. [760]

Nio has continued to pursue superior energy dispensing technology and currently operates liquid-cooled 500 kW fast-chargers. Depending on the BEV model and associated battery, if they have an 800-volt capability, they can charge the battery from 10 percent to 80 percent in twelve minutes.[761] This is important in the battle between old ICE cars which

---

[758] https://www.chevrolet.com/electric/living-electric/home-charging-installation

[759] CnEVPost, by P. Zhang, "Internal speech: William Li on NIO's new businesses, and why it's on right side of trend", Nov 29, 2022.

[760] Green Car Congress, "NIO launches its 1,200th NIO Power Swap Station in China", Nov 16, 2022.

[761] CnEVPost, by p. Zhang, "NIO unveils 500-kW ultra-fast charger that can charge EVs from 10% to 80% in 12 minutes", Dec 25, 2022.

can fuel up in ten minutes or less and BEVs that traditionally take 30-45 minutes to charge up. Nio's latest fastcharger is but one example of an industry trend where BEV and charging manufacturers are making increasingly capable chargers to reduce charging times. When BEV charging time equals that of filling up a tank of gas, a big reason not to transition to BEVs from a population of ICE drivers spoiled by fast refueling times has been removed.

There is nothing new with Nio's charging network approach compared to a Tesla or an Electrify America – it's just another piece of their operational business model. What is different is an idea Elon Musk and Tesla rejected years ago – battery swap stations. Beginning in 2020, Nio began providing its BEV owners Battery as a Service (BaaS) where Nio owners can sign up for the Nio battery swap plan. Nio's battery swap stations are relatively modest affairs where an owner drives into the station or they use their Nio app and the car self-parks. Then, machines automatically remove the existing battery from beneath the BEV and replaces it with a new, fully charged battery.

Once the car is fully parked and in place inside the changing station, it takes three minutes to make the change. Overall, the entire process takes about five minutes. The process requires no interaction with a human and the BEV owner is automatically billed for the change under their BaaS plan. This brings battery swap times equal to or below that of fueling an old ICE vehicle. I recently timed myself parking my 2018 Toyota Camry hybrid at a gas station and filling it up and then driving off and did it in three minutes flat. (I recently traded the Camry in and bought another Tesla Model Y.)

So, what are the advantages of using the Nio battery swap plan? For one, it is fast and convenient if there is a swap station nearby. This is good for people living in apartments with no ability to charge at home. Also, consider the needs of service industry fleets like cab companies, Uber drivers or police cars that may need a fast change for operational tempo reasons. This could also work in a military setting with batteries charged by small modular nuclear reactors.

Most importantly, this service increases the longevity of a BEV as one of the major concerns of every BEV owner is getting a bad battery that fails early or simply having to change it out at the end of its service life. Battery replacements are expensive and start at about $10,000.00 USD depending on the vehicle and battery and only go up from there. Importantly for the consumer, using BaaS saves them almost $11,000.00 USD on the initial price of their Nio BEV as compared to buying the BEV and battery together. A BaaS subscription costs around $150.00 USD a month or $1,800.00 a year, thus it takes six years to equal the $11,000.00 price of owning the battery itself.[762] As we can see, it is beneficial to Nio if a BEV owner opts for the BaaS subscription plan and keeps their car longer than six years.

Without a doubt, Nio's battery swap operations in China have been very successful. By November 2022, Nio had more than 1,200 battery swap stations installed. They were in major urban areas as well as travel corridors and transportation hubs. By 2025, they intend to exceed 4,000 stations. On average, Nio owners execute 30,000 battery swaps a day. Since Nio had about 300,000 cars sold at that time, 10% of owners swapped their battery on any given day. Also, some 23,000 owners had upgraded their original battery to a more capable battery with greater range.[763]

For the number of cars they have manufactured, Nio has the most robust charging infrastructure available in China for its brand. As we have seen, Tesla has a well-developed supercharging network as well, but it is proportionally smaller than Nio's. It is interesting to note that the #2 BEV producer in the world, BYD, decided not to build out their own proprietary network but is moving forward in a JV with Shell to establish a charging network. Nio's battery swapping capability helps them stand out from their competition and the data shows that in dense urban areas, BEV owners will frequently use battery swapping stations and they do want to upgrade their batteries.

An example of Nio's second-generation battery swap station. Nio's goal is to provide battery swapping in three minutes or less. Nio's software enables their vehicles to self-park. (by Nio)

---

[762] https://www.nio.com/news/nio-launches-battery-service

[763] Green Car Congress, "NIO launches its 1,200th NIO Power Swap Station in China", Nov 16, 2022.

EVOGO

The battery swap concept has been criticized as being more expensive than simple fast-chargers and for having much in-demand batteries unnecessarily sitting in swapping stations. However, Chinese battery giant CATL observed Nio's swap operations for two years and believed in the utility of that business model. Consequently, at the start of 2022, CATL announced their entrance into the battery swap business by launching their own enterprise called EVOGO. Specifically, EVOGO is under Contemporary Amperex Energy Service Technology Limited (CAES), a wholly owned subsidiary of CATL.

EVOGO's first battery swap partner was with FAW Group Corporation, a state-owned auto group, who designed their Bestune NAT EO5 BEV for purpose built online ride-hailing services (i.e., Taxis). The Bestune NAT (Next Automatic Taxi) has a 250-mile range and a right-side sliding door to optimize urban operations. Judging from the name, we can guess the NAT was developed with an eye towards eventual Full Self Driving technology becoming mature. When using CATL's battery swap stations, the NAT gets a new battery in three minutes. It is interesting to note that the NAT has been reported to use both BYD's lithium iron phosphate batteries and CATL's three-way lithium battery.[764]

The CATL/FAW connection becomes more intriguing with the fact that FAW developed the NAT in conjunction with the established ride-hailing service DiDi Global Inc. DiDi went public with an IPO in 2021 and is listed on the NYSE as DIDI with a $17.7 billion USD market cap. Previously, DiDi went to war against local ride-hailing rival Kuaidi Dache in the China market until they both agreed to stop the market bloodletting and merge in 2015. The merger of DiDi (backed by multimedia giant Tencent) and Kuaidi Dache (backed by e-commerce Godzilla Alibaba) resulted in a lock on 95% of the ride-hailing market in China.[765] Adding to DiDi's continued ride-hailing expansion, they bought out Uber China in 2016.

The CATL/FAW/DiDi nexus will provide a laboratory for battery swapping operations to see if they offer superior dynamics, or even if they are strongly complementary, to supercharging. This could potentially be big business for CATL as DiDi is

---

[764] https://autoelectro.cn/electric-car-faw-bestune-nat-e05.html

[765] TechCrunch, by J. Russell, "China's Top Two Taxi-Hailing Services Confirm That They Will Merge.

commonly cited as having 500 million annual ride-hailing users. Also, DiDi has stated their intent to pursue the electrification of their fleets and their desire for 1 million robotaxis by 2030.[766] This is interesting, because a robofleet conducting continuous operations (the underlying assumption is that they are employing FSD technology) can have their batteries recharged through CATL's battery swap platforms without the need for a human driver. In contrast, current supercharging technology requires a human to plug and unplug the charger and, thus, aren't suitable for 24/7 robotaxi fleets.

Chargepoint and Blink Charging

Finally, we are going to take a brief look at three different public EV charging companies to compare their growth, earnings, and current trajectories. It is useful to understand their place in the overall lithium value chain.

Let's start with ChargePoint, a California based company founded in 2007 and trading on the NYSE as CHPT. Their stock topped at $46.00 USD in December 2020 and has declined to $10.00 USD in January 2021. Their market cap in January 2023 was $3.44 billion USD. They are primarily U.S. based but operate in fourteen different countries and growing. Just so the reader knows, if they do their own research on ChargePoint's annual returns, their fiscal year rather oddly runs from January 31 to January 31.

For fiscal year 2020, ChargePoint took in $91,893,000.00 USD of revenue from their networked individual charging systems. However, these same systems cost them $87,083,000.00 USD to operate them, leaving them a profit of $4,810,000.00 USD or just over 5% in profit. Their charging service subscriptions earned them $40,563,000.00 USD in revenue at a cost of $20,385,000.00 USD. This resulted in a profit of $20,178,000.00 USD or almost 50% which is quite impressive. However, due to a variety of operating costs like research and development, marketing, and sales, general and administrative and the like, ChargePoint closed the year with a net loss of -$197 million USD.[767]

In 2021, ChargePoint increased their networked charging systems revenue to $174,350,000.00 USD at a cost of $147,814,000.00 USD for a profit of $26,536,000.00 USD – a healthy 15%. For their subscription services, they earned revenues of $53,512,000.00 USD at a cost of $31,190,000.00 USD which is a profit of $22,322,000.00

---

[766] Reuters, "China's Didi aims for 1 million robotaxis on its platform by 2030", Jun 23, 2020.

[767] ChargePoint, Q4 Fiscal 2022 Financial Results, March 2, 2022.

USD or an almost 42% profit. They finished the year with net losses decreasing to -$132 million USD which is a 33% change in the right direction. [768]

In 2022, ChargePoint increased their networked charging systems revenue to $363,622,000.00 USD at a cost of $318,628,000.00 USD for a profit of $44,994,000.00 USD, a declining margin of 12%. For their subscription services, they had revenues of $85,296,000.00 USD at a cost of $51,416,000.00 USD which is a profit of $33,880,000.00 USD or an almost 40% profit. This is still very good but is a 2% drop from 2021. Their net losses for the year ballooned to -$342 million USD. An enormous move in the wrong direction.

Blink Charging is a Florida based U.S. public charging company that was founded in 1998 and trades on the NASDAQ as BLNK. They peaked at $48.83 USD a share in February 2021 and then dropped steadily to $7.40 a share in January 2023. Their market cap in January 2023 was $611 million USD. Most of their charging assets are in the U.S., although they have expanded into Europe. As compared to ChargePoint, they are much smaller business as is reflected in their financial reports. ChargePoint has more than 1,400 employees while Blink has only around 200.

In 2020, revenues for product sales were $4,432,423.00 USD at costs of $2,859,559.00 USD for a 35% profit. They earned $772,540.00 USD in charging service revenue with costs of $397,377.00 USD for a 48% profit. Network fees brought in revenues of $344,819.00 USD while costs were much higher at $515,953.00 USD for a -50% loss. Also, host provider fees cost $265,272.00 USD while warranty/repairs/ maintenance cost $331,000.00. Overall, they had revenues of $6,230,231.00 USD with revenue costs of $4,713,921.00 USD which put them in the black $1,516,310.00 USD for a 24% profit. However, overarching operating costs ensured they ended the year at a net loss of -$17.8 million USD.[769]

In 2021, Blink continued to grow. Product sales more than tripled to $15,480,000.00 USD. Product sales costs were $11,670,000.00 USD resulting in a $3,810,000.00 USD profit of almost 25%. Their charging services revenues quadrupled to $2,978,000.00 USD while sustaining costs of $707,000.00 USD. This resulted in profits of $2,271,000.00 USD or a whopping 76%. Blink earned $667,000.00 USD in network fees while keeping its costs low at $454,000.00 USD. The remaining $213,000.00 USD represented a 32% profit. However, Blink ate $1,386,000.00 USD in host provider fees. They also ate another $892,000.00 on warranty/repair/maintenance fees, almost triple from the year

[768] Ibid.

[769] Blink Annual Report 2020.

before. Overall, Blink finished the year losing -$55.1 million USD, more than tripling the losses from 2021.[770]

In 2022, product sales again tripled to $46 million USD while associated costs were $31,428,000.00 USD resulting in a $14,572,000.00 USD profit of almost 32%, an increase of 7% from the year prior. Their charging services revenue increased significantly to $6,866,000.00 USD while sustaining costs of $1,466,000.00 USD. This resulted in profits of $5,400,000.00 USD or a whopping 78% or 2% higher than the year prior. Blink earned $4,370,000.00 USD in network fees, a huge increase from 2021, while keeping costs low at $1,463,000.00 USD for a $2,907,000.00 USD profit of an amazing 66%. However, Blink ate $3.9 million USD in host provider fees and another $2,795,000.00 on warranty/repair/maintenance fees, more than triple from the year before. Overall, Blink finished the year losing -$91.5 million USD, significantly more than in 2021.[771]

Closing Thoughts

While the consensus is that there are not presently enough fastcharging stations in place, that fact will not hold up the BEV transition. Ironically, we discovered with Japan, that having a robust BEV charging network doesn't automatically ensure an accelerated transition to BEVs if there aren't other incentives to do so. As we have seen, there are many different companies moving forward with charging networks and this will only accelerate moving forward. Charging networks are technologically simple, relatively inexpensive and can be placed just about anywhere.

For these last reasons, the barrier to initial entry into the BEV charging business is relatively low. If a company manufactures their own BEV charging stations, then they can control their costs, but they are also eating all the costs of the necessary start-up equipment and other overhead. If Company 1 pays Company 2 to install a level 3 DC fastcharger which Company 1 will subsequently manage, it costs around $50,000.00 USD and goes up from there depending on a host of factors. However, a company can start small and build out incrementally depending on how their operations go. Tesla started building out very small numbers of superchargers in strategic locations and now has the single largest fastcharging network in the world.

While the barrier to initial entry is low, the barrier to a profitable charging network

---

[770] Blink Annual Report 2021.

[771] Blink Annual Report 2022.

is quite high. As we looked at ChargePoint and Blink, they all had one important thing in common – they were all in the red operating at a net loss. Elon Musk believes Tesla's own supercharger network runs about a 10% profit which is a pretty low margin. For a pure-play charging company to be profitable they must build out a charging network at scale while annually dispensing large amounts of electricity. What that amount of electricity is, I don't know, and it depends on the company and how efficient they are. For instance, ChargePoint says they have dispensed 145 million separate charges yet they are far from being profitable.

The present competition among charging companies will continue with no single entity achieving network dominance. It would be interesting to see if consolidation takes place in the future with a large charging company buying out another. Then, we might see how much electricity must be dispensed for a charging company to become profitable. Until then, we may have to watch the prominent charging companies continue to grow to see how many and what kind of charging stations it takes to deliver enough electricity to get in the black. The two companies we looked at are many years away from achieving profitability and might not be in the black until 2030.

BEV manufacturers with their own proprietary charging network provides them an advantage over their peers, but only slightly so. A proprietary charging network does allow a BEV manufacturer to offer charging incentives, provides ease of charging and thus encourages owners to stay in the charging network vice going outside it. As a low margin business, I don't presently see profits from a proprietary network being significant enough to be a key ingredient in putting a BEV manufacturer in the black. However, it depends on volume.

A topic to discuss in relation to this is vertical integration as we see BEV manufacturers increasingly going upstream to secure battery minerals. When running a charging network, the owner, let's say Tesla, doesn't control the source of the electricity and thus doesn't control the price of the electricity dispensed through their charging stations. Therefore, pricing at fastchargers will reflect regional conditions and they can be up or down depending on the complexities of the energy markets involved.

Could we see in the future, as charging networks get much bigger and eventually profitable, a move to secure upstream electricity sources to manage costs and thus increase profits? EVgo's 100% renewable energy model and Tesla's Virtual Power Plant line of effort makes me think this could be possible. As Tesla's BEV fleet grows to millions and its supercharger networks number in the hundreds of thousands, is it time for them to become their own original clean energy provider to supply their proprietary charging empire? I think this is within the art of the possible and will be interesting to watch how the topic develops over time.

Looking Ahead

1. Does the reader think the world will adopt a universal charging infrastructure to include the charging port? It would "only" take the major car manufacturing countries of China, Japan, South Korea Germany, France, and the U.S. to agree on a solution. Or is this a non-issue since charging port adapters are cheap and easy to make? I believe the different charging formats will continue in parallel, but the Japanese-centric model will fall off.

2. Does the reader think charging networks and the electricity they sell is the new oil? As gas stations and ICE vehicles go extinct and are replaced by electric charging stations worldwide, isn't this reality self-evident? Will we eventually see consolidation in the charging networks as they form new Big Electricity cartels just like Big Oil did? Are the charging networks the new oil or are the upstream energy providers who generate the electricity the new oil providers? When will we see charging companies and BEV manufacturers recognize the need to move upstream in order vertically integrate their business model and insure themselves from electricity inflation?

3. Over the Chinese holiday season on January 26, 2023, Nio owners conducted 60,000 battery swaps in a single day.[772] Does the reader think battery swapping services will continue to grow steadily as we have seen or hit a deployment plateau? Will swapping stations ever surpass charging stations or will they merely run in parallel to one another as they both have different uses? While battery swapping has taken off in China, do you see this same business model working in Europe, North America, Japan and elsewhere? Will battery swapping become a niche market, perhaps getting and maintaining traction only in fleet services like taxicab and long-haul companies?

4. In February 2023, Tesla agreed to open 7,500 superchargers to other BEV fleets by 2024 in a deal with the Biden Administration. However, the government

---

[772] Opletal, Jiri. "Nio surpassed 60,000 battery swaps daily in China." Car News China, Jan 26, 2023.

will pay for any expenses to do so using the $7.5 billion USD made available through the *Bipartisan Infrastructure Law*. Was this a smart move for Tesla and how much do you think they received in subsidies, $500 million USD? What will the impact be on Tesla charging network revenues and profits if their energy dispensing doubles? Does this strengthen or weaken the Tesla brand now that its charging network is no longer proprietary?

5. Does the reader think there needs to be a robust charging infrastructure to encourage BEV adoption and if so, what kind of numbers do we need to make that happen? However, as we saw with Japan, a robust charging network doesn't guarantee BEV adoption if national policies do not encourage it. Is the current pace of charging network acceleration adequate as the CEO of ChargePoint says? What is the charging network like where you live, is it adequate or lacking? How do we solve the lack of adequate charging in apartment building complexes where they can't get home charging? What would your policies look like to solve this challenge?

A battery recycling engineer works through the reclamation process. As there is no standardization among lithium-ion battery manufacturers, to include those used in BEVs, batteries are taken apart by hand before being processed. This is a time-intensive operation. *(by Getty Images)*

One of two Redwood Materials buildings comprising its HQs in Carson City, NV. They are also developing a recycling center in Reno-Tahoe Industrial Park about 45 minutes away. *(by Author)*

Nikola Tesla, working in his laboratory, was originally hired by Thomas Edison to develop an electricity transfer system superior to DC (direct current) technology. Tesla did just that, developing what we know as AC (alternating current). The two would later have a falling out and wage a destructive war against one another over primacy of their competing systems. *(by Getty Images)*

A Tesla Model Y charges at a bank of superchargers. *(by Author)*

CHAPTER 19

Battery Energy Storage Systems

"The issue of great importance shall be to know: what is the capacity of Earth? And what is the charge if it is electrified?" – Nikola Tesla

Battery Energy Storage Systems (BESS)

An often-overlooked aspect of the downstream global lithium value chain is the growing battery energy storage system (BESS) enterprise. Importantly, BESS is needed to operate in conjunction with renewable energy systems like solar power and wind generation. To store unused energy from their intermittent electricity generation, a storage solution is required and BESS is often ideal. BESS is also useful in other ways such as replacing natural gas-powered plants that provide quick response energy to the grid but are extremely expensive to operate.

Peaker plants are a great example, one of many, of how antiquated most the world's national grid systems are. These grids are mostly based on centralized power plants fueled by some form of fossil fuel like coal or natural gas. This power generation model was developed in the late 1800's and became the norm worldwide. Since then, very little has been done to modernize these over-centralized systems whose primary characteristic is high carbon emissions which warm our Earth. Lithium-ion BESS have the potential to dramatically disrupt these existing systems.

In order to grasp the potential magnitude of the coming disruption in established energy markets, we need to understand the size of the total addressable market (TAM) for BESS. One assessment puts the 2022 global BESS market at $4.4 billion

USD in value with a forecast of attaining $15.1 billion in value by 2027.[773] However, estimates vary widely and some assess the present and future BESS market value at more than double that provided above. In the U.S., there was no significant BESS market until 2020. After that, the deployment of BESS increased rapidly to almost 5 gigawatts of storage in 2021 and 30 gigawatts of planned storage to be deployed by 2025.[774]

What does the current grid system look like in the U.S.? In 2020, 4.12 trillion kilowatt hours of electricity was generated in America. 40% of this electricity was generated by natural gas plants, 19% from coal, 1% from petroleum, 20% from nuclear and 20% by renewables. It is this 60% of fossil fuel generated electricity that is steadily being replaced by renewable energy. This is the market segment that will be disrupted the most by the introduction of BESS. However, the 20% market segment powered by renewables also requires the introduction of BESS at scale.[775]

As additional background for understanding the subject, the U.S. has some 7,300 individual power plants of all types that are interconnected by 160,000 miles of high-voltage power lines and millions of miles of low-voltage power lines. These plants and lines provide power to 145 million customers across the country. The national grid is divided into three sections: the Eastern Interconnection, the Western Interconnection and ERCOT (Electric Reliability Council of Texas). Furthermore, there are 66 balancing authorities, most of whom are utilities, which are responsible for managing the regional distribution of electricity.[776]

To set the stage for our first BESS topic, it helps to understand California energy policy. To start, the State of California is pursuing carbon neutrality by 2045 to align with the carbon reduction goals of the Paris Agreement. This means they are cutting carbon emissions across all sectors of their state economy. Part of their pathway ahead is cutting all fossil fuel consumption by 86% which means greening their electrical grid. The subsequent mass deployment of low-carbon wind and solar electricity generation in California requires a similarly massive deployment of BESS to store this energy. At

[773] https://www.marketsandmarkets.com/Market-Reports/battery-energy-storage-system-market-112809494.html

[774] https://www.eia.gov/todayinenergy/detail.php?id=54939

[775] https://www.epa.gov/green-power-markets/us-electricity-grid-markets

[776] https://www.eia.gov/todayinenergy/detail.php?id=27152

the end of 2022, California had 4 GW of lithium-ion BESS with the understanding that they would need 48 GW by 2045.[777]

The Moss Landing BESS

In 2018, Vistra Energy answered California's call for increased battery capacity, winning the project to build a BESS at Moss Landing near Monterey. In a fitting example of how green energy is replacing high-carbon emitting electricity generation in California, the battery is built on site at a decommissioned gas fired power plant. Presently, the Moss Landing battery is the biggest BESS in operation anywhere in the world. The project was begun in 2018 and commissioned in 2021 at a cost of $400 million USD. The battery plant was constructed in two stages involving an initial 300 MW capacity and then an additional 100 MW. The current total battery capacity provides 400 MW/1600 MWh of electricity meaning it can provide 400 MW of electricity for four hours. This can power up to 400,000 homes, depending on their energy usage, during peak energy usage times in the state.[778]

In early 2022, Vistra reached an agreement with PG&E (Pacific Gas and Electric) to provide increased capacity at Moss Landing through a 15-year contract. This Phase III expansion would provide an additional 350MW/1.4 GWh capacity, bringing Vistra's total power generation to 750MW/3 GWh. This additional battery capacity will come online in the summer of 2023. However, Vistra doesn't plan to stop there. If California requests more capacity at the location, Vistra envisions doubling the existing battery footprint to 1.5 GW. Vistra estimates this would power over one million homes. As California has 14.5 million homes according to the U.S. Census Bureau, they would need thirteen more of these BESS projects just to address residential power.[779]

South Korean company LG Chem provided the batteries for Vistra at the landing and have since spun off their battery division as LG Energy Solutions (LGES) in 2020. LGES used their Transportable Rack TR1300 LIB systems with proprietary JH4 energy cells for the project. For the initial Phase 1 of the project, LGES provided 4,500+ TR1300

[777] https://www.energy.ca.gov/news/2022-11/california-energy-commission-approves-31-million-tribal-long-duration-energy

[778] https://www.nsenergybusiness.com/projects/moss-landing/

[779] https://investor.vistracorp.com/2022-01-24-Vistra-Announces-Expansion-of-Worlds-Largest-Battery-Energy-Storage-Facility

battery racks which were then arrayed in an existing building that met required ventilation requirements. It is interesting to note at that time in 2018, that California determined there were no better U.S. or North American options for this BESS project.

Eight years before the start of the Moss Landing project, in 2010, LG Chem Michigan (LGCM) stood up a battery manufacturing plant in Holland, MI to produce battery cells for the Chevy Volt. When the Volt was discontinued, LGCM transitioned to supplying batteries for the newer Chevy Bolt. However, both were under-selling models and would never be substantial moneymakers for LGCM. More importantly, LGCM had an established presence in the U.S., a proven base of operations. LGES saw that the BESS market, both public and residential, was growing in the U.S. and that their primary automotive partner was expanding their BEV lineup. Consequently, in 2022, the renamed LGES announced it would invest $1.7 billion USD to expand its existing Holland plant.

LGES understood that it wouldn't be competitive in the North American BESS market if it continued to rely on a build-in-South Korea-and-ship-overseas business model. This is because domestic BESS manufacturers like Tesla were coming online and the U.S. government was incentivizing an onshore battery supply chain. Thus, LGES' expansion from an estimated 5 GW/year production capacity to a 25 GW/year output allowed them to meet both increased BESS and BEV (like GM's Ultium battery platform) requirements while meeting new U.S. government directed battery sourcing guidelines.

LGES historically built its batteries with a NMC (nickel-manganese-cobalt) chemistry because nickel offers high energy density as does cobalt along with an added measure of stability in the cathode. However, nickel is expensive with extensive environmental concerns. Cobalt is also pricey and has documented child labor risks stemming from extraction operations in the Congo. Consequently, LGES has begun moving away from NMC chemistries in their batteries as have other battery makers like CATL and SVOLT. LGES is developing new LFP (lithium-iron-phosphate) batteries for its residential battery storage units which are less expensive, have fewer branding risks and improved cycle life. There is less of a concern for maximum energy density for long-term battery storage at fixed sites because space isn't as much of an issue as compared to a BEV. These batteries will be made in their Holland, MI manufacturing plant starting in 2024.[780]

---

[780] PV Magazine, by M. Maisch, "LG Energy Solution unveils new battery storage solutions, moves to LFP", May 18, 2022.

Let's transition back to the Moss Landing for an update. California wasn't done growing the site as a major battery hub with just the Vistra/LGES project. In 2022, Tesla brought online a 182.5 MW/730MWh battery at the landing which was coordinated by PG&E. This is commonly referred to as the Elkhorn battery project. This was in line with PG&E's goal of being carbon neutral by 2040 and providing it's 16 million customers with fossil fuel free electricity. To provide this capacity, Tesla installed 256 of its lithium-ion battery Megapacks. Unlike the Vistra Energy BESS, PG&E bought and now owns Tesla's BESS with Tesla providing maintenance through a 20-year contract.[781] Over these two decades, it is estimated PG&E will save its customers $100 million USD in lower electricity costs.[782]

Hornsdale Power Reserve

Far from the coast of California, across the Pacific Ocean, the state of South Australia has been running its big battery at the Hornsdale Power Reserve (HPR) since late 2017. Importantly, growing its BESS capacity is integral to SA's goal to achieve carbon neutrality by 2050. Developing a robust BESS enterprise is crucial in reducing 67% of SA's current carbon footprint. To start, 25% of SA's emissions are from the transportation sector, meaning they need a low carbon grid to power their BEV fleet. 32% of emissions are from the energy sector, another area where large-scale battery deployment is crucial for transitioning off fossil fuel power generation. Finally, 10% of their carbon footprint is from fugitive emissions from fuels which batteries are needed to eliminate: no fossil fuels = no fugitive emissions.[783]

The HPR is owned by Neoen, a French renewable energy company with headquarters in Paris who has 5.4GW of capacity across its various projects. Tesla provided the batteries for the project with an initial capacity of 100MW/129MWh that was later upgraded by Tesla in 2020 with an additional 50MW/64.5MWh for a total of 150MW/193.5MWh. It is interesting to see that LGES' batteries cost California $100

[781] Teslarati, by S. Alvarez, "Tesla's giant Moss Landing Megapack battery storage project: How is it doing now?", March 23, 2022.

[782] Monterey Herald, by G. Wheeler, "Energy storage in Moss Landing: A smoky challenge to a new chapter", June 12, 2022.

[783] https://www.environment.sa.gov.au/topics/climate-change/south-australias-greenhouse-gas-emissions

million USD per 100MW of capacity while Neoen paid just $63 million USD ($90 million AUD) for its initial 100MW capacity from Tesla.[784]

Of note, Neoen intentionally paired the HPR battery with their adjacent Hornsdale Windfarm project that came online in 2017. The windfarm consists of 99 wind turbines with a 316MW capacity producing up to 1 terawatt over the course of the year, enough to power 225,000 homes.[785] The initial 32 wind turbines were Siemens SWT-3.2-113 Direct Drive model wind turbines that don't use a gearbox in order simplify the turbine and reduce long-term maintenance costs.[786] Siemens provided the windfarm with generator step-up (GSU) transformers that step up the stored energy at a local substation from 33kV to 275kV to enter the grid.[787]

A point of discussion between fossil fuel advocates and clean energy proponents is that only fossil fuel power plants can provide inertia (balance in the grid between supply and demand) to a grid. Specifically, the idea has been pushed that only spinning turbines that have physical mass, and powered by fossil fuels of course, can provide grid inertia. This is simply not true as the HPR has proven. The South Australian grid requires six GW-seconds to maintain the needed inertia.[788] This becomes a simple math equation of providing enough virtual inertia from a battery to stabilize the grid. The HPR currently uses Tesla's Virtual Machine Mode (VMM) to provide this virtual inertia. Tesla's VMM is just one of several programs offered from their Energy Software suite. Tesla's VMM is integrated with their grid-scale batteries or Megapacks which have bult-in inverters that control the voltage from the batteries to the grid.

This comes into play with Frequency Control Ancillary Services (FCAS), a system within the National Energy Market which works to maintain the grid at a constant frequency of 50Hz. Power to the grid must be constantly adjusted to keep the frequency within the Normal Operating Frequency Band of 49.85Hz-50.15Hz. Power demand and supply is kept within the band and as close to 50 Hz as possible to keep the grid

[784] Renew Economy, by G. Parkinson, "Revealed: True cost of Tesla big battery, and its government contract", Sept 21, 2018.

[785] https://hornsdalewindfarm.com.au/our-wind-farm/#helping-climate

[786] https://www.power-technology.com/projects/hornsdale-wind-farm-jamestown/

[787] https://www.siemens-energy.com/global/en/offerings/references/transformer-for-largest-storage-battery.html

[788] https://hornsdalepowerreserve.com.au/learn/

stable and avoid blackouts. The HPR using Tesla batteries has a significant advantage over fossil fuel powered systems because they can respond in milliseconds and provide precise amounts of energy.

Most importantly, the HPR can provide their energy services much cheaper than their fossil fuel competition. In 2018, the HPR saved Australian consumers $26 million USD. In 2019, it saved consumers $75 million USD. In one incident, when immediate power for the grid was required over a five-hour period, HPR saved consumers $9.8 million USD. The HPR has provided energy at prices as low as $176.00 USD/MW as opposed to fossil fuel generators costing as much as $9,000.00 USD/MW.[789]

However, the HPR has hit some speedbumps along the way as it matures as a power source. During a four-month period in 2019, the HPR failed to provide the FCAS services it had promised to the Australian Energy Market Operator (AEMO). This was an unintentional failure on the part of HPR involving a firmware update from Tesla. Regardless, the Australian Energy Regulator sued Neoen resulting in $900,00.00 in fines. Also, Neoen paid back AEMO $3.3 million in contract fees for the services it did not provide. [790]

In 2020, Neoen's energy storage segment raised $20.87 Million USD, a significant increase over their 2019 storage segment revenue of $10 million USD.[791] The increase in revenue was mainly due to the Hornsdale battery expansion and its associated energy sales. Specifically, most of the company's energy segment revenues were due to successful energy distribution related to frequency control services. However, Neoen recognized there was a growing profit to be made in energy arbitrage. This is where the HPR stored cheap energy saved during the day and then sold it back to the market, usually in the evening, at higher prices.

Total Neoen storage segment revenue increased only 5% in 2021 as compared to 2020, despite the HPR running at increase capacity and new battery projects coming online in Finland and Victoria, Australia. However, the reason for this relatively small increase was because the HPR had done so well in 2020 with non-recurring gains that could not be repeated in 2021. Specifically, in Q1 2020 a tornado severed the

[789] Teslarati, by R. Suba, "Tesla "big battery" in Australia is becoming a bigger nightmare for fossil fuel power generators", Feb 28, 2020.

[790] PV Magazine, D. Carroll, "Tesla big battery operator fined for power rules breach", June 30, 2022.

[791] Neoen 2020 Annual Statement.

Heywood Interconnector, the power lines connecting the South Australian grid to the Victorian grid. This meant that the HPR battery worked overtime to provide FCAS power generation, bringing in a lot of unexpected revenues.

In the first half of 2022, Neoen's battery storage operations in Australia brought in $34.6 million USD of revenues. This includes revenues from the HPR, their 300MW/450MWh Victorian Big Battery (Tesla Megapacks), their 20MW/34MWh battery (Tesla Megapacks) in the Bulgana Green Power Hub also in Victoria and the Western Downs battery (Tesla Megapacks) in Queensland. Neoen also began developing their 100MW/200MWh Capital Battery project in Canberra in Q4 2022 and their Blyth West 200MW/400MWh battery in South Australia in Q1 2023.[792]

For the full year 2022, 18% of Neoen's revenue came from their global BESS projects and 43% of overall revenue came from their combined operations in Australia. Thus, $99.8 million USD came from their energy storage efforts out of $548 million USD total revenue for the year. This was a 2.7 times increase in storage project revenue as compared to 2021. Neoen has a future 40 MW/40 MWh BESS project in the works at the Storen Power Reserve in Sweden with an operational date of 2024 and an 8 MW/8 MWh storage project in Antugnac, France with a ready date of 2024.[793]

China's Dalian Vanadian Redox Flow Battery (VRFB)

Dalian Rongke Power took a different technological approach to energy storage and instead of pursuing a lithium-ion model, they stood up a vanadium redox flow battery. Unlike a LIB, a flow battery has two different tanks that circulate electrolytic liquids that are pumped pass a membrane positioned between two electrodes. Flow batteries haven't achieved the same level of adoption as lithium-ion ones because they have lower energy density and lower energy efficiency. However, VRFBs have the advantage of being safer to run, have a lower carbon footprint, lower lifetime costs and are expected to run at full efficiency for at least 20 years.

The Dalian VRFB was initially designed for a 100MW/400MWh capacity with plans to double this sometime in the future. The battery came online on October 30, 2022, and is now connected to the grid. This first 100MW phase cost $266 million USD which is much higher than the Moss Landing battery at $100 million USD per

---

[792] Neoen, Half-Yearly Financial Report, June 30, 2022.

[793] Neoen, Full-Year 2022 Results, March 1, 2023.

100MW.[794] While VRFBs may be more cost efficient over time, most customers would probably balk at the 166% up front price difference.

Vanadium is relatively plentiful and is usually collected as a coproduct from steel slag. China produces 70% of the world vanadium supply and is thus a byproduct of their large steel production enterprise. Vanadium pentoxide is used in making electrolyte solutions for VRFBs and is sold by the pound and the ton. At the end of March 2023, vanadium pentoxide 98% flake sold for $19,937.42 USD in the China market.[795] Obviously, an unusually high price point for vanadium will increase the costs of any associated redox batteries. Since vanadium is used mainly in steel alloy production and only 2% is used for VRFBs, its use in steel drives its market price.[796]

In 2022, approximately 100,000 metric tons of contained vanadium was extracted worldwide. Only four countries dominated production: China 70,000 with tons, Russia 17,000 tons, South Africa 9,100 tons and Brazil 6,200 tons. There is an estimated 26 million tons of vanadium reserves on our planet. For the North American market, there are no efficient options with short supply chains; the best choice is most likely Brazil and then South Africa. The same can be said for Europe as their only efficient option is Russia which comes with its own problems as we have seen with Russia's invasion of Ukraine in 2022. As with other problem minerals, substitution is an option, and one could consider replacing vanadium with nickel in flow batteries.[797]

Since the price of vanadium pentoxide per ton is much cheaper than lithium, Chinese VRFB manufacturers can drop their overall costs if they scale up. Also, China's National Energy Administration banned the use of lithium-ion ternary batteries for medium and large-scale storage solutions in June 2022 due to fire hazard concerns. Obviously, this ban will give a boost to LFP BESS who already own 51% of the Chinese storage market.[798] This also gives a boost to VRFB storage solutions since they are more stable and less prone to fires.

---

[794] Santos, Beatriz. "China connects world's largest redox flow battery system to grid". PV Magazine, Sept 29, 2022.

[795] https://www.metal.com/Other-Minor-Metals/202110220002

[796] https://www.bushveldminerals.com/about-vanadium/

[797] U.S. Geological Survey, Mineral Commodity Summaries (Vanadium), January 2023.

[798] "Ternary lithium battery cannot be used in battery storage power system". takomabattery. com, July 2, 2022.

From a strategic lithium conservation perspective, China can use vanadium as a substitute in BESS projects to preserve much more expensive and scarce lithium for EV batteries. In fact, vanadium can be defined as a critical mineral specifically for strategic substitution purposes. As China shifts its critical mineral supply chains away from vulnerable foreign sourcing, vanadium is one area that they can onshore their industry to achieve independence.

The Chinese steel industry already sees the long-term economic potential in VRFBs and is investing in this downstream opportunity. The Panzhihua Iron and Steel Group (PISG) is the largest vanadium producer in China and accounts for an estimated 15% of world vanadium products. In October 2022, PISG and Dalian created a JV named Sichuan Vanadium Rong Energy Storage dedicated to the production of vanadium battery electrolyte solutions for the VRFB industry. This joint project aims to meet the forecasted demand of 290,000 tpa of vanadium pentoxide by 2030.[799] At $20,000.00 USD per ton, that is a $5.8 billion USD market. We will need to keep our eye on this space to see how VRFBs develop moving forward.

Residential Batteries

The BESS market goes beyond utility scale energy storage and is expanding into the residential sector at an accelerated pace. One research company estimated the size of the global residential battery market in 2021 at $9.87 billion USD with it forecasted to grow to $27.8 billion USD by 2030.[800] Another estimated the size of the global residential battery market in 2022 at $7.3 billion USD with a prediction that it would double to over $15 billion USD by 2027.[801] I have seen a dozen different reports all with different estimates, some of them wildly so. Consequently, I have concluded that no one has the complete data to know how big the market is. I will hazard my own guess that this is a multi-trillion-dollar market with well under 1% of penetration to date. The opportunity is massive.

---

[799] Vanadium-titanium share research report: With the wave of energy storage, "titanium" is no longer "vanadium". Min.news, March 23, 2023.

[800] https://www.globenewswire.com/en/news-release/2022/10/10/2530898/0/en/Global-Residential-Battery-Market-Size-to-grow-27-8-Billion-by-2030.html

[801] https://www.thebusinessresearchcompany.com/report/residential-battery-global-market-report

The goal for the residential battery business is maximum penetration of the TAM (Total Addressable Market). In the U.S. alone, that is 142 million residences. If each home buys an $8,000.00 USD battery, that is $1.1 trillion USD. Canada has an estimated 15 million homes[802] and Mexico more than 31 million[803] – another $368 billion potential for the North American TAM. In the European Union there are an estimated 197 million households, which equates to a potential $1.5 trillion TAM.[804] Most estimates put total global residences at more than 2 billion homes.[805] If each residence spends $5,000.00 USD for a home battery, that is $10 trillion USD. Of course, not every home will purchase a battery, nor can they afford to, but this gives an idea as to the size of the TAM the industry seeks to penetrate.

Without a doubt, Tesla understands this data as does their Tesla Energy division specializing in both residential and utility scale BESS. Tesla Energy also works in the smart grid space, but we'll address just their battery business in this section. For residential BESS, Tesla manufactures their Powerwall that is designed for homeowners and small businesses who desire secondary power generation during emergencies like a power outage. Powerwall is very much in line with Tesla's intent of reducing global carbon emissions and advancing individual energy independence and resilience.

To begin, their standard lithium-ion Powerwall has a 13.5 kWh capacity, weighs 310 pounds, and are designed to connect up to ten of them together in tandem. A single Powerwall starts at around $10,500.00 USD but if you purchase two, they are $8,500.00 USD apiece. As a cost comparison, 1.35MW of Powerwalls from Tesla costs $850,000.00 USD while the same 1.35MW Vistra Energy bought from LGES cost them $1.35 million USD – quite the pricing disparity. In the U.S. as of 2023, a Powerwall also qualifies for a 30% federal solar tax credit that brings the price of a single unit down to $7,350.00 USD. However, to get the discount your Powerwall must be 100% charged from solar panels.[806]

[802] https://www.globaldata.com/data-insights/macroeconomic/number-of-households-in-canada-2096147/

[803] https://www.statista.com/statistics/877252/number-households-mexico-housing-type/

[804] https://ec.europa.eu/eurostat/statistics-explained/index.php?title=Household_composition_statistics

[805] Architecture & Design, "How many houses are in the world?", Nov 11, 2021.

[806] EcoWatch, L. David, "How Much Does the Tesla Powerwall Cost?", Jan 13, 2023.

Tesla Powerwalls were first manufactured in low production volumes in 2015 out of their Giga Nevada factory. Over time, Tesla continued to perfect their processes and increase volumes. In Q2 2022, Tesla produced 37,600 Powerwalls with the understanding that they would continue to ramp up production further moving forward.[807] At the end of Q2 2022, they had achieved a 6,500 weekly run rate of Powerwall units.[808] If they can sustain that production tempo, they have the installed capacity to produce 338,000 Powerwall units annually. As we mentioned earlier, California alone has some 14.5 million individual homes, meaning there is a large addressable market for Tesla and the overall residential battery business to fill. For Tesla, or any manufacturer, to make a significant impact in this space, I would like to see them make and sell 1 million units annually and then double it. And then triple it.

The residential BESS sector is competitive and Tesla is not the only show in town. As with the charging sector, the technological and financial barriers for initial residential BESS entry is low. As discussed, LGES has been making excellent residential BESS units in the U.S for several years now. In Europe, Siemens Energy stood up a residential power division in 2019 and has since partnered with Northvolt for battery acquisition. Arch-rival BYD, with their well-developed battery mineral supply chain reaching back to 1995, sells their modular Battery-Box design with cobalt-free lithium-iron-phosphate (LFP) chemistry. Also, the leading BEV battery maker in the world, CATL, began moving into the BESS sector several years ago with their own lithium-iron-phosphate (LFP) products. While LFP batteries have lower energy density than LIB storage solutions, space isn't much of a concern with residential and commercial storage solutions. I expect LFP battery chemistry to eventually dominate the BESS market.

Smart Grids are the Future

Our dumb, dirty, and decrepit energy grids date back to the early 1880's when Thomas Edison made the first practical system that dispensed electricity to local consumers in Manhattan. While a miracle of modern technology at the time, our grids have become a symbol of man's high carbon, technological backwardness. Our original grids were based on an overcentralized model powered by polluting fossil fuels. Since then, this

---

[807] Inside EVs, by S. Loveday, "Tesla Cranking Out 6,500 Powerwalls, 9K Battery Packs A Week In Nevada", Sep 12, 2022.

[808] Ibid.

140-year-old model has received only slight incremental modifications that have done nothing to change the original character of the system that Edison set in motion. It is long past the time for radical change.

The pressing need to decarbonize our societies, accompanied by a growing global lithium economy, has spawned new ideas to overhaul our antiquated fossil fuel grids. The current accelerating trend is to replace fossil fuel power generation with the mass deployment of low carbon means such as solar and wind. Along with this is the idea that our grids should be increasingly decentralized and much less reliant on the old, centralized hubs of power generation. Additionally, these modern grids understand the need to be interconnected with a diverse ecosystem of power dispensing systems that are intelligently managed.

How big is this old beast that modern smart grids are steadily slaying? In 2022, the U.S. alone had a 1.2 terawatt power generation capacity. Natural gas provided 44% of this capacity, coal 18.5% and low carbon generation 30%.[809] This means about 63% of the U.S. power generation capacity remains to be disrupted by green energy alternatives. In 2021, revenues from electric companies totaled $424 billion USD. Going into 2022, the total market cap for investor-owned U.S. power companies surpassed $1 trillion USD.[810]

One of the key components of the smart grid is decentralized power generation. The idea is that every residence, every business, every building, and every structure that has a roof can and should have solar panels installed. The concept is that every individual residence becomes its own individual utility, its own source of independent power generation. This concept blows up the Edison model of centralized power generation where the individual customer purchases electricity from the large utility. With the individual model, the homeowner provides all or most of their own power and the old, centralized power source acts as a strategic backup to be used sparingly and only in emergencies.

The potential for disruption in the U.S. residential solar market is significant. In 2020, only 3.7% of homes had residential solar (out of an estimated 142 million households) and only 1.6% of commercial buildings (out of 5.9 million estimated

---

[809] American Public Power Association, by P. Zummo, "America's Electricity Generation Capacity", March 2022.

[810] https://www.eei.org/en/resources-and-media/industry-data

structures).[811, 812] A study by NREL (National Renewable Energy Laboratory) determined that there was more than 8 billion square meters of available roof space in the U.S. that could provide 1 terawatt of energy.[813] In some states, there is enough roof space and regular sunshine to power the needs of their entire population.

Importantly, for mass residential solar adoption to take place, prices must come way down. The data shows that the higher a homeowner's income, the higher the associated solar adoption rate. Similarly, the lower the household income, the lower the associated adoption rate. For example, I received an estimate on our house to install solar at $100,000.00 minus a 30% federal tax incentive which came out to a total of $70,000.00. Uhm, no, that isn't going to work when my electric bill is only $250.00 USD a month. It would take me 23 years to pay off the installation costs.

But there are several ways to skin this cat. One way is for a local utility to put their solar panels (that they own) on a residential roof. This provides the utility with instant access to the space they need and, in return, they provide the homeowner a discount on their monthly electric bill for doing so. Another method of implementing the same concept is through a shared solar project. With this model, a group of homeowners agree to have solar panels installed on their roofs by a third-party business who manages the overall operation. But in this case, the third-party doesn't have sole ownership of the solar panels nor the electricity produced. There can be any number of arrangements between the homeowners and third-party such as cost sharing, profit sharing, and rent-to-own options.

Regardless, let's imagine that we have solar panels on our roof as one part of the equation. Next, to continue building out our smart grid, we need a residential BESS unit installed which is far less expensive than the solar system. The solar panels from our roof provide energy during the day that we can use immediately. Also, the solar panels send energy that we don't use to our battery for use at night and long-term storage. We can stack as many batteries as we want depending on how much they cost and how much energy we want in reserve. If we still have excess solar, we sell this back to the utility for a profit.

---

[811] PV Magazine, by R. Kennedy, "Nearly 4% of U.S. homes have solar panels installed," Oct 28, 2022.

[812] https://www.eia.gov/todayinenergy/detail.php?id=46118

[813] https://www.energy.gov/eere/solar/solar-rooftop-potential

Now let's add to this system a BEV where our solar system charges our car as it is plugged-in inside our garage or carport. Importantly, our car becomes part of our energy management system where, when required, we can draw power from our car battery to power our house. This concept is called V2G (Vehicle to Grid), V2H (Vehicle to Home) or V2B (Vehicle to Building). However, a car must have the technology to participate in bidirectional charging – Teslas do not. Ironically, Nissan has long manufactured its cars with the ability to participate in V2G charging when plugged into a purpose-built V2G charger. Moving forward, a car without the ability to participate in a V2G smart energy system is at a value disadvantage to those that can.

Ingrained in the smart house energy system, also referred to as a Virtual Power Plant (VPP), is the ability and intent of selling energy back to the larger grid at a profit. For example, a house would store energy during the day in its home BESS and BEV and then sell it back to the grid in the evening when electricity was sold at higher prices. Therefore, a home would act like a miniature battery powered peaker plant that can store and sell energy at rates cheaper than traditional fossil fuel powered ones. This works well while smart grids are growing and disrupting the existing fossil fuel powered grids, but profit margins will become tighter when everyone adopts the technology.

Now that we understand how a smart house works, let's image this system implemented at a national scale with 150 million structures in the U.S. all outfitted with solar panels and batteries. Then include a national fleet of 200 million BEVs connected via home and public V2G charging outlets. 150 million structures each with a 15kW battery provides 2.25 terawatts of capacity. 200 million BEVs each with a 70 kW battery provides another 14 terawatts of capacity. With this much capacity sharing electricity with the grid as required, there are no grid stability problems. If California had this implemented at the State level in the summer of 2022, they would not have had to implement rolling blackouts due to overdemand during peak hours.

Smart Grids in Action

As I write this, VPPs and intelligent grids are still very much in their infancy with no systems operating at any sort of meaningful scale at the present. This leaves a lot of unanswered questions that will only be answered once these concepts achieve mass adoption. However, we do have examples at much smaller scale of how smart grids play out. If you have solar panels or a solar roof, a residential BESS, a BEV powered by your home utility and sell excess energy back to your established local utility, then you already know the fundamentals of a residential VPP. Now, let's look at some larger examples.

Let's deal with the 800-pound gorilla in the room first: Tesla Energy. They are magnitudes further along than their peers in pursuing smart grid systems. As we mentioned before, California has suffered from under capacity in its grid. As a response to that, California residents with solar panels and a Tesla Powerwall can participate in a VPP pilot program sponsored by PG&E and Tesla. This VPP program supports a joint Emergency Load Reduction Program (ELRP), a five-year pilot program that began in 2021. In that first year, PG&E achieved 150MW of VPP capacity able to respond to a short-notice grid demand.[814]

Participating Powerwall owners received $1.00 USD per kWh and up to $10.00 USD per event that discharged their electricity to the grid. This was not a lot of money, but it illustrates the idea that homeowners can be part of an interactive grid and earn money by doing so. Tesla Powerwall owners determine how much energy they are willing to reserve for an event through their Tesla app. In 2021, Tesla forecasted participating VPP members would provide at least 20kWh throughout the year. At the end of the year, PG&E would calculate the amount of energy dispensed by each VPP member and Tesla would then pay out the money due.[815]

By Q3 2022 Tesla had over 4,600 VPP participants supporting the grid. There are approximately 50,000 Powerwall owners in California whom Tesla would ultimately like to have participate, but they must provide better incentives to capture them. In 2022, VPP participants received $2.00 USD per kWh discharged per event with no limit for total amount of energy provided. During a three-week period before and after Labor Day weekend there were ten separate events where PG&E requested assistance to stabilize the grid. During those events, Tesla VPP participants contributed a total of 287MW to the grid.[816]

Across the country from California, in New England, Vermont has a relatively

[814] Business Wire, "25,000 PG&E and Tesla Customers Invited to Form World's Largest Distributed Battery to Support Electric Grid Reliability", July 07, 2022.
[815] https://www.tesla.com/support/energy/powerwall/own/tesla-pge-virtual-power-plant-pilot
[816] https://www.tesla.com/support/energy/tesla-virtual-power-plant-pge#2022-performance

green grid and buys a lot of hydroelectricity from neighboring Quebec. However, a continuing concern is grid disruption due to extreme weather events. In response, Green Mountain Power in Vermont has been building out their own VPP system since 2017 to enhance grid stability and resilience. By the summer of 2022, they had over 4,000 Powerwalls online and supporting the grid in case of emergency events. According to their calculations Green Mountain Power saved customers $3 million USD in 2021 through use of their decentralized VPP network and $1.5 million USD on a single event in 2022.[817]

Texas too has suffered from extreme weather events such as severe snow/ice events (February 2021) and heat waves (July 2022) that have crippled their grid for a variety of reasons. Their centralized fossil fuel model is neither resilient nor intelligent and Tesla knows this. In Texas, we see Tesla going far beyond being just a partner teaming up with an existing utility. In 2021, Texas Energy Ventures LLC filed an application to become a retail energy provider (REP) in the state of Texas, which was approved that same year. The Texas energy infrastructure, like every U.S. state grid, is ripe for disruption by a low-carbon smart grid.

Most of the energy distribution in Texas is coordinated by ERCOT (Energy Reliability Council of Texas) who manages the input of private companies operating in this deregulated sector. ERCOT has a big task: handling energy for 26 million people, providing oversight of 680 power generating plants (including coal, natural gas, nuclear, solar and wind) and coordinating the sale of electricity from 494 separate power generation companies.[818] The Texas energy market is large, complicated, and competitive. However, they all operate from the same basic business model implemented by Thomas Edison in 1882.

In order to blow up this existing business model, Tesla is building out a clean energy VPP that looks much different than the current players in the market. Like they did in both California and Texas, Tesla is selling their Powerwall and solar roof/solar panel packages to build out their VPP. Tesla participants opt in and get credit towards their electric bill when selling stored energy to the grid, specifically, when energy market prices are high and Tesla can sell their cheap solar energy at maximum profit. Tesla

---

[817] Tesmanian, by E. Fox, "Green Mountain Power Has VPP Consisting of 4,000+ Tesla Powerwalls in Vermont", Aug 22, 2022.

[818] https://quickelectricity.com/texas-electricity-explained/

makes profits when there are extreme price disparities in the energy markets like when Texas was selling electricity for $9,000.00 USD a MW in 2021.[819]

Let's be clear here about moving forward with Tesla's VPP model. They can't simply build solar farms and largescale BESS and be competitive as an energy provider – everyone is doing that. They need to lower the costs of their solar roofs/panels and residential Powerwall to the point where mass adoption takes place. If the incentives aren't there, it will never happen. Also, they need to make a concerted effort to get in the V2G game as just one of their Tesla BEVs has the same energy capacity as five Powerwalls. They are leaving a lot of capacity on the table by excluding that part of the VPP market.

To have a truly different energy business model, Tesla needs a million customers with solar roofs/panels, Powerwalls and V2G BEVs all connected to the larger grid. They must get to the point where their million separate households collectively become their power generation and they don't require separate solar farms and battery plants. They also must reach the point where they aren't just gaming the grid with its price disparities and are providing fundamentally cheaper low-carbon electricity in a reliable and resilient manner. Tesla needs their entire lithium battery and energy enterprise working together in an overlapping ecosystem at scale – that's what will differentiate themselves from their competitors.

Vehicle 2 Grid Is Creeping Forward

The VPP model and associated battery peaker plant disruption is moving at a fast pace compared to ongoing V2G implementation. At present, there are no V2G operations going on at scale and the concept is merely in the early pilot phase. However, for the lithium economy to expand and reach full potential, this must change. There are approximately 1.4 billion cars on the plant – that is the TAM V2G businesses must pursue.[820] If all these cars eventually become BEV models with a modest 60KW battery each, we are staring at an 84-terawatt capacity, a number the casual energy student probably cannot comprehend. That's a lot of lithium cheese to leave on the table.

Since 2020, Nissan has been advancing their V2G concept even though themselves, as a BEV company, lag far behind the competition. For example, Nissan participated in

---

[819] Reuters, "Texas cuts $9,000 power price cap after February freeze", Dec 3, 2021.

[820] https://hedgescompany.com/blog/2021/06/how-many-cars-are-there-in-the-world/

a one-year British Electric Nation project where Nissan BEV owners plugged their cars into 100 separate V2G bi-directional chargers. The project was sponsored by Western Power Distribution in partnership with CrowdCharge, a low-carbon emissions company. The purpose of this now completed trial was to show that BEV owners were willing to charge their vehicles at low-peak hours and then discharge their stored energy during high-peak hours like the established energy arbitrage model Tesla's VPP uses.[821]

Like residential BESS, the trial showed that users can save costs on their electricity bills using the V2G model. Nissan Leafs were chosen for the trial because their CHAdeMO charging technology allowed bi-direction energy exchanges. One of their findings was that V2G could have profound implications for fleet services. Just think of a fleet of taxis, police cars, town vehicles or buses. If 20% of them are plugged in at any one time, they can establish a continual grid balancing system. Also, if there are enough vehicles in the fleet sitting static at home station, one may no longer need a static BESS because the BEV fleet has become a mobile BESS. It's redundant.

Ridesharing company Revel out of Brooklyn thought the same thing as they instituted a V2G operation in 2022 along with NineDot Energy and Fermata Energy. While Revel is known for offering up an all-electric fleet of Teslas, they use Nissan Leafs (Tesla is missing out on this opportunity) for their three V2G bi-directional charging stations provided by Fermata. These vehicles are connected to the NYC grid through an agreement with Con Ed (Consolidated Edison, a power provider and a descendent of one of Thomas Edison's original companies). From 2 pm-6 pm, Revel and partners provide support to the grid at peak hours at the highest prices.[822]

While this pilot program is microscopic, let's not be held back conceptually. Instead, let's look at the art of the possible and where future trends will bring us. Out of 3.1 million total households in New York City, 1.4 million have provided data that they own a vehicle of some type.[823] This is the TAM to be attacked. Moving forward, BEV companies want these residents to own 1.4 million of their products. Similarly, established power companies and innovative pseudo-power companies like Revel want

[821] https://electricnation.org.uk/2022/06/21/home-energy-bills-reduced-by-vehicle-to-grid-project/

[822] https://fermataenergy.com/article/revel-fermata-energy-ninedot-energy-launch-first-v2g-system-on-nycs-grid

[823] https://edc.nyc/article/new-yorkers-and-their-cars

these 1.4 million vehicles to have an installed V2G capability. If they each have a 60kW battery, that equals 84GW of capacity for potential grid services. If NYC's entire private and government fleets are BEVs with a V2G capability, the city doesn't have a grid stability problem. The city's real challenge becomes providing this BEV/V2G mobile battery enterprise with clean renewable energy to charge from.

Final Thoughts

Our dumb, dirty, decrepit power grids are slowly becoming greener as ancient dinosaurs like coal plants go extinct. Admittedly, on a global scale, this is an uneven process. Most people, like me, want a clean grid as soon as possible. We have seen with various large scale BESS projects in this chapter that batteries play a crucial piece in this ongoing transition. Batteries can replace inefficient gas peaker plants, provide grid inertia and stability while storing vast quantities of energy from intermittent sources like solar and wind. While other kinds of battery chemistries certainly have potential, presently, it is the LIB that makes this all possible.

Not only do grids need to become cleaner faster, but they also need to become intelligent as well. Large, centralized power generating models are inefficient relics prone to disruption. The democratization of electricity generation as networked across millions of household roofs and managed by purpose-built software is the way ahead. Mass adoption will remain elusive until incentives go up and prices go down. The companies that recognize this now and proceed forward as first-movers will benefit the most. Likewise, the future fleets of BEVs driving all around us will collectively become the world's largest mobile battery enterprise. This dynamic army of batteries-on-wheels will store more useable energy than humanity has encountered in any other format to date. This, too, will be made possible by the lithium-ion battery.

1. What rate of penetration does the reader expect to see moving forward reference BESS as they replace existing fossil fuel power generation facilities like peaker plants? Will it continue to be a slow grind or will it accelerate at some point? If so, what causes mass adoption? Is it merely better pricing and improved technology or is there a conceptual or even a political tipping point?

2. What is the reader's opinion on using low-charge EV batteries in BESS as a second life market? While EV batteries require more energy density to move relatively heavy vehicles, they can still perform many more years of service

as static energy providers. Is it cost effective to do so? What pathways do we have to develop now to grow the space?

3. When will the LIB lose its dominance in the BESS market? Will vanadium batteries continue to grow in popularity and eventually push out LIB models as they are more cost effective over time? When will sodium-ion batteries achieve technological maturity in the BESS space? What are the strategic implications of the democratization of BESS using cheap and plentiful minerals available to most anyone?

4. While smart grids and VPPs are still very much in their very early stages, does the reader see these intelligent energy management systems taking off in the near future? Will the existing traditional utility companies pursue intelligent management technology on their own or will this necessary change have to come from the outside through a forcing function?

CHAPTER 20

Global Value Chain Disruption

"COVID-19 could have a significant negative impact on our revenue, profit and business if it affects the markets in which we operate, our customers or our suppliers." – SQM Annual Sustainability Report, 2020

COVID-19 as Lithium Value Chain Disruptor

The global LIB industry is prone to disruption in a variety of ways, none of which are unique to the battery minerals space. There are different levels of disruption depending on the circumstances: global, regional, and local. Disruption can be broad or narrow, planned, or unexpected, temporary, or permanent. We have seen several examples of disruption in the lithium enterprise since the end of WW II (hydrogen bomb programs, Rhodesia sanctions, government post-stockpiling dumping, overproduction & soft prices) so history should serve to teach us about future possibilities. However, the world had not experienced a global pandemic in recent memory with such profound economic effects. It is therefore useful for us to learn from this experience to be better prepared for similar future events.

The COVID-19 pandemic of 2020-2022 disrupted the global lithium enterprise in many ways. Mainly, it served to suppress production in the lithium value chain, limiting the growth of lithium, batteries and BEVs to modest gains. Production at many levels of the value chain was slowed down and/or temporarily halted which delayed production, deliveries, and increased costs. While the lithium enterprise was disrupted, it did not shut down because industry-wide adaptations evolved to overcome pandemic challenges and meet continuing demand. Let's see what this looked like across the key industries.

Chilean lithium miner SQM estimated that the world produced some 307,000 tons of LCE in 2019, increasing slightly to 330,000 tons in 2020 and then growing significantly to 500,000 tons in 2021.[824] Thus, world lithium production increased just 7.5% in 2020 as the pandemic surged and government countermeasures were at its height. The following year, in 2021, when many COVID restrictions were relaxed or lifted, production increased 52% from its 2020 levels. In 2022, world LCE production reached 689,000 tons. We can conclude that the disruption in global lithium extraction was significant but temporary.

Various elements of the global lithium enterprise were affected differently depending on their own unique situations. For example, the state of Nevada deemed mining an "Essential Business" in April 2020.[825] This meant Albemarle's lithium brine operations remained open, but employees had to follow appropriate health measures like masking and social distancing. SQM in Chile also remained open and pursued comprehensive mitigation measures like rapid tests, quarantines and limiting travel for employees. SQM sold 45,100 tons of LCE in 2019, increasing to 64,600 tons in 2020 and then skyrocketing to 101,100 tons in 2021.[826] There was no obvious negative impact to SQM's production stemming from the pandemic.

However, non-productive lithium operations did face closures. For instance, development of Lithium Americas' brine project in Argentina was put on hold several times in 2020 to comply with national COVID health guidance.[827] As of March 2023, their Jujuy brine operation, a JV with Ganfeng Lithium, was still not up and running. Similarly, Bacanora Lithium put their pilot plant in Sonora, Mexico on hold for several months in 2020 in accordance with Mexico's health guidance.[828] Bacanora was subsequently bought by Ganfeng Lithium and their Sonoran project remains under development. The delays due to COVID pushed these companies' eventual openings to the right by several months but did not interrupt any ongoing production.

While global lithium production was suppressed to a degree, how did this impact

---

[824] SQM Annual Report 2019, 2020, 2021.

[825] Nevada Health Response, "Gov. Sisolak Guidance: Directive 003 – Essential Businesses", updated 4/16/2020.

[826] SQM Annual Reports 2019, 2020, 2021

[827] Mining.com, by C. Jamasmie, "Lithium Americas to restart Argentina project", Aug 17, 2020.

[828] Bacanora Lithium, "Sonora Lithium Project and Covid-19 Update", May 28, 2020.

global battery production? SNE Research estimated that 118 GWh of battery storage was produced in 2019, increasing to 147 GWh in 2020 and then exploding to 297 GWh in 2021.[829] This 25% increase in 2020 indicates that there was enough "slack" in the global lithium supply chain before 2020 that the pandemic didn't significantly impact downstream LIB production. This slack took the form of bags of previously refined lithium sitting stacked in environmentally controlled warehouses around the globe waiting to be shipped when purchased by battery companies. One can guess that battery production would have been higher in 2020 without the pandemic, but growth was still significant.

In one example, Tesla and Panasonic's joint effort at Giga Nevada was disrupted for several months in 2020 with Tesla temporarily laying off 75% of its employees and Panasonic pulling out its entire workforce for a two-week period.[830] At one point in the summer of 2020, despite implementing comprehensive health guidance, Tesla had the most recorded cases of COVID by any single business in the county with 117.[831] However, manufacturing plants like Giga Nevada (as was mining) were deemed as an "Essential Business" by the Governor of Nevada so they weren't subject to long-term closures like bars and brothels.

What was the result? Tesla Energy, who makes Powerwalls and Megapacks, earned revenues of $1.5 billion USD in 2019, $1.99 billion USD in 2020 and $2.78 billion USD in 2021.[832] They clearly weren't impacted much by the pandemic. Panasonic Energy, who does 90% of its battery business with Tesla, produced 28.8 GWh of batteries in 2019, just 27 GWh in 2020 and then 36.1 GWh in 2021.[833] While Panasonic was negatively impacted with a 6% production dip in 2020, Tesla replaced this potential loss with increased battery production from LG Chem. Overall, Tesla weathered the storm in 2020 by benefiting from relationships with two strong battery sources.

If battery production increased, then we would expect to see the same reflected

[829] SNE Research, https://www.sneresearch.com/kr/home/

[830] Tech Crunch, by K. Korosec, "Tesla partner Panasonic is shutting down its operations at Nevada gigafactory", March 20, 2020.

[831] Reno Gazette Journal, by A. Damon & S. McAndrew, "Tesla Gigafactory tops list of workplaces with most Washoe County coronavirus cases", Sept 28, 2020.

[832] Tesla Annual Report 2020.

[833] SNE Research, https://www.sneresearch.com/kr/home/

in world BEV manufacturing and we did. According to EV Volumes, 2.2 million BEV & PHEVs were produced in 2019, increasing to 3.2 million in 2020 and then climbing to 6.7 million in 2021.[834] This 45% increase in 2020 indicates that there was considerable slack in the battery supply stream as well. The big jump in production numbers from 2020 to 2021 indicates BEV manufacturing was disrupted in 2020 due to the pandemic. Car manufacturers had to implement health measures just like the lithium and battery businesses and these restrictions suppressed production.

The biggest BEV factory in the world, Tesla's Giga Shanghai, was shut down for a two-week period in January-February 2020 as were many other businesses in Shanghai.[835] Tesla had to close its factory again in December 2022 when another outbreak hit Shanghai. They weren't alone. Luxury BEV manufacturer Nio had to close both its factories in Hefei for several weeks in both April and October of 2022 due to COVID outbreaks.[836] As late as Q4 2022, the #2 BEV manufacturer in the world was still being impacted by COVID outbreaks in China. BYD estimated that they produced 2,000-3,000 less cars a day because of employees staying home due to sickness.[837]

While lithium extraction, battery and BEV production were suppressed in 2020 and largely recovered in 2021, the costs of doing business skyrocketed through the period 2020-2022. At the start of 2020, global maritime shipping companies planned to cancel routes and consolidate others as carrier demand slumped. In fact, major shipping firms canceled 1,000 planned voyages in H1 2020. However, as millions of people around the world increasingly stayed home due to government mandated lockdowns, they began ordering large quantities of goods online which now required increased shipping capacity. This violent cracking of the global supply chain whip quickly created a shipping deficit, driving up prices. [838]

In early 2020, average maritime shipping rates for a 40-foot container fell below

---

[834] https://www.ev-volumes.com/

[835] The Verge, by A. Hawkins, "Tesla says China has ordered its Shanghai factory shut down over coronavirus fears", Jan 29, 2020.

[836] Reuters, "China's Nio suspends production due to COVID measures", Nov 01, 2022.

[837] CnEVPost, by L. Kang, "BYD facing daily production loss of at least 2,000 units in recent days as some workers infected with Covid", Dec 23, 2022.

[838] United States International Trade Commission, "The Impact of the COVID-19 Pandemic on Freight Transportation Services and U.S. Merchandise Imports"

$1,500.00 USD. These were reasonable rates. Mining companies used containers to ship battery minerals like lithium, nickel, and cobalt. Battery manufacturers shipped finished products like anodes, cathodes, and battery grade lithium hydroxide. BEV companies shipped everything they needed to support their vehicle production lines from tires and seats to aluminum sheets and electric motors. By September 2021, these shipping containers hit $10,278.00 USD apiece, greatly inflating the costs of goods shipped. Of course, these costs were passed on to the consumer. By the end of 2022, prices had plummeted back down to $2,000.00 USD.[839]

Let's apply these prices to a standard 40-foot shipping container that itself weighs 3,750 kilograms and can be loaded to a maximum weight of 26,300 kilograms.[840] This allows 22,550 kilograms of remaining shippable weight. Let's say a company ships 500 of these containers a year. At $1,500.00 USD per container, the expense is $750,000.00. At $10,000.00 USD the cost is $5 million USD. That is a significant price increase and a large amount of unforecasted expense for a company to eat. What does the company do in response? They either accrue more debt, pass the expense onto the consumer or both. What is the alternative to maritime shipping, is rail better?

Shipping via train is an option but it depends on geography and the business model in question. For example, a company can't move lithium concentrate from Australia to China by train, it must go by maritime shipping. However, there is the Eurasian rail connecting Europe to China, built as part of Beijing's ongoing Belt and Road Initiative. The average container rates (16,000 kilograms) from China to Europe remained amazingly flat during the pandemic. In February 2020, the rates were $2,722.00 USD per container and exactly one year later, in February 2021, they were $2,750.00 USD. A year later, in February 2022, average container prices "jumped" to $3,087.00 USD, a mere 10% increase from two years earlier. [841]

Consequently, for a two-year period, from October 2020 to October 2022, it was cheaper to ship BEV related products via the Eurasian rail than it was by maritime shipping. But there was a catch. BEVs were not allowed to be shipped via rail in China until September 2022 because of HAZMAT regulations. This meant Chinese car makers would have to truck their BEVs 2,500 miles from Shanghai to Xinjiang Province

---

[839] Drewry World Container Index

[840] https://www.icontainers.com/help/40-foot-container/

[841] https://index1520.com/en/

on the border with Kazakhstan before they could load their finished products onto a rail line. Chinese car manufacturers determined this wasn't worth it. Additionally, to this day, the Chinese Ministry of Commerce still prohibits the shipment of EV batteries via rail in China due to HAZMAT rules, although this could change in the future. Regardless, China now has a realistic method of transporting its BEVs via rail as a potential hedge against future maritime shipping rate inflation.[842]

On the land, rail competes with trucking for the ground movement of freight. Historically, shipping by truck costs twice as much per ton-mile than rail but it is also more flexible, which is why 70% of freight in the U.S. is transported by road. During the pandemic, U.S. truck rates were significantly impacted, rising almost 62% before coming down slightly. At the start of 2020, dry van contract rates were $2.10 USD per mile before climbing to $2.40 USD a mile by the end of the year. These contract dry van rates kept climbing in 2021, reaching $2.95 USD a mile by the end of December. In 2022, rates climbed still further to a high of $3.25 USD a ton-mile by mid-summer before coming back down a little to $2.95 USD at the end of the year. [843]

To put this in practice, Tesla's Nevada gigafactory is a 250-mile drive from its Fremont factory in California. At a $2.10 a mile rate, the cost for a single truck to make the trip is $525.00. If we cost the highest rate of $3.25 per mile, the trip is now $812.50. A hundred trips at $2.10 costs $52,500.00 USD while a hundred trips at $3.25 costs $81,250.00 USD, an increase in transportation costs of 55%. Most companies are hostage to these inflationary rates and always will be, but look at the position Tesla is in. As Tesla ramps up production of its own Tesla Semi trucks in 2023, it can control future dry van rate inflation by moving its own freight with its own fleet of electric powered semis which it acquires at the true cost of its own manufacturing. Also, Tesla will charge its semis with its own proprietary network of megachargers that it also manufactures in-house that serves as a hedge against charging inflation.

And what about air freight? Couldn't all the companies involved in the lithium value chain simply fly their batteries and raw materials around the world as needed? Depending on a host of factors, average air freight before the pandemic cost

[842] https://www.railfreight.com/railfreight/2022/09/21/electric-vehicles-but-not-batteries-are-allowed-on-china-railways/

[843] Owner-Operator Independent Drivers Association Foundation, Freight Rate Survey 2021 & 2022.

$2.50-$5.00 USD per kilogram and then rose to $4.00-$8.00 a kilogram.[844] This means a single metric ton priced at $3.50 a kilogram cost $3,500.00 USD and, later, that same metric ton priced at $6.50 per kilogram cost $6,500.00 USD. Today, flying one metric ton from Los Angeles to Shanghai costs upwards of $10,000.00 USD.[845] Obviously, air freight is not cost effective for large volume, high weight goods like batteries. While air freight costs suffered less inflation than maritime shipping during the pandemic, it was never a viable option (and never will be) for heavy shipments like raw materials and finished battery products.

Overall, the increased costs of all forms of transportation, created inflationary pressure that in turn increased the prices of raw battery minerals, finished battery products and the final BEV end-product. The higher prices throughout the lithium value chain meant fewer consumers could or would purchase lithium products and thus contributed to suppressing theoretical maximum production capacity during the pandemic. However, suppression of the lithium value chain in 2020 was more a product of restrictive health measures since transportation inflation lagged COVID lockdowns by a year or more.

The chief culprit for transportation inflation from 2021-2022 was maritime shipping rates which peaked in September 2021, up more than 500% from the start of the pandemic in January 2020. Importantly, the worldwide lithium enterprise could not escape this vulnerability because its intercontinental business model relied mostly on maritime shipping. By definition, this far-flung architecture was and is prone to inflationary and other physical kinds of disruption. But we know the solutions to this problem.

One mitigating measure for this disruption-prone model is building cost-efficient long-distance ground-based rail with the Chinese-built Eurasian corridor serving as an example. Let's also think of an Africa-European rail corridor and a north-south corridor for the Western Hemisphere. For sure, rail freight costs need to come down, but something to consider is that the comparative speed of rail reduces opportunity costs when compared to maritime shipping. Another obvious solution is shortening these elongated supply chains by sourcing raw materials locally and collocating battery and BEV manufacturing plants in the actual markets that they serve. As we discussed

---

[844] https://www.freightos.com/freight-resources/air-freight-rates-cost-prices/
[845] Ibid.

earlier in this book, the U.S. and the EU are both moving towards this model, but it will take many years to get there, perhaps by 2030.

Russia's Invasion of Ukraine in 2022

Russia's invasion of Ukraine in February 2022 has resulted in ongoing high-intensity warfare between the two armies with no end in sight currently. Prior to the war, neither country played a significant role in the lithium value chain. Hence, the largest European war since 1945 has had little impact on the business of extracting battery minerals, manufacturing batteries or producing BEVs. As can be seen with lithium value chain production data for the year 2022, any disruption caused by Russia's invasion has been minor and transitory at best. This could change. However, possible second and third-order effects generated from this war may have significant repercussions in the future, depending on how international dynamics evolve between the world's two largest economies: the U.S. and China.

Of interest to us is the sanctioning of Russia for its invasion and what its effects are on the global lithium value chain. To start, the U.S. and the EU placed various ineffective, half-hearted sanctions on Russia in 2014 after Putin invaded Crimea and eastern Ukraine. After Russia's second invasion in 2022, the West enacted far more significant sanctions on Russia to include leading personalities, companies, and commodities. For instance, the EU has sanctioned 1,473 individuals, 205 entities, frozen $21 billion USD in Russian assets and blocked another $300 billion USD of the Russian Central Bank.[846]

However, these sanctions only partially affect the Russian economy and are designed specifically not to negatively impact the EU's own economy. Russian battery minerals are not on the list. Naturally the "hurt-Russia-don't-hurt-Europe" principle the sanctions are based on creates some bizarre contradictions of policy. To better understand how sanctions affect the Russian battery mineral enterprise, we need to look at the Russian mining sector and lithium value chain.

Russia has a large and well-developed mining sector that accounted for an estimated 16.7% of its GDP in 2019. The majority of Russia's $419 billion USD in exports comes from its diverse minerals industry (63%) with petroleum, natural gas and ferrous metals being the top three minerals sold, combining to make up 30% of exported

---

[846] https://www.consilium.europa.eu/en/policies/sanctions/restrictive-measures-against-russia-over-ukraine/sanctions-against-russia-explained/

minerals. There are 16,900 different mining companies in Russia with 3,500 extracting metallic ores like nickel, manganese, and cobalt. Nickel, cobalt, and graphite are the only battery minerals of significance that Russia mines. Notably absent from Russia mining efforts is lithium.[847]

From a battery minerals perspective, Russia's most prolific battery mineral is nickel, followed by graphite and then cobalt. Russian company PAO GMK Norilskiy Nickel a.k.a. Nornickel has a near monopoly on the nickel sector in Russia, producing over 99% of it annually. Nornickel not only extracts almost all Russian nickel, but it also processes and refines it in its own facilities, achieving a degree of vertical integration. Russia exported 134,000 tons of nickel in 2019 with 99% of this going to Switzerland and the Netherlands. Another nickel miner, ZAO NPK Geotechnologiya, has a standing relationship with China whom it ships nickel concentrate to, a key ingredient in high-nickel battery cathodes.[848]

In 2022, Russia mined 220,000 tons of nickel or only 6.7% of the global production of 3,300,000 tons.[849] To put Russia's contribution in perspective, Indonesia produced almost half of the world's nickel at 1.6 million tons. While a relatively small amount, Russia does produce upwards of 17% of the world's Class 1 nickel (battery-grade, 99.8% purity).[850] In order to supply European customers, Nornickel has a long running nickel and cobalt refining operation in Harjavalta, Finland that has been open since 1959. Harjavalta is in southwest Finland, about 20 miles from the coast and the Gulf of Bothnia. In 2020, Nornickel's Harjavalta plant produced 63,400 tons of refined nickel.[851]

Cobalt is extracted by Russia in small quantities; in 2021 they produced 7,600 tons or just 4.5% of global production. World production in 2021 was 170,000 tons with the Democratic Republic of the Congo (DRC) producing the vast majority with 120,000 tons, Australia 5,600 tons, the Philippines 4,500 tons and Canada 4,300 tons. There is

[847] U.S. Geological Survey, by E. Safirova, 2019 Minerals Yearbook, Feb 2023.

[848] Ibid.

[849] U.S. Geological Survey, Mineral Commodity Summaries – Nickel, January 2023.

[850] Mining.com, by C. Jamasmie, "Nickel Needs | Russia accounts for 17% of global production capacity for Class 1 nickel, used in electric vehicle batteries", March 30, 2022.

[851] https://www.nornickel.com/business/assets/kola-division-finland/

no significant extraction of cobalt in Europe although Finland produces about 1,000 tons a year and plans to develop additional extraction operations.

Russia produces only modest amounts of graphite, extracting just 15,000 tons or a little over 1% of global production that was 1.3 million tons in 2022. China, by far, produced the most graphite at 850,000 tons, followed by Mozambique 170,000 tons, Madagascar 110,000 tons and Brazil with 87,000 tons. Other European countries produce graphite like Norway with 10,000 tpa and Turkey 2,900 tpa. Ukraine produced 10,000 tons in 2021 but dropped to 3,000 tons after the Russian invasion. With 1.3 million metric tons produced worldwide in 2022, this small change hardly mattered to the global graphite value chain.[852]

Russia produces very little manganese, extracting just 57,000 tons of it or 0.25% of global production in 2022, which was 20 million metric tons. South Africa produced by far the most manganese at 7.2 million metric tons and has enormous reserves estimated at 640 million tons. Gabon came in second with 4.6 million tons, Australia with 3.3 million tons and China with 960,000 tons. The only European country with significant manganese reserves is Ukraine with 140 million tons. Presently, from the perspective of manganese, Russia has no impact on the battery industry.[853]

While lithium is not a mineral currently sanctioned against Russia, Moscow is conscious that they are vulnerable to such an action as they import all their lithium needs that run about 9,000 tpa of LCE. Russia, much like the U.S. and China, neglected their own domestic lithium industry because they found it cheaper to import abroad from the Lithium Triangle. To secure their vulnerable lithium supply chain, Nornickel signed a cooperation agreement with the State Atomic Energy Corporation Rosatom (ROSATOM) in 2022 that included a JV to develop a lithium operation. The two are looking specifically at the Kolmozerskoye lithium deposits in the Murmansk region. Both companies have experience working in cold, remote locations and they will need these skills if they are ever to bring this subarctic open pit mine to a productive state. The operating costs in such a harsh polar environment will be considerable.[854]

In 2021, Chile provided Russia 68% of its needed lithium, the U.S. provided another

[852] U.S. Geological Survey, Mineral Commodity Summaries-Graphite, January 2023.

[853] U.S. Geological Survey, Mineral Commodity Summaries-Manganese, January 2023.

[854] Batteries News, "Battery Materials – Nornickel and Rosatom Sign Cooperation Agreement", May 3, 2022.

14%, Argentina 11%, Bolivia 3.8%, and China 2.4%. There was reporting that both Chile and Argentina shut off Russia from their lithium contracts after the invasion, or 79% of their annual needs, but this has remained unconfirmed. When S&P Global contacted Chilean lithium producer SQM about these reports, SQM stated that they were continuing to fulfill their standing lithium contract with Russia. Albemarle did pause its lithium shipments to Russia and Livent confirmed that they didn't have any standing business relationship with Russia.[855] In the meantime, Russia can make up their lithium shortfall from their strategic partner, China.

When it comes to BEV adoption, Russia is far behind the rest of Europe with new purchases of BEVs at about 1% of overall sales. Although Russia has many BEV start-ups, none of them are successful or produce competitive BEVs at scale. Can the reader name just one Russian-made BEV? I can't and I wrote a book on it! One of the leading manufacturers is Motorinvest, who makes licensed copies of a Chinese sedan. These vehicles are built from Chinese parts in cooperation with state-owned Dongfeng Motor Corporation, who has previously used solid-state batteries made by Ganfeng Lithium.[856] Since western auto makers have pulled out of Russia due to its invasion of Ukraine and won't provide them BEV technology, it makes sense that they are partnering with China.

With no BEV production of any notable size, it's not surprising Russia has no associated battery industry either, although they have made initial plans to move into this space. In 2021, Russia enacted government subsidies for BEV and battery manufacturers as well as other incentives to encourage the development of a BEV charging network, which only has an estimated 134 charging locations.[857] To support Moscow's tentative move into the battery space, ROSATOM announced in 2021 their intent to build a 3 GWh EV battery factory in Kaliningrad. Importantly, ROSATOM bought a 49% share of South Korean battery manufacturer Enertech International who has the technology and intellectual capital to operate the plant.[858] The battery plant will be built on the prop-

---

[855] "Russia no longer receives lithium carbonate from Chile, Argentina: ministry". S&P Global, April 13, 2022.

[856] Interfax News Agency, "Lipetsk-based Motorinvest begins serial production of electric vehicles under Evolute brand" Sep 28, 2022.

[857] https://www.electromaps.com/en/charging-stations/russia

[858] Electrive, "Rosatom to build battery factory in Kaliningrad", Sep 20, 2021.

erty of ROSATOM's nuclear power plant facility. The location gives ROSATOM a battery foothold in eastern Europe as well as access to a nearby seaport for logistics.

Before we address each part of the Russian lithium value chain through the lens of sanctions, we must address the voluntary divestment of Russia by private corporations. A Yale University research team led by Professor Jeffrey Sonnenfeld has identified 1,000 foreign companies who have voluntarily pulled out of Russia since their invasion. The decision to leave by these companies is an example of Professor Sonnenfeld's idea that "doing good, is doing well", meaning that withdrawing from Russia hasn't hurt their businesses. It is interesting to note that Chinese companies have decided to stay in Russia which should not surprise anyone as they are strategic allies.[859]

Let's start with a discussion on sanctioning Russia's EV battery sector, an industry that is non-existent. Obviously, there are no active battery plants to sanction but ROSATOM's future Kaliningrad plant could be targeted if the war in Ukraine is not resolved by the time it comes online (if it ever does). From a critical minerals security perspective, it would make no sense for European BEV manufacturers located in NATO countries to develop supply chain dependencies on Russia. Then again, many people said the same thing about Europe relying on Moscow for its energy supply, but they did that as well.

The topic gets more interesting understanding that previously mentioned Nornickel is working with German chemical company BASF to build a battery precursors plant adjacent to the Nornickel facility in Finland.[860] From a supply chain security perspective, does it make sense for Europe to source finished nickel and cobalt products from Russia and to develop associated supply chain dependencies on them as well? Ironically, BASF received an "A" rating from Yale's research team because they announced that they were winding down all operations in Russia. But BASF had no problem continuing to do business with Nornickel in Finland because the Russian nickel provider had not been formally sanctioned.[861] Did BASF leave Russia because it

---

[859] https://som.yale.edu/story/2022/over-1000-companies-have-curtailed-operations-russia-some-remain

[860] https://catalysts.basf.com/news/basf-and-norilsk-nickel-enter-exclusive-negotiations-to-cooperate-on-raw-material-supply-for-battery-materials-production-in-europe

[861] Reuters, "BASF says 2022 battery chemical production start in Finland in doubt", April 29, 2022.

looked bad reputationally to stay? But continuing to do business with Russian companies in Finland was okay because it received less public scrutiny?

What is even more intriguing is that Finland continued to allow Nornickel to run their Harjavalta facility even after the Finnish parliament voted 184-7 to enter the NATO military alliance a year after Russia's invasion.[862] Some of Finland's freight train companies refused to transfer further shipments of Nornickel raw materials to Harjavalta as of January 2023 in order to "do good and do well", but other Finnish train companies had no problem picking up the service.[863] Thus, we are confronted with the contradiction that Finland feels threatened enough by Russia's invasion of Ukraine to join NATO, but they'll continue to allow Nornickel's Harjavalta operation to run, helping to fund Moscow's war machine right next door. Profits over policy, it appears.

Like the battery industry, there is no credible BEV industry in Russia to sanction except a few start-ups. Regardless, many of the major western car companies have voluntarily ceased operations in Russia to include Ford, Mercedes-Benz, Toyota, BMW, and VW Group. The void left by these western auto makers has already been filled by Chinese companies like Geely, Chery, Dongfeng and SAIC to name just a few. In 2022, more than 30% of all car sales in Russia were already Chinese models.[864] There is no doubt that future BEV, battery, and charging infrastructure developments in Russia will come from Chinese brands. We can expect the Chinese companies to conduct all the technical operations in any JV with Russian companies since Moscow does not have the R&D capability nor the intellectual capital in this space to do it themselves. Also, the existing Eurasian rail corridor built as part of China's Belt and Road Initiative ensures a ready means for transportation of Chinese cars and associated material.

As Russia produces negligible amounts of cobalt, manganese, graphite and no lithium, the only battery mineral that could be sanctioned to any effect is nickel. And as they have a near monopoly on the Russian nickel market, we are only talking about

[862] AP News, by J. Tanner, Finland's Parliament gives final approval for NATO bid", March 1, 2023.

[863] Railfreight.com, by M. van Leijen, "Will anyone transport nickel from Russia to Europe next year?" Dec 22, 2022.

[864] Reuters, G. Stoylarov, "Exclusive: Chinese grab Russian car market share after Western rivals depart", Dec 08, 2022.

Nornickel. As we mentioned before, battery minerals in Russia have not been sanctioned to include Nornickel. However, the U.S. placed sanctions on Nornickel's owner, Vladimir Potanin, at the end of 2022, ten months after Russia's invasion. While the U.S. and the UK have sanctioned Potanin, the EU has not, revealing the many holes in the West's sanction regime.

The sanctions freeze Potanin's U.S. assets, might lead to the seizure of his $120 million USD yacht and bars him from entering the country, all of which does little if anything to impact the sale of Nornickel products. The sanctions also target Potanin's investment firm Interros and their bank Rosbank, which again has no direct impact on Nornickel sales. These actions may inconvenience Potanin if he and his companies were exceptionally tied to business operations in the UK and U.S. but will certainly ensure Potanin and his business enterprise focus their efforts elsewhere like Europe, China, Asia, and South America. [865]

In February 2023, the U.S. Department of the Treasury issued a determination targeting the "Metals and Mining Sector of the Russian Federation Economy". The document is intentionally broad and vague, giving the Treasury and Department of State wide latitude to sanction personalities and entities operating in that space. The four Russian companies listed by Treasury provide various metal services for the Russian military such as ammunition production. To keep the sanctioning of these four companies in perspective, as we mentioned earlier in this chapter, there are at least 3,500 Russian companies in the metal mining business. There was no targeting of a specific commodities industry and no mention of any battery minerals.[866]

The prevailing wisdom of why the U.S. and the E.U. have conspicuously not sanctioned Nornickel is to avoid destabilizing the global nickel markets. This is not unreasonable. After Russia invaded Ukraine in February 2022, many professionals in the metals space were concerned with the associated market uncertainty. Market uncertainty can lead to volatility. This volatility played out on the LME (London Metal Exchange) when nickel prices rose precipitously from $25,000.00 USD and skyrocketing to the $100,000.00 USD mark on March 08, 2022, and putting on a "short squeeze".[867]

---

[865] Forbes, by D. Saul, "U.S. Sanctions Russia's Second-Richest Man Vladimir Potanin", Dec 15, 2022.

[866] https://home.treasury.gov/news/press-releases/jy1296

[867] Ahead of the Herd, "Nickel goes parabolic on historic LME short squeeze", March 09, 2022.

This meant some investors bet that nickel prices would fall, and when they rose rapidly instead, these short sellers were forced to cover the margin calls. The cost of margin calls for some companies ran into the hundreds of millions of dollars. Because of the volatility, LME suspended nickel trading for the day, canceled nickel contracts, and temporarily halted the physical movement of the commodity. A year later, the Financial Conduct Authority investigated LME's decision to cancel nickel contracts worth billions of dollars and to ensure measures were in place to prevent future chaos.[868] This is the kind of metals volatility the U.S. and EU want to avoid as sanctioning Nornickel can create market conditions (sustained high prices) that have a negative global economic impact. Thus, Nornickel may be "too big to sanction".

For arguments sake, let's say Nornickel is sanctioned by the U.S. and the EU and Russia can't sell its Class 1 nickel in either market. What does those sanctions look like? At present, there are no American or European battery makers available to even buy Class 1 nickel. All the battery factories in these two markets are Chinese, South Korean, or Japanese owned. Will these allies participate in the sanctions also? If Nornickel is sanctioned, they will pivot to the Asia market that owns most of the global battery space. For instance, If Finland forces Nornickel to shutter is Harjavalta nickel/cobalt operation, Nornickel would be forced to restructure its architecture. A viable option could be establishing a nickel JV with POSCO, a South Korean battery materials manufacturer who still operates in Russia. Although this may take three years and a $1 billion USD, it is a feasible course of action.

What if sanctions go one step further and prohibit the use of Russian nickel in batteries subsequently sold in the U.S. and EU? Once Russia ships finished Class 1 nickel to a Ganfeng Lithium or CATL battery manufacturing plant in China, how do we know where the various nickel feedstocks came from? How do we prove the origination of the battery mineral supply chain? Until the industry institutes an enforceable battery passport concept, who is to say where the nickel came from? The U.S. already can't determine what Chinese products were made using forced labor from Uyghurs. Similarly, end users also can't be certain if the cobalt in their batteries was sourced from child labor in the Congo. What makes the U.S. and EU think they can effectively keep Russian nickel, laundered through Chinese companies, out of western BEVs?

---

[868] Reuters, "UK regulator launches enforcement probe into LME nickel trading halt", March 03, 2023.

Doing Business with the Enemy

It is a curious reality that nations diametrically opposed to one another will continue to do business with each other as they capitalize on mutual short-term gains and willingly defer catastrophic long-term results. From a strategy perspective, each side believes they can use their immediate rewards to skillfully outmaneuver and inflict severe future consequences on their foe while avoiding these same costs for themselves. One may have thought that the U.S. and Europe would strangle Russia with severe sanctions from the day they invaded Ukraine, no matter the industry or commodity. As we know, this did not happen. Instead, the West pursued a strategy of gradually increasing pressure on Russia while still doing business with each other. Rarely will nations eliminate mutual trade unless they are in all-out war with one another. And then maybe.

Since we have some interest in the automobile industry due to the BEV's prominent role as a finished downstream product in the lithium value chain, let's investigate the European business operations of the Ford Motor Company during WWII. Specifically, let's understand the dynamics of Ford's operations in Germany under Nazi rule both before and after the onset of hostilities. While we observe the major elements of this relationship, let's assess it through lens of disruption. Let's learn why and how companies can be disrupted during a time of conflict or, equally, how their operations can remain resilient and adapt.

Ford's subsidiary in Germany eventually became known as Ford-Werke. It was formally incorporated in 1925 with the first production plant located in Berlin. 1920's Germany was a very difficult place to do business in with incredible levels of social instability, crushing inflation and the Great Depression coming in 1929. In 1928, Ford pursued a corporate restructuring plan for Europe, setting up nine separate Ford affiliates in neighboring countries with Ford, headquartered in Dearborn, MI, retaining 60% ownership of each.

Regardless of the many severe operational challenges in Germany, Ford-Werke successfully implemented their ruthlessly efficient "scientific management" business model that seemed to cut through the chaos to bring production certainty. In 1929, an estimated 30% of all cars registered in Germany were made by Ford. That same year, Ford amazingly ran a 30% margin on its Berlin enterprise valued at $3.75 million USD. However, the Germany auto industry was tiny at the time with Ford producing just 12,000 vehicles that year.[869]

---

[869] Holyoke Daily Transcript and Telegram, "Ford in Germany", March 10, 1930.

With Ford's European enterprise doing very well in the hardest of times, Ford decided to construct a much larger factory in the city of Cologne that became operational in 1931, two years before Hitler became chancellor.[870] Ford-Werke would face considerable difficulty after the plant was completed, running financial deficits every year until 1935 when it became profitable again. After the Nazi Party came to power, there were increasingly nationalistic pressures brought to bear on the automotive industry to support the regime and Ford-Werke was no exception. As an example of this, German auto manufacturing policy eventually mandated that upwards of 95% of all vehicle materials must be German sourced.[871]

In order to survive in an environment demanding maximal Germanness, Ford-Werke responded by filling its board of directors with a majority of German citizens, sold 15% of its stock to the German company I.G. Farbenindustrie, and tried to merge with another German automobile company.[872] Next, the Nazi Party pushed for standardization of all auto parts, meaning auto companies had to meet the "German Industrial Standard" or remain locked out of lucrative German government contracts. It became increasingly clear that standardization between vehicle types was not just for efficiency's sake, but in preparing the German auto industry for war. Ford-Werke ended up standardizing about two-thirds of its operations by 1936 to satisfy Berlin.[873]

Ford-Werke also participated in the Nazi regime's plan to stockpile foreign currency by accelerating exports just for this purpose, including selling Ford-Werke products to other parts of the global Ford enterprise. Ford-Werke, with the consent of Dearborn, also imported raw materials, like much needed tires, for is Cologne plant. However, this also entailed providing 30% of these materials to the German government.[874] By the end of December 1936, Dearborn also agreed to supply the Third Reich with thousands of tons of pig-iron.[875] With these actions, Dearborn no longer could

---

[870] Ford Motor Company, "Research Findings About Ford-Werke under the Nazi Regime", December 2001.

[871] Henry Ford Museum, Acc. 38, Box 14, Ford-AG Manager's Report, March 1933.

[872] University of Pennsylvania, *The Silent Partner: How the Ford Motor Company Became an Arsenal of Nazism*, by D. Warsh, May 2008, p. 58.

[873] Ford Motor Company, *Research Findings About Ford-Werke Under the Nazi Regime*, p. 20.

[874] *Research Findings*, p. 24.

[875] 2 NARA, RG 407, Entry 368B, Box 1032, Schneider Report, Exhibit 74, R. Schmidt Raw Materials Agreement Memorandum, August 6, 1945, p. 1.

claim to be merely supplying its Cologne subsidiary with needed materials. They had become a logistics arm for Nazi Germany.

While Ford-Werke was profitable, the $515,000.00 USD it earned in 1939 wasn't impressive when considering Ford had to keep the money it made in Germany. They couldn't take it out due to Third Reich currency stockpiling laws.[876] Also, Ford-Werke was constrained to a quota system for vehicle sales, selling just over 36,000 vehicles in 1938[877] compared to the almost 600,000 vehicles Ford sold in the U.S. that year.[878] At every step in the relationship between Ford-Werke and Nazi Germany, it appeared that the juice wasn't worth the squeeze, yet Ford never pulled out of the country and never halted their operations. One might have expected Ford headquarters to sever all connections completely and permanently with the Third Reich after they invaded Poland in 1939, but this never happened. Quite the opposite.

Ford-Werke continued to meet regime demands. This included collaborating with another German company in the operating of a new manufacturing plant in Berlin. Until its closure in 1941, this plant produced heavy off-road personnel carriers, making 1,837 of these Schwerer Personenkraftwagen (SPKW). Ford-Werke outfitted them with their own V-8 engines. The SPKW were multi-purpose, used by both the SS and Wehrmacht for their signal corps, as ambulances and as artillery, anti-aircraft, and personnel carriers. Including Ford-Werke's contribution, about 10,000 of these off-road workhorses were made.[879]

Ford-Werke continued contributing to the Nazi war-machine whenever the opportunity arose. For example, in June of 1940, the Luftwaffe asked them to produce 8,000 V-8 motors for barges which was assumed to support the pending invasion of England.[880] Ford-Werke accepted the contract. When Germany invaded and overran

---

[876] Simon Reich, *The Fruits of Fascism*, Ithaca: Cornell University Press, 1990, p.117.

[877] Hill, Frank, and Wilkins, Mira, *American Business Abroad: Ford on Six Continents* (Detroit: Wayne State University Press, 1964). p. 436.

[878] 4 Nevins and Hill, *Ford: Decline and Rebirth*, 1933-1962, Appendix I: Ford Motor Company Production Report, 1903 Thru 1955.

[879] https://www.quartermastersection.com/german/support-vehicles/563/s.E.Pkw

[880] NARA, RG 407, Entry 368B, Box 1032, Schneider Report, Exhibit 172, Schmidt Memo Re: LC8 Motors, July 20, 1945.

western Europe that summer of 1940, the captured Ford subsidiaries were given a special exemption to be managed by Ford-Werke instead of Nazi industrialists.

In December 1941, when Germany declared war on the U.S., there were over 250 American companies operating in the country.[881] Many of these companies were seized by the state to be managed by hand-picked men selected by the Reich. Again, Ford-Werke was given an exception because of its influential board members with close ties to the Nazi Party. Importantly, at this time of declared war between the U.S. and Germany, Ford-Werke and all its assets in-country were considered enemy property.[882]

We must ask the question, was this collaboration worth it? From 1939-1943 Ford-Werke had combined profits of $3.6 million USD or $906,000.00 USD a year.[883] These were the good years for Ford when the Nazi war machine rolled over Europe. But the end was near in 1943 with the colossal failure of the Germans at the Battle of Kursk and the total reversal of fortune in North Africa by the Afrika Korps. In 1944, the walls began to crumble all around the Third Reich, meaning supply chain disruptions cut into Ford-Werke's bottom line. That year, they suffered a loss of $1.09 million USD.[884]

In March 1945, the U.S. Army entered western Cologne, "liberating" the Ford-Werke plant, which could no longer be considered enemy property. For the first two full months of 1945 that Ford-Werke still operated under the Third Reich, they lost $228,000.00 USD.[885] But taking into account all of Ford's European subsidiaries like those in England, France and Denmark, Ford did quite well during the war years, pocketing almost $11 million USD in profits.[886] Of course, all of Ford's occupied European factories, excluding the one in England, transitioned immediately after capture to assisting the German war effort as that was the path to prosperity: large German government contracts.

Importantly for Ford, over the course of many allied bombing raids on Cologne, the Ford-Werke plant received relatively little damage and never ceased operations.

---

[881] *Research Findings*, p. i.

[882] *The Silent Partner*, p. 114.

[883] *Research Findings*, Appendix G.

[884] *Research Findings*, Appendix G.

[885] *The Silent Partner*, page 129.

[886] Hill & Wilkins, page 334.

Although the factory was considered enemy property and was employed directly by the Third Reich after 1939 to support its war economy, Ford Motor Corporation still submitted a claim for compensation for its losses in both Germany and Austria. If one thought Ford could not sink any lower as a corporate entity, they would be wrong. Accordingly, Ford asked for the astronomical sum of $7 million USD in compensation with a review panel later awarding them only $522,526.00 USD.[887]

As one would expect based on their corporate character, Ford fought this lowly amount, successfully getting it increased slightly to $785,321.00 USD.[888] This dogged fight for corporate compensation is indeed ironic when considering Ford benefitting greatly from Nazi slave labor for so many years (1941-1945). At their height, Ford-Werke employed some 2,500 coerced workers, to include the doomed prisoners of Auschwitz and Buchenwald.[889, 890] Afterall, nothing made more economic sense for Ford's bottom line than using discounted forced labor that had no future – no pensions or health care plans to worry about.

But the war was over, and Ford had successfully navigated the most ruinous war in human history, instigated by the most despicable genocidal regimes ever known. For sure, devastated Europe was still a difficult environment to navigate with many German cities in rubble and a new U.S.-Soviet Cold War looming on the horizon. However, Ford found itself in a strong position to take advantage of the post-war boom due to its network of European subsidiaries and the fact that its modern production plant in Cologne was in good shape and ready to get back to making cars. Maybe this was the prize Ford had waited for all along to exploit: a peaceful Europe with a growing economy filled with people needing to buy automobiles in pursuit of the "Ford Dream".

Lessons Learned

Let's compare Ford's actions in Nazi Germany with what's going on in Russia today. Most western auto companies have already voluntarily pulled out of Russia, disrupting their ICE market as well as any BEV cooperation they had under way. This is largely due to the relatively new development of an ESG (Environmental, Social, Governance)

---

[887] *Research Findings*, p. 108.

[888] *The Silent Partner*, p. 132.

[889] "Working for the Enemy."

[890] Independent, by A. Lebour, "Slave labour at Auschwitz used by Ford", Aug 19, 1999.

framework in the European and U.S. business space. Instead of the predatory capitalism Ford practiced in WWII, companies today are more likely to make decisions based on their company culture that includes the idea of what is right and wrong. However, a sense of morality is highly subjective as we can also tell from the long list of companies who have not pulled out.

Companies that haven't pulled out include China's Minmetals, Mitsubishi Heavy Industries, POSCO (through a Russian subsidiary), SAIC Motor, German auto supplier Bosch, and Toyota Tsusho just to name a few. Clearly, they have no problems doing business with Russia from an ESG perspective. There are a disproportionate number of Chinese companies who have not pulled. Dictators support dictators. This amorality is not surprising as China has continuing association with using child labor to mine cobalt in the Congo as well as using forced labor of minorities in its mainland businesses. In today's world, ESG principles can cause disruption in any industry to include the lithium value chain, but this disruption is most likely to be partial at best and unequally enforced.

Nornickel and Ford both serve as examples of being so important to the world economy that they are "too big to sanction". Sanctioning Nornickel in a serious manner, such as delisting it from the LME and rejecting its products in Europe and the U.S., could have a serious disruptive impact, maybe temporary, on both the company and the battery industry but it hasn't been done yet. Similarly, Germany and the U.S. both allowed Ford to skirt industry and even national guidelines because of its far-reaching influence in the global auto industry.

Back in the U.S., Washington never held Ford accountable for its wartime support to the Nazi regime that fought and killed U.S. soldiers using Ford manufactured products. Because Ford had such an outsized impact on the American, global, and to a lesser extent, German, economies they were able to use their political influence and power to successfully navigate the most disruptive period in the 20th Century. Many smaller, less influential companies did not do so.

A modern example today of outsized influence like a Henry Ford and Ford Motor Company must be Elon Musk and Tesla. To start, Tesla received special exceptions to establish the first independently owned and operated BEV manufacturing plant in China. Tesla's Giga Shanghai makes one think of Ford-Werke in Cologne, which is still in operation today and is transforming into a BEV production site. Henry Ford had an authoritarian mindset and supported the Nazi regime for a variety of reasons to include his deeply held antisemitism.

Elon Musk has also been observed to have an authoritarian personality and to side with China and Russia on the issues of Taiwan and Ukraine.[891] Would Tesla headquarters allow its foreign subsidiaries in Russia and China to employ forced labor? Would Tesla close its operations in a country engaged in war against the U.S.? Ford didn't in WWII and neither did GM for that matter. Has the culture of the U.S. auto industry evolved since then? Would U.S. auto companies today make ethical decisions based on the U.S. national interest and not their bottom line?

What might the disruption to the global lithium value chain look like if Russia's war against Ukraine expands and China takes a more active role in supporting their ally, Putin. Is the West going to line up against the East and start a Cold War 2.0? If Nornickle is too big to sanction now, how is the West going to effectively sanction Ganfeng Lithium and CATL. What would happen if Australia cut off its supply of hard rock lithium concentrate to the China market? We know what would happen, most of China's lithium enterprise from midstream processing to BEV production would grind to a halt. China knows this.

In early March 2023, CATL divested itself of its holdings in Australian lithium producer Pilbara Minerals and bought a China-based lithium company, Sinuowei Mining.[892] Is CATL merely shortening its preposterous supply chain or hedging against future conflict? In a cold or hot war with China, would Tesla ride it out, leveraging their influence with both Beijing and Washington to keep their enterprise thriving even in wartime conditions? In turn, would CATL do everything it could to keep its Michigan plant producing batteries for its American customers regardless of politics? History may provide us answers.

Looking Ahead

1. Did industry, including the global lithium enterprise, learn deep lessons about their business models from the pandemic? Are they better prepared for future disruption, or did they just pursue reactionary policies to a bad situation, memory hole the entire experience, and then go back to doing business as usual because it's easier to do so? Often, engrained company culture trumps intelligent decisions.

---

[891] The Washington Post, by J. Menn & C. Zakrzewski, "Musk appeasement of Putin and China stokes fears of new Twitter policies", Oct 12, 2022.

[892] CnEVPost, by L. Kang, "CATL takes over Chinese lithium miner to lock in more material supplies", March 08, 2023.

2. The disruption of the global supply chain during the pandemic showed how preposterously inefficient and fragile it was. Did nations and industry learn the correct lessons about supply chain resilience? Are they making meaningful changes to build more durable models which means shortening the current far-flung structure through more intelligent design such as onshoring, regionalization and substitution?

3. Warfare can be very disruptive depending on a whole host of factors. Sanctions are one form of disruption that can have serious impact depending on the target and how they are employed. Poorly thought out and weakly enforced sanctions can be sidestepped. Sanctioned companies can be surprisingly resilient if they are agile, creative and have a dispersed business architecture. Should companies build a resilient architecture in anticipation of disruption?

4. Will we see the continued rise in the importance of ESG principles as a disruptive element in future conflicts? Will there ever be a global definition and understanding of ESG or will it remain subjective and regional? What new ideas will arise to potentially disrupt the economies of bad actors? Will nations continue weak policies relating to corporate actions in warzones?

Norilsk Nickel's Nadezhda plant located in north-central Russia in the Arctic Circle. The Siberian town of Norilsk is considered one of the most polluted in the world where acid rain has destroyed surrounding forests for many miles. The average life expectancy in Norilsk is a full decade below the rest of Russian society. *(by Ninara)*

Vladimir Putin meets with Xi Jinping on February 4, 2022, in Beijing for the Winter Olympics. Three weeks later, Russia would invade Ukraine. Because of their strategic cooperation, it would be hard to effectively sanction Russia's battery mineral industry. Moscow could easily sell all its battery mineral products to the Chinese battery industry. *(Official Kremlin Photo)*

A German *Maultier* half-track made by Ford-Werke. These vehicles were
good in muddy terrain, snow, sand, and were used extensively on all
fronts including against American troops. *(Author Collection)*

A German SS unit drives a *Schwerer gelandegangiger Pkw* towing an anti-tank gun. These rough
terrain vehicles were made by Ford-Werke using Ford's excellent V-8 engine. *(by Bundesarchiv)*

Made in the USA
Middletown, DE
11 October 2023

40579335R00265